Immigrants on the Hill

Immigrants on the Hill

Italian-Americans in St. Louis, 1882–1982

GARY ROSS MORMINO

UNIVERSITY OF MISSOURI PRESS
Columbia and London

University of Missouri Press, Columbia, Missouri 65201
Originally published by University of Illinois Press, 1986
Printed and bound in the United States of America

5 4 3 2 1 06 05 04 03 02

Cataloging-in-Publication Data available from the Library of Congress
ISBN 0-8262-1405-3

∞™ This paper meets the requirements of the American National Standard for Permanence of Paper for Printed Library Materials, Z39.48, 1984.

Printer and binder: Thomson-Shore, Inc.

To Lynne

Contents

Preface to the 2002 Edition

First love, best love. In the words of Yogi Berra, poet laureate of Elizabeth Avenue, my homecoming was "deja vu all over again." I first fell in love with the Hill as a young graduate student in 1970; as a fifty-something professor of history, I remain infatuated with this well-ordered community in southwest St. Louis.

Following the publication of *Immigrants on the Hill* in 1986, I drifted far from St. Louis, far from the Hill. I feared for my beloved Hill. In August 2001, I returned for a brief visit. How could this single neighborhood resist the relentless forces of urban decay and white flight, gentrification and affluence, the Internet and cultural convergence?

Physically, the Hill has changed little. The neighborhood remains cordoned off by highways and natural barriers. Emblems of St. Louis's industrial past—brick kilns, iron foundries, and stove factories—stand silent. In many cases, local leaders have ingeniously converted abandoned warehouses and buildings into meeting halls and community gathering places. Restaurants and bakeries break up rows of modest but lovingly cared for homes. The Hill exudes the feel of a very special place.

In an age of increasing homogeneity and globalization, the Hill retains its historic ethnic character and vibrancy. Most of St. Louis's ethnic neighborhoods are gone. Little Italy, located on the city's near north side, is now only a memory. New civic monuments tower over the once glorious community. While the population of St. Louis has declined by a staggering half a million persons between 1950 and 2000, families wait on lists hoping to move to the Hill. Still largely Italian American, but no longer exclusively so, the Hill exerts a powerful and positive ethnic identity. The immigrants are mostly gone, but their heritage survives. Lombard dialect is taught in the schools; third-generation Italian bakeries and specialty shops provide an aura of permanence. Boccie, a game enjoyed by old-timers in the 1970s, has become a sport of the masses. St. Ambrose Church functions as an anchor, as it always has. Clusters of neighbors gather on street corners to talk; priests enjoy lattes at fashionable cafes. The Hill remains a well-ordered society amid seeming chaos: lunch and evening crowds spill onto sidewalks while drivers prowl for precious parking spots.

The Hill has long enjoyed a reputation for home-style dining. But tastes change. Ruggeri's, once the most popular restaurant in the area, closed in the 1980s. Rau's department store, a fixture for decades, also closed its doors. The beloved Ravarino and Freschi Macaroni Company and Rose's Tavern no longer exist. Even the North Italy America Club, part of the Hill since the nineteenth century, is a memory. New institutions have emerged. Mom-and-pop grocery stores and corner taverns have been replaced by upscale cafés and specialty stores. Northern Italian cuisine became suddenly fashionable, and the Hill capitalized on its Lombard roots. Long before New York bistros discovered northern Italian cooking, Hill residents had enjoyed risotto Milanese, Bel Paese cheese, and Volpe's prosciutto. Today, Charlie Gitto's, Lorenzo's Trattoria, Zia's, Dominic's, and Giovanni's enjoy immense popularity, even while locals curse the accompanying traffic.

The Hill endures. I feel privileged to have been an observer these last three decades.

Acknowledgments

This book is an outgrowth of my intellectual curiosity in seeking answers to questions of ethnicity on a local level, and it also has stirred questions of a personal nature. I was first touched by the immediacy of the immigrant experience in 1965, as stoop-backed men and rosary-clutching women filed by my grandfather's coffin. I became intrigued by their stories, guilty that I had not really understood what my grandfather's life had been like and had not asked more questions. From the mountainous village of Alia in Sicily to the sugar fields of Louisiana and the industrial town of Wood River, Illinois, a small band of Sicilians had stayed together. It was an odyssey that only struck me later as Homeric. Rosolino Mormino had laid bricks at the Standard Oil Refinery so that my father could be a machinist at the Shell Oil Refinery so that his son could be a writer.

During the decade this book has been part of my life I have amassed debts too great to repay with a single acknowledgment. It seems all too appropriate to draw instead on a Hill folktale. On August 27, 1947, St. Louisans honored Lawrence Peter ("Yogi") Berra at Sportman's Park. Yogi climaxed the evening with a memorable witticism, asking the crowd "to thank everybody who made this night necessary." May I too thank everybody who made this book necessary.

I benefitted immensely from a year in Italy, 1980–81, under the auspices of the Fulbright-Hays Commission, which allowed me the time and opportunity to travel throughout Italy and discuss the project with students and faculty at the Università di Roma. Father Gianfausto Rosoli graciously shared his ideas and magnificent collections of immigration materials at Centro Studi Emigrazione. Ernesto Milani guided me through the backroads of Varese and Cuggiono. Zia Concetta Mormino and Carmelo Colura welcomed back one of their kin as only family can.

The months spent on the Hill in St. Louis permitted me to study the neighborhood from within. The indomitable Tina Fuse performed myriad roles as landlady, counselor, diva, guide, and friend. So many families and individuals generously opened up their hearts and shared their memories that I can only thank the community collectively. Brickmakers and clay miners added an important dimension to this study, sharing their feelings and lives in many ways. Not everyone there will agree with my interpretations; I only ask that they try to understand them.

In St. Louis, Raymond Pisney of the Missouri Historical Society encouraged this study. Professor James Neal Primm of the University of Missouri at St. Louis read the manuscript and thus saved me from many embarrassing errors.

I am deeply indebted to former teachers who awakened my interest in history and laid the groundwork for this study. Professor James Graham Provan of Millikin University encouraged me as a young history student to strive for excellence. Professor Roger Lotchin of the University of North Carolina at Chapel Hill guided me through earlier papers in graduate school and patiently oversaw my doctoral dissertation. Their unflagging standards, keen insights, and personal attention left a profound impression.

Friends and colleagues at the University of South Florida have goaded me and nursed this work through crisis and calm. Jay Dobkin, Harvey Nelsen, Jim Swanson, David Carr, and Charles Wrong read portions of the manuscript, offering their encouragement and insights. John Belohlavek and Ray Arsenault generously gave their hearts and tennis elbows to see this work published. My writing was enriched by their collegial conversations over many cups of café con leche. Dean Wallace Russell's support also is greatly appreciated.

George Pozzetta of the University of Florida, Richard Long of Hillsborough Community College, and Luciano Iorizzo of SUNY–Oswego read the manuscript and provided invaluable suggestions. Fortune Bosco, the last of the Renaissance men, was always available to translate an arcane phrase and to discuss the decline of the West.

A special debt of gratitude is owed to Michael G. Copeland, Cecile L. Pulin, Peter Selle, and Nita C. Desai, whose expertise and patience enabled this manuscript to be completed electronically. Richard Wentworth, the director of the University of Illinois Press, patiently supported this project, offering needed encouragement. Theresa Sears, assistant editor at the press, guided this book through the Scylla and Charybdis of publication.

Finally, this book belongs to my family, and I hope it speaks as eloquently as the brick walls my grandfather laid and the straight Illinois furrows plowed by the Wheelers. My daughters, Amy and Rebecca, infused my study with their passion for life, and my wife, Lynne, shared the frustrations and inconveniences. She cheerfully—and sometimes not so cheerfully—accompanied me to St. Louis and to Italy so I could complete my work. Neither the dedication nor these few words can ever express how much her love eased this manuscript through its many passages.

Introduction

We shall be as a city upon a hill,
the eyes of all people are upon us.
John Winthrop

Once there were many Little Italies and Dago Hills; alas, they have grown fewer. Such has been the case in St. Louis, Missouri. If an arbitrary event can trumpet the death of one Italian neighborhood and the renaissance of another, Hill Festa Day 1973 qualifies as such a date. How ironic that time and circumstances should intersect on that insufferably hot August day, marking one more summer of despair for Little Italy, another day in the neighborhood's march to destruction. The once-proud colony was on urban death row.

It was not always so. For a time Little Italy glittered as one of St. Louis's ethnic jewels, succeeding but never replacing the glories of Kerry Patch and the Ghetto. In its heyday between the two world wars the enclave bristled with excitement: the cacophonous voices of street vendors boasting "Fish, *Pesci freschi—Che bella insalata!!*" punctuated by the staccato machine-gunning of Egan's Rats or the scribblings of journalists such as Theodore Dreiser and Harry Rosencrans Burke.

Armed with tape recorder, I set out in 1973 to find remnants of a fallen civilization. Memories awakened of kindred spirits Dreiser and Burke, unabashed lovers of city sidewalks, who searched and described this same northside neighborhood decades earlier. Dreiser had haunted these streets in 1892, working the beat for the *St. Louis Globe-Democrat*, a paper he later left, having written a theater review for a performance he never attended. He had sensed that the near north side was on the cutting edge of urban and ethnic change, as the Irish fought a rearguard action against encroaching Jews and Italians. "It was all so dirty, so poor, so stuffy, so starving," he confessed, ". . . long-bearded Jews and their fat wives . . . rag pickers, chicken-dealers and feather sorters all."[1] Burke, a sympathetic reporter for the *St. Louis Star-Times*, patrolled Little Italy in the 1920s and 1930s. "Largely the population is Italian," he rhapsodized in 1923. "You will also find a big percentage of foreign-born Jews. . . . Thus it is a life which one does not know, yet a life one can glimpse carefully as one passes and those glimpses are pregnantly suggestive of poverty and thrift, of struggle and success, of dirt and cleanliness, of sorrow and humor, of sordid living and the bright dreams of romance." It was, he reflected "not a bad place to wander about in search of impressions."[2]

How disenchanted Burke and Dreiser would have been in 1973. Time had exacted a terrible toll on the city's north side. The neighborhood reeked of neglect and abuse, as blueprints plotted a new convention center for the area. Vague reminders of the hurly-burly past were scribbled on abandoned tenements: Evola's Barber Shop, D'Angelo's Meat Company, St. Patrick's Church, Columbus Square, Our Lady Help of Christians. The crumbling walls of the doomed buildings, marked like diseased pines, offered little resistance to the omnipresent wrecking ball. Nick Evola would soon leave the neighborhood. An emigrant from Palermo, Evola cut (not styled) hair practically from the moment he walked through Union Station in 1913; for sixty years he lived and worked in Little Italy. "I like barbering," Nick explained, "God has been good to me."[3] Fortune has smiled less kindly on the patrons of the skid-row Sunshine Mission at 612 Martin Luther King Drive. The asylum's motto stares at you like Uncle Sam's accusing finger: "No case is too hopeless for Jesus."

The fate of Our Lady Help of Christians, the Italian church at 1010 Cole, was still uncertain in 1973. Originally built for Methodists, in the 1890s the church had served as a Jewish synagogue. Our Lady Help of Christians now symbolized the area's turbulent past. Its crusty, soul-searching pastor, Father Edward Filipiak, plainly lamented the case of a similar church in the area. "The damn trucking firm bought the church and turned it into a garage," roared the belligerent priest. "In the future all the cities all over the country will be condominiums. Where are those people going to go to church? . . . I'm telling you, I'm Polish," he proudly noted, taking an occasional swig from a can of Falstaff. "If I would be taken away from down there, my heart would sink—twenty-seven years! I baptized kids over there that finally married and I baptized their kids! You know, it's a family to me."[4]

His family, a small congregation of Italian-Americans, had moved long ago to the suburbs but returned each Sunday in a defiantly pious gesture of tradition. "Monsignor said he wanted to phase out Our Lady Help of Christians," bristled Mary Greco, one of the loyal parishioners. "Monsignor told us, 'Why can't you go to any other church?' Because they don't have the tradition we have! Every statue in that church is not from the United States, but from the provinces in Italy. Madonna della Grazie—from Terrasini. Santa Fara—from Cinisi. Madonna del Ponte—from Partinico. . . . I belong to St. Catherine's but don't go there because you walk in there and it's like you're walking in a bar—too modern!"[5] It made me think of the 1905 description of the Feast of Corpus Christi in Little Italy, of "freshly scrubbed alleys and lanterns, mandolins, zithers, flags and candles."[6] Reminisced Rose Cusamano, a former resident of Little Italy and a Sicilian immigrant, "With nothing we was happy . . . we knew more about religion than they do today. We were very close. We were all Italians. Our days was different."[7]

Our Lady Help of Christians became a considerable liability—a church amid potentially valuable urban real estate. Silently expunged by writ of the city planner, the church was destroyed in the fall of 1975. But Father Filipiak staunchly refused to leave the neighborhood. "If it's a slum, I hope I die in it," he insisted.[8] He did. Permitted to relocate to the nearby Shrine of St. Joseph, a church built in 1843 and the site of authenticated miracles, which unfortunately were in short supply in 1979, Father Filipiak characteristically took up the lost cause of St. Joseph's, which the Jesuits had ignored for decades. His loyal congregation from Our Lady Help of Christians followed him to his new church. But when parishioners arrived for mass on September 30, 1979, they found police searching for clues to the murder of Edward Stanislaus Filipiak. Three sixteen-year-old youths from the Cochran Housing Project had robbed the seventy-nine-year-old priest, binding his legs and arms and tying a pillowcase over his head, causing suffocation. A police lieutenant somberly told reporters, "He lived almost like a dog and he died like a dog. But he died for what he believed in." The event shocked St. Louisans, 1,500 of whom attended his funeral.[9] While his death may have saved the Shrine of St. Joseph, even martyrdom could not save

Little Italy. Today it resembles a chic adult development, sporting affluent townhouses (one named after Columbus Square) and businesses catering to the convention crowd.

As church fathers eulogized Edward Filipiak, and elegized Little Italy, urban planners battled over superlatives to salute the lusty health of the Hill. The pulse of the Hill was strong in 1973, and it is even stronger today. Tens of thousands of St. Louisans have attended the neighborhood's annual Hill Day, discontinued because it was too successful! But the health of a district must be measured in ways other than how many roast pepper sandwiches and buckets of beer are consumed. The history of the Hill runs much deeper than ethnic festivals or "Kiss Me, I'm Italian" buttons. To say that the Hill experienced a rebirth in the 1970s is profoundly mistaken, for it had never died.

The Hill was born in the old country. Immigration historians have long recognized that local history must be more than state and area events. Indeed, the history of this neighborhood in southwest St. Louis transcends its parochial boundaries and is interwoven with national economic patterns and international movements of ideas and people. On April 25, 1981, the citizens of Cuggiono, a small village in Lombardy which had sent to St. Louis the bulk of the Hill's population, hosted a "Cuggionesi in America" celebration. Almost 500 inhabitants—all related to St. Louis brethren—crowded into the San Rocco Club to hear me feebly attempt to explain in Italian what had happened to their *parenti* (relatives) once they had left to seek their fortunes on *la Montagna* (the Hill). An aging farmer asked what had happened to his cousin, who had worked as a fireman at the brick kilns around 1907; a young student wanted to know whether the streets in America were gilded; a parliamentary delegate rose to her feet, assuring the gathering that, yes, Cuggionesi in America had few wants. An elderly priest sat quietly through the entire proceedings, then cornered me and posed only one question: "Have they kept the faith?" The Cuggionesi not only kept the faith, I told him, they survived. In a country where almost everyone is from somewhere else, where new is better, the legacy of Cuggiono still stands, a monument to immigrant inspiration and perspiration. The lustre of the neighborhood has brought the fifty-two-block enclave national publicity. *Time*, the *Christian Science Monitor*, *Sports Illustrated*, *Attenzione*, the *Tampa Tribune*, National Public Radio, and *The Today Show* have all lauded the ethnic vibrancy of the colony.[10]

What occurred from steerage to success? Why has the Hill survived while most other ethnic neighborhoods have long since deteriorated? Essentially, the creation and sustenance of a community preserved the Hill. Rowland Berthoff maintained in *An Unsettled People* that "the nature of modern urban life was essentially uncommunal," that until Americans stopped moving so much and rededicated themselves to a sense of community, our social malaise would continue.[11] Clearly the Hill, in comparison to other ethnic and urban colonies, has traveled a very different path of development. Early residents, after a period of settlement, erected communal institutions that have continued to sustain and maintain individual and family allegiance. Immigrants on the Hill clustered together in an isolated and exclusively Italian enclave where most inhabitants sank tenacious roots, refusing to leave the colony despite limited economic prospects. I do not contend that the same processes occurred in Boston, San Francisco, or Tampa, for in many respects the Hill was—and is—unique; in other ways, the colony's territorial persistence reflects the history of ethnic enclaves, such as New York City's Little Italy, San Francisco's North Beach, Boston's South End, and "the Burg" in Trenton, New Jersey.

The physical existence of the Hill speaks reverentially of the neighborhood's history. Equally eloquent are the many voices of inhabitants who have ensured that this history will not be a dreary compilation of census data and newspaper accounts. Interviews buttress the foundation of this book, which is, perhaps, as it should be. Few archivists cared to preserve documents from the Hill; consequently, little traditional history exists in libraries or museums.

It is true that oral histories liberate us from total dependence on the written word, but how are we to separate the "facts" from the octogenarian ramblings about a past that never was? Barbara Tuchman has complained that while oral histories are being gathered at a furious pace, much of them consist of mindless trivia passed off as scholarship.[12] Trivial for whom? Significant and meaningful historical data can be generated if the historian asks intelligent, open-ended questions and analyzes the material with the same scrutiny as traditional sources.[13] I believe that oral history can and should be utilized as an essential methodology for immigration history, since immigration history is a study of *people*. Those who struggled and loved and worked can provide indispensable insights into their world. Indeed, without such interviews this study would have been reduced to collective portraits gleaned from census tracts and institutional histories written by elites. This account of the Hill is told mainly from the parish's view, not the archbishop's; from the workers' vantage point, not the owners'; from the bootleggers' cellar, not the courthouse. The immigrant perspective adds bands of color and a human dimension too often forgotten in many mobility studies. Discussions of picture brides and war grooms allow the historian and general reader alike to view the world of the workplace and playground. Like the slave narratives compiled during the 1930s, immigrant oral histories are not perfect sources, but they still must be recognized as profoundly important, because the interviews often constitute a unique resource, an insight from the immigrant and slave perspective. Sadly, most of the participants in the tapings for this study, done between 1973 and 1984, are now dead.

Oral tradition thrives on the Hill. The recollections of anonymous individuals has breathed life into the past. Many respondents reached back to the old country, where on cold winter nights the peasants told their stories. "Those old men had never been to school," remembered an elderly woman from Cuggiono, "but they were smart, anyway, the way they told the stories and made everybody laugh,"[14] A barber promised in 1973: "If you write this up, you're going to get some good material and it's no bullshit, it's all up and up stuff. It really happened."[15] We are reminded of the encounter between the poet Ronald Blythe and an elderly farmer in Akenfield, England. "What songs did ye sing Davy?" Blythe asked. Davy responded, "It's not the songs, it was the singing." The point for Blythe, and for me, is that it was not so much the individual responses but the rapturous anthem of spirit conveyed in collecting data from extraordinary people.[16]

A study based on interviews always exposes itself to criticism in that its conclusions, when drawn from oral sources, may not be representative of an entire community. Studying a "successful" neighborhood can be a self-fulfilling exercise: those who have not "kept the faith" have most likely moved away and hence escaped the tape recorder; those who remain behind are thus, by nature of the selective process, both stable and supportive. In the research design of this manuscript the conclusion of a "successful" community was not predetermined. Interviews were conducted along the lines of neighborhood themes and personal experiences. No systematic basis of selecting interviewees was made, aside from a conviction that individuals who performed critical roles in the community's power structure—priests, politicians, and journalists—should be interviewed. Most of the interviews, however, were with individuals who had achieved neither success nor fame: elderly immigrants, laborers, housewives, and parishioners. Virtually anyone who would sit down and talk was given an audience. From taverns to rectories, nearly 100 interviews were conducted, and a diverse and appealing portrait of an ethnic community emerged in these peoples' life histories.

Future historians may well look back on 1983–84 as the year of Italian-American recognition. Names like Paterno, Valvano, Massimino, Altobelli, Lasorda, Pacino, Stallone, Scorsese, Coppola, Iacocca, D'Amato, Domenici, DeNiro, Giamatti, Curti-Smeal, and Rodino testify to the sheer accumulative achievement of Italian-Americans. The Census Bureau confirms the image: Italian-Americans no longer resemble stereotypical blue-collar, tenement-dwelling *cafoni* (rubes). According to Alfred J. Tella, adviser to the Census Bureau, Italian-Americans have arrived: their presence in white-collar positions mirror national averages; they have moved to the suburbs and have no more children than the average American family. "It's the story of a three-generation success," says Stella, noting that there are now about fifteen million Italian-Americans.

The *New York Times Magazine* conferred special status on Italian-Americans in the form of a May 15, 1983, cover story: "Coming Into Their Own." Observed feature writer Stephen Hall: "Among white ethnic groups, there is probably no other culture that has so conscientiously and successfully husbanded its traditional values—from the close-knit family structure to the exuberant celebration of feasts—into the present moment." Just when readers thought it was safe to escape from Italian-Americana, Mario Cuomo delivered an impassioned address at the 1984 Democratic National Convention, a speech filled with ethnic nostalgia and a yearning for the old New Deal coalition. If Cuomo won the minds of Democrats, Geraldine Ferraro won their hearts, with her triumphant vice-presidential nomination. *CBS Sunday Morning News* devoted a cover story to the Italian-American political phenomenon, "It's Our Turn Now," reminding viewers that until John Pastore became governor and later senator of Rhode Island in the 1950s, no other Italian-American had held such a high office.

Lest history degenerate into a cataloguing of ethnic gifts and who's who, we must ask not how many Italian-Americans have made the front page of the *New York Times*, nor how many hot tubs these ethnics have in suburbia, but rather how success is measured. If Italian-Americans have been slow to assimilate and late in climbing America's social and economic ladders, is it simply because they measure success by a different yardstick? Italian-American history is a study of neighborhoods and communities, a heritage of person-to-person, group-to-group relationships. It emphasizes the primacy of personal and ultimate relations in family and communal institutions, and celebrates a struggle to achieve dignity and control over the quality and shape of life in urban-industrial America. Success is more often measured not by mobility through white-collar suburbia but by preservation of family and community. By this standard Italian-Americans have succeeded, making their way to the mainstream via different routes.

Historians and social scientists have long been fascinated by the Italian-American neighborhood, its origins, its culture, its tenacity and persistence. A number of outstanding studies on the Italian-American experience have been published in recent years. These monographs, by Josef Barton, John Briggs, Dino Cinel, Luciano Iorizzo, Thomas Kessner, Sal Mondello, Humbert Nelli, Donald Tricarico, Rudolph Vecoli, and Virginia Yans-McLaughlin, have established new parameters of research and scholarship. These authors examine the impact of various Italian-American settlements and, more significantly, assess the importance of mobility, family, labor militancy, and migration patterns through the agenda of immigration history. My study is different in that it focuses on the evolution of one neighborhood over a period of 100 years.

The definitive history of the Italian-American experience still awaits its historian. The task of interpreting the saga of six million immigrants, who left varied landscapes and settled in every state in the Union, is clearly a formidable assignment, but studies at the local level, both in Italy and the Americas, will facilitate this task. Thus far, the bulk of the research has focused on the premigration experience and ends in the 1920s, with the formal Immigration Restriction Acts; to get a full picture will require studies that extend up to the present.

My interest in the Hill was motivated in part by a process of self-discovery and self-identification, in part by a desire to find a relevant past rooted in primary social relationships and institutions. How did immigrant settlement succeed in developing distinctive communal values? What is a community? How can we explain the persistence of Italian-American neighborhoods?

NOTES

1. Dreiser, *Book About Myself*, 219.
2. Burke, *From the Day's Journey*, 155.
3. Interview with Nick Evola, July 29, 1973.
4. Interview with Fr. Edward Filipiak, Aug. 14, 1973.
5. Interview with Mary Greco, Sept. 16, 1973.
6. *St. Louis Republic*, June 25, 1905, iv, p. 4 (hereafter cited as *Republic*).
7. Interview with Rose Cusamano, July 30, 1973.
8. Interview with Fr. Edward Filipiak, Aug. 14, 1973. *St. Louis Post-Dispatch*, Oct. 14, 1975, p. 1 (hereafter cited as *Post-Dispatch*); *St. Louis Globe-Democrat*, Jan. 27, 1975, p. 6-a (hereafter cited as *Globe-Democrat*).
9. *Globe-Democrat*, Oct. 1, 1979, p. 1; *Post-Dispatch*, Oct. 1, 1979, p. 1; *Globe-Democrat*, Oct. 4, 1979, p. 17.
10. Michaels, "St. Louis," 27; "The Hill, St. Louis," *Christian Science Monitor*, Feb. 13, 1973, p. F1; Deford, "They Call It a Game," 116–20; "Report from the Hill," *Today Show*, NBC television, Jan. 23, 1976; Horrigan, "Little Italy Now," 65–69; Cassidy, "No Blues in St. Louis," 30–37; Otto, "St. Louis on Independence Day," B1; Edwards, National Public Radio, Sept. 27, 1985.
11. Berthoff, *An Unsettled People*, 389.
12. Tuchman, "Significant and Insignificant," 9–10.
13. See Bodnar, *Workers' World; Oral History Review*, past issues; Thompson, *Voice of the Past*.
14. Ms., Rosa Casettari collection, box 1, folder 2, University of Minnesota, Minneapolis, Immigration History Research Center (hereafter IHRC).
15. Interview with Charles Rancilio, July 14, 1973.
16. Greele, "Movement Without Aim," 127–54.

1 The Mound City

Meet me in St. Louis, Louie,
Meet me at the Fair.
Don't tell me the lights are shining
anywhere but there.
Meet Me in St. Louis (1944)

"First in shoes, first in booze, and last in the American League," chanted St. Louis civic boosters not too many decades ago. Alas, today the city claims supremacy neither in shoes (importing slippers from Naples) nor in beer (displaced by upstart Los Angeles), and the beloved Browns callously departed for Baltimore (where they began winning). A slogan, a song, a book, a movie, a World's Fair, all once trumpeted the splendors of St. Louis, called at various times the "Mound City" and the "Gateway City."

Now, the city that helped give birth to jazz is singing the blues. Not since the Gilded Age—when brassy Chicago outdistanced St. Louis—have Gateway leaders been so melancholy. The 1980 census tabulated a litany of urban disasters: between 1950 and 1980 the population of St. Louis plummeted from 857,000 to 453,000, a 47 percent decline, the highest percentage loss of any large city; since 1950 St. Louis has lost one-quarter of its housing stock due to abandonment. In reality the city has not so much died as surrendered its population to outlying areas in Illinois and Missouri. St. Louis, which has not expanded its boundaries since 1876, contains a land mass of only 61 square miles; by comparison, Chicago commands 224 square miles. In 1900 two of every three people living in the designated Standard Metropolitan Statistical Area resided within the city limits; by the 1970s that figure had fallen to fewer than one in four.

A city built for the steamboat, railroad, and factory system had fallen prey to the internal combustion engine, suburbia, and the Sunbelt.[1] But there was a time when St. Louis basked in the urban spotlight, a time when German beer barons sneered at Milwaukee and sternwheelers crowded the levee. A frontier heritage, river-boat culture, Creole settlements, graceful neighborhoods, and a distinctly ethnic flavor gave the Mound City, in the words of Ernest Kirschten, "a touch of catfish and crystal."[2]

The colorful history of modern St. Louis dates from the turbulent struggle for empire in the remote but promising Mississippi Valley. The year 1763 saw Pierre de Laclede Liguest sail up the Father of Waters in an attempt to regain for France the lucrative fur trade of Upper Louisiana. His keen eye caught the imposing limestone bluffs that guarded the first elevated land mass south of the confluence of the Mississippi, Illinois, and Missouri rivers. Geography clearly blessed Laclede's choice for a new settlement. Protected from perennial floodwaters, the site afforded easy access to the Mississippi while the hinterland offered excellent farmland and timber for future settlement. Laclede boasted with unpardonable pride that this place would become "one of the finest cities in America."[3]

When American dragoons arrived in 1804 to assay Jefferson's timely purchase the city had already been prospering for half a century. Three flags over St. Louis had given it a lusty, cosmopolitan character, an infusion of French and Spanish culture steeped in the raucous influences of mountain men, Indians, and slaves. Symbols of the past and future existed side-by-side: prehistoric Indian mounds gave way to Gallic mansions and gristmills. The Mound City from which Lewis and Clark marched west in 1804 resembled a European village, as its European designers had intended. This "anachronistic beginning" imparted a legacy that helped shape the geographical and social bases of modern St. Louis. A Creole aristocracy, dominated by entrenched landed and commercial interests, retained positions of power and prestige. French and Spanish land grants created future obstacles to growth and a litigious nightmare.[4]

"St. Louis will become the Memphis of the American Nile," prophesied the American statesman Henry Brackenridge in 1811.[5] The city prospered briefly following the War of 1812 but then stagnated throughout the 1820s. Although it still retained vestiges of a frontier town in 1830, change wafted in the air. Most visibly the city's profile was undergoing a transformation: fur traders, once guarantors of prosperity, drifted away from the Mississippi Valley; and French residents, once numerous, were being overshadowed by new arrivals. The city's 5,852 inhabitants looked to the future, and in 1830 that future was the Mississippi River,[6] although eventually it would be water that lockset St. Louis's growth. With the arrival of two small steamboats in 1812 and the regular appearance of sidewheelers by the 1820s, St. Louis was cast in the role of a major station on the thriving river trade. By 1832, 596 steam-driven vessels paddled their goods to and from the city, a figure that increased to 2,105 in 1844.[7]

The bustling river trade meant more to St. Louis than a colorful backdrop for Samuel Clemens. "The first time I ever saw St. Louis," wrote Mark Twain in *Life on the Mississippi*, "I could have bought it for six million dollars, and it was the mistake of my life that I did not do it."[8] Twain's loss was St. Louis's gain. The city grew from 16,469 persons in 1840 to 77,000 in 1850. "St. Louis is a most striking town as seen from the river," remarked a visitor in 1847. "For some distance the river is lined with piles of lofty and massive warehouses, indicating the existence of an extensive heavy business. The wharves are thronged with crafts of different kinds, but from the inland position of the town, the steamers greatly predominate. The city is handsomely built, chiefly of brick."[9] The city's relationship with the river affected its living and working patterns. Geographically the river culture tied St. Louis to an interregional network of trade and exchange; spatially the town evolved parallel to the river in a north-south axis three times longer than it was wide. River traffic and natural barriers, such as Chouteau's Pond and Mill Creek, blocked westward development for decades.[10]

The august age of steamboating created an aura of urban supremacy, a smug security in the belief that geography had predestined the Mound City for greatness. Boosters pointed to the city's advantageous natural factors. Abundant sources of Missouri iron ore, lead, zinc, gypsum, and salt, and fabulous deposits of cheap bituminous coal from central and southern Illinois, supplied St. Louis with the raw materials necessary for an industrial base. From the smelters and foundries, factories and millshops, poured forth an impressive array of steamboat machinery, cast-iron stoves, nails, lead paints, and barrel staves. Farmers from Illinois and Missouri shipped their bountiful surpluses downriver to turn St. Louis into a major center for flour and meal refining, meat packing, and brewing. St. Louis was, on the eve of the Civil War, a bustling, industrialized trade entrepôt.[11]

America's trek westward assured St. Louis of its role as a gateway city.

"St. Louis is the starting point from civilization for savagedom," observed the 1857 gazetteer *Appleton's Illustrated.* The Show-Me State shared in the prosperity, adding thousands of new residents during this phenomenal growth of the Mississippi Valley. Hannibal's favorite son, Mark Twain, described this feverish era in *The Gilded Age.* Missouri is "the place for a young fellow of spirit to pick up a fortune," ballyhooed the irascible Colonel Eschol Sellers in a meeting at St. Louis's Planter's Hotel. "The whole country is coming up. . . . The richest land on God Almighty's footstool is lying right out there."[12]

The Civil War only temporarily halted the impulse toward urban greatness. Logan Uriah Reavis articulated this philosophy in his now-classic paean *St. Louis: The Future City of the World and Its Impending Triumph.* Indeed, the triumph seemed at hand. The opening of Eads Bridge in 1874 promised to fulfill the city's destiny. After all, had not census takers in 1870 discovered a dynamic city that had doubled its 1860 population—all accomplished in spite of a divisive war. Officially St. Louis ranked as the nation's fourth largest city in 1870; unofficially, as Neal Primm has painstakingly recounted, the 1870 census count was fraudulent, "rotten bacon in the barrel." In reality William McKee, publisher of the *Missouri Democrat* and patronage agent for President Grant, had recruited a corrupt cadre of census enumerators to inflate the St. Louis total over its rival Chicago.[13] St. Louisans, falsely comfortable in their numerical superiority, expressed disbelief and outrage on discovering in 1880 that Chicagoans outnumbered them. The 1880 census revealed that St. Louis had officially grown only 11 percent, but in truth the Mound City had enjoyed an impressive decade of growth, a fact obscured by the skewed data of 1870.

The census fiasco precipitated a recurring historical debate: how to explain Chicago's triumph over St. Louis. Wyatt Belcher's *The Economic Rivalry Between St. Louis and Chicago* (1947) advanced the enduring thesis that the more sedentary St. Louis leaders, rooted in a premodern, preindustrial Creole setting, allowed the more aggressive Yankee businessmen from Chicago to outhustle them. To prove his theory, Belcher pointed to Chicago's prescient decision to invest in the future of railroads, while St. Louis remained wedded to the river, a decision based more on sentiment than acumen.[14]

Historians Neal Primm, Glen Holt, and Christopher Schnell have demolished the Belcher thesis as being interpretively simplistic and factually wrong. First, St. Louis was, in 1870, neither dominated nor monopolized by Creole leaders; Belcher simply confused social status with economic power. Second, the failure of St. Louis to become *the* rail hub of the Midwest did not occur because of any lack of effort by its leaders or an idyllic fascination with steamboats, but because of the more compelling locational advantages of Chicago, as well as postwar migration and immigration patterns.[15] In spite of Chicago's dominance, St. Louis did become a major rail center, shifting the city's axis from a north-south orientation to an east-west one. Eads Bridge dramatized the new era, as rail traffic brought millions of visitors and workers to and through St. Louis. In fact, by 1900 some twenty-two rail lines carried 1,000 passengers daily into Union Station at Eighteenth and Market streets. New settlements followed the train tracks; and as railroads probed the valleys west of the city, homes were being built atop the hills.[16]

If St. Louis never matched the astronomical growth of Chicago, the metropolitan area nonetheless experienced dramatic gains in the second half of the nineteenth century. Both the character and the composition of the city underwent major changes, most noticeably in the ethnic makeup of its inhabitants. George Featherstonaugh, an English commentator, noted after visiting St. Louis in 1834 that "the population of the place is oddly mixed up."[17] Just as the steamboat and railroad transformed the urban economy, so would the first great invasion of immigrants in the 1840s recast cityscapes and workplaces. The 1840s famine in Ireland and crop failures in southern Germany unleashed a tidal wave of immigrants, many of whom came to settle in the Midwest.

Like Gaul from which its founder came, St. Louis was divided into three parts, in this case German, Irish, and American (slave and free). The social upheaval taking place there was evident in the 1850 census, which showed that St. Louis was the most ethnic city in the United States: almost 60 percent of the city's population at that time was foreign-born. Residential patterns, once fixed by river habits, now began to reflect class, racial, and ethnic divisions. Newly arrived immigrants sought low-cost housing near their place of employment, carving out Irish and German enclaves on the north and south sides.[18] These two ethnic groups comprised the majority of the expanding population base in the 1840s and 1850s. By 1850 there were 22,571 Germans and 9,719 Irish immigrants settled in St. Louis; by comparison, barely 20,000 of the Mound City's residents were born in Missouri. For every Irish and

German immigrant who remained in St. Louis, scholars now believe that many others funneled through St. Louis, presaging its nickname as the Gateway City.

Prospective German farmers, propelled by the lure of western soil and the heady accounts by such publicists as Gottfried Duden, flocked to St. Louis to prepare for the journey westward, to work and save for the future, and to purchase farming and other implements.[19] Ethnic enclaves continued to sprawl along the city's north and south sides, and by 1890 St. Louis had attracted 66,000 foreign-born Germans, representing nearly 15 percent of the city's population.[20] Foremost among the German colonies was the Soulard district, near the breweries. But one could not speak of a coherent, geographically bounded German community, as in Milwaukee or Cincinnati.

These failed revolutionaries and highly skilled craftsmen from the Rhenish region imprinted their lusty life-style on St. Louis culture and work. Brewmasters such as Eberhard Anheuser and Adolphus Busch, through an alchemy of Missouri grains and old-world artisanship, created a vast industry and discovered an appreciative clientele to consume their lagers and ales. A widespread institutional network ministered to the immigrants. Carl Schurz, Emil Praetorius, and Carl Danzer debated dialectics and sectionalism in the *Westliche Post* and the St. Louis Hegelian Society. The masses preferred the earthier open-air beer gardens and the various *vereine*, which all shared an utter contempt for the city's Sunday blue laws. The turnverein, a highly structured athletic association, survived the transplant to the New World, stressing not only physical fitness but also the retention of German culture, scholarship, and coeducational activities. But overall, the turners fragmented rather than unified the German immigrants in St. Louis, who never did become a homogeneous group.[21]

German immigrants adjusted easily to the American political system. "The foreign character of St. Louis is again signally illustrated by the election of Mr. Wahl," editorialized the *St. Louis Post-Dispatch* in 1879. Founded by the Hungarian immigrant Josef Pulitzer, the newspaper keenly perceived the importance of ethnic politics. "The Mayor of St. Louis is a German," it was pointed out. "The Lt. Governor of the state is a German. One of the Judges of the U.S. Court is German. The last Republican candidate for Governor was a German. . . . And of the seven morning dailies, four are German."[22] Perhaps the best known of the German politicos was "Onkel" Henry Ziegenham, who, when the city refused to install a modern lighting system, quipped, "We got a moon yet, ain't we?"[23]

If the Germans boasted the largest immigrant group in St. Louis, the Irish were the most colorful. For Irishmen home rule became a reality with the creation of the great enclaves, Kerry Patch and Tipperary. Fed by refugees from County Kerry, the Celtic colony in St. Louis sprawled along the northwestern edge of the downtown area and was a constantly shifting district, ebbing and flowing with northwestern in- and out-migrants. "Kindly and brutal, prim and riotous, pious and profane," wrote Frank O'Hare, "Kerry Patch was staunchly self-contained."[24]

The 1880s and 1890s served as watershed decades for St. Louis. Demographically and industrially the city lagged behind Chicago, "Hog Butcher for the World," which modernized its industrial base and attracted hundreds of thousands of immigrants to furnish the raw labor. In St. Louis the "new" immigrants from southern and eastern Europe never achieved the scale of migration and labor that occurred in Chicago, and the "old" immigrants, the Irish and Germans, retained their numerical advantages. In 1880, for instance, St. Louis had 350,900 residents, of whom 54,901 were German, 28,536 Irish, and 7,750 English, Welsh, and Scotch. If one counted second-generation progeny, perhaps two-thirds of the city's population came from these groups.[25]

While St. Louis continued to expand in the late nineteenth century, relatively few new immigrants put down roots along the Mississippi. The figures and percentages pale in particular when compared to the more dynamic economies of Chicago, Detroit, and Cleveland, where Slavs and other Europeans anchored the expanding heavy industries. The decade of the 1890s—a pivotal period during the early stages of immigrant dispersion—was hard on St. Louis. The depression devastated the city's industrial base, which increased only 2 percent during that period.[26] While St. Louis's economy remained highly diversified, it lacked the dynamic quality of Chicago, Detroit, and Cleveland, which generated and refined new economies of scale in petroleum, automobiles, meat processing, and steel. Immigrants were leaving Italy and the Austro-Hungarian Empire because of economic reasons, and where they settled in America was determined predominantly by economic-familial factors.[27]

The 1910 census provides a clear picture of the direction in which St. Louis was going. Overall the city claimed 687,029 residents, making it the fourth largest in the nation. However, comparing the proportion of foreign-born whites to the general population, at 18.3 percent St. Louis ranked thirtieth relative to cities of more than 100,000. This was roughly equal to Denver, Toledo, Syracuse, Albany, Cincinnati, and Baltimore—cities normally not regarded as major destinations for new immigrants; among cities with over half a million inhabitants, only Baltimore had fewer immigrants. Analyzing the composition of St. Louis's foreign-born residents, it becomes apparent that the city had failed to attract appreciable numbers of Italians, Slavs, Greeks, and Jews. There were more Scots than Greeks, more Canadians than Rumanians, and six times more Germans than Italians. The city counted 12,119 Russians (Jews), 7,594 Italians, 8,759 Hungarians, 11,171 Austrians (Slavs from Poland, Yugoslavia, and Czechoslovakia) and 1,312 Greeks; Germans constituted the largest group, with 47,765.[28] World War I drastically curtailed immigration, so the figures did not substantially change in 1920 (see Table 1), except for a 19 percent increase among Italian immigrants (to 9,067) and a 56 percent increase among Greeks (to 2,049). The Germans and Irish registered significant losses between 1910 and 1920, the former declining from 47,765 to 30,089, while the latter slumped from 14,268 to 9,244, indicative of the aging profiles of both groups. The 1920 census

Table 1. White Foreign-born Population in St. Louis, 1920

Country of Birth	*Number*	*Percentage*
Austria	5,587	5.4
Canada	1,935	1.9
Czechoslovakia	3,479	3.4
England	3,892	3.8
Germany	30,089	29.1
Greece	2,049	2.0
Ireland	9,244	9.0
Italy[a]	9,067	8.8
Poland	5,224	5.1
Rumania	1,200	1.2
Russia	13,067	12.7
Sweden	898	0.9
Yugoslavia	1,686	1.6
Total	103,239	93.7

Source: *Fourteenth Census of the United States, 1920, Population—Missouri*, vol. 3, Table 13.

[a]Of these, 2,070 (2.0 percent overall) lived on the Hill.

allows for a more detailed examination of nationalities from the Balkans and eastern Europe, but the numbers remain scant (1,686 Serbians and Croatians, 1,200 Rumanians, 3,479 Bohemians and Slovaks, and 5,224 Poles).[29]

On the eve of the jazz decade the economic bombshell called Prohibition shattered St. Louis. Adding numerical insult to economic injury the city fell to sixth place nationally, behind New York, Chicago, Philadelphia, Detroit, and Cleveland—all major centers of immigration. St. Louis had, however, attracted a large Afro-American community; by 1920 some 69,854 blacks constituted 9.0 percent of the population, in contrast to Chicago (4.1 percent), Milwaukee (0.5 percent), and Cleveland (4.3 percent). In 1916 St. Louisans overwhelmingly endorsed the nation's first segregation ordinance, which mandated residential quotas.[30]

The failure of St. Louis to draw more immigrants in the late nineteenth and early twentieth centuries can be attributed to factors other than mere urban rivalry. Relatively large numbers of Slavs, for instance, settled to the east in Illinois, just across the Mississippi River. After 1900 the east side swiftly evolved into an industrial matrix of iron foundries, oil refineries, slaughterhouses, and leather tanneries. Industrialists, taking advantage of new economies of scale, inexpensive land, compliant governments, the availability of Illinois coal, and the facility of barge and rail traffic, built factories in East St. Louis, Granite City, Wood River, Alton, Belleville, Madison, Venice, and Roxana. Manufacturers in Illinois also were able to avoid payment of Missouri's controversial bridge tax. While the combined populations of Madison and St. Clair counties barely exceeded 100,000 in 1880, by 1920 there were over 25,000 immigrants huddled in eastside quarters alone, such as Granite City's "Hunky Hollow," which prior to 1910 had housed the largest concentration of Bulgarians in the United States. Immigrants constituted the work force for a manufacturing complex that increasingly competed with St. Louis and won. Between 1904 and 1909 Madison and St. Clair counties lured nearly as many new factories as St. Louis, and by 1929 the metropolitan eastside district laid claim to nearly one-third the area's manufacturing products.[31]

St. Louis may not have achieved the distinction of becoming the most prominent immigrant center in America, but immigration nonetheless profoundly shaped this metropolis. Although the "new" immigrants did not replace Germans and Irish in numbers and impact, Italians, Jews, Slavs, and Greeks did greatly influence the city. Headlines trumpeted their presence in 1900–1925: "GREEK AND LATIN INVASION HAS REACHED ST. LOUIS," and "DEATH OF KERRY PATCH," and "GHETTO ARISES OUT OF KERRY PATCH."[32] The inimitable Jack Ryan recorded with a touch of bravado the precise moment of the decline of Kerry Patch: "About my block, of which I was so proud, there were no foreigners on it. The neighbors were the McClanns, the O'Reillys, the Haggartys, the O'Briens, the Noonans, the O'Roarkes. Johnny Corrigan's Block? It became ruined. A family named Schweitzer moved in."[33] "The old St. Louis is vanishing," observed the *Post-Dispatch*, May 18, 1912. "There will be regrets for the disappearances of its German sections, of its Kerry Patch, of the many attractive features that gave a distinctive quality to the town. But St. Louis is still a cosmopolitan city."[34] "Contrasted to Chicago," confessed Theodore Dreiser, "it [St. Louis] was not a metropolis at all. . . . I learned in time to like it very much, but for the things that set it apart from other cities, not for the things by which it sought to rival them."[35]

Little Italy and the Ghetto both frightened and fascinated St. Louisans at the turn of the century. Although Syrians, Croatians, Macedonians, Poles, and Hungarians also concentrated in ethnic clusters, the print media seemed transfixed by the Italian and Jewish enclaves, in part because they existed just a notebook's throw from the offices of the fourth estate. Italian and Jewish immigrants, attracted by employment opportunities in the downtown shoe factories, garment shops, and fruit-and-vegetable markets, flocked to the cheap housing of the northside tenements. Labor agents and *padroni* frequently hawked transients and gangs for railroad work. Quartered in the center of the city and characterized by patterns of high density and rapid geographic mobility, Little Italy and the Ghetto both fit the classic portrait of an ethnic enclave.

City dailies frequently spotlighted the bizarre traits of these newcomers. "St. Louis is a cosmopolitan city with a foreign population within her borders gathered from the far corners of the earth," observed the *Globe-Democrat*. "It is not necessary to cross the Alps to see the 'picturesque peasantry' of southern Europe. One only has to wander into 'Little Italy' to see lazzaroni, with only the Blue Bay of Naples lacking to complete the picture. . . . It is not necessary to sail through the Straits of the Dardenelles to see the Russian Jew or cross the Levant to get a view of a sad-eyed Syrian woman."[36] "If all the different kinds of people in St. Louis wore on the streets of the city all the different kinds of costumes they wore in their native countries before they came here," the paper later promised curiosity seekers, "we might put a fence around the city and charge an admission fee."[37] Reporters delighted in the exotica of the foreign enclave, such as the rag peddlers' exchange, the warring factionalism between ethnic sects, and the parade of barefoot Italians honoring the Virgin Mary.[38]

The hurly-burly of Little Italy and the Ghetto offered bohemians an ethnic oasis, but St. Louis's more affluent classes preferred the comforts of the west side. Neighborhoods there radiated the distinctive patterns of religion, ethnicity, and class. Subdivisions catering to middle-class life-styles attracted increasing numbers of families, leaving blacks and immigrants behind in tenements and ghettos. The rhythm of the turn-of-the-century city, an urban historian has suggested, "while often frantic, had a definite pattern, a pattern that consisted of a constant ebb and flow between the percussion and brass of downtown and the more subtle sounds emanating from the periphery."[39] Like other cities St. Louis was in a constant process of sorting out races, classes, and ethnics in an economic and geographic matrix. Where once the Chouteaus and first families of St. Louis built mansions in the downtown district, the horse-drawn trolley and later the electric streetcar allowed the middle and upper classes to escape to the first suburbs, city beautifuls. Between 1890 and 1910 the proportion of St. Louis's population living west of Grand Avenue rose from 12.9 percent to 27 percent. The nickel trolley fare enabled executives and many middle-class workers to live miles away from their places of employment in the center city.[40]

Not all St. Louis immigrants huddled in downtown tenements, heard the singsong of the hurdy-gurdy, or sold bananas at curbside stalls, however. Just as the new order and technologies had ordained some immigrants to the downtown area, so had it decentralized the urban economy, allowing certain industries to take advantage of extended rail lines and cheap raw materials. Such an industrial and extractive complex evolved, known as the Cheltenham district, with a work force that, once German, was by 1900 composed of Italian laborers. An Italian colony grew out of this industrial complex, an ethnic enclave destined to become one of the most enduring in America. Geographically isolated and culturally insulated, "Dago Hill" struck contemporaries as a distinct contribution to the city's vibrant life-style. "Sixty thousand immigrants entered the United States in 1900," began an account of life on the Hill. "Where do they go? And what do they do? And how do they live?" The author confessed that he had many unanswered questions after his brief tour of the colony.[41]

The enclave proved difficult to penetrate. During its formative years Italian immigrants labored long hours for pittance wages and lived in boardinghouses. Cordoned by rail lines, iron foundries, brick factories, and the sewage-strewn River des Peres, the community breathed an aura of legend, and more than one journalist was tempted to find the colony's pulse. Exotic and historic as the city, the site on which the Hill was situated had come a long way since 1764. West of the fur-trading post known as St. Louis lay an arcadia, where gentle hills and broad valleys lined the banks of the meandering streams, the *Petite Rivière* and the *Rivière des Pères* (anglicized to Mill Creek and River des Peres). The rolling woodlands and mineral springs along the River des Peres tantalized early speculators, such as the Swiss merchant-trader Charles Gratiot, who sought to amass an immense tract of land for speculation. Related by marriage to the powerful Chouteau family, Gratiot in 1785 petitioned Spanish authorities for a land grant. The 5,700-acre tract, comprising much of present-day southwest St. Louis, has since been called the Gratiot League Square. By the time of Gratiot's death in 1817, few settlers had disturbed this virgin land.[42]

Much of the Gratiot League south of present-day Forest Park and west of Kingshighway had been sold by 1830, including a large parcel to William Sublette, the famous mountain man and fur entrepreneur. Derrick A. January, a wholesale grocer, also maintained a large estate in the vicinity. Sublette envisioned his property as a suburban retreat, which he dubbed Sulphur Springs (the locale was later called Fairmount Heights), and in 1834 he began construction of a permanent stone residence, in addition to a number of guest cottages. Married to Frances Hereford in 1844, he died shortly thereafter, and in 1848 his heirs sold 388 acres to David Graham. Graham, in turn, sold smaller tracts to Thomas Allen, a financier, who leased the resort to William Wible. The area was renamed Cheltenham, in honor of Wible's birthplace, the famous spa by that name in England, and it enjoyed brief fame as a fashionable refuge for the urban weary.[43]

Transportation would play a significant role in Cheltenham's evolution from a spa to an industrial hive. Improvements on the Manchester Road in the 1830s made travel to St. Louis possible. The Pacific Railroad completed five miles of track from St. Louis to Cheltenham in 1852, the first trans-Mississippi rail venture, thus opening the area to economic development. Later, in 1876, St. Louis absorbed Cheltenham in the city's last annexation.[44]

Into the sparsely settled outpost came one of the most bizarre groups to grace the Gateway City. Several hundred Frenchmen, disciples of the revolutionary Etienne Cabet, purchased twenty-eight acres of Cheltenham property in 1858. The controversial Colonie Icarienne had drifted into St. Louis in the mid-1850s, after unsuccessful ventures in Texas, Louisiana, and Illinois. The Icarians, determined to succeed in their millenarianism after Cabet's death in 1856, erected a community center, library, and theater, but the communal experiment ended in failure in 1864.[45]

Factionalism in general, and geography in particular, doomed Cheltenham as a utopian dream. "The intermittent fever," complained a malarial-crazed resident in 1860, "was as regular in its semi-annual visits as the appearance of the springtime and fall."[46] The perennial fevers may have been spread by the already contaminated River des Peres. On August 4, 1872, the *St. Louis Times* lamented that the "cottage and spring have both fallen into bad repute and the odor of one is nearly as bad as that of the other."[47] Ironically, environmental factors also assured the area's economic promise. Glacial drifts and Paleozoic formations had created valuable loessial clay and shale deposits in the district.[48] This Cheltenham seam had been discovered before the Civil War by an English laborer who, while drilling a well, penetrated a vein of clay resembling the famous Stourbridge fire clay of England.[49] "Nowhere in the United States," a geologist calculated, "is the clay so perfect for fire clay and terra cotta as in St. Louis."[50]

Urban America's insatiable demand for new technological and building materials in the last half of the nineteenth century brought about an expansion of the Cheltenham works. Fire brick, used as a refractory lining in locomotives, smelting, and iron furnaces, came from St. Louis. Systematic extraction of the Cheltenham seams was begun in 1854–55 by the Evens and Howard Fire Brick Company, an establishment organized by Charles P. Chouteau. The success of this firm opened the way for a dozen similar brick and tile factories by the 1880s. The Hydraulic Brick Company belonged to the poet T. S. Eliot's father.[51]

Terra-cotta became an important local industry after the Chicago fire of 1871, because of its cheap cost and fire-proof qualities. Most of the local terra-cotta was shipped west of the Mississippi. Winkle Terra Cotta

Company began operation in 1883, followed quickly by two other factories in the district.[52] In addition to its use as a roofing and decorative tile, terra-cotta also was utilized as an important material in the construction of modern sewage lines. Noted one authority, "a clay is required which will burn to a hard, dense body and which will produce a dark-colored ware. The shales of St. Louis are well suited."[53] Eventually three sewer pipe factories linked the Cheltenham Valley, producing by 1907 $1.3 million in hardware. Only the state of Ohio manufactured more sewer tile than Missouri.[54]

From a health spa in the 1840s to a French commune in the 1850s, Cheltenham was destined to become one of the leading clay centers in America by the turn of the century. Intricate tunnel networks undermining the district fed the industrial complex, which city booster James Cox lauded as "the largest terra cotta factory in the United States . . . the largest press brick, fire brick and sewer pipe factories in the United States."[55] "The great fire brick and terra cotta companies of St. Louis," added the *Globe-Democrat* in 1907, "have an eminent place in the history of their respective industries. The sewers of far western cities and the furnaces of eastern manufacturing plants, in fact the whole country today, is employing St. Louis brick for various purposes."[56] By 1908 the yearly output of clay products for the city was valued at $6.4 million.[57]

An expert geologist once remarked that Cheltenham clay could easily be used in the manufacture of the finest pottery in the world.[58] But the local industries preferred sewer pipe and fire brick which, rather than attracting master potters, attracted thousands of unskilled laborers. As the district changed from spa to industrial hive, so too did the population shift from the French blue-blood, trappers, Icarian communists, German miners, and black mule skinners, to Lombards and Sicilians. Today the mines are used as dumping grounds, and the tile factories have long since changed tenants. But the last of Cheltenham's occupants, the descendants of Lombards and Sicilians, have staunchly refused to leave the neighborhood. What historical circumstances joined together to bring about this flight of people to an isolated industrial community in southwest St. Louis? Was it an act of fate that caused several thousand immigrants to cross two continents to form a city on a hill?

NOTES

1. *1980 Census of Population and Housing, Missouri*, Table 2; "St. Louis Sings the Blues," *Time*, May 4, 1981, p. 34; Darst, "Prufrock with a Baedeker," 28–34; Advisory Commission on Intergovernmental Relations, *Trends in Metropolitan America;* Jackson, "Metropolitan Government versus Political Autonomy," 445.

2. Kirschten, *Catfish and Crystal.*

3. Foley and Rice, *First Chouteaus*, 5; Wade, *Urban Frontier*, 5–24.

4. Holt, "Shaping of St. Louis," 44–45.

5. Brackenridge, *Views of Louisiana*, 123–24.

6. Primm, *Lion of the Valley;* Green, *American Cities*, 46–66; Hodes, "Urbanization of St. Louis"; Holt, "St. Louis's Transition Decade."

7. Holt, "Shaping of St. Louis," 148, 272; Primm, "Locational Factors," 10.

8. Twain, *Life on the Mississippi*, 192.

9. Mackay, *Western World*, 34.

10. Holt, "Shaping of St. Louis," 121–81; Hodes, "Urbanization of St. Louis," 24–25.

11. Primm, "Locational Factors," 10; Holt, "Shaping of St. Louis," 140–81.

12. Twain, *Gilded Age*, 130–31; Dorsett and Dorsett, "Rhetoric vs. Reality"; Schnell and Clinton, "New West."

13. Reavis, *St. Louis;* Lauer, "St. Louis and the 1880 Census"; Primm, "Locational Factors," 12.

14. Belcher, *Economic Rivalry.*

15. Primm, *Lion of the Valley;* Holt, "Future of St. Louis"; Holt, "Shaping of St. Louis," 350–57; Schnell, "Chicago vs. St. Louis."

16. Primm, *Lion of the* Valley, 311–12; Kouwanhoven, "Eads Bridge."

17. Featherstonaugh, *Excursion Through the Slave States*, 1:259.

18. *Sixth Census of the United States, 1850, Missouri*, 134–38; Ward, *Cities and Immigrants*, 51–85, 105–25; Holt, "Shaping of St. Louis," 162–63.

19. Bek, "Gottfried Duden's Report"; Goodrich, "Gottfried Duden." See also Conzen, *Immigrant Milwaukee.*

20. *Eleventh Census, 1890, Population–Missouri.*

21. Olson, "Nature of an Immigrant Community"; Saalberg, "*Westliche Post*"; Olson, "St. Louis Germans"; Wittke, "German Language Press in America"; Binz, "German Gymnastic Societies in St. Louis."

22. *Post-Dispatch*, Jan. 1, 1879; see also Rammelkamp, *Pulitzer's Post-Dispatch.*

23. Quoted in Muraskin, "St. Louis Municipal Reform," 48.

24. *Post-Dispatch*, Mar. 25, 1979, p. 18R; *St. Louis Star*, Jan. 21, 1912, II, p. 1 (hereafter cited as *Star*); Sullivan, "Constitutionalism, Revolution and Culture."

25. *Statistics of the Population of the U.S. at the Tenth Census, 1880*, Table 14, p. 518. Historians use the term "new" immigration to describe the major change in the origin of emigration after the 1880s. Older immigrants came predominantly from northern and western Europe, while newer groups originated from southern and eastern Europe.

26. Primm, *Lion of the Valley*, 346.

27. Barton, *Peasants and Strangers;* Holli and Jones, *The Ethnic Frontier.*

28. *Thirteenth Census of the U.S.: 1910. Population*, Tables 1, 5. In 1910 St. Louis outdistanced Cleveland in population, 687,029 to 560,663, but the latter dynamized its working-class elements with increasing numbers of Slavs and Magyars. Cleveland boasted 42,059 persons defined as "Austrians" (compared to 11,171 in St. Louis), 31,053 Hungarians (8,758), and 25,477 Rumanians (1,055).

29. *Fourteenth Census of the U.S.: 1920. Population*, III, Tables 12, 13.

30. Ibid.; Primm, *Lion of the Valley*, 435–50; Christensen, "Black St. Louis."

31. *Statistics of the Population of the U.S. at the Tenth Census, 1880*, Table 5; *Fourteenth Census of the U.S., 1920*, III, Table 12; Primm, *Lion of the Valley*, 311, 465; Thomas, "Localization of Business Activities," 1; "Foreigners Riot in Granite City," *Globe-Democrat*, Feb. 15, 1909, p. 1; "Armenians Flee in Race Battle in Granite City," *Post-Dispatch*, Aug. 18, 1904, p. 1; "Race War Closes Steel Plant in Granite City," *Globe-Democrat*, Sept. 16, 1909, p. 1; "Shooting Follows Fourth Race Riot," *Republic*, Sept. 17, 1906, p. 1; "Making Good Americans Out of the Hungarians of East St. Louis," *Globe-Democrat*, June 9, 1912, magazine; "Alton Bootblack, in Balkan Battle," *Post-Dispatch*, May 4, 1912, p. 1; "Foreigners' Strike Stirs Granite City," *Globe-Democrat*, Mar. 14, 1909, p. 1; "700 Americans Rout 1,000 Foreigners," *Republic*, Aug. 15, 1911, p. 4.

32. *Republic*, May 20, 1905, Oct. 1, 1910, p. 9; *Star*, Jan. 1, 1912; *Star and Chronicle*, Sept. 20, 1908, in Stevens Scrapbook, no. 46, pp. 184–86, Missouri Historical Society (hereafter MHS). See also Sullivan, "Hyphenism in St. Louis."

33. Ryan and Lannigan, *Happy Days Are Here Again*, 29.

34. Mihanovich, "Americanization of the Croats"; interview with Clement Mihanovich, Aug. 3, 1973. For a literary portrayal of Macedonian immigrants in St. Louis and the east side in Illinois, see Stoyan Christowe's *My American Pilgrimage* (1947) and *This Is My Country: An Autobiography* (1938). See also Myslinec, "History of the Catholic Poles"; *Republic*, Oct. 1, 1910, p. 9; "Rag Peddlers' Exchange," *Globe-Democrat*, Oct. 19, 1913, July 8, 1912, p. 12; *Post-Dispatch*, May 2, 1911, editorial; *Republic*, May 6, 1900; *Globe-Democrat*, June 23, 1907, magazine; "Plague Spot of America," *Post-Dispatch*, May 24, 1910, II, p. 1; "Slums in St. Louis as Bad as New York," *Star*, May 24, 1910, p. 1;

"Italian Catholics Will Parade Before Dawn," *Republic*, Dec. 7, 1900, p. 1; "The Italian Quarter," *Republic*, Sept. 9, 1900, magazine; "St. Louis Syrian," *Globe-Democrat*, Nov. 26, 1903, p. 16; "Assyrian Colony," *Republic*, May 20, 1900, II, p. 2; "Ghetto District Children," *Globe-Democrat*, Aug. 10, 1907, p. 2; "The Passing of the Hokey-Pokey Man," *Republic*, Nov. 16, 1913, magazine.

35. Dreiser, *Book About Myself*, 88.

36. *Globe-Democrat*, Oct. 7, 1900, p. 7.

37. Ibid., Feb. 3, 1907, magazine.

38. Ibid., Oct. 19, 1913; *Republic*, Dec. 7, 1900; *Globe-Democrat*, July 8, 1912, June 19, 1913.

39. Goldfield and Brownell, *Urban America*, 202.

40. Ward, *Cities and Immigrants*, 105–47; Saunders, "St. Louis," 559; Christensen, "Black St. Louis," 139; Hays, "Changing Political Structure."

41. *Globe-Democrat*, May 26, 1901, magazine.

42. Foley and Rice, *First Chouteaus*, 26, 38, 73–75; Brooks, "Some Views of Old Cheltenham"; Thomas, "Sequence of Areal Occupation."

43. Ibid.; Holt, "Shaping of St. Louis," 381.

44. Ibid.

45. Blick and Grant, "French Icarians in St. Louis."

46. *Sunday Morning Republican*, Nov. 9, 1856, p. 1.

47. *St. Louis Times*, Aug. 4, 1872 (hereafter cited as *Times*).

48. Thomas, "Climate of St. Louis," 4; Krusekoff, *Soil Survey*.

49. Reis and Leighton, *History of the Clay-Working Industry*, 120–21.

50. "Toilers of the Dark," *Globe-Democrat*, June 9, 1907, magazine.

51. Aschemeyer, "Urban Geography," 137–43; "St. Louis Business and Industry," MHS *Bulletin* 16 (Jan. 1960): 168–69.

52. Reis and Leighton, *History of the Clay-Working Industry*, 32; Glaab and Brown, *History of Urban America*, 137–43.

53. Aschemeyer, "Urban Geography," 72–79.

54. *Brick and Clay Record* 33 (Aug. 15, 1908): 21.

55. Cox, *Old and New St. Louis*, 29.

56. "Toilers of the Dark," *Globe-Democrat*, June 9, 1907, magazine.

57. *Brick and Clay Record* 33 (Aug. 15, 1908): 21.

58. "Toilers of the Dark," *Globe-Democrat*, June 9, 1907, magazine.

2 Lombard Roots
"The More You Leave, the More Sentimental You Get"

O Signore, che dal tetto natio ci chiamasti.
O Lord, that from our homes you summoned us.
Giuseppe Verdi, *I Lombardi*

Cuggiono embodies a postcard image so characteristic of northern Italy, a sprinkling of modernity and antiquity: weathered red roof tiles grace the Lombard sky, occasionally interrupted by a television antenna; the ubiquitous World War I memorial and the eerie silence of World War II; and a harmonious piazza containing the church, a café, and crowds of kinfolk animating piety, gossip, and politics. The cacophonous sounds of giggling children empty into the Gregorian caverns of an abandoned convent; an efficient city hall operates from a sixteenth-century baronial villa.

Within the Archivio Municipale of Cuggiono lay the fragments of yesterday and the proliferating record of the new bureaucracy. The 1880 Censimento di Cuggiono survives, noteworthy because of the meticulousness of the recording clerk and his penchant for observation. Of Francesco Margarita, born in 1841, the clerk wrote, "*era uno dei Mille*" (He was one of the thousand—a celebrated native who enlisted in Garibaldi's Red Shirts). The nineteenth-century scribblings leap from the pages. Across entry number 846—the Calcaterra family—the message "*America*" is scrawled in red. These cryptic notes, added years later, appear again and again: "*conjugata in America,*" "*America col marito,*" "*morti America sud,*" "*morti America nord,*" and "*osservazioni: tutto la famiglia in America.*"[1] How could such a picturesque town have surrendered so many of its sons and daughters to Argentina and the United States? And why did so few of them return to their roots?

Cuggiono encapsulates the three contrasting images of Italy popularized in nineteenth- and twentieth-century America. One view romanticized the Italy of Capri, Michelangelo, the Renaissance, and the Grand Tour.[2] In 1906 Archbishop John J. Glennon, increasingly agitated by the influx of southern and eastern European Catholics into St. Louis, retreated to this sentimental past that never was, asking why Italians would leave behind "their homes where there was peace and joy and sunshine . . . [and] the clear blue of the Italian sky?"[3] A second, contrasting view, yet equally distorted, depicted heroic immigrants casting off the yoke of political tyranny and voting with their feet for liberty and opportunity in America. The third view held that the immigrants had been violently uprooted from their primordial villages and were swept into the maelstrom of modern life and deracinated by the impersonal forces of industrialization and urbanism. In reality immigration has always been a terribly complex phenomenon. The idyllic Lombard town of Cuggiono served merely as a starting point for a multifaceted migration involving five continents and thousands of participants.

The study of Italian emigration has benefited immensely from the insights of many scholars. Historians have captured in particular the magnitude of this epic undertaking. "The Greater Italy is an empire—but a proletariat-empire," observed Robert Foerster in his classic 1919 study. "[Italy] bestrides the world like a Colossus—but a colossus arrayed in rags."[4] Carl Wittke painted his canvas with similarly broad strokes: "In whatever time frames are defined, the magnitude of Italian migration to the U.S. is staggering."[5] Eric Amfitheatrof utilized a familiar metaphor in his overview of the process: ". . . between 1881 and 1911 the land literally hemorrhaged peasants."[6] The European exodus to the Americas after 1800 constituted the greatest mass movement of people in history. (Josef Stalin once remarked that when one man is murdered it is a tragedy; when millions are exterminated it becomes a statistic. The same might be said for emigration.) This study is an intensive examination of emigration at the local level, one that, it is hoped, transcends raw statistics and instead portrays emigrants not as victims of a tragedy but rather as agents of change and architects of their own destiny.

The human volcano that erupted in late-nineteenth-century Cuggiono had its core deep within the stratum of European history. Surrounded on the great Lombard plain by small villages such as Inveruno, Marcallo, Robechetto, Buscate, Ossona, and Boffalora Ticino, Cuggiono represented a flat, fertile stretch of land so inviting to Huns, Goths, Romans, Lombards, and Franks that, as a Lombard proverb laments, "*Chi ha terra ha guerra*" (He who has land must fight). Kings and merchants, barbarians and archbishops, all coveted the prized bounty of Cuggiono. Originally settled by the Celts and named "Cusonum" and then "Cuzono" (meaning place near the woods) by the Gauls, Cuggiono began to re-emerge from the barbarian invasions in the sixth century. Charlemagne called the region "Seprio." The oldest document discovered in the town dates from 1098 and tells of Ottone da Cuggiono bearing witness to a contract.[7] During the next nine centuries the Cuggionesi would give to the world their grapes, oats, maize, and rice, and ultimately their sons and daughters.

The historian Fernand Braudel maintained that Lombardy offered the clearest example of the human conquest of nature. Land rich but water poor, the Lombards engineered an ingenious system of canals to irrigate the valleys and distinguish Milan as a great port city without a river. Begun in the twelfth century, the completion of the elaborate canal system in the sixteenth century signaled a new era, as influential families constructed villas along the rivers Ticino and Adda to replace the anachronistic castles.[8] A succession of powerful nobles dominated Cuggiono during the Middle Ages, with the commune occupying a strategic position as a bulwark on the Ticino. In 1185 a native son, Uberto Crivelli, ascended the papacy as Pope Urban III, reigning until 1187. In 1274 an army from neighboring Novara destroyed the Casteletto di Cuggiono. The following centuries witnessed a local power struggle between the families Clerici and Piantanida.[9] The Villa Clerici stands today as an awesome example of the power and influence generated by one Lombard *signore*.

The plight of the *contadini* (peasants) changed little as the fortunes of Italy vacillated between city-states, dynastic struggles, and foreign domination. A rural proletariat faithfully tended the lush fields of wheat, rice, corn, rye, oats, hay, grapes, and mulberries. The Spanish Inquiry of 1547, which studied Lombard property, concluded that the peasants owned less than 3 percent of the land.[10] Peasants in Cuggiono did not escape the torturous conditions of the nearby rice fields, an odious form of work; nor did Cuggionesi escape the scourge of the terrible plague of 1633, which reduced the village population from 2,500 to 1,250.[11] And again, in 1735, "there was a terrible sickness among the population," noted a church historian.[12]

In *la terra degli zoccoli*, the land of the wooden clogs, change came slowly. The *Inchiesta Agraria*, a nineteenth-century study of agrarian conditions, reported Lombard peasants clinging to primitive and outmoded tools. In 1907 landlords in Lombardy paid male farm laborers 30 to 40 cents a day, and 15 to 25 cents for women and children.[13] The peasants faced lives of unrelenting work and meager opportunities in exchange for survival. The Countess Martinengo Cesaresco observed in 1902 that this agrarian system could be maintained only where "an intense power of work and a primitive conception of life [existed]."[14] Lombard peasants were "slaves of the glebe," stated Luigi Torelli. Indeed, few opportunities for upward mobility existed in Cuggiono. The 1860 *Stato delle Anime* (State of Souls-Census) listed 708 adult males, of whom 574 were classified *contadini;* 118 claimed artisan status such as blacksmithing, bartending, or catering; only 13 were *borghesi* (small businessmen); and 3 boasted of noble status.[15]

This agrosystem, which had functioned efficiently if not equitably, faced irreparable cracks in its nineteenth-century foundation. Cuggiono, like Europe in general, rumbled from demographic and economic quakes that would eventually culminate in massive emigration. The gravest crisis faced by Cuggionesi involved a fundamental inability to support a burgeoning population (see Table 2). "In Cuggiono, we was so hungry we even steal from the pig," remembered an elderly emigrant.[16] In 1780 Cuggiono's population stood at 4,567, and by 1861 that figure had risen only slightly to 4,967; yet in the next twenty years it spiralled to 6,105.[17]

Table 2. *Old-World Villages of Origin*

Towns	*1861*	*1871*	*1881*	*1901*	*1911*	*1921*
Bernate Ticino	1,449	1,438	1,677	1,807	1,894	1,856
Boffalora sopra Ticino	1,556	1,598	1,623	1,957	2,115	2,178
Buscate	1,784	1,842	2,083	2,375	2,797	2,665
Castano Primo	3,628	3,930	4,349	4,831	6,250	6,015
Cuggiono	4,967	5,111	6,105	5,636	4,970	5,430
Inveruno	2,720	2,771	3,067	3,729	3,985	4,834
Marcallo	1,934	1,940	2,089	2,350	2,700	2,820
Ossona	1,284	1,269	1,356	1,561	1,796	1,905
Robecchetto con Induno	1,645	1,808	2,001	2,035	2,509	2,706
Nosate	463	528	539	555	504	460

Source: *Istituto Centrale di Statistica Popolazione Residenti dei Comuni al Censimenti* (1961), 136.

An examination of parish and communal records reveal that Malthusian pressures were at work. Cuggiono literally swarmed with *bambini* in the period following the Napoleonic era. In 1839 there were 159 children baptized at the parish of San Giorgio, a figure that grew to 237 in 1869 and further increased to 262—a commune record—in 1879.[18] There was a definite, direct correlation between rates of emigration and previous birthrates.[19] The local natural rate of increase in population plummeted after 1900, indicative of the drainage of manpower wrought by emigration. By 1923, for example, fewer than 100 births were being recorded each year; and only half a dozen times after World War I would Cuggiono welcome 100 or more births. Emigration fever had struck in Cuggiono, a community of disaggregation.

Land in Cuggiono was owned almost entirely by nobles who lived in Milan and who refused to sell their fields to the peasants who worked them. (Historians Robert Foerster and Giuseppe Badi have estimated that absentee landlords held 90 percent of the land in late-nineteenth-century Lombardy.[20]) Cuggionesi, caught in a trap between an escalating population and survival as a landless proletariat, soon confronted a trauma brought on by Italian political-agrarian policies.

A litany of disasters crippled Lombard farmers in the decades before and after unification. The grapes of Cuggiono once were so renowned that natives named a street Via Buon Vino (Street of the Good Wine), but phylloxera ruined the arbors in 1750 and returned to ravage the crop a century later. A needless tariff war with France brought further ruin, compounded by increased agrarian competition from the Americas and the Black Sea region. A devastating nineteenth-century drought ignited Lombard peasants to action. Friar Don Rodolfo Terzaghi wrote that only the cultivation of the silkworm saved Lombardy from starvation and rebellion.[21]

In Cuggiono it was hoped that the introduction of *filande* (silk mills) might relieve the plight of the peasant family. A local proverb hinted, "The shadow of the mulberry is the shadow of gold." Silk, like meat, became an item to produce, not consume. The frenzied demand for silk after 1814, coupled with the adaptability of the silkworm in Lombardy, resulted in the building of scores of *filande* in the region around Cuggiono. Soon the smokestacks of the silk mills rivaled the feudal towers, but the stench exuding from the work floor and the exploitative conditions brought a whiff of modern industrialism. In Cuggiono the imposing feudal structure of the Villa Clerici was transformed into a *filanda* in the mid-nineteenth century and joined by another structure, called together Filande Bossi e Fossati.[22]

The Cuggiono mills employed nearly 800 women and children. Girls between the ages of five and twelve worked arduous twelve- and fifteen-hour days. "In the summer we started at four or five in the morning," remembered Rosa Cassettari, describing her initiation to the new work routine at the *filanda*. ". . . there were no belts and no machines to turn the reel. The machines were us little girls. All day we had to stand there by the wheel, turning and watching the thread as it wound around the cocoons. . . . The big room of the silkmakers was so full of steam you could hardly see. And in the summer we were sweating bullets."[23] The employers often reimbursed children with bags of cereal or rice, whereas the women earned about one lire a day (fifteen cents), an appalling wage made even more painful by the fact that the mills seldom operated more than 200 days a year. Life was never easy in Cuggiono, but family and village maintained associations of mutual aid. The silk factories ended the tradition of family work, however, and instilled in its place a new rigor of time work and machine discipline.

Interviews with immigrant women paint a poignant picture of Lombard life at the turn of the nineteenth century. Maria Imo, born in 1895 at Rubone, a small village near Bernate Ticino, was the third of twelve children. She prided herself on having been the first in her family to attend school, walking the two miles there and back in wooden clogs. At age eleven she began work at the mill at Casteletto di Cuggiono, and for six days a week, thirteen hours a day, she dropped the *gallete* (cocoons) into boiling water. "One day the government inspector come," she explained, "and the *Padrone* sneak me into toilet because I was too young."[24]

Maria Torno, born in the village of Nosate in 1884, was the youngest of four children. She considered herself lucky to have attended school from age six to eleven. On her eleventh birthday she was graduated to the fields—*divanti delle bestie!* (behind the oxen). At age twelve she obtained work at an *establimento* at Legnano, weaving sheets on large looms. To get to work Maria Torno walked several miles to Castano, took the train to Castalanza, then trod several more miles to Legnano. Like many other children apprenticed at the mill, she remained there for a fortnight, returning home every other weekend. She remembered the hard times: "We ate *pan giallo* [corn bread], *minestra* [soup], pasta, *polenta* [corn mush] and meat maybe twice a year—*una vita di miseria* [a life of misery]. Once we killed the ox because it was too old to work and we had meat."[25]

In 1948 the Italian filmmaker Di Santis shocked audiences with his neorealistic portrayal of Lombard rice workers, in *Riso Amaro* (Bitter Rice). But many immigrants already knew the brutal conditions of the *risaie* (rice plantations). For rural Italians children were commodities—to be loved, for sure, but also to assist the family—and in the late nineteenth century this meant time in the rice fields for many Lombard youth. An immigrant recalled the experience: "One summer I went with other little girls and boys to work in the rice fields. We had to go a long ways on a wagon and sleep in a big barn that was there. In the rice fields we had to stand with our legs in the water and pull the weeds. For food we gotta big bowl of rice three times a day. . . . For pay our mothers for each one a big bag of rice after the harvest."[26]

The Catholic church, through offerings on saints' days and the liturgical tradition, attempted to relieve the plight of peasants and millhands. From the pulpits of Cuggiono a powerful ethos was articulated, binding the village faithful in a cohesive religiosity. The village priest, like the *campanile* (bell tower) of San Giorgio, loomed over the inhabitants. Carlo Cattaneo wrote of the priest in 1841 that he was "the keystone in which all the lines of life center." His ubiquitous presence penetrated the village: he was often a teacher, a school inspector, an informal magistrate, and an arbitrator between the mills and parish.[27] Nuns, too, played active roles in ministering to the Lombards. "Daytime, all us girls have to work in the silk factory," remembered one immigrant, "but Sunday afternoon we was often sitting around with the sisters, and then they tell a story—story to make us good, about the saints . . . they was *Suore di Carità* (Sisters of Charity)."[28]

In the primordial collectives of Cuggiono and Inveruno, Catholicism exerted a force that carried well beyond the Sunday sermon. Cuggionesi vividly recall the priestly influences: "I heard about the plays the new priest was making in the hall," recreating events that had occurred in the 1870s. "I couldn't wait to see them. And because they were for the church, Mama Lena gave me a few *centesimi*. . . . Oh, those plays were good! . . . the young priest was wonderful the way he taught the young men and girls . . . everybody was coming to see the plays of Father Bruschetti."[29]

The peasant church forged an amalgam of fantasy and reality, piety and ritual. The Madonna reigned as the supreme protectress of humankind. A worker in Cuggiono recalled once being pulled into the mill looms, "but the Madonna helped me," she swore. "She made my head go all around with the wheel so it would come out again at the end. Sure it was the Madonna."[30] The Cuggionesi venerated La Madonna del Carmine as their patron saint, and testimonials to her curative powers abound. "Something was the matter with my legs—pretty bad," explained a former resident of Cuggiono. "We had a miracle. We go up there [Alps] and we had a miracle."[31] The Madonna might cure the blind and heal the lame, but to stave off starvation and seek new channels of relief required the probing of new alternatives.

The success of the risorgimento depended on a delicate balancing of the idealism of Garibaldi and Mazzini and the realpolitik of Cavour and the House of Savoy. The unfulfilled revolution of the 1860s and 1870s shattered any illusion that Italy's rural classes would improve their standard of living. Some historians hold that Italian leaders modernized Lombardy and Piedmont on the backs of the peasants. The despised *macinato* (grist tax) served this precise purpose.[32]

The Cuggionesi would have preferred to reform and control their economic lives. Women worked for wages at nonagrarian pursuits, and still the family teetered on the brink of disaster; parents leased their children to the new industrial barons, but family suffering continued. Individuals then sought to organize, and in April 1881 peasants and artisans formed La Società di Mutuo Soccorso degli Operai e Contadini di Cuggiono (The Society of Mutual Support of Workers and Peasants of Cuggiono). Such societies sprang up throughout Italy in the late nineteenth century in an attempt to provide a safety net for workers who were increasingly alarmed at falling through the economic webbing.[33]

Peasants and artisans quickly sensed that mutual aid provided at best a local anesthetic to a national problem, one that in fact required an international solution. By the 1860s and 1870s the unrelenting demands imposed by accelerating birthrates and diminishing economic opportunities at home forced the Cuggionesi to seek alternatives beyond the Madonna del Carmine and the silk mills of Lombardy. Migration, and later emigration, became a safety valve for the embattled residents and in the next sixty years steadily stripped the town, its young men and women moving across five continents. For their globetrotting prowess the Cuggionesi became renowned as the "Genoans of Lombardy."[34]

Ironically, the very forces that constricted Lombard mobility at home propelled northern Italians to the mines of Germany and the hearths of

France. Industrialization, with its twin corollaries of urbanization and modernization, dislocated vast numbers of Europe's agricultural workers between 1860 and 1920. Modern plows and mechanical reapers, manufactured in European and American factories, displaced the peasants, who in turn were drawn to the industrial districts to trade a *zappa* (hoe) for a work apron.[35]

Migration to Milan, just twenty miles away, offered a flicker of hope to many Cuggionesi. A tram connecting Cuggiono and the provincial capital, begun in 1880, facilitated that movement. Other peasants and day laborers flocked to the metropolis in search of jobs as personal servants and factory workers, with a significant proportion of workers in tobacco, textiles, garment making, domestic service, and the rubber industries being comprised of women. Fully 70 percent of Milan's growth in the late nineteenth century consisted of rural migrants. The city's population surged from a quarter of a million inhabitants in 1861 to over half a million by 1900. The International Exposition, held in 1881, showcased the Lombard city to the world but served as a backdrop for the series of urban and labor strikes and unrest that wracked Milan between the 1870s and 1900.[36]

Migration, once undertaken to preserve the village, became an end to itself. Emigration from Cuggiono did not occur simply within the crude confines of a push-pull model. To understand its dynamics within Cuggiono we must reconstruct the options and patterns existing within Italy after 1860.

Decades before the Statue of Liberty captured the attention of Italian emigrants, other sirens called Lombards and various Alpine laborers to migratory passages. Northern Italians had long scythed rye in Germany and harvested Swiss oats in a traditional seasonal migration to neighboring countries. Called *rondini* (swallows), thousands of Lombards spent several months in migratory movement each year but always returned to Italy to harvest local crops.[37]

In 1859 a celebrated entrepreneur-*padrone*, Ercole Belloli, organized a company of Cuggionesi to help construct the fortress of Bilbao and a railroad in Spain. Returning to Lombardy with the outbreak of the War of Risorgimento, these people organized a military unit and fought with Garibaldi, utilizing their skills at building fortifications. After the war the journeys of Belloli's company rivaled those of Marco Polo, matched only by a group of local women who were sent to China to learn silk breeding. Belloli's imposing tombstone in Cuggiono, a conspicuous shrine molded in bronze, depicts the eternal *padrone* exhorting his *paesani* to lay more track. An elderly Italian remembered Belloli as "the impresario of construction."

Between 1865 and 1880 Cuggionesi dug a canal in the Suez, constructed a railroad in the Belgian Congo, laid track between Constantinople and Bulgaria, and blasted rock at the Saint Gotthard Tunnel in Switzerland. "We survived the St. Gotthard" became a breastplate for veterans of the dangerous project in which thousands of Italians died blasting tunnels in the Dolomites and Swiss Alps.[38]

"Lombards are leaving Italy, cursing and in tears," cried an Italian deputy in 1868.[39] Another Milanese official complained later, "Everything is getting dearer, life is getting dearer, one cannot live."[40] Since the fields and mills of Cuggiono could no longer support its inhabitants, emigrants would support Cuggiono. Thus far, "push" conditions had exerted inexorable pressures on the village. But as John S. MacDonald has argued, emigration involved more than economic deprivation. Some of Italy's poorest provinces, such as Siracusa, generated low rates of emigration. Cuggiono was no poorer than hundreds of other towns, yet the fever to leave raged there.[41]

Scholars have suggested a complex interrelationship between land tenure, economic stratification, cultural attitudes, and emigration. Areas dominated by concentrated landholding, such as the Po Valley, traditionally had low emigration rates. Yet Cuggiono, ruled by a handful of families and marked by a maldistribution of wealth, witnessed heavy emigration. MacDonald contended that such disparities in income often fostered militance in the form of collective associations and class struggles. Pelizza da Volpedo's famous painting of *Il Quarto Stato* (The Fourth Estate) depicts the agrarian conflict in north Italy. Such areas of associational activity and militance also held low emigration rates, suggest both MacDonald and Barton.[42]

The Cuggionesi pondered their future. They could do nothing, which meant stagnation; they could rebel, but agrarian riots offered little more than cathartic release; or they could reform, though collective associations could do little to change the essential rigidity of their society. Continental migrations to Germany or France yielded short-term fixes but did not diminish the fundamental problems of land hunger, overpopulation, and pessimism. As long as the land barons steadfastly refused to yield power or sell land, life in Cuggiono would stifle the ambitious. With reluctance mixed with promise, Cuggionesi looked beyond the silk towers and church steeples to the future. America was not, as Abraham Lincoln proclaimed, the last best hope on earth; to Cuggionesi it was the best last hope. It piqued the ambition of individuals in ways not measured by census reports, bewitching them and their families with an intoxicating taste of self-betterment and familial dignity.

Overseas migration from Italy, which began as a trickle in the 1860s and 1870s, became a human tidal wave by the 1880s, with approximately 100,000 persons leaving Italy every year; by the end of the decade that figure doubled. The 1890s witnessed 300,000 Italians emigrating annually, and in the decade and a half preceding World War I, over 500,000 Italians departed each year. Transatlantic migrations peaked in 1913 when almost a million people left Italy.[43] Northern Italy was the most active region during the early stages of emigration. In 1870, for instance, the alpine provinces sent tens of thousands of Udinesi and Piemontesi to France, Austria, and Switzerland. The province of Milan was distinguished not so much by absolute numbers of emigrants as by the adventuresome points of destination, such as Russia and India.[44]

The destinations of Italian emigrants shifted dramatically in the early 1870s. Argentina and Brazil, eager to open new coffee and rubber plantations, attracted fabulous numbers of Italians. By 1895 more than two million Italians had migrated to South America, where they made significant contributions to the labor movement and to modernization of the local and national economies. Large numbers of Italians from the northern provinces participated in the South American expeditions, and as many as two-thirds later returned to their natal villages to purchase land. By the decade of the 1890s, as the proportion of southern Italians emigrating to the Americas began to rise, their destination shifted dramatically to the United States.[45]

Just as Lombards had scoured the contours of Europe and Africa for bread and work, so too did they seek their fortunes far and wide in the Americas. Within a brief span of time after 1880 at least four distinct streams of emigrants left Cuggiono, each establishing a separate but interrelated colony. In 1880 a group of Cuggionesi left for Buenos Aires, part of a greater movement of one million Italians who arrived in Argentina between 1861 and 1900. Also in 1880 a handful of Cuggionesi sailed for North America, their destination being the copper mines of Calumet, Michigan. A *padrone*, Pietro Cucchi, who had organized previous migrant camps in Germany and Switzerland, arranged this venture. Sailing from Le Havre, France, the group arrived in New York on October 16,

1880, whence they proceeded to Detroit. While awaiting passage to Calumet they chanced to meet a Tuscan statue vendor who directed them to a Genoan restaurateur. There they discussed their prospects with a local Neapolitan who encouraged them to remain in bustling Detroit. Convinced of the short-term advantages of remaining in the city, the Lombards soon found work with the Michigan Central Railroad and sent for their kinfolk. By 1897 the Cuggionesi boasted the largest Italian settlement in Detroit, which included 62 families and a Mutuo Soccorso Lombardia di Detroit, a mutual aid society, formed by 117 Lombards in 1889.[46]

Paralleling the Lombard exodus to Detroit was a third group of Cuggionesi who sought work in Williamson County, Illinois, the center of a newly exploited bituminous coal belt. Lombards who settled in the town of Herrin, like their counterparts in Detroit who had hoped to mine copper, had no experience mining coal. But recent technological changes had resulted in a shift from skilled to unskilled labor, and the Cuggionesi earned their reputation with the pick and shovel. By 1900 over 26,000 Italians, principally from Lombardy and Piedmont, could be found in the coal mines of Illinois, Pennsylvania, and West Virginia.[47]

The fourth, and ultimately the most successful, foreign adventure for Cuggionesi began in 1882. A vivid account of Cuggiono at this time was left by a perceptive raconteuse, Rosa Cassettari (the account was later published as *Rosa*, edited by Maria Hall Ets). "That summer," she told a friend, "after the work in the fields was done, Beppo could find no more work in Bugiarno [the fictional Cuggiono], so he joined one of those gangs going to America. I was sad to lose him."[48] Unfortunately, no records outlining the exact nature of the work agreement have been discovered, but most likely agents from the Big Muddy Coal and Iron Company secured the services of Cuggionesi through a local *padrone*. Once at Castle Garden, the immigrants traveled by rail to the lead mines of Union, Missouri.

Disenchanted with the grueling life-style, temporarily out of work, a half dozen Lombards from Union, Missouri, found themselves on the St. Louis levee in the early 1880s. A Genovese saloon keeper, Giuseppe Boggiano, welcomed the refugees to the Mound City, having himself arrived in the United States in January 1882. (Examination of the passenger list of the SS *St. Germain* reveals that Boggiano left Italy with seven companions, one of whom was Giovanni Merlo. Merlo is a very popular Lombard name, and there is the possibility that Giovanni Merlo migrated from Cuggiono to Genoa and then to St. Louis, where he served as a surveyor of urban prospects.) Strong backs were needed at the Evens and Howard clay pits, the publican Boggiano informed the weary travelers. The next morning he escorted Luigi Caloia, Giovanni Calcaterra, Luigi Oldani, Luigi Berra, and Luigi Genazzi to the brick kilns, nestled on the banks of the River des Peres, far away from urban encroachment. "The men were hired that day," wrote Angelo Sala. "That night they looked around for a boarding place, but the farmers in the area would not take them in, the settlement then were mostly German families. . . . So these men went back to Evens and Howard where a railroad boxcar was made into temporary quarters."[49]

Locals residing in the sparsely settled outpost reluctantly approached the new workers. Hugo Schoessel, born in Cheltenham—then a hill overlooking St. Louis—in 1884, was one of the first to breach the social barrier. Leaning back in his rocker in 1973 he narrated the "comin' of the Eye-talians." "I was about five years old. There was a bunch of . . . —colored people—living over there, and they were awful reckless you know. And the first Eye-talians come over here. . . . About half a dozen men got together and rented the house and batched it [bachelors]. . . . The Germans who were here—they mistreated the first Eye-talians. . . ."[50] Laughing, the sprightly ninety-year-old German-American pointed his finger north, toward Shaw Avenue, and recalled his childhood: "In the evening they had an accordion. They played music sitting out in the yard and singing and us kids used to hang on the fence listenin' to 'em. We thought it was funny because we didn't understand it. And then after a while they send for their friends and their brothers . . . and that's how they got started here!"[51] And send for their friends and brothers they did. Despite the less than cordial reception, Lombards visualized the work camp as something more than a brick factory and clay mine—for them it was a new beginning.

Paesano loyalties, kinship ties, and a fluctuating economy generated feverish traffic among the Italian settlements in Illinois and Missouri. Job skills in the lead, coal, and clay mines were interchangeable; hence, when the mines periodically closed or nativist antagonisms boiled over, Lombards migrated to the most prosperous and stable of the camps, St. Louis. By the mid-1890s several hundred Lombards and a sprinkling of Sicilians infused a degree of stability to the colony, already called "Dago Hill" by the locals.[52]

The nucleus of a colony thus was born. Lombards dubbed their new home *la Montagna* (literally the mountain). Local storytellers explain that the name originated during the first winter of settlement. The brick kilns lining the river basin constantly needed refiring, and the men, to avoid freezing in the cruel St. Louis winters, rode on horses down and back up the hill, which seemed more like a mountain.[53] The epithet carried little romance at the time, however. This dedicated vanguard paid a heavy price in loneliness, privation, and sacrifice as they helped clear the urban wilderness. "Tommaso lived very frugally," wrote a reporter describing one of the first Italian miners on the Hill. "Bologna, garlic, and black bread is ordinarily what may be found at his table during the noon hour, and at supper it is very much the same except that a cheap bottle of wine is sometimes added." Confessing his amazement, the proprietor of the clay mines added, "Tommaso spends 25 cents a day for living expenses and I do not remember that during my connection with the company (1882–1907) this old fellow has missed a day in the mines."[54]

Equally observant of immigrant parsimony was Julius Selvaggi. Founders of the city's first Italian banking and postal order firm, Selvaggi and his father ministered to the needs of their compatriots. "You don't understand all these immigrants like I do," the spry octogenarian exclaimed. "For a buck and a half (they) hit that streetcar track all day, eat garlic and onion and a half-loaf of dago bread so they could save money and send it to their family." Shaking his head he sighed, "You don't know what those fellows went through . . . but all these men were faithful to their families. . . . I wish I had the money they sent back—millions! . . . On Sunday [when they deposited their money] we had to get a policeman to keep people in line."[55]

Although concern for the family remained the lodestar, family life was singularly absent during the first decades on the Hill. Young men typified the first stage of migration. Possessed with the sole aim of earning enough money to begin a new life or maintain an old one, the sojourners extended their meager incomes through cooperative boardinghouse arrangements, a common immigrant institution. Before 1900 only a handful of women assumed responsibility for the care of the boarders. As many as ten men crowded into makeshift shanties and other groupings of ten men shared rooms in twelve-hour shifts.[56]

Typical of the early pioneers was Carlo Gualdoni. He arrived on the Hill from Cuggiono in October 1886, twenty-two, single, and ambitious. An imposing five feet eight inches tall, weighing 200 pounds, Gualdoni sought his fortune deep in the clay pits. After toiling in the mines for five years he returned to Lombardy to secure a life partner, Angelina Calcaterra. The couple then set off for St. Louis, and their first son was born on the Hill on December 4, 1892. Louis Jean Gualdoni would ascend from the clay mines to become power broker of the Hill and one of the most influential Democratic figures in the state.[57]

Maria Torno was just a baby when the first vanguard left Cuggiono. In 1904 she married Angelo Torno (no relation), who had worked as a *contadino* until migrating to France with a group of Lombards to labor in the iron foundries and tanneries of Marseilles. Angelo Torno accompanied a handful of *paesani* to St. Louis in April 1904, boarding with relatives on Wilson Avenue. As soon as he had saved enough money from his job at the Laclede Christy brickyards, he sent for Maria, who joined him in March 1905. The Torno family rented a three-room house at 5300 Shaw Avenue and took in four boarders; Maria was responsible for all the cleaning, laundry, and cooking. The Tornos eventually purchased a home at 2236 Edwards, where they resided for thirty-six years.[58]

Disparagingly called "birds of passage" by locals, immigrants such as Carlo Gualdoni had originally hoped to earn a few hundred dollars and return to Lombardy as wealthy men (60 percent of Italian immigrants did repatriate).[59] A few, such as Luigi Genazzi, earned their fortunes and returned to Italy *un pezzo grosso* (literally a big piece). But most of the early immigrants between 1882 and 1900 chose to remain on that hill in St. Louis for the simple reason that they could never buy land in Cuggiono. Their decision to sustain a colony in St. Louis drastically changed the destinies of both the Hill and Cuggiono. An ethnic beachhead had been secured, a pioneering endeavor of great import. Lombards had cleared the urban frontier, and their experiences in the uncharted waters of economics, ocean travel, ethnic relations, and urban survival became life lessons for the next generation of fellow travelers. They were the first link in the great chain migration that would evolve into the largest settlement of Milanese outside Lombardy. In the beleaguered village of Cuggiono people anxiously awaited news of the experiment.

The year was 1900. A long-awaited letter arrived in Cuggiono, postmarked St. Louis, Missouri, United States of America. Young Antonio Ranciglio watched intently as his mother desperately tore open the envelope sent by her husband; family and friends gathered nearby gasped as the precious lire spilled out, the bounty of America. Even more forceful perhaps than the paper currency was the eloquent message that came with it: "Here I eat meat three times a day," proclaimed Alessandro Ranciglio, "not three times a year!" A blacksmithing stint in Milan had persuaded Ranciglio to set sail for America in hopes of reviving his trade and perhaps returning to Lombardy a wealthy man. No bird of passage was he, however. Dramatically, the blacksmith had made his life choice: better to shoe mules in St. Louis than starve in Cuggiono. "*Fare fortuna, trovare l'America*," he advised *paesani* (To make a fortune, find America). He bluntly instructed his young wife: "I'm not going to come back there. Cuggiono! I want you to take Tony and come here on the Hill. There's an abundance, a lot of work and I'd like to live here. . . . If you don't come here, I don't come back!"[60]

America-mania had struck Cuggiono like an epidemic, the very air charged with stories of fabulous wealth to be had on a mountain in Missouri. "Those early settlers," remembered Nick Correnti, "made maybe 50, 75 cents a day and they would write back to Italy about the gold that was to be made in America."[61] Even more exhilarating than a letter stuffed with promises, however, was the sight of a Luigi Caloia or Carlo Gualdoni swaggering down the trodden path, a gift-laden tote bag slung over one shoulder, dressed in a rakish store-bought suit, and wearing a pair of St. Louis Browns. Maria Griffero recalled precisely her first touch with the *americani*. "Oh look," she remembered thinking as she viewed the sojourners in the village square. "Go to America, come back with everything. Somebody go to America and build a house. Oh, they look a lot different from us!"[62] The returning heroes confirmed the peasant proverb, "For by their shoes ye shall know them."[63]

Cuggiono would never be the same. "America was a magic word," mused Leo Erutti, one of the many who was wooed by that siren voice. "You know," he said, "America was a land of promise, for people of ambition, the thing to do—to be romantic—especially for youth."[64] Another contemporary explained, "One is born with the idea of going to America. It is a contagion that cannot be resisted."[65]

Although it may have seemed that America-mania infected all of Italy at once, the phenomenon was actually endemic, striking villages and regions with varying degrees of intensity. Cuggiono represented one of only a handful of villages in the province of Lombardy to record an absolute loss of population during the period between 1881 and 1931 (from 6,105 to 4,475);[66] of more than 200 towns and villages, most others marked impressive population gains.

Immigration functioned as a sensitive barometer of opportunity. The

Lombard historian Antonio Annoni estimated that about 300 Cuggionesi emigrated every year during the early 1890s and nearly 2,000 lived abroad, sending home nearly half a million lire every year.[67] The savage depression of 1894 drastically curtailed emigration. The Italian historian Arrigo Serpieri detailed the dynamic interchanges between economics and movement in his 1910 study. During the five-year period 1896–1900 an average of only 23 emigrants left Cuggiono each year. But during the subsequent period, 1901–5, an average of 188 Cuggionesi emigrated every year, including 283 in 1905. While Cuggiono supplied the most emigrants, the neighboring villages of Inveruno, Marcallo, Castano, and Buscate also lost an annual average of 71 inhabitants to emigration during the period 1901–5.[68] These villages also claimed representatives in St. Louis. In 1950 a historian in Cuggiono estimated that 3,000 *paesani* had left altogether. It appears, he wrote, that they form whole neighborhoods "of *paesani* in *S. Louis Mo*, a *Herryn Illinois e Detroit*."[69]

An Italian proverb warned prospective emigrants, "Whosoever leaves the old road for the new, knows what he is leaving, but not what he will find." Not so for Cuggionesi. Harried travelers from Lombardy were bolstered by bulwarks of help built up by previous migrants. Immigration, as Frank Thistlethwaite has argued, was *not* an undifferentiated mass movement of peoples.[70] Order prevailed in the madness of international travel. Immigrants needed advice, interpreters, encouragement, money for travel, and guides for the trip; on arrival they sought a job, housing, and a culture. Former emigrants met these needs and in the process encouraged migration and directed its relocation in the new country.

Emigration robbed Cuggiono of its young men and women and their future children and may have shaped its demography in still another way. The church archives of San Giorgio reveal that an incredible 159 of 287 children born during 1882 and 1883 died in infancy. Residents attribute this to an epidemic of "*mal grup*—a knot in the throat," or diptheria.[71] Did this calamity spur the townfolk to emigrate, or were these deaths a sign of a society trapped with its men in America and too many mouths to feed? Regardless of motivation, Cuggionesi left Italy in torrents. If a deteriorating economy pushed Lombardy to the brink of rebellion, the Hill pulled them over the edge to America. Clearly, emigration was fueled by more than economic deprivation.

No metaphor better describes the intimate relationship between the Hill and Cuggiono than "the chain." Contemporaries frequently used the image to describe the patterns of group settlement. The commissioner-general for immigration noted in 1907 that letters and return visits of *americani* forged "endless chains . . . link by link" between European villages and American cities.[72] These elaborate patterns between the Hill and Lombardy rapidly built up the colony after 1900. The basic formula precipitating wide-scale emigration was repeated time and again in the period 1880–1924. Young men obtained money from the family of *paesani* in America, came to the Hill, secured a job, and frugally saved money to send for wives, prospective brides, children, and relatives. Then this group would return as *americani*, dazzling and assisting a new generation who had never known Maria Torno or Carlo Gualdoni.

Chain migrations moved clusters of individuals, households, and villagers across space via a continuum of makeshift stations. Forged in primary social relationships, the regeneration linkage of human assistance functioned during the early stages of the migratory process. It was a rare emigrant who left Cuggiono alone. A network of constantly shifting arrangements necessitated considerable experimentation, probing the new economic orders and combating bureaucratic resistance. The chain metaphor suggests rigidity, but in reality the process was chameleon-like. It encouraged cunning, teaching immigrants to falsify medical information and seek lines of least resistance, to cushion the shock of adjustment and recruit new laborers.[73]

The chain migration phenomenon channeled millions of Italians into the Americas, linking individuals and groups to specific economic niches and settlement patterns. What later became stereotypical—Italian fruit vendors and Polish foundry workers—reflected more the economic flow of migration patterns and less the innate work habits of these people. Thus, distinct Italian communities were carved from old-world locales: Sicilians from Santo Stéfano di Quisquina settled in Tampa while their island compatriots from Melilli gravitated to Middletown, Connecticut. Dino Cinel's *From Italy to San Francisco* offers an outstanding analysis of these processes.[74]

The Cuggionese experience illustrates the flexibility and regenerative nature of migration. On July 28, 1906, the SS *Lorraine* docked in New York harbor. Aboard were five Cuggionesi, two of whom were heading for Detroit, two for Joliet, Illinois, and one for the coal mines of Westville, Illinois.[75] During periods of economic slack these immigrants became migrants, shuffling between the Lombard colonies. In March 1905 the SS *La Touraine* arrived in New York with ten individuals from Marcallo who were destined for St. Louis (all had relatives there).[76] The Monti family represents the flux of migration. Born in 1888 in Bernate, Stefano Monti left for the Illinois coal fields in 1913. In 1920 he married a woman from Bernate in Oglesby, Illinois. The following year their first child was born in Hillsboro, Illinois, and in 1925 they moved to the Hill.[77]

Time has not eroded memories of the great chain migration. "When my sister came to America," Angelina Merlo fondly reminisced, "she wrote me and she say, 'Don't stay in Italy, come here it is better!' I'm glad I came over. I come over the 15th of May (1920). I got married the Fourth of July. My sister bought the house for me. I still live in it. Fifty-five years."[78] Angelina Bianchi, born in 1887 in Cuggiono, recollected her moment of fortune. "Someone [an *americano*] came to help me," she remembered, "and I told them I don't want to die, I wanted to go to America."[79]

America beckoned, and Lombards who set their sights on the Hill marched lockstep and sidestep on the well-traveled path of experience. The Lombard connection enabled Cuggionesi to ease their way through the rites of passage, the immigrant maze rife with pitfalls for the uninitiated. First came the most important and agonizing of the stations—the decision to leave the *paese*. The Dantean journey, which Virgilian comrades carefully plotted, proceeded along a familiar itinerary: the farewell, the train depot at Milan, the long ride to the port of Le Havre, the voyage, endless lines at Ellis Island, the rapid excursion to the heartlands, the emotional reunion at Union Station, and finally baptism on the Hill.

Immigration demanded, above all, economic decisions. How to finance the endeavor? Would a job await in St. Louis? What if one miscalculated and arrived during hard times? Steamship tickets exacted sacrifices, costing thirty-five to forty dollars for the Le Havre cruise, in addition to five to ten dollars for the rail ticket from Milan to Le Havre. Once in New York sixteen dollars brought the financially exhausted traveler to St. Louis.[80] Considering the typical Italian immigrant brought less than fifteen dollars in capital, there is little wonder that so many of them remained on the East Coast. Sheer relentless purpose and sacrifice were necessary for the few thousand immigrants who arrived on the Hill.

Cuggionese financed the exodus in a variety of ways. "In the old country I didn't have five cents," lamented Paul Alagna. "My brothers had to send me money for the trip." Once in St. Louis he reciprocated the favor: "But if you was by yourself and live here like a hobo and save a few pennies here and there, you'll save quite a bit. Three or four dollars a week!" Interrupting, Alagna's wife explained, "You see, he sacrificed for his mother and sister who were still in Italy."[81] For Angelina Puricelli a trip to America depended on the health of the family cow: "My father wrote and said that when the family cow had a calf he would sell it and have enough money to send me. If I had waited for the calf I would still be in Italy because *la vacca è morta* (the cow died)!"[82] Family belts were tightened, and she left Lombardy in 1911.

Whether buoyed by family prosperity or encouraged by successful *paesani* on the Hill, young men by the boatload sought their fortunes in America. The number of parish marriages reflected the demographic imbalance wrought by emigration, or else the changing attitudes toward that institution because of new options: 67 marriages took place in Cuggiono in 1867, cresting at 72 in 1876, then dramatically falling to an average of only 42 throughout the 1880s. Between 1900 and the late 1940s Cuggiono persistently recorded more deaths than births. Meanwhile, in the immigrant enclave of St. Louis the number of births increased each year, from 167 in 1908 to 273 in 1914, and so on, the majority of these being Lombard Americans.[83]

Left behind in Italy were young women uncertain of their future, given the diminishing number of men. Some women entered the church; others dedicated themselves to caring for their families, since the elderly seldom emigrated. Still others became "picture brides," a much-celebrated sorority. "You know what those are?" asked Lou Berra, proclaiming that he had sailed to America comforted by a group of bewildered brides-to-be:

> Well in those days people came to St. Louis, young fellows not married, and they got a job and worked and saved their money and they figured, "Well, I ought to get married." Well, true to old country tradition the family kind of advised and steered you when you got to be of marriageable age. So, "Mama, I think I'm ready to get married. Do you know any nice girls who would have me?" And the Mama knows all the families over there and so she goes over, "My son, he is doing real well in America and looking for a wife and I know your daughter and we know your family . . . wouldn't it be great for both of them to get together."[84]

Maria Imo Griffero sailed to America, an anxious picture bride. Asked about her previous acquaintance with the groom-to-be, she confessed, "Not really well. . . . The family real nice because it was the same little town, Cuggiono!" She described the etiquette of her arranged marriage: "First he write his sister-in-law, 'See, I've intentions to get married and I ask my family first to get intentions to call you.' . . . So he wrote to me, 'Would you like to come and marry me?' He sent me a picture too but when I meet him more better than the picture . . . was really nice and fat and dressed like a soldier. . . . So he sent money so I went to a place in Cuggiono and got *passaporto*."[85]

While oral sources add a human touch to the life histories of picture brides, parish documents and naturalization records reveal other dimensions of this phenomenon of marriage and family constitution. The St. Louis portrait mirrors the findings of Dino Cinel, who also utilized naturalization data. Cuggionesi settling on the Hill in St. Louis arrived, on the average, as bachelors or married men without their families; only 8 percent of the men came to St. Louis with their wives and families. The typical Lombard male married eight years after emigration, and the choice for a bride was generally a *paesana* from the same old-world village, almost always a woman from Lombardy. The average man married at age twenty-seven and fathered his first child eight years after emigration. Lombard women were typically seven years younger than their husbands and married soon after arriving in America.[86]

The Hill evolved as a typical immigrant colony in the sense that during its formative years the men outnumbered the women. Consequently, women were in great demand as brides, domestics, and co-workers. The rigors of work, the loneliness of the immigrant colony, and the atomizing of families placed great pressures on Italians to fulfill their prescribed duties of union. Old-world traditions and new-world realities left little room for premarital romance. Working-class Italians intent on establishing a new life in a strange land could little afford the extravagance of an emotional courtship.[87]

Parish and government files depict the mobile nature of emigrants after arrival in America. Scores of future brides and grooms were born in Detroit, Herrin, or Joliet, only to return to Italy as children and then emigrate later to the United States. A typical case is Carlo Ravetta and Luigia Carnaghi, married in St. Louis on August 15, 1912. Both were born in Detroit, both emigrated to Cuggiono, and both emigrated later to St. Louis, where they remained after their marriage.[88]

Hopeful picture brides and failed farmers were all on the move. Tearful farewells, gesticulated in a thousand courtyards, traumatized the participants. In the tiny village of Ossona, not far from Cuggiono, Angelina Coco Merlo bade her last anguished farewell: "When my father take me to the station, he grab me by the neck and start cry. I cry and he cry and he say, 'Angelina, Angelina, I no see you no more.' I say, 'I come over again, don't worry daddy. . . . I no gonna stay in America.' He grab me by the neck—he no wanna me go. He start crying, that poor man."[89] "Oh, I never forget," recalled another veteran. "My family all gather, my poor grandfather say, 'For me, its just like a funeral.'"[90]

The odyssey augured life, not death. Promises to return, faithfully sworn, would rarely be fulfilled. Maria Torno philosophized the dilemma: "When I came here, I was on a cattle boat. It was so unpleasant, I decided never to go back. And if, when I lived there, Italy had been nice, I never would have left."[91] Giovanni Garagiola, who never once missed a day's work at the St. Louis brickyards for fear of losing his job, was later urged by his more successful son Joe to accept the gift of a plane ticket to Italy. His father agreed, Joe said, "as long as it was a round-trip ticket!"[92]

A Frenchman once wrote that to go away is to die a little. For those who remained in Cuggiono and witnessed the exodus of family and neighbors, staying behind was the price they paid for being satisfied with the status quo, for being elderly or sick or unwilling to change. Not to have left meant not to have been born again; it also meant death for seventy Cuggionesi during World War I. And yet emigration freed the town: the birthrate declined markedly as Cuggiono was robbed of future inhabitants; wages rose dramatically because of the sudden shortage of labor; and remittances from America improved the quality of life. War and modernization eventually ended the reign of the town's ruling nobility. Much later emigrants would recall with nostalgia *la via vecchia*. "The more you leave, the more sentimental you get," reflected Maria Griffero.

Grieving fathers, wailing mothers, and jealous kinsmen were left at the crossroads, at least for the time being. As the ox cart slowly rumbled down the ancient path, the Old World vanished. Ahead was the castle for trains, where pandemonium reigned. A Lombard and a missionary to the immigrants, Bishop Giovanni Baptiste Scalabrini, noted in his diary the emotional setting of the Milan train station:

> In passing through the station I saw the vast hall . . . filled by . . . individuals poorly dressed and divided into several groups. Their faces, burned brown by the sun, were worn and etched with deep wrinkles of hard years of toil in the fields. . . . All of them were directed toward a common goal.
>
> They were the emigrants. . . . They left . . . some called by relatives who had preceded them in the voluntary exodus. . . . They were going to

> America where they had heard the oft-repeated cry that there was work, well-rewarded work. All you needed were brawny arms and a strong will.[93]

Once on the train the landscape changed dramatically. The crystal Lombard lakes, alpine tunnels, and rolling provinces of France rushed by the huddled travelers. "I loved the ride," insisted Frank Gianella, "I was not scared. A fellow from the Hill, Angelo Calcaterra, was home on visit and brought me there."[94] The French port of Le Havre teemed with human freight as many people were forced to wait for days to book passage to New York. The delays exposed them to the omnipresent rogue, the bunco man, but the dangers and inconveniences merely strengthened the common bond and security of *paesani.*

Contemporaries called immigrant conditions "animal-like." "Cattle boats" became a common nickname for the steamships that carried these people to the Americas. "Never since the world began," a reporter noted, "have such loads of human freight been carried as those that are now being unloaded in New York harbor."[95] Steerage on *La Touraine*, whose cramped quarters reeked of the thousands of passengers, offered few luxuries. "You eat, you puke," Antonio Ranciglio graphically remembered. "See, it was third class steerage—pretty bad. Hot, seasick—two weeks!"[96] Snorted Carmelo Cacciatore, "We were packed like a suitcase—suffocating."[97] "Then one day we could see land," exclaimed Rosa Cassettari, "America! The country where everybody could find work. Where wages were so high no one had to go hungry."[98]

Counting their currency for the hundredth time the masses were herded into the red brick buildings of Ellis Island. For centuries inhabited only by gulls and oysters, Ellis Island now amplified waves of commotion. Nervous murmurings reminded all of the ruinous reputation of *La Isola delle Lacrime* (The Island of Tears). *Paesani* rehearsed with their companions answers to the dreaded questions: "Who paid your passage?" "Are you an anarchist?" "Where are you going?" They would later remember New York in a variety of ways: "My God," Charles Rancilio recalled his father saying, "the first thing we saw were the *corvi* [literally black crows—Negroes]. I thought to myself, 'What kind of country is this?'"[99] Leo Erutti confirmed the culture shock: "Upon my arrival . . . I saw so many dark people—I thought they were Africans! The only thing that bothered me was they knew the language!"[100]

New York City had its less serious side as well. Awaiting departure a sleeping Sam Russo was awakened by a vendor who casually deposited an apple in his lap and then tried to collect the outlandish sum of one dollar. Russo calmly munched the gift and apologized for his debt. The man finally stormed away, minus both his apple and his dollar.[101] Charles Rancilio recalled a story about his father's encounter with the legendary banana, ironically a fruit by which Italians would grow wealthy. "He bought this strange looking fruit from a peddler—he called it a banana. Then he saw this *corvo* [black] eating a banana. 'So that's how you eat it,' he said. 'What a crazy fruit that is!'"[102]

Loaded with excited and ever-wiser passengers the trains steamed out of New York toward the Midwest. At St. Louis *paesani* anxiously awaited the new arrivals at the depot. "We'd go to Union Station," laughed Antonio Ranciglio, "and that would be a big thing. We'd go down on a streetcar . . . wait, wait. We'd go across the street where a lot of Lombards had a saloon. We'd get a big schooner of beer for a nickel and there'd be a table with roast beef, ham, bread—a free lunch. We'd look forward to that. Then we'd go back and wait for the train."[103] The reunions were tumultuous. "Ohh, man—hugging, kissing. Boy it was wonderful," recalled Sam Russo.[104] "My two brothers were there for me," reminisced Angelina Merlo. "Ohh, they saw me, one kiss me, the other grab me."[105]

Greenhorns, new to urban America, gasped at the splendor and vastness of Union Station, the skyscrapers, and even such commonplaces as the Model T. "I'll never forget my cousin Tony," roared an elderly gentleman. "We had bought a new Chevrolet in 1920 and Tony came over in 1921. We came out of the station and got into the car. He gasped, 'Oh—you kidding—automobile?' he figured, 'Man, you millionaires!' Over there you couldn't even buy a bicycle! Was he surprised!"[106] Reunited with family, safely snug in the automobile or trolley, the final leg of the long journey was only ten minutes from the station to the Hill.

Safe at last in the insular ghetto, families could celebrate. Gifts were carefully unwrapped, revealing a family Bible, a votive candle, a treasured heirloom. Maria Ranciglio proudly presented her husband with three sprigs from the ancient fig tree that had stood in their backyard. (In the Old World the fig tree symbolized life, and after each child's birth the placenta was buried near the tree.) The nurtured sprigs grew into a tree at the rear of 5223 Bischoff Avenue, the Ranciglios' home for seventy-five years, next to the blacksmith shop where Alessandro Ranciglio taught his son, Antonio, an honored trade.

Such was the pattern of immigration to the Hill. Lombards arrived in

St. Louis, not uprooted but transplanted. Cuggionesi had safely crossed the ocean on a human bridge constructed of family and *paesani* timbers. Immigration was a disruptive experience but not an alienating one, a reintegration process that greatly eased the trials of settlement. Once on the Hill these chains of migrants, tempered by the rites of passage, determined Italian social structures and helped to mold a highly cohesive colony. Clearly, the inexorable pull of the Hill was stronger than the push of Lombard agricultural conditions. Cuggionesi who had learned the ABC's of urban life forcefully translated their experiences to *paesani*. Sickened by ruthless landlords and a bleak future, the peasants saw the magnetic letters and the examples of the *americani* as irresistible guidepaths to colonization of the hill on a city.

What evolved on that hill in St. Louis holds special interest for the immigration historian. We might expect that such a colony, given the extraordinary international work habits of its settlers, would have experienced high rates of geographic mobility, a rapid turnover of inhabitants, and periods of instability. Rather, the Hill has become one of the most stable, immobile, and cohesive ethnic colonies in the United States. Its evolution from immigrant colony to Italian-American community helped to create new alliances and new challenges.

NOTES

1. *Censimento di Cuggiono* 1880.
2. Baker, *Fortunate Pilgrims.*
3. *Republic*, Apr. 23, 1906, p. 11.
4. Foerster, *Italian Emigration of Our Times*, 504.
5. Wittke, *We Who Built America*, 406.
6. Amfitheatrof, *Children of Columbus*, 138.
7. Badi, *Cuggiono*, 1–5.
8. Braudel, *Mediterranean*, 1:72; Perogalli and Favole, *Ville dei Navigli Lombardi*, 69–72.
9. *La Storia di San Giorgio;* Badi, *Cuggiono*, 5–14.
10. Braudel, *Mediterranean*, 1:75.
11. Cipolla, *Cristofano and the Plague*, 15; *Il Baco la Seta nella Storia.*
12. Quoted in Badi, *Cuggiono*, 59.
13. *Rosa* draft, IHRC, MS. 18; Ermanno Olmi's *Tree of the Wooden Clogs* (1979) was filmed near Cuggiono; *Inchiesta Agraria* 6:70; *U.S. Immigration Commission: Emigration Conditions in Europe*, 156.

14. Foerster, *Italian Emigration of Our Times*, 112.

15. *Censimento di Cuggiono* 1880.

16. *Rosa*, MS., 21.

17. *Istituto Centrale*, 136; Badi, *Cuggiono*, 42.

18. *Liber Baptizatorum Sancti Giorgi.*

19. Thistlethwaite, "Migration from Europe," 90.

20. Personal interviews in Cuggiono, Italy, Dec. 1980, Apr. 1981; Foerster, *Italian Emigration of Our Times*, 111; Badi, *Cuggiono*, 59.

21. Foerster, *Italian Emigration of Our Times*, 106–26; Greenfield, *Economics and Liberalism*, 19–38.

22. *Il Baco da Seta nella;* Greenfield, *Economics and Liberalism*, 38.

23. Ets, *Rosa*, 76–77.

24. Interviews with Maria Imo Griffero, July 25, 1973, Oct. 27, 1975.

25. Interview with Maria Torno, June 19, 1973.

26. Ets, *Rosa*, 76–77.

27. Quoted in Greenfield, *Economics and Liberalism*, 116.

28. "Stories in the Barn," Rosa Cassettari Papers, IHRC, MS., 5.

29. Ets, *Rosa*, 121.

30. Ibid., 76.

31. Interview with Antonio Ranciglio, May 29, 1975.

32. Smith, *Italy*, 107, 151.

33. *Statuto della Società.*

34. Annoni, *Cuggiono e Zone Vicine*, 22.

35. Stearns, *European Society in Upheaval*, 78–86.

36. Tilly, "Working Class of Milan"; Tilly, "Urban Growth."

37. MacDonald, "Some Socio-Economic Emigration Differentials," 67.

38. Ibid., 22–24; Badi, *Cuggiono*, 36–37; interviews in Cuggiono, Italy, Dec. 1980, Apr. 1981.

39. Quoted in Dore, "Some Social and Historical Aspects," 98.

40. Quoted in Tilly, "Working Class of Milan," 31.

41. MacDonald, "Italy's Rural Social Structure."

42. Ibid.; Barton, *Peasants and Strangers*, 27–47; Briggs, *An Italian Passage*, 1–14.

43. Carpi, *Dell' Emigrazione Italiana;* Gilkey, "Effects of Emigration, 4–45.

44. Carpi, *Quadro Statistico.*

45. Foerster, *Italian Emigration of Our Times*, 279–89; Gilkey, "Effects of Emigration," 4–45; Baily, "Italians and Organized Labor"; Baily, "Adjustment of Italian Immigrants."

46. Vismara, "Coming of the Italians"; Re, *Michigan's Italian Community*, 18. Calumet, the place not chosen, did attract a large number of Italians. Nativist hostility contributed to the infamous affair in 1913 which resulted in the

deaths of seventy-three Italian children. Woody Guthrie immortalized the event in song:

The 1913 Massacre
Take a trip with me in 1913
To Calumet, Michigan and copper country
I'll take you to a place
Called Eye-talian Hall . . .

47. Foerster, *Italian Emigration of Our Times*, 349–50; *Globe-Democrat*, Aug. 8, 1907, p. 1; Manfredini, "Italians Come to Herrin"; Marchello Papers, folder 23, IHRC; interview with Fred Giacoma, Sept. 20, 1973.

48. Ets, *Rosa*, 84.

49. Letter from Giovanni Schiavo to the author, Nov. 3, 1973; interview with Theresa Sala, Aug. 7, 1975; letter from Angelo Sala to the author, Aug. 18, 1975; List or Manifest of Alien Passengers for U.S. Immigration Office, Jan. 20, 1882, SS *St. Germain*, from Le Havre, National Archives.

50. Interview with Hugo Schoessel, July 10, 1973.

51. Ibid.

52. *Post-Dispatch*, Jan. 23, 1898, p. 5.

53. *Il Pensiero*, Aug. 18, 1929, p. El.

54. "Toilers of the Dark," *Globe-Democrat*, June 9, 1907, magazine.

55. Interview with Julius Selvaggi, Aug. 15, 1973.

56. 1900 U.S. Manuscript Census, St. Louis, National Archives.

57. Naturalization petition, Carlo Gualdoni, 1925; interviews with Louis Jean Gualdoni, Aug. 13, 1973, July 30, 1982.

58. Interview with Maria Torno, June 19, 1973; *Hill 2000* 4 (May 1975).

59. Cinel, *From Italy to San Francisco*, 1; Caroli, *Italian Repatriation.*

60. Interview with Antonio Ranciglio, May 29, 1975.

61. *Post-Dispatch*, May 5, 1941.

62. Interviews with Maria Imo Griffero, July 25, 1973, Oct. 27, 1975.

63. Steiner, "Returning Emigrants," 701.

64. Interview with Leo Erutti, July 2, 1973.

65. Quoted in Gilkey, "Effects of Emigration," 158.

66. *Istituto Centrale*, 136–38. During the period 1881–1914 northern Italy averaged approximately 33 births per 1,000 inhabitants, a very high level of population growth. *Statistiche Sul Mezzogiorno d'Italia*, 61.

67. Annoni, *Cuggiono e Zone Vicine*, 22.

68. Serpieri, *Il Contratto Agrario*, 38–41.

69. Badi, *Cuggiono*, 60.

70. Thistlethwaite, "Migration from Europe," 80.

71. Archivio di Chiesa di San Giorgio, Cuggiono.

72. *Annual Report of the Commissioner-General for Immigration*, 60–61; MacDonald, "Chain Migration."

73. Tilly, "Migration in Modern European History," 53; Hareven, "Family Time and Industrial Time," 373–75.

74. Cinel, *From Italy to San Francisco*, 26–28.

75. List or Manifest of Alien Passengers for U.S. Immigration Office, vols. 1670, 1671, 1672, July 1906, National Archives.

76. Naturalization records, vol. 129, 1931.

77. Ibid., vols. 1112, 1113, Mar. 1905.

78. Interview with Angelina Merlo, Aug. 6, 1975.

79. Interview with Angelina Bianchi, Aug. 28, 1973.

80. Interviews with Julius Selvaggi, Aug. 15, 1973, and Mrs. Joseph Riggio, June 10, 1973. The Selvaggi and Riggio families pioneered the steamship-immigrant postal service among St. Louis Italians.

81. Paul Alagna, interviewed by Gayle Swiler, Nov. 13, 1973, St. Louis (tape on file at University of Missouri at St. Louis, Oral History Collection).

82. Interview with Angelina Puricelli, July 12, 1973.

83. *Liber Conjugatum Sanet.*

84. Interview with Lou Berra, July ll, 1973.

85. Interviews with Maria Griffero, July 25, 1973, Oct. 27, 1975.

86. *Libro dei Matrimonie Santo Ambrogio*, St. Louis Archdiocesan Archives; naturalization records, 1907–40; Cinel, *From Italy to San Francisco*, 168–69.

87. Yans-McLaughlin, *Family and Community*, 93–95.

88. *Libro dei Matrimonie*, 1:207.

89. Interview with Angelina Coco Merlo, Aug. 6, 1975.

90. Interviews with Maria Griffero, July 25, 1973, Oct. 27, 1975.

91. *Hill 2000* 4 (May 1975).

92. Interview with Joe Garagiola, June 19, 1984.

93. Felici, *Father to the Immigrants*, 125.

94. Interview with Frank Gianella, Aug. 1, 1975.

95. *Post-Dispatch*, May 18, 1902, II, p. 8. *La Touraine* was able to carry over 1,200 passengers; by comparison the *Mayflower* brought over only 102 immigrants.

96. Interview with Antonio Ranciglio, May 29, 1975.

97. Interview with Carmelo Cacciatore, May 28, 1975.

98. Ets, *Rosa*, 164–65.

99. Interviews with Charles Rancilio, June 28, July 14, 1973.

100. Interview with Leo Erutti, July 2, 1973.

101. Interview with Sam Russo, Sept. 10, 1973.

102. Interviews with Charles Rancilio, June 28, July 14, 1973.

103. Interview with Antonio Ranciglio, May 29, 1975.

104. Interview with Sam Russo, Sept. 10, 1973.

105. Interview with Angelina Merlo, Aug. 6, 1975.

106. Interview with Antonio Ranciglio, May 29, 1975.

3 The Formation of a Community, 1900–1930

To be deeply rooted in a place that has meaning is perhaps the best gift a child can have.
Christopher Morley

The Gateway Arch dominates the St. Louis skyline, a symbol intended by its immigrant architect, Eero Saarinen, to consecrate the mobile spirit of Americans. At the turn of the century St. Louis stood on the restless crossroads of east and west, north and south. Few residents of that city needed reminding that America was a nation on the move. Although St. Louis had not become one of the great centers of the new immigration, large numbers of southern and eastern Europeans were not deterred from using the Gateway City as a staging point for their migrant labors.

"Union Station," a 1903 commentator noted, "attracts 10,000 laborers passing through St. Louis during March and they expect more in April. . . . They are of all nationalities and the majority cannot speak English."[1] Another report proclaimed, "the Greek and Latin invasion has now reached St. Louis."[2] Still another source told of "100,000 men a year passing through St. Louis" and described how "the labor agent scouts along Market Street, through the Greek and Italian colonies, picking up recruits to fill the great army of railway laborers which St. Louis expects to supply to the country annually."[3] By 1900 clusters of Greek, Jewish, German, Irish, Hungarian, and Slavic colonies dotted the inner city and urban fringes of St. Louis, offering to most newcomers a temporary refuge, a halfway house where settlers worked in hopes of moving upward and outward. Most historians concur with Stephan Thernstrom's assessment that many of these immigrants could be expected "to vanish from [the colonies] before ten years had elapsed."[4]

Yet there were exceptions. Urban observers have long noted the extraordinary endurance of Italian-American neighborhoods, but most scholars hold that such territorial persistence was not necessarily a residual carryover of the original inhabitants. South Village in New York City, Taylor Street in Chicago, and Boston's West End, for instance, experienced several successive waves of Italian populations.[5] St. Louis's Hill was one of several hundred Italian colonies in 1900, yet early in its development commentators declared *this* was no ordinary ghetto. "Successful Cooperative Colony in St. Louis" was the headline of a 1901 *Post-Dispatch* story that pointed out the salient features of the settlement: "Six hundred Italians, a community store and saloon, the North of Italy tongue, a $500 flag, a rented mass in a German-Catholic Church, a Garibaldi society and an anti-Garibaldi society, Italian bread for the bakeries, and a $2 fine for fighting in a conspicuous place. All these things has Dago Hill unique among the communities of St. Louis."[6] Readers scanning the urban dailies half a dozen years later discovered another feature-length article dealing with the colony: "Once a place of lawlessness, it is now a settlement of thrifty sons of Italy. Nowhere else could be found a more ideal settlement with respect to social, business and religious relations."[7]

The turn-of-the-century journalists would not be the last to ascribe to the Hill the quality of "uniqueness." Clearly, vast forces—some generated by the directions of urban America, others dictated by the vagaries of local ecology, and still others by the destinies of the inhabitants—influenced the formation and originality of the Hill. Like the proverbial bent twig, the colony's formative period was critical to the future of the enclave. During the period 1900–1930 three distinct, yet interacting factors underpinned the foundations of the Hill: settlement patterns underscored stability and portended cohesion; residential and environmental trends created an identifiable ghetto; and ethnic antagonisms between Lombards and Sicilians fostered group rivalries and institutional growth.

SETTLEMENT PATTERNS

Once little more than a mining camp, the Hill changed drastically after 1900 as its social complexion took on the hues of a community. The 1908 Sant' Ambrogio parish census captured an immigrant colony flush in the midst of a dynamic growth prompted by streams of new residents and a natural increase sanctified by the church. There were nearly 3,000 inhabitants, and men continued to outnumber women by a six-to-one margin, a characteristic common to immigrant communities in the early stages. The church conducted 60 marriages that year, a figure that remained steady for a decade. Parents marched steadily to the baptismal font in 1908, as 167 babies received blessings from the church fathers. Remarkably, over half the adult women on the Hill gave birth during a single year, a dramatic example of fecundity.

The number of births increased each year, to 273 in 1914, a reflection of the increasing number of women in the community. If births were many during these early years, deaths at the parish level were few: only 64 in 1914, and 55 in 1925. By comparison, in Cuggiono, Lombardy, a town twice the size of the Hill, only half as many baptisms and marriages occurred in 1908. The growing number of brides and children on the Hill served to reinforce the most notable feature of the colony—a virtual absence of anyone over fifty years of age. In 1910 fewer than 2 percent of the Hill's inhabitants had been born before 1860, a demographic statistic not unusual for immigrant colonies. Grandparents preferred to remain in the old country; immigration was a phenomenon to be experienced and endured by the young.[8]

Ethnically the colony had also changed by 1900. No longer was it the exclusive domain of Lombards, for Sicilians had discovered the Hill. Although northern Italians outnumbered southerners three to one, the staccato Lombard dialect was not the only language in the area mines and factories. The arrival of the Sicilians inaugurated a generation of bitter ethnic quarreling between northern and southern Italians. In 1907, to discourage open conflict, a Lombard mutual aid society imposed a two-dollar fine for fighting. In spite of the new antagonists an element of domestication began to envelop the rough-edged labor camp.[9]

Growth, interrupted only by war and depression, characterized the first half-century of the colony's existence. Between the early 1880s and 1900 the enclave evolved from a primitive collection of shacks housing a handful of sojourners to a crude community numbering 700. Weekly streams of new arrivals between 1900 and 1914 buoyed the population. Despite the temporary halt to immigration during World War I and the repatriation of some pioneers, in 1920 the Hill was home to 2,651 foreign-born Italians and 1,410 second-generation residents. In the early 1920s a number of new residents arrived before the restrictive quotas, as well as scores of displaced southern Illinois miners. By 1930 the number of first-generation Italians had fallen slightly to 2,264, but birthrates—

the highest of any district in St. Louis—boosted the second-generation cohort to 2,983. As late as 1930 foreign-born residents comprised almost 40 percent of the Hill's population, which was double that of any other census precinct in St. Louis.[10]

Much of the stability and continuity of the Hill can be attributed to the colony's settlement and migration process. The data gleaned from 600 Hill Italian naturalization petitions filed between 1906 and 1930 make it possible to paint a collective portrait of the colony (see A Note on Sources). These petitions represent almost half of the immigrant males on the Hill and provide not only a detailed description of the immigration process but also critical information concerning geographical and occupational mobility.

The typical Lombard emigrated from Cuggiono as a twenty-year-old, single male, born in 1890, who set sail from Le Havre, France, and arrived in New York within ten days. Lombards, mindful of their final destination, proceeded promptly to St. Louis after processing at Ellis Island. Dino Cinel argued that in San Francisco northern Italians were more adventurous in moving out of the ethnic enclaves.[11] Such was not the case in St. Louis. Consider Antonio Gioia. Born in Cuggiono in 1885 he left Lombardy in August 1902, purchasing steerage tickets at the Agenzia di Pinel in his hometown with funds forwarded by Giuseppe Gioia, a successful merchant on the Hill. Setting sail aboard *La Città di Genova*, Antonio Gioia departed Le Havre on August 7, 1902, and arrived in New York on August 17; just two days later he stepped onto the Union Station platform in St. Louis. Gioia found work immediately at his uncle's saloon at 5256 Pattison Avenue. In 1907 he received his first papers, a necessary prelude to citizenship; naturalization was granted in 1913. Gioia continued to reside at 5226 Pattison Avenue, the only home he had known since 1902.[12]

Contrast this experience with that of Giuseppe Visconti. Born in Cuggiono in 1888, at the age of seventeen Visconti departed with twenty cousins for Austria, where they worked on a railroad for a *padrone* from nearby Varese. Two years later Visconti returned to Cuggiono where he farmed for the Calcaterra family. In 1909 he chose to immigrate to America and purchased one third-class ticket for 297 lire. To save money Visconti and seven Cuggionesi walked to Magenta, where they boarded the train to Le Havre. They embarked on a French liner, *La Gascogne*, and arrived in St. Louis within a month. Visconti obtained a job at the local brickyards, but after seven months of toil he migrated to Herrin, Illinois, to mine coal. The 1912 strike disrupted work, and Visconti journeyed to Joliet, Illinois, where a scattering of Lombards had settled. He labored in the sewers of that city until 1916, when he migrated to Detroit, to still another colony of Cuggionesi. Visconti remained in Detroit until the depression, returning to Cuggiono in 1933.[13]

These two cases illustrate the dichotomy of the Lombard experience on the Hill. Immigrants like Antonio Gioia tended to predominate, permitting historians more opportunity for study, but we will never know how many Giuseppe Viscontis filtered undetected from one immigrant colony to another, shuffling from bad times to a hopeful future. The evidence, however, clearly shows that individuals migrated to rather than from the Hill, and the Gioia case is typical of the immigrant experience on the Hill.

The Sicilian experience differed from the Lombard passage in several respects. Among other things Sicilian males were on the average five feet five inches tall, or three inches shorter than their Lombard counterparts. The typical Sicilian immigrant had been born in 1890, was unmarried, and was twenty-one years old at the time of arrival. Unlike Lombards, who had originated from a tight cluster of villages around Milan, Sicilians migrated in equal numbers from the towns of Catania and Augusta on the eastern coast, and Casteltermini, Belmonte Mezzagna, and Palazzo Adriano in the province of Palermo. The magnetic lure of the Hill pulled less forcefully for Sicilians than Lombards; 63 percent arrived there within one month after emigration, as opposed to 87 percent of the Lombards. Whereas southern Illinois served as the seasoning ground for Lombards, many Sicilians had spent time in Louisiana.[14]

The life histories of Giuseppe Urzi and Pietro Castellese parallel the Sicilian experience on the Hill. Born in 1893 at Santa Venerina, a provincial town near Catania, Sicily, Urzi left Italy in May 1909, arriving in St. Louis one month later. In 1920, at age twenty-seven, he married an eighteen-year-old Catanesa. He spent the rest of his life working at unskilled jobs in the brickyards in St. Louis, eventually becoming a truck driver in the 1930s. Castellese was born in Parco, Palermo, in 1884, leaving Sicily at age fourteen. Six months after arriving in New York he made his way to the Hill, where he too remained for the rest of his life, working as a laborer and molder at local foundries. In January 1915 he married a Catanesa and they reared six children. Such marriages between Sicilians from two different island provinces were quite common on the Hill.[15]

During the period 1900–1924 local immigration patterns dovetailed with international movements except when local vicissitudes disrupted traffic. The years 1905, 1906, and 1907 witnessed the largest single number of immigrants arriving on the Hill. Joseph Riggio, a steamship agent and immigrant banker from Palazzo Adriano, Palermo, explained the heavy influx: "We used to sell maybe a thousand steamship tickets a year. Once, for four months, somewhere around 1907, there was a steamship war and passage could be had for only $5. That year the Hill built up fast."[16] The 1908 national depression gripped the local brickyards and clay mines with particular severity. "I worked [only] two-three hours each day to earn expenses," reminisced a melancholic Leo Erutti. "Many were out of work the whole year [1908]. I would not write my folks in Italy about it—I was too proud to admit my mistake." A desperate Erutti left St. Louis for Germany, a country bent on war with an economy primed for production. Fortuitously, he returned to the Hill in 1913, where he remained for the rest of his life.[17] After 1914 Ellis Island took on a hauntingly silent air. The number of Italians immigrating during the entire period 1915–19 constituted less than one-half that of a single year, 1907. The war, plus a bitter 1917 strike at the brickyards, dramatically halted the flow of Italians to the Hill. Not one of the 600 naturalization petitions studied indicates arrivals on the Hill during 1917 or 1918.

Once the guns of Caporetto and the Piave were silenced, a beleaguered Italy and a relieved Hill braced for one last spectacular exodus. The colony received large numbers of immigrants during the period 1920–23, the final gasp before immigration restriction. Humbert Nelli postulated that the affluence of the 1920s enabled Chicago Italians to disperse throughout the city and suburbs. For the Hill the 1920s proved to be a decade of institutional maturation and internal growth, in part a reflection of the lassitude in the St. Louis economy, in part a result of local dynamics.[18]

The Hill was infused with the vitality and energy of still another population base in the 1920s: during that decade several hundred Lombards fled southern Illinois for the sanctuary of St. Louis. The Immigration Restriction Act may have curbed the international flow of traffic but not the motivation to seek a better life once in America. Immigration, generally described in terms of the original move to cities, also included secondary movements of migrants.

Southern Illinois inflicted a grievous price on immigrants who settled in coal-mining towns such as Herrin, Murphysboro, Tamaroa, DuQuoin, and West Frankfort. Williamson County attracted the lion's share of immigrants in southern Illinois's "Little Egypt." Immigrants from northern Italy began arriving in southern Illinois in the early 1880s. By 1899 there were 3,016 Italian miners laboring in the Illinois coal fields (8 percent of the work force), a figure that increased to 18,489 in 1910; 1,607 mined in Williamson County alone. The 1910 census lists sizable numbers of Italians, Russians, Belgians, Finns, Poles, Lithuanians, Welsh, and English miners scattered throughout the county but living principally in Herrin. Interestingly, most of the Italians in 1910 claimed an ability to speak English, an attribute not shared by their kinfolk in St. Louis. Most likely, mining officials imposed English as a lingua franca given the polyglot work force.[19]

In the abandoned coal shafts and deserted company towns of Little Egypt lie the remains of many immigrants victimized by mining accidents, economic exploitation, and nativist excesses. In 1907 twenty-three Italians perished at the bottom of the number eleven mine at West Frankfort; in 1915 eleven immigrants, including six Italians, were sent to a permanent grave by an explosion in Panama, Illinois.[20] Yet Italian immigrants frequently found mining safer than walking the streets of southern Illinois.

It is difficult to separate myth from reality, such as the 1909 account of how 150 Italians, "crazed by drink," took over the town of Marion, Illinois. The *St. Louis Globe-Democrat* attributed the violence to alcoholism and the Black Hand.[21] The period 1914–20 witnessed several outbreaks of violence. In October 1914 Albert Piazzia, operator of a poolroom in Willisville, Illinois, shot two locals during an attempted robbery. Outraged citizens marched to Pickneyville, where a crowd of 500 broke into the jail and hanged Piazzia.[22] The following year a mob composed of 600 local residents battered their way into a Johnson City jail and seized Joseph Stranzo, an Italian accused of murdering an area farmer. Stranzo maintained his innocence even as vigilantes pumped the first of several hundred rounds into his body. "The lynching of Stranzo," editorialized the *Globe-Democrat*, "was the culmination of a reign of terror which began in Williamson County a year ago and which was attributed to the Black Hand society. Twelve mysterious murders have occurred in that time."[23] A third episode flared in August 1920, when natives of West Frankfort, frustrated by the economic malaise gripping southern Illinois, sought a scapegoat in the form of Italian immigrants accused of moonshining and extortion. During two nights of rioting local mobs firebombed the Italian quarters, killing 1 immigrant, injuring 30 and destroying $20,000 in property. One reporter estimated that at least 250 Italians departed for St. Louis.[24]

The Ku Klux Klan ruled "Bloody Williamson" during the 1920s. Provoked by chianti, Catholicism, and crime, the Klan attacked Italians in a series of confrontations. Wizard Glenn Young's hooded hoodlums delighted in smashing up wedding receptions. Efforts by Italians to assert themselves were met with predictable violence. During the 1920s a Lombard, John Garavaglia, broached local custom in attempting to organize the Italians of Herrin into a political bloc. In October 1926 the Klan attacked Garavaglia outside the county courthouse, pistol-whipping the immigrant into unconsciousness.[25] The death of Grand Wizard Young (killed in a shootout) and the demise of the Invisible Empire (by debauchery and hypocrisy) failed to ameliorate the economic misery in southern Illinois. King Coal had simply collapsed.[26]

Bloody Williamson was less than 100 miles from St. Louis. Hundreds of displaced Illinois miners rejoined family and kin on the Hill, pointing out the importance of secondary migration movements. During the 1920s and 1930s perhaps as much as 15 percent of the Hill's external growth originated from southern and central Illinois as Lombard miners left for St. Louis. To Italian immigrants related by blood and custom the Hill was not "superficial, anonymous and disorganized," as Louis Wirth depicted the city, but rather a haven of organization and meaning.[27] Consider the case history of Mauro Belossi. Born in Buscate, Lombardy, in 1880, he left Italy for a peripatetic career in the Illinois coal fields. The birthplaces of the Belossi children accentuate the mobility involved in mining: Herrin, 1905; Christopher, 1912; Belleville, 1920. The Belossis moved to St. Louis in 1920 and remained on the Hill, as Mauro exchanged his mining pick for a waiter's apron.[28]

To appreciate the Hill's settlement patterns one must compare and contrast that colony's experience with other St. Louis ethnic groups/enclaves, viz., Greeks, Russians, Jews, Hungarians, and Italians. The Greeks of St. Louis appear to have been the most geographically mobile and dispersed ethnic group. In the Mound City, as elsewhere, Greeks actively entered the restaurant, confectionery, shoeshine, and entertainment enterprises.[29] Economically, the small Greek community of St. Louis could support only a limited number of such endeavors, hence the Greek population became geographically decentralized. Possibly because of their economic pursuits Greeks apprenticed themselves in other cities before migrating to St. Louis. Only 37 percent of the 167 Greek nationalization petitions I examined, the lowest comparative figure, revealed emigration directly to St. Louis. In addition, a very high number of Greek men (75 percent) were unmarried at the time of naturalization, a factor reinforcing their mobile status.

Jewish immigrants in St. Louis congregated in "the Ghetto," a sprawling district bordering Little Italy and Little Poland on the near north side. Once settled most Jews worked in the nearby garment and shoe factories, or entered the commercial trades as peddlers and small businessmen. Of the 600 samples I studied, 56 percent of these people migrated directly to St. Louis, a figure higher than the Greeks but considerably lower than Hill Italians (78 percent). Disembarking from New York, the Jewish center in America, many elected to begin their careers there before moving west.

The Hungarian enclave was in south St. Louis among the city's famous breweries and foundries.[30] Fully 72 percent of the 325 Hungarians living in the Soulard district could be found in St. Louis within one month after immigration, a rate of settlement second only to the Hill.

St. Louis was also the home of another Italian community comprised of several thousand Sicilians hailing from Cinisi, Partinico, Castelvetrano, and Palermo. These immigrants congregated in the densely populated downtown enclave known as Little Italy. A sample of 350 petitions reveals that only 55 percent of the Sicilians moved directly to St. Louis, a figure lower than Hill Sicilians (65 percent) and much lower than Hill Lombards (87 percent). The presence of at least two Cinisi and several colonies of Palermitani in New York City may explain their hesitation prior to migration to St. Louis.

Hill Italians, contrasted to other ethnic groups, were not only remarkably settlement-oriented in their migratory patterns but also extraordinarily stable once they arrived in St. Louis. Every social indicator from 1900 to 1982 verifies the exceptional permanence of the Hill and its residents. Fully 96 percent of the Italians who emigrated there between 1900 and 1925 and who later petitioned for citizenship could be found residing in the same house or within the old neighborhood during the three- to five-year period required for naturalization. Only 5 percent, chiefly saloon keepers and restaurateurs, moved to other areas of St. Louis. While naturalization petitions contain a natural bias—that is, individuals wishing to become citizens would be more likely *not* to move—

significant differences appear when comparing ethnic groups or neighborhoods using the same criteria.

Contrast the stability of the Hill to the transiency of Little Italy. Only 62 percent of the latter's residents could be found within the borders of the enclave between the first and second citizenship, 38 percent having fled from the area to midtown or north St. Louis. The proportion of all St. Louis Italians living in Little Italy ranges from 50 percent in 1910, to 41 percent in 1920, to 27 percent in 1930; on the Hill the figures reflect a more permanent neighborhood: 21 percent in 1910, 24 percent in 1920, and 24 percent in 1930.[31] Also pertinent is the fact that during the period 1906–30 only 1 Sicilian out of a sample of 350 migrated from Little Italy to the Hill, while no Lombards or Sicilians moved downtown from the Hill, emphasizing the social distance between the two Italian colonies. Keep in mind that in 1930 half of St. Louis's Italian immigrants lived outside the city's principal ethnic ghettos, indicative of the residential fluidity of the immigrant colony.

If naturalization statistics represent only the more permanent members of an ethnic group, there is additional evidence to document the Hill's reputation for stability and permanence. *Gould's St. Louis Red-Blue Book* published household-by-household, block-by-block directories of the Gateway City from 1921 to 1928. A survey of the principal streets on the Hill during the period 1921–26 reveals that fully 60 percent of the heads of households could be found residing at the same house after the six-year lapse. In Little Italy only 11 percent of the families could be similarly located after five years. North Ninth Street, for example, in the heart of Little Italy, was almost completely unrecognizable in 1926, as 96 percent of the households had changed occupants since 1921. Cooper and Shaw avenues on the Hill, however, registered only a 6 percent change in new residents during the same period. The 1920s inaugurated a tremendous boom in home construction on the Hill, and one suspects that much intra-neighborhood mobility occurred, as had happened with individuals petitioning for citizenship. The bizarre spellings employed by city directories prohibit name indexing and individual checks.

Several other studies conducted between the First World War and the New Deal verify the Hill's exceptional stability. The community became a laboratory for sociologists intrigued by the colony's reputation and fascinated by the neighborhood's durability in the midst of chronic urban decay. "The brick houses are an index of immigrant progress," wrote reformer Ruth Crawford in 1916, "because in the majority of cases they are owned by the Italians themselves. . . . These immigrants have come to stay. . . . Dago Hill is a splendid part of the city for a growing industrial community to develop."[32] Donald Cowgill declared in his 1935 study, "Fairmount Heights [the Hill] was one of the most stable areas in the city." The Washington University sociologist found only 9 tracts in the city, out of a total of 128, that registered less geographic mobility than the Hill. Furthermore, most of the household moves during this period involved intra-neighborhood shifts.[33]

Elmer Shorb Wood, a graduate student and social worker on the Hill during the Great Depression, also noted low rates of geographical mobility. In 1933 Wood circulated questionnaires to forty families and found that thirty had not moved within the last five years; six had moved only once and four had moved twice. All retained residence within the neighborhood during the entire period. Local school officials confirmed Wood's conclusions. The principal at Shaw School told Wood that his school had fewer transfers than any other school in the city. In a 1984 interview Wood recalled discussing the phenomenon of stability on the Hill with his Washington University mentor, Professor Stuart McQueen. "From all I can figure out," Wood remembered telling McQueen as they examined census reports, "no one is moving from this place [Hill]. They are not hedge-jumping." McQueen concurred.[34]

Journalists extolled the Hill's continuity and promise. Claudio Delitala, the editor of *La Stampa Italiana*, a newspaper based in Little Italy, declared, "Italians have gone to the Hill with the intention to remain. They may move from a frame house to a more pretentious brick home; they may go from one street to another, but they stay on *la Montagna!*" Amy Bernardy, an experienced student of immigration, on a tour of midwestern Italian colonies for *Bolletino dell' Emigrazione* in 1911, described the Hill as an "*extra-urban* [suburban] community where almost everyone owns his own house. . . . it is almost an oasis of rest where residents live with plenty of space and light. . . . compared to the rest of St. Louis, Dago Hill represents the best of America, and a vengeance for the name, Italian immigrant."[35] Father Salvatore Polizzi, a former pastor at St. Ambrose Church and a perceptive student of ethnic life, suggested that "over 90 percent of the people living on the Hill today [1970s] are descendants of the original settlers and have never lived in any other section of the city."[36]

AMBIENTE ON *LA MONTAGNA*

Lombards and Sicilians emerged from premodern, old-world villages to the modern, industrial expanse of St. Louis yet discovered not the anonymous and hostile modern city but the recreation of a Little Milano. One of the most striking features of the Hill during its formative period was the colony's high degree of ethnic homogeneity, spatial isolation, and cultural independence. "Where I come from in St. Louis is called the Hill," Lawrence ("Yogi") Berra once told a reporter. "It's strictly an Italian neighborhood, except I can remember one German family that lived in the same block with us."[37] Few outsiders resided in the fifty-two-block Italian section of the city bounded by Macklind, Northrup, Kingshighway, and Southwest avenues, a fact verified not only by Berra's recollection but by city directories, voting lists, and censuses.[38]

The concentration of Italians in neighborhoods has long been a salient feature of immigrant life; indeed, in 1910 blacks were substantially less segregated than Italians.[39] An earlier generation of urban scholars, most notably those of the Chicago School of Sociology, painted a portrait of the immigrant neighborhood characterized by ethnic homogeneity. Recently historians such as Sam Bass Warner, Jr., Kathleen Conzen, Howard Chudacoff, and Stephan Thernstrom have reexamined the nature of the ghetto as a factor in immigrant life, insisting that immigrants rarely huddled in homogeneous, distinct, separate residential areas. According to Thernstrom, the extent to which white, foreign-born newcomers clustered together "has often been exaggerated." Warner and his colleague Colin Burke contend that "such ghettos as did exist were probably not the uniform environments that the [ghetto] interpretation implies."[40] Clearly the Hill goes against the grain of the revisionist interpretation, certainly an exception to the immigrant rule.

Italian immigrants generally established colonies in the older sections of central cities, often neighborhoods previously settled by Irish and Jewish immigrants. St. Louis's Little Italy bears witness to this pattern. But the Hill was sparsely settled when the first Italians arrived in the 1880s, with clusters of homes occupied by Germans and Afro-Americans dotting the area overlooking the valley factories. By 1910 the Hill had clearly been taken over by Italians, although several individuals withstood the onslaught. The 5232 Pattison Avenue Baptist Church, an Afro-American church, seemed an unlikely survivor, yet it coexisted in relative harmony with its new neighbors. In 1910 Walter Williams ministered at the church and worked in the clay mines; in the 1970s Joseph Smith headed the congregation. "He is the third generation in that house [5347 Pattison]," explained the area mailman. "They [Smith and his wife] walk around this Hill and color does not seem to come out of them. I've seen them on the corner talking to northern Italians, southern Italians. . . ." Such enlightened sentiments did not always characterize Italian-black relationships. Several bitter conflicts grew out of the labor disputes at the area factories, and by 1930 only a handful of blacks resided within the Hill's precincts, a figure that remains virtually unchanged in the 1980s.[41]

To appreciate fully the import of the Hill's ethnic-residential solidarity one must understand complementary ecological factors. The physical environment, reinforced by the early aspirations of the immigrants, clearly played a constraining and restraining role. The editor of *La Lega* complained without success to the Public Service Commission in 1914: "There is in this city a district inhabited by over 5,000 souls, which as regards street railway services is completely isolated from the rest of the city."[42] Until the 1920s the Hill was isolated from St. Louis; insular and provincial, the colony functioned as an ethnic, industrial island miles from downtown St. Louis. Not until the age of jazz did the neighborhood acquire intra-urban and streetcar terminals.[43] When reformers discussed the necessity of establishing a settlement house in the area in 1915, an organizer noted "the difficulty of reaching the place. . . ."[44]

Modern transportation and the sprawl of St. Louis reached the Hill in the 1920s. Physical barriers continued to separate the neighborhood from its surroundings, in part the result of unconscious development. The River des Peres, streets such as Kingshighway, and the existence of brickyards, rail lines, and foundries effectively cordoned off the Hill. But more compelling than an industrial hedge were cultural barriers imposed by residents. The urban environment performed a constraining role only as long as immigrants wished. In his perceptive study entitled *A City People*, Gunther Barth described how the late-nineteenth-century department store, baseball park, and entertainment industry introduced immigrants to an exciting urban culture. But this urban panorama of St. Louis, described by Walt Whitman in *Specimen Days* as "store-streets, showy modern, metropolitan, with hurrying crowds, vehicles, horse-cars, hubbub . . . rich goods, plateglass windows, iron fronts, often five or six stories high," was a world few Italians on the Hill experienced prior to the 1920s.

"The six hundred Italians on the Hill are at once a part and apart from the great city," the *Post-Dispatch* observed in 1901. "The city contributes to their daily life only the schoolhouse, the mail carrier and the policeman. They have everything else."[45] This observation was echoed by scores of residents, including Silvio Pucci, a businessman who proudly boasted, "We were a self-sufficient neighborhood."[46] *La Montagna* afforded its colonists the continuity of culture, the commonality of language, and the cohesiveness of group/kin/family solidarity. Literally and figuratively, many original settlers never left the neighborhood. "Never!" an emphatic Lou Cerutti exclaimed. "We had stores here, we had doctors, drug stores, every corner had a grocery store. I thank God my Mom must have been fifty years old before she crossed Kingshighway. . . . they didn't have to leave."[47]

The bus ride to Sportsman's Park widened the social vistas for Joe Garagiola's generation, but his immigrant parents clung desperately to the sanctity of *la Montagna*. The broadcaster reminisced that "downtown as far as Hill mothers and fathers were concerned, was the place you went to take your citizenship test. Otherwise, downtown was as far away as the Duomo in Milan."[48] Nor had Garagiola's parents tuned in to the electronic rhythms of modern America. In 1930 over half the homes in metropolitan St. Louis had a radio, but on the Hill just 18 percent of the residents followed the consumer fad, placing themselves near the bottom of census districts in that category.[49]

Two incidents illustrate the provinciality of the Hill, the first involving a leading Italian journalist and the second concerning an illiterate laborer. Luigi Carnovale emigrated from Calabria to command the Italian pavilion at the 1904 World's Fair in St. Louis. Having successfully launched two newspapers in Italy, the talented Carnovale chose to remain in St. Louis and establish a career as a journalist to the immigrants. He quickly founded the city's first Italian paper, *Il Pensiero* (The Thought), and a monthly periodical, *Gazzetta Illustrata*. He fancifully expected to unite the Italian colonies with his persuasive pen. "We must collectively unite in a show of spiritual and fraternal solidarity," he wrote in his first column; "we must form bonds that connect all the Italian colonies."[50] His financial and literary struggles are eloquently captured in his autobiography, *Il Giornalismo degli Emigranti Italiani del Nord America*.

In 1904 Carnovale attempted to distribute his papers outside the Italian churches in the hopes of recruiting readers. "We generously offered the Italian parishioners free newspapers," he reminisced. "Many frowned, others bit their lip in a threatening manner, and some lowered their heads like rams." On another occasion the intrepid journalist attempted to penetrate the veil of the Hill. As a southern Italian he frowned on the restrictions imposed by the North Italy American Club, which only accepted members "from Rome up." Nonetheless he selected this society as a bridge to the colony.

> I arrived at the building of the North Italy America Club which rises on a hill given the name "Dago's Hill." On the ground floor I see a large hall, where the members, seated around numerous tables are intent upon studying and refining themselves, playing *briscola* and *tresette* [card games] and gulping down enormous tankards of beer, chatting, shouting, and swearing like demons. . . . There is nearby another lecture hall. I mean beerhall. I find here, surrounded by his bigshots, the president of the society who is also honoring Bacchus. I ask permission to present *Il Pensiero* to the members, and he gives it, not without having first consulted with tears of tenderness, the bottle of whiskey. . . . At the sign of the president, I begin to speak. I say, "It would be dutiful and useful for the Italians to read a newspaper written by their brothers in the beautiful language of Dante, with the goal of illuminating the conscience of immigrant workers, and protecting the dignity of the Italian name in America." . . . Having said this, I and my friends began to walk around the room offering copies of the newspaper free to members. But the members crouched down in their chairs and held their noses pointed to the ground. . . They appeared to be mummies. . . . Yes, not even one copy could we give them. That is, one copy we did give them, to the deserving president who, from high on his chair witnessed undaunted our failure. To console us for our sickly shame, or maybe to display his intellectual superiority, he even set about to open the newspaper, slowly, almost majestically. . . . After having barely opened it, he begins to read it . . . then the secretary whispers something in the ear of the grand marshall. Both smile, laugh and puff out their cheeks so not to burst. Alas, the Mister President—the president of a society is reading the newspaper holding it upside down![51]

Carnovale shortly thereafter left for Chicago where he became a renowned journalist for *La Tribuna Italiana Transatlantica.*

Some thirty years later, in 1934, Elmer Shorb Wood, a student of the neighborhood, observed an unemployed brickmaker who had lived on the Hill for many years. A friend finally procured a construction job for the man and graciously walked his *paesano* to the nearby worksite. The immigrant failed to return home that evening. "Three days later, and at the point of exhaustion," quipped Wood, "the Italian reached *la Montagna*, having been hopelessly lost once away from the sheltered environment."[52]

The cultural fabric of the colony, a textured weave between patterns of spatial isolation and residential segregation, was quilted in a number of other critical areas, including the distinctive trademarks of regionalism, involving marriage characteristics and ethnic rivalries.

ETHNIC RIVALRY AND GROUP RELATIONS

"Deny thy father and refuse thy name," Juliet pleaded with her Romeo, an oft-repeated cry heard on Italy's Balkanized peninsula. Capulet and Montague, Catholic and heretic, Guelf and Ghibilline, monarchist and republican, Alta Italia and the Mezzogiorno, all emblazon a trail of historic strife. From this milieu Lombards and Sicilians came to St. Louis to make their fortunes and unknowingly forge new ethnic identities.

Immigration, while drawing on the boundless wellspring of kinfolk and townfolk, cast individuals and families into a more complex society. The social bases of immigration, industrialization, and urbanization resulted not in the destruction of folkways and values but rather in reorganization and reidentification. Immigrants came to the Hill not as Italians but as Cuggionesi and Catanesi. Village loyalties mattered far more than the recent tug of nationalism, a concept few Italians comprehended. The elaborate nationalizing process that enveloped France in the late nineteenth century, so eloquently described by Eugen Weber in *Peasants into Frenchmen*, did not occur in Italy.[53] Instead, regional alliances superseded village loyalties: Cuggionesi and Inverunesi became Lombards, and Catanesi and Augustini became Sicilians. The movement from localism to regionalism, a phenomenon evident in San Francisco during the same period, served as a source of tension, organization, and debate until World War II.[54]

Immigration precipitated a welter of new identities, a psychic hurdle described by Charlotte Gower Chapman in her study of the Sicilian village of Milocca: "In America he will be an Italian to all members of other nationalities. In Sicily he will be a Millochese. In Milocca, he tends to remain a Piduzzana [clan] who has moved."[55] *Campanilismo*, an intense variant of localism which taught Italians to distrust strangers who could not hear the toll of the village bell tower (*campanile*), hindered inter- and intraregional as well as national efforts of cooperation. Edward Banfield argued that in southern Italy amoral familialism—the all-pervasive hold by the family—sapped all energies and prevented any meaningful social relationships outside the family household. Joseph Lopreato attacked

Banfield, holding that the lack of cooperation between Italian peasants was due to the precariousness of the economy, not amoral familialism.[56]

Campanilismo also exerted a centrifugal influence on town life in northern Italy. Art historians note the traditional rivalries between Cremona and Modena, Venice and Padua, Pistoia and Lucca, over which town had amassed the most impressive art treasures or erected the most magnificent piazza. The villages and towns west of Milan competed fiercely with one another over religious shrines, grazing rights, and communal honor. A rich oral tradition helps to capture these regional vignettes, which often took the form of vigorous satire. Inverunesi delight in telling how the inhabitants of Cuggiono wished the Festa della Madonna del Carmine to continue, so they drove a nail into the clock to stop time. The villagers of Buscate, insist the Cuggionesi, once decided to put donkeys on their roofs to eliminate trimming. They hoisted up the hapless animals by the neck and then wondered why they were dead when they reached the top. The housewives of Boffalora were said to wrap their chickens in diapers to keep the eggs from rolling into the canals, and the men of Arconate supposedly were celebrated for their great bodies and little minds.[57] In a remarkably short time those historical forces were channeled into a source of regional pride.

"Marry women and buy oxen from your village only," counseled an Italian proverb, a bromide infused by the ethos of *campanilismo*. In Lombardy and Sicily custom and tradition dictated the tenets of marriage, a profound step in the preservation of family honor.[58] For hundreds of years Cuggionesi had only married Cuggionese, Catanesi married only Catanese. Immigration expanded the horizons and tested the outer limits of marriage.

Marriage reinforced and reidentified the fundamental allegiances of the first-generation residents on the Hill. Between 1900 and 1930 in St. Louis, Hill Italians almost always (99 percent) married Italians. More significantly, however, Cuggionesi did not always marry Cuggionese, nor did Catanesi always marry Catanese. Immigration broadened the boundaries of marital acceptance from a local to a regional parameter. In part this reflected the exigencies of immigration, since men outnumbered women until the 1940s. While Cuggionesi may have preferred mates from their village, matrimony records reveal that between 1907 and 1930 some 40 percent of the immigrants from Cuggiono married Lombards from the surrounding villages or St. Louis–born Lombard-Americans (60 percent married spouses from Cuggiono). Most typical was the example set by Giovanni Merlo and Giuseppina Puricelli, both born in Cuggiono and married at San Ambrogio on the Hill in October 1913.[59] The 1912 union between Pietro Berra of Cuggiono and Luigia Griffachi of Castano Primo, however, illustrates the emerging importance of regionalism.[60] While it became acceptable for a Cuggionese to select a life partner from the neighboring villages, it was anathema to consider marriage to someone beyond the pale of Lombardy or northern Italy. In 1911 Antonio Naggi of Buscate married Maria Amighetti of Cremona.[61] Buscate lay in the network of villages of origin; but Cremona, while in Lombardy, was not an important source of emigration. Only a handful of such marriages occurred, demonstrating the regional limits of matrimony before the 1930s.

Sicilians, commonly depicted as overly protective and devoutly suspicious, exhibited a greater willingness to marry individuals born outside the provincial birthplaces than Lombards. While Sicilians almost always married Sicilians, over half the Sicilian marriages performed at San Ambrogio Church between 1907 and 1930 involved mates born in different provinces of Sicily. For instance, in 1912 Giuseppi Belfranca of Girgenti married Giaconia Paglicca of Palermo.[62] One may explain this broadening tendency toward regionalism among Sicilians as a response to diffused immigration patterns. Since residents of no one Sicilian village populated the Hill, immigrants were encouraged to select marriage partners from other Sicilian locales. Like their Lombard counterparts Sicilians steadfastly refused to marry outside their regional loyalties.

On the whole the Hill's marriage patterns mirrored tendencies in other Italian communities. During the early decades of the twentieth century Italians almost always married Italians, generally mates from the same province. In Buffalo, New York, as late as 1930, about 75 percent of all Italians continued to marry Italians, a rate similar to the Hill and paralleling the findings of Ruby Jo Kennedy for New Haven, Connecticut, and Josef Barton for Cleveland, Ohio. But whereas Italians on the Hill began to intermarry with non-Italians and outsiders only during and after World War II, such customs had begun decades earlier in Chicago. Nelli postulates that this was a result of "mixing in the immigrant colony" and the mobile nature of Chicago Italians.[63]

It would not be until the 1930s and 1940s that second-generation Lombard- and Sicilian-Americans crossed the marital Rubicon and intermarried. The defiant antagonisms between Lombard and Sicilian immigrants remained an essential and unavoidable feature of the Hill throughout the period 1900–1930. Thus *campanilismo* had become *provincialismo*. The lines of division had been clearly drawn: Lombard versus Sicilian.

Lombard and Sicilian relationships quickset in the St. Louis milieu. Regional stereotypes, the products of centuries of folklore and custom, served as a major obstacle to the unification of Italy. "We have made Italy," a cynical but perceptive deputy once proclaimed, "now we must make Italians." Little wonder Lombards in St. Louis treated Sicilians as pariahs. "Plenty them little black fellows here, but they all downtown," a Lombard gleefully explained to an inquiring reporter in 1901, pointing out that the Hill had as yet attracted few "black fellows" (i.e., Sicilians). "They [Sicilians in Little Italy] push the banana carts. North Italian works. Only one or two South Italians on the Hill." But Sicilians eventually came to the Hill. Northern Italians felt culturally and racially superior to southern Italians, commonly depicted by Lombards and the American press as Mediterranean savages prone to the stiletto and by nature lazy. As late as 1932 Rose Pilla, a staffer at the St. Louis International Institute, could write, "Many people often make the assumption that the people of Northern Italy are superior to those of Southern Italy. It is also an assumption of the Italian people themselves. A Southerner stands in awe of a Northerner." The U.S. Bureau of Immigration reinforced these entrenched biases, classifying Italian immigrants as two different races, northern and southern.[64]

Ethnocentric Lombards brought to the Gateway City their deeply rooted prejudices against southern Italians. "The people from Toscana," Rosa Casettari explained, "they're not good like the people from Lombardia. But they're not bad like the people from Sicilia. I should say not! Lombard is the last in the world to do wrong things."[65] On another occasion Rosa likened northern and southern Italians to the Holy Ghost and the Devil.[66] While outsiders may have viewed the Hill as a conglomeration of Italians, in reality profound internal divisions existed. "The Italians on the Hill," Lombards emphasized to a reporter in 1901, "are particular they be recognized as people from north of Italy. . . . They want the world to know that they did not come from the south or Sicily. They say that they are a lighter complexion, larger of frame and further advanced in intelligence than their countrymen from the south."[67]

During the formative period, Lombard-Sicilian relations were at best bifurcated and strained. "Lombard good people," whispered Angelina Merlo, an elderly northerner, who then cautioned, "but I tell you, we didn't talk much with the Sicilians [in the old days]. The Sicilians talk with themselves. The Lombards talk with themselves."[68] A thoughtful Isidore Oldani, Jr., confirmed this ethnic breach: "Back in those days, you know a Lombard and Sicilian, they were as far apart as could be."[69] Sam Russo recalled his 1913 baptism to America. An emigrant from Catania in Sicily, Russo secured a job at Winkle's Terra Cotta Factory, an establishment employing mainly northern Italians. "Oh, them Lombards treat Sicilians lousy," he lamented. "The young Lombards—they hate us. . . . These guys all the time call us, '*Terra brucciata!* You come from burned ground!' They say, 'Sicilian no good—Black Hand!'. . . They say, 'Before you leave work, we're going to give you a good beating.' After work, they beat me, right, left, right. . . . Oh, you be surprised. Oh, they hate each other. . . . He's from the South. He's from the North. . . . I tell the truth!"[70]

Despite the colorful recollections of internecine violence, physical hostility rarely occurred. In 1911 an Italian official expressed surprise at how well the factions got along.[71] Lombards and Sicilians may not have approved of one another, but they were more concerned with the exigencies of survival. Residential patterns, for instance, were not reflective of regional segregation but followed supply and demand; the two groups lived interspersed with each other. In general wars were waged with words, not knives. Sicilians taunted Lombards, calling them "pigeons," and the latter countered with their sobriquet, "hatchets." "The nickname 'hatchets' started because the Lombards always thought the Sicilians were throwing hatchets at somebody," explained Roland DeGregorio, the local raconteur-mailman. "Well 'pigeons' got started because the Sicilians thought that whenever northern Italians talked in their dialect, they sounded like pigeons going 'coo coo, coo coo.'"[72] It should be noted that over time many residents became adept in both the Lombard and Sicilian dialects.

Lombards and Sicilians forged new economic and social relationships during the period of settlement on the Hill. In the process the interaction of people moved from an individual and family level to one of larger organizations. Easing the transition between the Old World and the new, St. Louis Italians founded a score of mutual aid societies. Genoans founded the city's first Italian society, the Società Unione e Fratellanza Italiana, in 1886. Three years later the association hired an instructor to teach in the proposed Italian grammar school, but the grandiose plans were dashed on the rocks of fiscal uncertainty and Genoan assimilation.[73]

In 1892 a group of Genoans organized the Cavalleria Italo-Americana to celebrate the 400th anniversary of the voyages of Columbus. The fraternity purchased flamboyant uniforms and with their handsome steeds and plumed helmets became fixtures at local parades.[74] In group attire, function, and composition, the Italo-American Cavalry was far removed from the societies soon to spring to life on the Hill.

The immigrant mutual aid societies were rooted in nineteenth-century Europe, as peasants and artisans organized in response to the new order.[75] A spurt of organizational fever swept Italy during the period after 1860, including the birth of La Società di Mutuo Soccorso degli Operai e Contadini di Cuggiono (The Society of Mutual Aid for Workers and Peasants of Cuggiono), on April 30, 1870. Founded for the promotion of morality and concord among workers, the society also provided funds for sick and indigent *paesani.*[76]

Cuggionesi exported their mutual aid network to St. Louis. To guard against future uncertainties, members who had joined the society in Lombardy retained their good standing when they joined the sister organization in St. Louis, Il Nord Italia America Società (soon anglicized to the North Italy America Club, or NIAC). Lombards who repatriated to Italy could rejoin La Società di Cuggiono and claim benefits, as was evident by a number of surviving letters in the Archivio.[77]

Founded in 1897, the NIAC served as the Lombard flagship for several decades, an institution that preserved that group's hegemony. The organization fulfilled an old-world dream of *Ticinia*—the unification of villages along the Ticino River in western Lombardy.[78] The NIAC coalesced Cuggionesi, Inverunesi, Marcallesi, and other Lombards into a powerful political and social voluntary association. "Entering the Hill from the east, one finds upon Shaw Avenue a two-story structure bearing the letters NIAC," observed one journalist at the turn of the century. "This is the community clubhouse and saloon . . . a society including practically all of the Hill. It has a membership of 375."[79] The noted immigrant commentator Amy Bernardy described the NIAC as a unifying force for the colony's Lombards, particularly after church on Sunday when members crowded into the club for beer and entertainment.[80]

The first president of the society, Luigi Caloia, was born in Cuggiono in 1859, where he acquired an education and business skills. Immigrating to St. Louis in 1886, Caloia quickly became a leader and was dubbed "the Mayor of Dago Hill" by the American press. According to a 1907 newspaper article, "The word of Luigi Caloia is law and he has his countrymen well organized. To him the Italians in trouble come for relief. They recognize Caloia as a power to be used in their interest. Luigi Caloia is a well-educated Italian who thoroughly believes in his race and controls a good number of votes."[81] It is unclear where Caloia derived his power; according to the 1910 census he worked as a laborer.

If Caloia's NIAC directed the political fortunes of the Hill, the economic domain was ministered by the Nord Italia America Mercantile (NIAM), a corporation that antedated the NIAC by one year. "This is the most interesting institution on the Hill," exclaimed a reporter describing the North Italian American Society Cooperative Store, located at 5226 Shaw Avenue. "It is a combination meat market and grocery . . . and does a rushing business every day and night. The store sells produce and meat a trifle below current prices and the first of the month, the profits are divided among the shareholders. They are frequently considerable, the butcher averaging $300 in receipts every Saturday."[82] A 1901 member explained: "The profits are put into improvements. The saloon is now less than three years old and the store less than two. . . . This spring, for instance, we bought at a cost of $500 a hand-worked Italian flag."[83]

Louis Jean Gualdoni began his long career on the Hill as a stock boy for the NIAM in the early 1900s. "The reason why I mention all this about the cohesion on the Hill," Gualdoni reminisced, "well, it all began with this here North Italy America Society. . . . If you belonged to the North Italy Club, you had credit, an open account at the store and the store was cooperative, they sold everything at cost. And I'm telling you, that was wonderful! Everybody bought their meats and groceries there, and at Christmas, they give you a big turkey, and at Thanksgiving, a big bag of groceries."[84] The NIAM co-op experiment lasted fourteen years, from 1896 to 1910.

The NIAC continued to prosper in the decade following 1910 as new arrivals joined the society. In the era prior to social security and workmen's compensation, before mass unionization and an activist church, immigrants sought security and protection in their fraternal orders. Terrified at being exiled to the poor farm or buried ignominiously in the potter's field, clansmen were guaranteed sick benefits and a decent funeral. Monthly dues of 50¢ (1900–1915) entitled Lombard members to free doctor's care, $6 a week in sick benefits, and a $259 death indemnity.[85] "Most of the time they [mutual benefit societies] helped you get a job," explained Silvio Pucci. "All the societies had free doctor's care and so much a week if you had to stay home from work because you were sick.

Money was scarce in those days."[86] "Hell, a stranger in a strange land," mused Lou Berra, a lifelong member of the NIAC. "Sure you belonged to it."[87]

One of the most important functions of the society was to ensure immigrants the accoutrements of a meaningful funeral. Before the first funeral parlor on the Hill, the Calcaterra establishment in the 1920s, fraternal societies maintained an honor vigil around the casket of the deceased *paesano*. "The day of the funeral, members would form an entourage," explained undertaker Frank Borghi, "and in a final gesture of tribute, would march by the home of the deceased. Because you see, owning a home meant so much to these immigrants."[88] For members, the Italian way of death had a special meaning. "Funerals were really something," exclaimed Lou Berra. "Ariotti got his band . . . the neighborhood band. . . . If you died, then everybody took half a day off from work and the band came along and walked to the church. Then everybody got into one of those cabs, four in a cab, horse-driven cabs, and then went out to Peter and Paul [cemetery] . . . which was all right because we made a stop at every saloon on the way. There was one on every corner in those days!"[89]

The NIAC embodied an extension of the highly cohesive process by which *paesani* were carefully shuffled from Lombardy to the Hill. Once settled Lombards rallied under the regional banner of the North Italy America Society. It embodied what Philip Gleason has called a "tangible organizational reality" within which newcomers could identify themselves and declare their solidarity with kindred folk.[90] Sicilians, by contrast, never achieved the success of centralizing power in one mutual aid society. First, old-world divisions and suspicions prevented a Sicilian equivalent of *Ticinia*. Organization beyond village lines proved virtually impossible because of the blinders of *campanilismo*, although marriages did penetrate these boundaries. Second, the Sicilian family usurped loyalties and energies that might have tempered the effects of localism. Third, Sicilian immigration patterns to the Hill were more disruptive than the Lombard influx. Moreover, since Sicilians arrived at a later period than the Lombards the latter naturally viewed the former as "outsiders" and "intruders." Fourth, northern Italians arrived with strong, identifiable regional loyalties since nearly all had originated from a small cluster of villages. Not so with the southern Italians, for they traced their origins from geographically diverse parts of the island: Augusta and Catania on the east coast; Belmonte Mezzagna, Palazzo Adriano, and Casteltermini from the central region of Sicily; and Termini Imerese and Palermo from the northern province.

On the Hill, Sicilians exhibited diverse organizational behavior. In 1904 southern Italians founded the Società Unione Sicilia e Principe Piemonte. Open to all sons of Italy (unlike the NIAC) but membered chiefly by Sicilians, the SUSPP served as the southern rival to the powerful NIAC. Financially, the SUSPP offered the most impressive program of any of the Sicilian mutual aid societies. In 1927, for example, dues of $1 a month entitled its 329 members to free doctor's care and sick benefits of $5 a week. The family of the deceased received a handsome benefit of $500, unusually high for that time.[91] As more Sicilians migrated to the Hill after the turn of the century, the number of mutual aid societies proliferated. For example, Sicilians from Augusta founded in 1913 the Megara Augusta, and a score of societies reflecting old-world loyalties quickly followed.[92]

Efforts to unify the mutual aid societies, both on the Hill and in the city, failed. In 1910 representatives from several fraternal orders met to study the benefits of collective action. Arguments in favor of consolidation looked impressive on paper: financially, families of deceased members would receive $1,200 in benefits; politically, Italian-Americans would become a force to be reckoned with; and socially, cooperation might erode accumulated prejudices. However, individual societies roundly rejected the plan.[93] Only once, motivated by the intense demands for Americanism during the First World War, did Italian fraternal orders band together in a Federation of Mutual Societies,[94] which quickly dissolved after the war.

Mutual aid societies served a vital role in the recrystallization of old-world traditions and as a social-economic safety net in the new urban world. Their organizational impetus weakened, however, between 1925 and 1930, a period of vibrant institutional growth within the colony's religious, recreational, and political voluntary associations. Declining membership, financial insolvency, the duplication of services by private insurance firms, and the depression all weakened the hold of the mutual aid society. "See, in the early days the societies played an important part," explained Sam Chinicci, "but in my generation, the second, they lost significance."[95] The NIAC, strongman of the fraternities, slumped from 1,400 members in 1913 to 475 in 1927.[96] As members aged the weakened societies were less able to meet the heavy financial obligations. Joe Correnti explained how his father, a member of the Garibaldi

Society, was unable to pay hospital expenses in the early 1930s because the organization ran out of funds. "Why didn't I join the mutual benefit societies?" asked Correnti, who was born on the Hill in 1907. "See, I was second generation, my father first. See, we were Americanized. Our thoughts and ideas were a heck of a lot different than our fathers'. . . ."[97]

COMMUNITY

By the mid-1920s the Hill had evolved from a primitive mining camp into an enclave of 5,000 Italian-Americans, served by a church, mutual aid societies, political parties, an athletic league, and schools. The colony was poised for change, as some institutions declined in importance (mutual aid societies) while others grasped for power (the Democratic party, youth gangs, and the Catholic church). A new generation was maturing, more American than Italian, and this second generation would instill dynamism and leadership within the new power structure.

The Hill had evolved from an immigrant colony—one of many in polyglot St. Louis—to an ethnic community, noteworthy for its cohesion, stability, and permanence, increasingly rare qualities as Kerry Patch and the Ghetto dissolved. The metamorphosis had occurred almost imperceptibly. Giovanni Schiavo declared forthrightly in 1929 that "the Hill is a true community." The pioneering historian catalogued this finding: "It has its church, its branch library, its clubs, its shops, its music store, its drug store, its lawyers, its physicians, its family theatre, its poor rooms, its factories, its businessmen's associations, its boys' band, its 'speak easies'."[98] The prescient Schiavo concluded, the Hill "is indeed one place where some sociological theories do not find confirmation, where prejudgements are shattered, where environmentalists are vindicated."[99]

But what is a community, really? That question, observed Thomas Bender, "has been central to the analysis of social and political life at least since Plato and Aristotle inquired into the character of the Greek polis."[100] In 1955 George Hillery, Jr., found ninety-four definitions of the word "community." During the last several decades, however, social historians have achieved some pioneering work in the field of community studies.[101] There now appears to be a core of agreement around which community studies converge. The sociologist Gideon Sjoberg defined a community as a "collectivity of actors sharing in a limited territorial area as the best for carrying out the greatest share of their daily activities."[102] Thomas Bender described a community as a "network of social relations marked by mutuality and emotional bonds."[103] Harold Kaufman conceived of community "as a social unit of which space is an integral part; community is a place, a relatively small one. . . . community indicates a configuration as to the way of life, both as to how people do things and what they want—their institutions as collective goals."[104]

In the beginning the immigrant colony was a means to an end. In time the Hill became an end in itself, a community of place and will. If Lombard and Sicilian immigrants lived their lives in divided camps, their institutional accomplishments enabled the second generation to reap the communal harvest. Above all, immigrants remained on the Hill, investing their individual energies in houses, institutions, and hopes. Successive generations of the same families, not successive waves of new faces, built a community. Immigrants did not work on the Hill and live elsewhere, nor did they worship downtown or shop in other neighborhoods. The community was self-contained, total. Before World War II most Italian-American residents lived, worked, and played entirely on the Hill, spending vastly more time with one another than with outsiders. A community need not consist of individuals who spend all their time together, however; rather, it must, as Martin Buber insisted, "consist of people who, precisely because they are comrades, have mutual access to one another and are ready for one another."[105] That time would come in the 1920s.

The Hill generated a vigorous cultural and institutional flowering beginning in the 1920s. Organizations rooted in religion, recreation, politics, and crime all flourished, binding the first and second generations in a cohesive communal network. If community organizations exert their greatest influence in the arena of personal contact and territorial culture, the Hill fostered splendid examples of public will. Self-interest and individual capitalism did not degenerate into an abscess of privatism, resulting in the out-migration of the entrepreneurially successful. The successes of saloon keepers and shop owners did not destroy the communal spirit but merely replaced and improved archaic and outmoded institutions. The excesses of Prohibition did not bring about moral decay but merely provided communal wealth and pride.

Robert Wiebe, in his brilliant study *The Search for Order, 1877–1920*, described how after 1880 the United States evolved from a society of "island communities" based on autonomy, informality, and face-to-face relations, to a centralized, formalized society of bureaucratic impersonality and functional specialization.[106] But as Herbert Gutman and

John Bodnar have demonstrated, pockets of premodern, preindustrial communities existed and persisted in the midst of the new urban, industrial nation.[107] One such community was the Hill. Isolated by environmental factors, the Hill evolved on the edge of a modern metropolis. Immigration had not devastated Hill families nor had urbanism deracinated their culture. Lombards and Sicilians had not transplanted their culture intact. Immigrants adapted their values, tacking their sails to the winds of urbanization. Assimilationists, such as Robert Park and Ernest Burgess, long argued that immigrant neighborhoods would disappear in time, happy victims of the melting pot.[108] But the Hill stubbornly has refused to disappear, its loyal inhabitants defiantly resisting the temptations of the American dream of suburbia.

The decade of the 1920s closed one stage of immigration history and launched a new era on the Hill. The Immigration Restriction Act of 1924, coinciding with the declension of mutual aid and old-world regional rivalries, augured a new set of values, symbolized by the rise of the second generation, the age of jazz and the allure of bootlegging, and reconstituted attitudes toward politics, religion, and recreation. The first decades of the twentieth century inaugurated a long process of interaction between immigrants and their new environment. Lombards and Sicilians adeptly adjusted to the colony isolated from the urban pressures of downtown St. Louis. Until the 1920s the modern urban bureaucracy had barely penetrated the Hill. In turn, Italian immigrants clung to their environmental sanctuary, refusing to learn English or participate in the political process. Immigrants sought identity and security through an elaborately fashioned cloak of kinship ties, community relationships, and job structures.

NOTES

1. "Migratory Laborers: Following the Birds," *Post-Dispatch*, Apr. 1, 1903, II, p. 1.
2. *Republic*, May 20, 1906, p. 7.
3. "Selling 100,000 Men a Year in St. Louis," *Post-Dispatch*, May 8, 1910, magazine.
4. Thernstrom, *Other Bostonians*, 221.
5. Tricarico, *Italians of Greenwich Village*, xvi; Gans, *Urban Villagers;* Suttles, *Social Order of the Slums*.

6. *Post-Dispatch*, May 26, 1901, magazine.

7. *Republic*, Sept. 1, 1907, magazine.

8. *Libro dei Matrimonie* and *Registro Morturorum*, 1914–25; *Post-Dispatch*, May 26, 1901; 1910 Manuscript Census, St. Louis, National Archives, 380–84; Archives at San Giorgio Church, Cuggiono.

9. *Libro dei Matrimonie; Republic*, Sept. 1, 1907, magazine.

10. *Twelfth Census of the U.S.: 1900*, vol. 100, St. Louis, sheet 8; *Thirteenth Census of the U.S.: 1910. Population*, II, Missouri, Tables 1, 5; *Fourteenth Census of the U.S.: 1920. Population*, III; *Fifteenth Census of the U.S.: 1930. Population*, III, Tables 9, 18; Fletcher, Hornback, and Queen, *Social Statistics of St. Louis*, 9–17.

11. Data gathered from naturalization petitions, 1906–36. Few women petitioned for citizenship until the late 1920s. Since Italian women typically received less schooling, and since married women and children were granted citizenship when the husband or father was naturalized, there was little reason for women to apply for citizenship until the Nineteenth Amendment. Even after 1919 few Italian women applied for citizenship. Cinel, *From Italy to San Francisco*, 116.

12. Naturalization petition, Antonio Gioia, 1913; information supplemented by the Gioia family in Cuggiono and St. Louis.

13. "La Storia di Giuseppe Visconti." The Visconti family compiled the biography as part of a school project, for which this author provided advice.

14. Naturalization petitions, 1906–36.

15. Naturalization petitions, Giuseppe Urzi and Pietro Castellese, 1936.

16. Riggio, quoted in *Post-Dispatch*, May 19, 1941.

17. Interview with Leo Erutti, Aug. 1, 1973.

18. Nelli, *Italians in Chicago*, 204.

19. "I Minatori Italiani di Carbone Bituminoso," *Bolletino dell' Emigrazione* 2 (1914): 11–14; Hubbs, *Pioneer Folks and Places*, 131; *Globe-Democrat*, Sept. 10, 1907; *La Lega Italiana*, Mar. 11, 1915 (hereafter *La Lega*); *Immigrant and Coal Mining Communities; Immigration Commission Report: Immigrants in Industries*, "Bituminous Coal Mining in the Middle West," vol. 24, Tables 313–17; U.S. Manuscript Census, Williamson County, 1910.

20. *Globe-Democrat*, Sept. 10, 1907, p. 1; *La Lega*, March 11, 1915, p. 2; Angle, *Bloody Williamson*. In 1922 Williamson County vaulted to national notoriety when local thugs slaughtered twenty-three strikebreakers. Angle maintains the county's reputation for violence preceded this incident; between 1839 and 1876 the county recorded fifty murders (pp. 72–73).

21. *Globe-Democrat*, Dec. 6, 1909.

22. Ibid., Oct. 13, 1914, p. 1.

23. Ibid., June 11, 1915, p. 1.

24. Ibid., Aug. 8, 1920, p. 1; *Star*, Aug. 9, 1920, p. 3.

25. *Post-Dispatch*, Feb. 13, 1923, magazine, Apr. 16, 1924, p. 23.

26. Bernstein, *Lean Years*, 258–91; *Post-Dispatch*, Oct. 2, 1927, p. 1.

27. Naturalization petitions, 1920s, 1930s; Wirth, "Urbanism," 168.

28. Naturalization petition, Mauro Belossi, 1924.

29. Stellos, "Greek Community of St. Louis." The Skouras brothers invested in a St. Louis movie theater, later known as Fox Studios. Salutos, "Greeks of Milwaukee."

30. Konyu, "Hungarians in Missouri."

31. *Thirteenth Census of the U.S.: 1910*, 632; *Fourteenth Census of the U.S.: 1920. Population*, II, 752, and *Population*, III, 632; *Federal Census for Metropolitan St. Louis, 1930*, 60–75.

32. Crawford, *Immigrant in St. Louis*, 22.

33. Cowgill, "Residential Mobility," 31–32.

34. Wood, "Fairmount Heights," 52–53; interview with Elmer Shorb Wood, May 17, 1984.

35. *La Stampa Italiana*, Aug. 19, 1927 (hereafter cited as *La Stampa*); Bernardy, "Sulle condizioni," 63.

36. Polizzi, "Edwards Street Overpass," 3.

37. Berra, *Yogi*, 33.

38. *Twelfth Census of the U.S.: 1900*, vol. 100, reel 8; *Gould's St. Louis Red-Blue Book*, 1921–28; Voting Registration Lists, 1900, 1910, 1920, 1930, Municipal Archives, City Hall, St. Louis.

39. Lieberson, *A Piece of the Pie*, 263; Thernstrom, *Other Bostonians*, 209.

40. Thernstrom, *Other Bostonians*, 232; Conzen, "Immigrants"; Warner, "Cultural Change and the Ghetto"; Chudacoff, *Mobile Americans*, 40; Nelli, *Italians in Chicago*, 53; Lopreato, *Italian Americans*, 42.

41. Interview with Roland DeGregorio, Aug. 18, 1973; 1910 Manuscript Census, St. Louis, 381.

42. *La Lega*, Nov. 6, 1914, p. 1.

43. Keating, "A Study of Americanization," 40.

44. *Central Blatt and Social Justice*, Aug. 1915, 126.

45. *Post-Dispatch*, May 26, 1901.

46. Pucci, "My Memories of the Hill."

47. Interview with Lou Cerutti, Aug. 7, 1975.

48. Garagiola, *Baseball Is a Funny Game*, 3.

49. *Federal Census for Metropolitan St. Louis, 1930*, 120–21; *Social Statistics of St. Louis by Census Tracts*, 10.

50. *"Cosa Dobbiamo Fare?" Il Pensiero*, Aug. 27, 1904.

51. Carnovale, *Il Giornalismo*. For Carnovale's experience in Chicago see Nelli, *Italians in Chicago*, 120, 157, 167; *Il Pensiero*, Aug. 17, 1929.

52. Wood, "Fairmount Heights," 59–60.

53. Weber, *Peasants into Frenchmen.*

54. Cinel, *From Italy to San Francisco*, 196–227.

55. Chapman, *Milocca*, 27.

56. Banfield, *Moral Basis of a Backward Society;* Lopreato, *Peasants No More*, 151.

57. Interviews in St. Louis, 1973–84. See Villari, *Italian Life*, 9–10. "Each little town for many centuries led its own independent life, had its own policy, its own manners and customs, its own artistic development, its own parties, its own aristocracy, bourgeosie, and working class, and each was a little world unto itself."

58. Salomone-Marino, *Costumi e Usanze*, 179–91; Covello, *Social Background*, 168.

59. *Libro dei Matrimonie*, vols. 1, 2, 3, 4, 1907–30, Archives, San Ambrogio, St. Louis; I, Oct. 5, 1913, 307.

60. Ibid., I, Mar. 31, 1912, 177.

61. Ibid., I, Feb. 12, 1911. The imbalance of immigrant men over women is illustrated in this 1907 story about recreation on the Hill: "If there be not enough women for each man have just as much fun" (*Republic*, Sept. 1, 1907, magazine). According to the parish census at St. Ambrose, men outnumbered women in 1907 by 1,976 to 353.

62. *Libro dei Matrimonie*, I, Apr. 7, 1912, p. 179.

63. Yans-McLaughlin, *Family and Community*, 256–58; Kennedy, "Single or Triple Melting Pot," 56; Barton, *Peasants and Strangers*, 168–69; Nelli, *Italians in Chicago*, 194–98.

64. *Post-Dispatch*, May 26, 1901, magazine; Odencrantz, *Italian Women in Industry*, 168; Covello, *Social Background*, 15–34; Tricarico, *Italians of Greenwich Village*, 6–7; Iorizzo and Mondello, *Italian-Americans*, 4, 30; Foerster, *Italian Emigration of Our Times*, 325; IHRC, St. Louis International Institute, 1932, Box 6.

65. Ets, *Rosa*, 209.

66. Casettari-Ets MS., IHRC, 93.

67. *Post-Dispatch*, May 26, 1901.

68. Interview with Angelina Merlo, Aug. 6, 1975.

69. Interview with Isidore Oldani, Jr., Sept. 10, 1973.

70. Interview with Sam Russo, Sept. 10, 1973.

71. Bernardy, "Sulle condizioni," 19.

72. Interview with Roland DeGregorio, Aug. 18, 1973. The Sicilians' difficulty in grasping the nuances of Lombard dialect were shared by a Viennese officer who in 1771 remarked that in Lombardy "the peasants babble their words so they cannot even understand one another." Quoted in Berkner, "Recent Research," 213.

73. *Società Unione*, 1–30; *Libro di Letture Graduate;* interview with Mario

Pertici, President of SUFI, Aug. 14, 1973. A small colony of Genoans, born in Chiavari, had settled in St. Louis in the 1850s and 1860s and helped inaugurate the wholesale fruit and vegetable business there.

74. *Italo-American Cavalry Pamphlet.*

75. Horowitz, *Italian Labor Movement;* Barton, *Peasants and Strangers*, 48–63; Tilly, "Working Class of Milan," 335.

76. *Statuto degli Società.*

77. Archivio Comunale, Cuggiono. Four 1901 letters explore various financial aspects of benefits and expenses from immigrants in St. Louis.

78. Interviews in Cuggiono, Italy, Mar. 1981.

79. *Post-Dispatch*, May 26, 1901.

80. Bernardy, "Sulle condizioni."

81. *Republic*, Sept. 1, 1907; *Twelfth Census of the U.S.: 1900*, vol. 100, sheet 8; *Thirteenth Census of the U.S.: 1910*, Daggett Avenue. Caloia had become an American citizen, so his power may have been political.

82. *Post-Dispatch*, May 26, 1901.

83. Ibid.

84. Interviews with Louis Jean Gualdoni, Aug. 13, 1973, July 30, 1982.

85. *Il Pensiero*, Aug. 17, 1929. This issue marked the twenty-fifth anniversary of the Italian weekly and contains an excellent survey of the community organizations.

86. Pucci, "My Memories of the Hill."

87. Interview with Lou Berra, July 11, 1973.

88. Interview with Frank Borghi, manager of Calcaterra's Funeral Parlor, July 18, 1973.

89. Interview with Lou Berra, July 11, 1973.

90. Gleason, *Conservative Reformers*, 10.

91. *Il Pensiero*, Aug. 17, 1929.

92. Ibid.

93. "Minutes, 1910," *Società Unione E Fratellanza Italiana Historical Review* (St. Louis, 1966).

94. "Minutes, 1917," ibid.

95. Interview with Sam Chinicci, Aug. 8, 1975.

96. *La Stampa*, Aug. 19, 1927.

97. Interview with Joe Correnti, Apr. 30, 1976.

98. Schiavo, *Italians in Missouri*, 59.

99. Ibid.

100. Bender, *Community and Social Change*, 3.

101. Hillery, "Definitions of Community," 118.

102. Sjoberg, "Community."

103. Bender, *Community and Social Change*, 7.

104. Kaufman, "Interactional Conception of Community," 89.

105. Buber, *Paths in Utopia*, 145.
106. Wiebe, *Search for Order*, xii.
107. Gutman, *Work, Culture and Society;* Bodnar, "Immigration and Modernization."
108. Park, Burgess, and McKenzie, *City*, 191.

4 Making It in St. Louis: Work and Community

Work hard, work always,
And you will never know hunger.
Italian proverb

The streets of the New World, immigrants had fantasized, were paved with gold. Once shuffled through Ellis Island they quickly learned three salient facts: "first, the streets were not paved with gold; second, the streets were not paved at all; and third, they were expected to pave them."[1] Italians arriving on the Hill learned a fourth lesson: they were expected to mine the clay and fashion the bricks that lined the industries of a growing country.

OCCUPATIONS

"Every morning, in the old days as now," wrote the celebrated columnist Harry Brundidge in 1936, "an army of workers stepped down the steep paths to that district formerly known as Cheltenham, to work in the clay mines and tile factories."[2] Mining seemed scarcely akin to urban life, yet hundreds of St. Louisans toiled beneath the ground to exploit the clay deposits that were transformed into terra-cotta and firebrick. Lombards predominated in the ranks of the clay-mining profession, an occupational bent characteristic of earlier Lombard migrations. "Oh, those Lombards were a hardy lot," reminisced Antonio Ranciglio. "They were all Lombards, only one Sicilian—I only knew one Sicilian who worked in the clay mines. Why? Why don't you find a Jew in the brickyards? Italians are hard-working people!"[3]

Ethnic occupational clustering, such as Lombard miners, characterized American industrial history. The Chinese laundry, Italian fruit stand, and Greek sweetshop were the products of social stereotyping and economic circumstance.[4] The structural transformation of the local economy had created thousands of low-skill jobs, and Lombard settlers acted as labor recruiters for prospective immigrants, thus satisfying familial needs as well as guaranteeing the mine owners a steady supply of cheap and reliable labor.

Teams of Lombards intricately tunneled the area's subterranean caverns. "Clay mines are just like coal mines," explained a hoary veteran. The work involved hand-mining operations, since modern earth-moving equipment had not been adopted during Cheltenham's peak years, 1860–1930.[5] "See, you had a shaft going straight down in a cage," recalled a former miner. "They gave you a stall, your stall. When you dug the clay you got so much a ton, 35–40¢ a ton. Put it in a boxcar. The mule would then pull it to a cage. But you had to furnish the drill, pick, shovel and ammunition. After a day's work, they'd put the dynamite in there and break up the clay for the next day."[6] After years of intensive operations an intricate tunnel network had been constructed beneath the Hill. "It seemed we had traveled for miles before we had arrived at the end of that subterranean road," an exhausted reporter wrote in 1907. "We came upon several Italian miners who were attacking a point in the mine with their shining picks. Others were loading a mule train with lumps of porous clay of a white color about the size of an ordinary lump of coal."[7]

The fabled Missouri mule accompanied the miners into the damp and dangerous tunnels. Few knew the stubborn creatures better than Antonio Ranciglio, who, born in Lombardy in 1901, learned the honored and relevant trade of *fabbroferrario* (blacksmith) from his father, Alessandro Ranciglio. "When I was fifteen, I went into the mines to make custom shoes for the miners' animals," Ranciglio reminisced. "Hydraulic Brick Company had 500 mules to haul brick. Missouri mules—all white. See, they were smaller than normal mules so their shoes had to be specially made, six instead of the usual eight nails in their hooves. The mules never came out of the mines. They went blind and died within the mines."[8] Puffing incessantly on a foul-smelling, coal-black De Nobli cigar, a philosophical Ranciglio thought over his years of hard labor. "I tell you this," he firmly insisted, "we Italians gave the owners an honest day's work. When I start [1915], I make 11¢ an hour, 10 hours a day! But more important," he added, hammering out a stonemason's chisel on a tripping device the city's 2,500 blacksmiths used in 1915, "there is the consolation of knowing that I can take a piece of steel and make it do what I want it to do. If I can make a good chisel, it is the accomplishment, the achievement of doing good work."[9]

Fear permeated the mines. "The farther you proceed in the mine," cautioned a journalist, "the colder it becomes; we were compelled to pause for reasons of a cave-in seriously injuring several workmen. This place has been the scene of several calamities, owing to the loose condition of the soil."[10] Sighed Antonio Ranciglio: "Bad air, damp mines. Men who work there all have bad lungs. Men would call me over to sharpen their drills. They would pay me a quarter and the quarter was all black!"[11] Recollected Robert DeMatti, another former miner: "Very, very dangerous. The top and the bottom was limestone, in between the fire clay, white clay. Pieces of rock came down and hit you on the head. No helmets, just cloth hat and carbide light. . . ."[12] "When miners get old they'd all walk like this," said Ranciglio, mimicking a hunchback to poignantly emphasize his point.

If the mines enfeebled the old they provided youth with much-sought jobs. "Back then you went into the clay mines at thirteen," reminisced Louis Jean Gualdoni, who quit school to enter the trade in 1905. "I worked in the mines as a cager," he recalled. "In those days they had the mules, nothing electrical to move those carts with clay in it. They had a mule to carry clay over to the shaft to hoist it up. And they always had a youngster as a cager to put it on the elevator. In those days it was dangerous, a slide could come and cover you up. An uncle of mine was killed in the mines."[13] Once the cager had transferred the raw materials to the outside, the clay was loaded onto railroad cars and taken to the factory yards for three years of curing, after which the materials were ready for processing. "We got the clay," explained a worker, "then we would grind it and pulverize it, rub it over a screen, and then it went through a press and the driers where the men burned it. We kept three shifts going."[14]

Work at the brickyards, manned by both Lombards and Sicilians, was more complex than labor in the mines. Tasks included the setting, burning, offbearing, firing, and wheeling of the clay products. The setters and burners placed the green brick in the kilns, the firemen lit the kilns, and the offbearers wheeled away the brick after it had been baked. The process varied, depending on the final design of the product; terra-cotta demanded more handwork than firebrick.[15] If workers in the brick factories escaped the ever-present fear of mine cave-ins, they nevertheless endured onerous conditions. "My father was a fireman," recalled Sam

Chinicci, a Sicilian immigrant. "He used to fire the kilns. Worked under a German foreman. That was really hard work because I used to go down as a young boy and watch them, and many times they would work straight through for 48 hours."[16] "They [the German foremen] treat us like mules," exclaimed Antonio Cesare. "I work in brick yards. I make brick and tile. Work like a mule, push wheelbarrel, sixty bricks. Break my back."[17] Today these veterans bear gruesome identification. "Just look at their hands," Lou Fuse moaned. "Their knuckles are all broken."[18]

From the turn of the century until the depression Italian laborers comprised the most important ethnic work group at the Cheltenham factories. At certain plants Lombards and Sicilians commanded nearly all the lower-paying positions. "At times the number of Italian employees was 95% of the total number of employees," recollected an official at Evens and Howard Sewer Pipe Company.[19] The Cheltenham industrial complex dominated the local economy until the 1930s. In 1900, 90 percent of the Hill's male work force (325 men) were employed at the clay mines and brick factories.[20] By the depression only 30 percent of the community's male workers labored at these concerns.[21] As the precious clay deposits were exploited new industries absorbed the surplus work force.

During the period after 1910 heavy and light industries gravitated to the Cheltenham locale. Two of the most important sources of employment were the Carondelet Foundry and the Banner Iron Works, which by 1930 employed 11 percent of the colony's males (205 jobs).[22] The Quick Meal Stove Company, which introduced the gas-burning Magic Chef oven in 1929, erected an immense factory at 2001 Kingshighway in 1910 and employed more than 100 neighborhood workers during the 1920s and 1930s.[23] Joining the industrial network was the McQuay-Norris Company, which built a spacious plant at Southwest and Cooper avenues in 1919. The factory manufactured piston rings and engine parts and employed 75 residents in 1930. In the decade after 1920 Cheltenham experienced an economic renaissance. Eighteen companies selected sites and located plants in the industrial valley, including the National Bearing Metals Corporation, Liggett and Myers Tobacco, the Forest Park Highlands Amusement Corporation, and several low-grade foundries and shoe companies.[24] On the eve of the depression 144 Italian-Americans worked at the nearby shoe factories, while hundreds of others were dispersed throughout the local economy.[25]

WAGES AND OCCUPATIONAL MOBILITY

Italian immigrants brought to America little capital and few skills valuable to an urban-industrial society, other than strong backs and a dogged willingness to work long hours for minimal wages. The great majority of the settlers were *contadini* (peasants) and *braccianti* (a term loosely translated as laborers, derived from the Italian word for arm). In 1907 laborers averaged only forty cents a day in Lombardy, even less in Sicily.[26] An earlier study revealed that Italians brought an average of only thirteen dollars each to America, making them the most impoverished group to enter Ellis Island.[27]

At the turn of the century immigrant brickworkers earned between $1.35 and $1.50 a day, while miners averaged $1.75 a shift, although the latter were expected to supply their own equipment (drills, picks, shovels, and explosives). Wages had not risen since 1882, when officials had listed pay scales at Evens and Howard Company.[28] While many new industries entered the Cheltenham Valley after 1900, immigrant laborers enjoyed few benefits from the expansion. In 1912 unskilled laborers still earned only $1.50 for ten hours of work.[29] A social worker was prompted to describe the area as one of the least desirable industrial sectors in the city. "All the work is unskilled and offers no opportunity for advancement," complained Irving Crossland, a social economist. In addition he pointed out that the men "worked from 7 A.M. to 6 P.M."[30] Compared to contemporary immigrant groups, Hill Italians fared poorly in the economic marketplace. In 1907 northern and southern Italians averaged $2.23 and $1.95 for their daily labors, substantially more than the $1.50 earned on the Hill. In a study by the U.S. Immigration Commission, no ethnic group averaged less than the daily salary of Hill Italians[31] (see Table 3). Hill laborers made few great economic leaps after 1907. In 1917 brickworkers toiled ten hours a day for $2.10, while elsewhere St. Louis union laborers were paid $3.25–$4.50 for eight hours' work.[32]

Journalists described the Hill as "provincial" and "old-world," but no phrase captured the neighborhood's economic essence better than "blue-collar." From 1900 to the Second World War every economic index indicated that this enclave constituted one of the most thoroughly working-class districts in the city. Census takers in 1900 located 280 "laborers" and "miners" but only a handful of white-collar inhabitants: 3 saloon keepers, 2 grocers, and 4 grocery clerks. The 1910 census charts the progress of aspiring immigrants, but only a small number had graduated

Table 3. Average Rate of Daily Earnings for Male Immigrants, 1907

Country of Origin	
Croatia	$2.38
Germany	$2.29
Italy (North)	$2.23
Russia (Hebrew)	$2.20
Italy (South)	$1.95
Poland	$1.90
Bulgaria	$1.75
Greece	$1.58
Italy (Hill)	$1.50
Total	$2.11

Source: U.S. Immigration Commission, *Immigrants in Industries*, 23, p. 104.

to business lines: a total of 16 individuals—all but 2 were Lombards—claimed proprietor-manager status. Most of these positions involved immigrant services, typically grocers and saloon keepers.[33] The 1930 census and a 1934 local study clearly indicate that the streets of the Hill were ungilded. Overwhelming numbers of immigrants and their sons toiled at the bottom rungs of the economic ladder. In particular the colony lacked a professional class; in 1934 only 6 Italians (.05 percent) claimed such status.[34]

The 1940 census provides the first comparative key to the neighborhood's economic profile. Precincts 13B and 13C, which perfectly conformed to the Hill's boundaries, were designated as the city's most working-class district.[35] In 1940 fewer than 1 percent of the colony's male work force had graduated to professional or semiprofessional status, compared to an overall St. Louis rate of 5.5 percent. The community correspondingly lagged far behind in the proportion of low-level, white-collar jobs. Only 3.1 percent and 8.1 percent of the area's males worked in the respective positions of proprietor-manager and clerical-sales, while fully 10 percent and 22 percent of their St. Louis cohorts were employed in these white-collar jobs. Overall, 37.7 percent of the Gateway City adult males in 1940 wore a white collar to work, contrasted with only 12 percent of the Hill.[36]

Economic fashions changed slowly in this small community, as blue-collars still predominated in 1940 (see Table 4). Italians were drastically overrepresented in jobs at the very bottom of the occupational ladder.

Table 4. Occupational Classification for Employed Males, Ages Fourteen and Older, 1940

St. Louis	*Number*	*Percentage*
Professional workers	9,509	4.3
Semiprofessional	2,762	1.2
Proprietors, managers	21,835	10.0
Clerical/sales	48,497	22.0
Craftsmen/foremen	40,806	18.4
Factory operatives	51,331	23.1
Service workers	23,345	10.5
Laborers	21,470	9.7
Total	221,421	
Hill		
Professional workers	8	.5
Semiprofessional	4	.3
Proprietors, managers	50	3.1
Clerical/sales	130	8.1
Craftsmen/foremen	217	13.5
Factory operatives	402	25.0
Service workers	215	13.4
Laborers	563	35.1
Total	1,600	

Source: U.S. Census Bureau, 16th Census, 1940, *Population and Housing*, Table 33.

Nearly four times as many workers were classified as "unskilled laborers" (35.1 percent) as in the city (9.7 percent). In other blue-collar lines the Hill's 1940 work force was more balanced in comparison to the city, running slightly behind in the percentage of craftsmen and foremen (13.5 percent to 18.4 percent) and ahead in the percentage of factory operatives (25 percent to 23.1 percent).[37]

A small but important service economy had evolved on the Hill by the 1920s. Groceries, bakeries, and taverns, designed to serve an Italian clientele, thrived in the concentrated ethnic enclave and in turn created jobs. By 1940, while only 3.5 percent of the male work force was employed in the professional or managerial-proprietor class (as opposed to 15.5 percent of male St. Louisans), fully 13.5 percent of the colony's men labored in the service sector as waiters, clerks, bartenders, and so on (contrasted to 10 percent of St. Louis men).

On the eve of Pearl Harbor few Hill immigrants or their sons had climbed from the bottom to the middle of the economic ladder. Was this economic malaise a local phenomenon, or was it characteristic of the larger urban Italian-American experience?

Josef Barton's pathfinding *Peasants and Strangers* traced the careers of Italian, Slovak, and Rumanian emigrants to Cleveland between 1890 and 1950. Overall, Cleveland's immigrants began their careers at higher stations and achieved more occupational mobility than their St. Louis counterparts. Sixteen percent of Italians born in 1870–90 began their Cleveland careers in white-collars jobs, whereas their Hill compatriots fared miserably in such pursuits: fewer than 1 percent had achieved such a foothold in managerial-professional lines in 1900, and as late as 1940 fewer than 4 percent of the immigrants and their sons had established themselves in these trades.[38]

In *The Other Bostonians* Stephan Thernstrom maintains that Bean City immigrants achieved steady upward mobility. A "mere" 10 percent of Boston's immigrants held white-collar jobs in 1910, a figure not reached on the Hill by first- and second-generation males until 1950.[39] Thomas Kessner, in his study *The Golden Door*, examines the process of mobility in New York City, 1880–1915. In 1950, 20 percent of the city's Italian work force occupied white-collar positions, the majority being shopkeepers and peddlers.[40] Interestingly, peddling—a vital trade for Italian immigrants in New York and elsewhere—offered little promise or employment on the Hill. The logistical difficulty in obtaining fruits and vegetables worked against the establishment of such enterprises there.

NEIGHBORHOOD BUSINESSES

A working-class ethos, carried by immigrants into the mines and factories, pervaded the Hill. If a community reveals its aspirations in the dreams of its workers, an examination of some immigrant success stories might help explain the Hill in another way.

Immigration historians have long pointed out how different ethnic groups have sought to carve their own economic niches in America. In 1915 *The Immigrant in St. Louis* was published. Its author, a young Vassar graduate named Ruth Crawford, had been intrigued by the economic leanings of the city's immigrants, and she expressed particular fascination with the comparative pursuits of Greeks and Italians. In 1915 St. Louis Italians (including Little Italy and the Hill) outnumbered the Greeks, 7,500 to 1,500, yet the Greeks proved far more adventurous in mercantile dealings than their Mediterranean counterparts, 402 enterprises to 268. Greek immigrants pursued certain types of businesses, particularly restaurants, confectioneries, shoeshine stands, and billiard parlors; in fact, fully 58 percent of Greek establishments were either restaurants or candy stores, an old-world legacy (see Table 5).[41]

Occupational patterns, however, imposed severe geosocial restrictions on the small Greek population, which simply could not support 140 restaurants, 94 confectioneries, 21 billiard parlors, 26 shoeshine shops, 19 coffee houses, plus assorted barbershops, butcher shops, and so on. Thus the gregarious Greeks by necessity catered to an "American" clientele and became the most widely dispersed ethnic group in St. Louis.[42]

Italian businessmen were clearly more colony-oriented than the Greeks. For instance, the grocery business—an important institution for Italian immigrants—languished within the Greek enclave (seventy-four Italian groceries vs. five Greek). Interestingly, the Italian-American restaurant, probably the most identifiable symbol of ethnic enterprise today, was not an avenue of mobility for first-generation Italians. They tended

Table 5. Business Enterprises of St. Louis Greeks and Italians, 1915

	Greek	*Italian*
Artificial flowers	0	1
Bakery	0	3
Barbershop	18	52
Billiard and pool parlor	21	9
Boardinghouse	8	2
Butcher shop	0	1
Cigar manufacturing	0	2
Coffee house	19	0
Commission merchant	0	4
Confectionery	94	0
Fruit store	0	13
Grocery	5	74
Restaurant	140	0
Saloon	6	95
Steamship agent	0	6
Shoeshine shop	26	0
Tailor shop	5	6
Other	60	0
Total	402	268

Source: Crawford, *Immigrants in St. Louis.*

to invest their savings in the ubiquitous corner saloon, which numbered ninety-five in 1915 (as opposed to five Greek saloons).[43]

Sicilians, in particular, found the barbering profession attractive. In 1915 there were fifty-two Italian barbers in the Mound City, many of whom had learned their skills on their native island. "My profession as a barber started while attending school in Augusta, Sicily," explained Sam Lisitano. "Half the day was spent in school and half the day I learned the trade as an apprentice in my cousin's barbershop. . . . I arrived on the Hill on Saturday and reported for work on early Monday."[44]

Italian-Americans also dominated the St. Louis fruit markets. In 1918 *Gould's Directory* listed 35 Italian fruit merchants, all of whom lived in the Sicilian Little Italy, which bordered the great open-air markets. Many of the Sicilians working in the stalls had previous experience in the old country.[45] The Hill, despite its Sicilian minority, held few attractions for fruit and vegetable dealers. As late as 1931 only one such establishment could be found on the Hill out of a total of 103 St. Louis Italian fruit dealers (wholesalers and retailers).

The Hill, miles away from the city's commercial district, held little promise to Sicilians in what was a traditional economic stronghold. Hill Italians purchased their greens and fruits not in open-air markets but in the local mom-and-pop grocery store. The corner grocery became one of the most popular avenues of upward mobility for Hill immigrants. Lombards and Sicilians demanded hard-to-obtain staples and preferred to deal with *paesani*, creating a natural outlet for enterprising merchants. "All the shopping was done in the neighborhood," remembered Joe Garagiola, "and in Italian!"[46] In 1931 forty-seven grocery stores dotted the colony.[47] Each institution, according to Harry Brundidge, was laden with an endless variety of enjoyment: "spaghetti, vermicelli, macaroni . . . but what about farfalle, rigatoni, mostaciolli, magalietti, conchille, ditalini . . . and the endless strings of garlic and red peppers, imported anchovie paste, Sardinian butter, gallon cans of virgin olive oil, tins of dwarfed, pear-shaped and very red tomatoes."[48]

"Every corner that didn't have a grocery store had a tavern," joked Lino Gambaro.[49] The neighborhood saloon continues to enjoy a healthy trade despite the national decline of that once venerable institution. "One outstanding type of business is the saloon," observed Elmer Shorb Wood in the 1930s. "At one intersection, three of the four corners are occupied by saloons."[50] Saloon keepers held exalted positions in the community. "Take Louis Merlo," laughed Bishop Charles Koester. "He was unbelievable! He had the greatest thing going. He went to mass at six o'clock in the morning, then came over at 6:30 to open his tavern. There would be the boys waiting for him before they went to work. They wanted to get their little shot in the beer. But at twelve noon every day and at six in the evening, everyone in the place answered the prayers or that was it!"[51] A penniless emigrant from Cuggiono, Merlo arrived on the Hill in 1900, working in the brickyards until he secured a job as a bartender, where most saloon keepers started. By 1918 Merlo had accumulated a sizable savings and purchased a tavern on the corner of Wilson and Cooper avenues, across from St. Ambrose Church.[52]

Bread and pasta, not Lemp Beer, was the Italian staff of life, and the Hill prided itself on its local delicacies. Immigrants could live in wooden shacks and endure backbreaking labor, but none could survive without the cherished *pane*. "The bread is baked at a local bakery after the local custom of Italy," a reporter noted in 1901, adding, "[It] is then molded in such a way that it can be broken off in chunks." By 1931 seven local bakeries were thriving, supplying residents with countless panettone-etched memories.[53]

Long thin loaves of Lombard bread and thick crunchy loaves of Sicilian bread were delivered daily to neighborhood homes by horse and wagon until the 1920s. Thrown on the porches, much as newsboys delivered *Il Pensiero*, bread was sold by the token, forty tokens for a dollar. Trucks eventually replaced horse-drawn wagons, but bakers still hawked their much-touted products. "I can still see Fazio's Bakery truck making the rounds, and hear the familiar cry of '*Abbiamo tuo pane*,'" remembered Joe Garagiola.[54]

Today a pilgrimage to the Hill necessitates a stop at the Missouri Bakery, which dates to turn-of-the-century New York, where Stefano Gambaro and Franco Arpiani began their careers as apprentices in the bakery of the Knickerbocker Hotel. Attracted to St. Louis by the 1904 World's Fair, the talented team gravitated to the Hill and opened a small bakery on Shaw Avenue. "It was always called the Missouri Bakery," reminisced second-generation owner Jo Arpiani, "because at that time it wasn't fashionable to be Italian! They [locals] threw rocks at our truck! My father and uncle didn't think, especially delivering to restaurants, that anyone with the name of Gambaro or Arpiani would be acceptable."[55] Now, laughed the baker-virtuoso, "we always put in our advertising, 'Gambaro and Arpiani's Missouri Bakery'."

Every evening, regardless of class or status, thousands of midwestern families indulged in Hill-baked bread, accompanied by a hearty helping of Hill pasta. If St. Louis advertised itself in 1910 as the spaghetti center of America, *la Montagna* could lay claim that it was "Macaroni Hill." "Each year," a reporter marveled, "St. Louis produces a million dollars worth of spaghetti, macaroni, and noodles. Over 325 skilled workers are required to make this output possible."[56]

Situated in the heart of the great wheat-raising belt and on the crossroads of America's transportation system, St. Louis was ideally suited to command the lion's share of the pasta market. In its heyday the Gateway City boasted ten macaroni plants, eight of which were located in Little Italy and one on the Hill. But whereas in 1919 there were 557 pasta factories, in 1927 the number had slipped to 353, a figure that plunged drastically with the onset of the depression.[57] While nationally the cutthroat competition and declining sales spelled disaster for the pasta industry, locally the Hill prospered, adding a couple more factories in the 1920s and 1930s. A familiar theme reappeared: the Hill served as an urban refuge, in this case as an economic asylum, for the displaced factories of Little Italy. The colony was able to offer to industrialists skilled craftsmen, Italian workers, nonunionized employees, and a local market for pasta.[58]

Today the Ravarino and Freschi Macaroni Company stands as the last such factory on the Hill. Internationally recognized, the R & F La Terminese brand is, according to Alphonse Ravarino, "the Rolls Royce of pasta!"[59] The firm's story is a curious blend of Horatio Alger and Mama Leone. Giovanni Ravarino was born in northern Italy in 1876. His father, a cheesemaker, sold prized wheels of *formaggio parmigiano* to the aristocrats at the Royal Palace in Torino. He persuaded the royal chefs to apprentice his son, aged eleven, in the imperial arts of haute cuisine. As a teenager Giovanni Ravarino became an accomplished chef, and by Piedmont standards he seemingly had it made. Yet the America fever struck even aspiring chefs, and in 1890 he set sail for St. Louis, where *paesani* had promised him work.[60]

In the Mound City Ravarino found work as a bartender in the saloon of countryman Mario Rossi. Soon the young man was placed in charge of the saloon's free lunch, hardly a challenge to a royal chef. In time Ravarino graduated from the corner saloon to some of the more prestigious eateries, and by 1895 he had accumulated enough funds to form the Italian Sausage Company with his brother-in-law, Giuseppe Freschi. The two immigrants achieved immediate success in the salami business and branched into the wholesale grocery line in 1901. In late 1914 Ravarino and Freschi shrewdly calculated that the European conflict would be a long one and consequently Italian imports would be suspended. "My Dad figured that with the abundant supply of semolina wheat right here in St. Louis, why not begin a pasta factory?" recollected his son.[61] In 1914 the first R & F Macaroni Company opened in the heart of Little Italy. From a daily production of only 4,000 pounds in 1914, R & F was processing 40,000 pounds a day by 1929. The company's special brand, La Terminese, received a gold medal at the Milan Exposition in 1922.[62]

These sketches of Italian immigrants' fortunes after passage to America illustrate several important points about their careers. First, old-world occupational skills were unquestionably valuable assets for success in America. Training in a Milanese restaurant or a Catanese barbershop proved valuable once on the Hill. Agricultural laborers were obviously less equipped to succeed in America as immigrants than were those who had training in urban skills. In *Peasants and Strangers*, Josef Barton similarly has observed that social background influenced both the first job and subsequent work experience of Cleveland's Italians.[63] Yet Barton's observation is only partly valid for the Hill, which leads to a second point—that few merchants *began* their careers as merchants or white-collar managers. The road to commercial or industrial success was seldom a direct route. Most businessmen came to the Hill with little capital; thus, most merchants paid their dues in the brickyards before slipping on a white collar. The road to commercial success was often laid on the groundwork of the saloon. At one time during their careers practically every local businessman was a saloon keeper.

Two of the most important enterprises on the Hill were not Italian at all but Jewish. Rau's Department Store (1902) and Spielberg's Furniture (1921) were indicative of the overall weaknesses in the Hill business class, at least before the 1930s.[64] In light of this dismal overall entrepreneurial record, how does one explain the failure of Lombards and Sicilians to achieve occupational success? Why had Hill Italians vis-à-vis eastern Europeans and other ethnics shown so little commercial bent? In perspective, to what can we attribute the laggard economic progress of Hill Italian-Americans before World War II?

THE REASONS WHY

Discrimination

One invitingly simplistic explanation of the Hill's economic malaise places responsibility on the "white native devils" who discriminated against the defenseless immigrants in the marketplace. The enclave's unusually low rate of population turnover buttresses the discrimination theory. Perhaps prejudice contributed to the ghettoization of the Hill and its consequent economic backwardness?

Certainly, mordant nativism existed in twentieth-century St. Louis.[65] A product of the dime novel and Sunday supplement, the image of the Italian immigrant wavered between romanticism and deprecation. Letters littered the editorial pages decrying the mongrelization of American purity. America faced an internal crisis as serious as ancient Carthage or Rome, warned one citizen. "The American race will eventually be wiped out by these alien hordes," he prophesied. "Even now every city has its Little Italy or Little Bulgaria, in which the people do not learn the English language, do little business except among themselves, and send all the surplus earnings back whence they came."[66] While some restrictionists feared the racial consequences of immigration, others attributed hard times to alien labor. "Why is it that industrious, intelligent Americans are compelled to remain idle when hordes of foreigners are working in all the factories?" asked C. Young during the recession of 1908.[67] "I have noticed foreigners, such as Italians and Greeks, sweeping the streets of St. Louis," an indignant resident announced that same year, "when at the same time these jobs could be given to the old men who have lived here the greater part of their lives and who are registered voters."[68] Many nativists possessed short memories. "Let's make a new slogan," demanded Mike O'Toole, "a job for an American first."[69] The rancorous ravings against the alien laborer were soon replaced by a problem of far greater dimensions: the hyphenated American. World War I and its regimented demands for 100 percent Americanism placed the immigrant in the national spotlight. The Lusk Committee reports richly document the government's efforts in St. Louis and elsewhere.[70] "America wants no more Little Germanys or Little Italys in its domain," demanded the *Globe-Democrat*.[71] A reporter from the *Republic* was shocked to discover whole townships of ethnic enclaves just a short drive from the Mississippi.[72] Yet few ripples from the World War I crusade reached the Hill, a virtual island until the 1920s. Like the Spanish Alcaldes of colonial America, the Hill obeyed but did not comply.

Nativist tracts make for interesting reading, but their economic impact mattered little. Racist editorials generally tell more about the letter writer than about the intended subject. One must look for more substantive reasons as to why Italians clustered in groups and advanced up the occupational ladder less rapidly than other groups. St. Louis Jews and Greeks, for example, were similarly rebuffed by racial and religious taunts yet fared well in the economic mainstream. Thomas Sowell argues in *Ethnic America* that "the existence and effectiveness of economic discrimination depend on far more than the existence or degree of prejudice against a particular group." The Japanese, for instance, suffered historic prejudice and legal discrimination at least as opprobrious as that encountered by Puerto Ricans, and yet the Japanese have mastered the American economy while Puerto Ricans continue to occupy the mudsill.[73] Clearly, forces within the ethnic community and the city loom more instrumental in shaping economic motivations than elements from without.

The Urban Factor—St. Louis

The economic doldrums of the Hill partly reflected the stagnating St. Louis economy. In one sense Hill Italian-Americans were victims of chance. The district they had settled offered few opportunities for blue-collar workers. But the problem amplified beyond the corridors of the Mill Creek Valley. Neal Primm has effectively demolished the myth that St. Louis, because of its diversified economy, survived the depression with relatively little pain. The depression devasted a languishing economy; between 1929 and 1939 St. Louis's share of the United States' manufacturing output dropped from 2.18 percent to 1.91 percent. Scores of factories relocated or built branch plants in rural Missouri and Illinois.[74]

Prohibition in particular devastated the city's south side. While the repeal of the Volstead Act in 1933 helped St. Louis in general, the opening of breweries did not help the Hill, since few residents worked at them. Moreover, the end of Prohibition ended the lucrative bootlegging operations. Yet other ethnic groups succeeded despite the St. Louis blues, perhaps because they were better equipped to grasp the intricacies of the urban economy.

Background Handicaps and Problems of Adjustment

Lombards and Sicilians arrived in St. Louis utterly unprepared for the harshly competitive urban environment. Rural skills, appalling rates of illiteracy, and the inability to speak the English language encumbered the new settlers. Oral histories and census materials indicate that an unusually high percentage of Hill Lombards and Sicilians were unskilled *contadini.* Historians have found that immigrants from agricultural backgrounds fared poorly in America compared to those who brought with them trades and skilled callings.[75]

An old-country proverb augured a bleak economic future for Hill Italians: "We who have no education must guide ourselves with our hands."[76] Rampant illiteracy fettered Italians. As late as 1930, 35 percent of the colony's foreign-born were illiterate, the highest rate in St. Louis.[77] In comparison only 1.9 percent of the Germans and 4.4 percent of the Jewish immigrants were unable to read and write their native language.[78] While old-world skills provide a yardstick by which to measure new-world progress, they alone could not guarantee success or failure—witness the limited gains achieved by the English-speaking Irish as opposed to eastern European Jews.[79] Immigration history demonstrates many examples of groups readily acquiring new job skills. Far more difficult to acquire were attitudinal changes, such as intra- and intergroup cooperation. Perhaps more critical than linguistic or educational skills were the more practical aspects of economic life, such as the effectiveness of labor unions.

Labor Unions

"The people of the Hill have been Americanized in a good many ways," applauded the *Post-Dispatch* in 1901. "One of the best proofs of this being the means employed to secure an advance from $1.35 to $1.50 a day in their wages at the brickyards last week. They struck. They gained their point."[80] If the immigrants won their point (a meager wage increase) it was a Pyrrhic victory, for the company also hoisted a victory flag—the brickworkers' union was denied recognition. On May 4, 1901, over 1,000 brick and tile workers struck against the Cheltenham industries. "Although the men are not organized into a union," the *Globe-Democrat* noted, "they seem to understand the situation and the effort to get them out was no great task. The great majority of the strikers are Italian. The labor required is not skilled in any particular branch."[81] Strike leaders cautiously advised their comrades to avoid violence. "When the men struck," wrote the *Post-Dispatch*, "they instructed the kiln burners to stay at their posts until the kilns should be burned sufficiently, this position being taken because the men did not wish to destroy property and abandoning the kilns prematurely would result in their loss."[82]

Organizing workers was an easier task than organizing an effective union. On May 8, 1901, strikers met at the North Italy America Club, where 700 men were initiated into the Central Trades Union of St. Louis.[83] No Italians were represented on the union organizing committee, yet they dominated the nascent union ranks.[84] The union arrived stillborn, however. Company clout overcame union muscle and workers' lack of resources. In attitude and atmosphere the Hill resembled mining towns of Illinois or Kentucky. Typical of the tough-minded company attitude toward employees with an inclination toward organization was a message posted on a fence outside the Laclede-Christy Fire Brick Plant: "All employees of this company who walked out Saturday morning, May 4 will please call at this office tomorrow afternoon (May 8) at 3:00 o'clock and get the balance of the money due them and consider themselves discharged. [Signed] T. T. Green, V.P."[85] In case anyone had underestimated the owners' belligerent attitude, a number of black strikebreakers were imported. Hill Italians quickly bolted the short-lived union and returned to their positions.

During the next two decades local and national leaders made repeated attempts to organize the Cheltenham Valley, which had acquired an unenviable reputation in labor circles. In April of 1912 the matter was brought to the attention of the *Post-Dispatch*. "My husband is a hardworking man," an employee's wife wrote, adding that he and his fellow workers had not received a raise since 1901. "He is a brickworker and receives only $1.50 a day for ten hours work. He works only 9–10 months a year. Under the circumstances, brickworkers ought to have a union. As I understand it, they seem to be the only class of working men who are not organized. And the poorest paid I know. [Signed] Mrs. L.P."[86] The letter was answered by William Van Bodegraven, of Chicago, secretary-treasurer of the International Brick and Tile and Terra Cotta Workers' Union. "Mrs. L.P. is not aware of the *repeated* attempts that have been made in that direction without success," he explained. "As late as the winter of 1910–11, an organizer of the I.B.T.T.C.W.U. spent several months in St. Louis in an effort to unite the workers of that city, of whom there are 2,000."[87] Van Bodegraven's dream of a brickworkers' phalanx was never fulfilled.

In March of 1917 several thousand laborers again struck, demanding a wage increase of four cents an hour to combat the dizzying wartime inflation. Strikers vented their frustration in rage; in one incident 200 employees at Evens and Howard cordoned off the plant to prevent strikebreakers from entering. During the melee two company guards were stabbed, and a striker, Domenico Ginnello, was shot. According to the newspapers, "the mob was composed mostly of Sicilian workers and carried signs, 'We fight for our daily bread' and 'We fight *per la vita*'."[88] A union was again organized, but the strikers' committee, composed of Sicilians Peter and Joseph Italiano, Giovanni Cataldo, and Tony Canzoneri, failed to sustain the movement. Italian workers had struck believing the war had ended the supply of new workers (i.e., immigrants).[89] However, they ignored a powerful new force: the black migration to the northern urban centers. Very possibly southern blacks were the only other group willing to work for such a menial wage and under such conditions. The Italian weekly *La Lega*, based in Little Italy, counseled the strikers: "We feel the time for a walkout has been badly chosen. First, because the federal government might step in. Secondly, because a great many [blacks] are being hired in St. Louis. May you succeed and persevere."[90]

La Lega's warnings were prophetic. Once again black scabs proved a nemesis to the frustrated brick and tile workers. Whereas in 1900 only 137 blacks were employed at the local industries (14 percent of the total), the number increased to 353 by 1910 (19 percent), rose to 649 by 1920 (45 percent), and then slumped to 495 in 1930 (42 percent).[91] The number of Italian-Americans employed at the industrial complex fell correspondingly as blacks replaced local white workers and Hill personnel who chose to work elsewhere. In 1900, 248 Italians worked at the brick and tile factories (27 percent of the total), the number rising to 961 in 1910 (52 percent), thereafter falling to 700 in 1920 (47 percent) and 571 in 1930 (48 percent).[92] The simultaneous exhaustion of the clay mines and the Great Depression devastated the Cheltenham brick, tile, and mining industries. In 1930, 17 percent of the factory workers in the area were unemployed or laid off without pay.[93] The employment situation would worsen, and by the time the American Federation of Labor was strong enough to unionize the industry, the Cheltenham kilns were cold.

If the community's conservative labor movement was wrecked by a combination of bad luck, inadequate resources, and entrepreneurial tenacity, the neighborhood radical coalition was dashed on the rocks of apathy. Symbolizing the utter rejection and comic failure of the Left was an attempt by the Communist party to radicalize the Hill's younger workers. "Some of the young men talk a great deal about communism," revealed an observer, "but they have little or no organization. . . . When the communists attempted to organize the employees of the tobacco factory recently, over 100 Italian girls signed up, but the attempt failed when the parents refused to allow the girls to go out at night to attend the organizational meeting."[94]

In retrospect, the failed labor movement froze wages in the short run; but in the long run a vigorous union movement could not have saved what was essentially a failing industry. What do the efforts of Lombards and Sicilians tell us about the Hill in particular and Italian immigrants in general? Blistering debates among historians over the nature of the Italian-American labor movement have resulted in little consensus. Italian immigrants, in Rudolph Vecoli's phrase, were neither "padrone slaves or primitive rebels." What appears clear is that immigrant working-class attitudes were shaped by a blend of values resulting from the old-world villages and new-world locales. Sicilians in Tampa, Florida, for instance, brought with them a sharpened sense of class conflict and radical values, hammered out in a series of agrarian protests culminating in the *Fasci* rebellion of 1894. In Tampa they found an industry and milieu that leavened their ideology.[95] Lombards and Sicilians in St. Louis came from no such background and found no such milieu.

Should not Italian immigrants on the Hill have fought a harder union battle or left the colony for better jobs elsewhere? They might have, but they did not. The question presupposes that immigrants were fundamentally economic creatures. While historians have dwelled on the heroic struggle by Italian immigrants at Lowell and Paterson, more typical were the workers who never joined a union and never participated in a strike. John Bodnar's extensive oral histories of industrial workers in Pennsylvania suggest laborers' discontent with social idealism and an affirmation of a pragmatic worldview that embraced job security as a means to family stability. Similarly, many of my interviewees stressed the paramount role of family preservation.[96] Working conditions may have been bad, wages may have been abominable, but as long as the family honor could be preserved, immigrants endured. The strength and resilience workers derived from their families reinforced the commitment to community.

Family and Fertility

Twentieth-century Malthusians, alarmed at immigrant life-styles, warned St. Louisans that southern and eastern Europeans were breeding themselves deeper into poverty and thereby threatening the city's general welfare. "The overproduction of babies is a crime and a sin," pontificated the director of Washington University's School of Social Economy.[97] The argument and its implications offer an explanation for the poor economic performance of Italian-Americans. Immigrants tended to have significantly larger families than native Americans and consequently offered less occupational assistance to their many sons.

Census data confirm reformers' suspicions that Italians were the most prolific group in St. Louis. Charlotte Rumbold reported in a 1907 study that the average Italian immigrant family was composed of 4.9 members, closely followed by the Poles (4.5), blacks (3.8), and Jews (3.7).[98] The Polish and Italian birthrates are impressive considering that most immigrant families were separated for two to three years during the prime childbearing period. Moreover, the immigrant population—a youthful cohort—continued to bear children.

The 1930 census charts the demographic changes in the St. Louis ethnic community. In 1930 the most fertile group in the city, the Poles, claimed a median family of 4.4, closely followed by the Italians (4.3). The median for all St. Louis foreign-born families stood at 3.5; demographic data for the Hill put the size of the family at 4.4. A 1935 study of the city's census tracts reports that precinct 13B (the Hill) claimed the largest family size in St. Louis at 4.58. Precinct 13C of the Hill had 4.19 persons per family.[99]

While census data correlate Italian fecundity and low economic achievement, this does not mean there was a direct relationship between the two variables. St. Louis Jews had large families, 4.2 members in 1930, yet they exhibited impressive occupational mobility. By contrast, St. Louis Greeks were the most celibate of the city's ethnic groups. They traditionally married late in life, a cultural factor that encouraged them to establish mercantile careers before considering family plans. However, in St. Louis a demographic imbalance kept many Greeks from the marriage altar. In 1930 Greek males outnumbered females 1,207 to 377.[100]

Historically, it is difficult to discern a relationship between sheer family size and group economic gains. If fertility differences alone were not a basic factor in determining economic gains, then perhaps the character and value structure of the immigrant family contain the key to that complex puzzle.

Family Values: Education and Children

Italian culture stressed the preeminent and paramount role of the family. Family obligations dominated and predominated working-class life and exerted a moderating influence on individual expectations. In the interrelationship between work and family a nexus of concerns agitated the lives of workers where survival, not working-class consciousness, became the lodestar of Hill Italians.

Children became handmaidens for family survival. Individual success for Italian-Americans militated against collective betterment. Not surprisingly, Hill Italian-Americans accomplished little in the educational realm. "My father's attitude was that he more or less raised children for productive means," recalled Sam Chinicci, a Sicilian who was born in 1908. "This is a pattern from the old country, you raised kids to work on the *lobo*, the small farm. Of course they loved us, but our first thing was to get a job to support the family income. All for our family. I was fourteen when I was taken out of school."[101]

Statistics point out two rather curious trends in the community's evolution. The 1930 census indicates that the Hill ranked first in the city in both the percentage of total population attending school and the percentage of males over age ten who were gainfully employed.[102] The explanation lies in the fact that local birthrates were high, but also that few students ever attended, let alone graduated from, high school. By 1940 Hill Italian-Americans held the dubious distinction of being the least-educated group in metropolitan St. Louis, a notoriety shared by Italians elsewhere. In the early 1930s only 11 percent of New York City Italian-American high school students graduated, whereas 42 percent of all such high school students in New York did so.[103] On the eve of Pearl Harbor the average Hill adult had barely obtained a fifth-grade education, compared to the average St. Louisan's eighth-grade education. Appallingly, only 17 individuals from the community's 1,600 males over age twenty-five claimed a high school diploma. Italian-American women fared only slightly better: 22 high school graduates from a total of 1,600 adult females. Black St. Louisans entered the labor market with higher educational qualifications; the average black male had completed the seventh grade.[104] (Education will be discussed in more detail in chap. 8.)

Hill parents customarily removed their sons and daughters from school at age fourteen, electing to collect immediate, albeit meager, dividends from a combined family income. Immigrants were reminded, "A family's wealth depends upon the number of hands it has."[105] When a Lombard miner was told that a law forbade the employment of his seven- and twelve-year-old sons, the immigrant exploded with indignation.[106] "The earnings of all members of the family are pooled together in a family budget," noted a community social worker in the 1930s. "Girls and boys are expected to participate in this until they marry."[107] Isidore Oldani, Jr., recalled: "I'll never forget, I got married in 1940 and never had I seen a paycheck in my life until two weeks before my wedding."[108] Early on youth became an active cog in the Cheltenham work force; in 1910, 15.5 percent of the brickworkers were young men aged fourteen to twenty, although quite likely the real numbers of child laborers ranged higher. An Italian adage counseled parents, "When hair begins to grow between the legs, one is fit to marry and work."[109]

Early employment knew neither regional nor sexual boundaries. "A fourteenth birthday means a work certificate and a farewell to studies," wrote Ruth Crawford, describing the plight of Hill females. "In their place, the little Italian girl begins sorting the great tobacco leaves."[110] Both Lombards and Sicilians endorsed the utility and necessity of child labor. A caseworker from the St. Louis International Institute described the comparative attitudes of a Lombard and Sicilian immigrant, both of whose daughters graduated from the grammar school and wished to go on to high school. "Scholarships were procured for both girls," explained the counselor. "The Sicilian parents resisted all explanations and attempts of persuasion to send their daughter to school rather than the factory. The Lombardian parents also resisted attempts to send their daughter to high school, but, because she could find no work, they let her go to school for one year, then, she too went to work."[111]

Italian-American women from the Hill found few outlets for their labors in the local economy. Virtually no women worked in the brick factories, clay mines, or iron foundries. In 1930, 106 women worked in the clothing industry, 35 in shoe factories, 38 in laundries, and 35 in the wholesale trades. Opportunities for women in the service economy (restaurants, etc.) had yet to open. Instead, in 1930 the largest single wage employer (158 jobs) was the Liggett and Myers Plug Tobacco factory—the world's largest—a short ride away at Tower Grove Avenue. A characteristic pattern emerged whereby young girls and women worked at the tobacco factory until they married. "I was no married," explained Angelina Merlo, an elderly Lombard immigrant. "I go work at Tobacco factory. A young girl—I got to pay my own way!" Typical, too, were the examples of Sara Calcaterra, Mary Valdone, Lena Berra, and Jennie Pizzini, immigrants ranging in age from fourteen to seventeen, who worked at the Liggett and Myers factory in 1910. Such factory work was deemed acceptable and was encouraged by immigrant fathers. An Italian official, after touring the factory in 1911, concluded, "In St. Louis, it is considered proper and right for women to work in the factories."[112] Fully 10 percent of the female employees at the Liggett and Meyers Plant on Tower Grove Avenue were Hill Italians, a figure increasing to 25 percent by the late 1920s.[113]

During the summer of 1931 a social worker surveyed area paychecks and disappointedly reported that female tobacco workers earned only between five and ten dollars a week.[114] This meager income buffered the edges of the depression for many families. For a pittance in wages the young girls endured nearly intolerable working conditions. "The atmosphere of these stripping rooms," complained Ruth Crawford in 1916, "is pungent and choking to the stranger."[115] Conditions had actually deteriorated by the 1930s when Elmer Shorb Wood reported several Italian women suffering from tuberculosis. "Those employed report unhealthy working conditions," wrote Wood. "The humidity is high and the air is filled with tobacco dust. Handkerchiefs are worn over their faces, and the white uniforms, which must be worn by workers in the stemming department, become red with tobacco dust."[116] "Real hard workers, the poor things," said Sam Chinicci, who witnessed the daily march of women past his filling station: "I saw them worn out, changing physically by the hard work. They came home dirty, smelling of tobacco and then they had to cook meals and do their housework. All economics. To buy their home. They made a real contribution, a tremendous contribution to the development of the Hill."[117]

A distinctive Italian attitude toward the role of family members and formal education unquestionably acted as a drag for individuals on the Hill. "When I think back, we [the Hill] may have ended up with more professional people," reflected a pensive Paul Berra, whose success was marked by his elevation to city treasurer and comptroller, "but our mothers and fathers just wouldn't let their kids jump into professional fields. They'd rather [let] them work in the mines."[118]

The Hill experience might puzzle an outsider. Why had thousands of immigrants and their families—in status an urban proletariat—remained rooted in a depressed industrial locale, especially when their toil had been so niggardly rewarded and their hope for future occupational mobility stalled? Nativism, rural handicaps, large families, a sluggish urban economy, and apathy toward education, all contributed to the Hill's stunted economic profile. Individually, none of the aforementioned factors created such an impact; compounded, the interactions resulted in an amalgam of resilient ethnic bonds but a weak economic infrastructure.

Yet how inadequate or atypical was this infrastructure? A number of recent studies have stressed the success orientation of European immigrants. Timothy Smith maintained that nearly all immigrants possessed a "commitment to the American dream" and an "indigenous thirst for education."[119] John Briggs, a Smith student, carried through this theme in *An Italian Passage*, a study of Italian immigrants in Kansas City and in New York's Utica and Rochester. Briggs depicted Italians motivated by an intense drive for individual advancement and proprietorship, a quest to fulfill stirrings first felt in nineteenth-century Italy. "Italian children seem to have fared at least as well as their classmates in schooling," noted Briggs, adding that "the colonies were culturally and materially prosperous."[120]

But how shall we define success? Traditionally it has been seen through the prism of white Anglo-Saxon Protestant America. Mobility was indispensable to success, a plank in the Protestant work ethic, defined as movement "up and out" of the ghetto. But as Mark Stolarik, among others, has suggested, there was another way of "making it" in America: "It was all right to be a blue-collar worker, to drop out of school at an early age, and to live in the same neighborhood all your life."[121] So, too, did Hill Italian-Americans reject at least part of the American dream. Although they were motivated by individual and familial aspirations, Hill residents preferred stability to mobility, community to suburbia. Individuals and families sank tenacious roots into their community.

One of the cruelest ironies of Italian-American history may be that the very strength and cohesiveness of the ethnic neighborhood arrested the occupational prospects of its sons and daughters. Canadian sociologist Raymond Breton has suggested that there may well be an inverse relationship between the "institutional completeness" of an ethnic community and the upward mobility of its members. The greater the degree to which a neighborhood organization fulfills the social requirements of its congregation, the Breton paradigm holds, the lesser the needs and opportunities for geographic and economic mobility.[122]

Nothing embodied the essence of community more than the home. Home ownership became the great trade-off, a capstone to the immigrants' relentless labors. No home, no community; no property, no dignity.

A HOUSE ON THE HILL

Louis Wirth, in his classic work *The Ghetto*, told of the anguished reaction of an elderly Jewish immigrant when his son proposed that the family flee the old neighborhood. The bewildered old man could not understand his son's contempt for the ghetto, but after much soul-searching he moved his family from Jefferson Street to Lawndale, where he changed his religious congregation, trimmed his beard, and discussed real estate with his upwardly mobile son.[123] Few residents on the Hill identified with this notion of "making it" in America. Hill Italians elected to improve their neighborhood through the collective mobility of residents, a familiar pattern among Italian-Americans. "From a community of shacks to a little bit of old Italy," wrote Harry Brundidge in his assessment of the Hill's evolution. More accurately the Hill enclave evolved from a collection of new-world shacks to a community of homes.[124]

Lombards fled Italy in part because of their propertyless plight. Less than 20 percent of the rural population in nineteenth-century Lombardy claimed proprietor or landholding status; in Sicily conditions were even more abysmal.[125] The quantum gains in property mobility among Sicilians and Lombards underscored the immigrant promise, "He who crosses the ocean, buys a house."[126] The immigrant voyagers soon discovered the price of such legends.

Early settlers on the Hill accommodated their meager resources and noble intentions by resorting to boardinghouses. In 1890 the Hill's residential district consisted of ten austere shacks, each housing a dozen men.[127] Workers shared expenses to finance the migrations that followed. Reformers were aghast at the living conditions. "On Dago Hill, 175 Italians were found living in thirty-four rooms," observed Ruth Crawford, adding that two shifts of men often occupied the same room.[128]

Italian women provided a critical need and played a pivotal role in the early household economy. A young Cuggionesa was told by a returning emigrant in the 1880s that "those men in the . . . mines of Missouri need women to do the cooking and washing." On arriving in Missouri she was instructed to "cook, make beds, clean sheets, and wash clothes . . . for men."[129] Immigrant families accepted boarders, generally *paesani*, to stretch their meager incomes and to facilitate countrymen and kinfolk in the adjustment process. Typical was the arrangement documented in the 1910 census at 5123 Pattison Avenue. Carlo Ferrario had arrived in St. Louis in 1906, followed shortly by his wife, Josephine. Two children resulted from the reunion. Ferrario, a Lombard, worked at the clay mines while Josephine reared their family and took care of four boarders, Lombard immigrants who worked at the brickyards.[130] Women performed innumerable duties under these arrangements. Sam Chinicci recalled: "My mother, besides having six kids, had maybe ten *bordanti* [boarders]. My poor mother. I can still remember her at five in the morning making the fire and boiling the clothes. . . . the men would live there until they had a place of their own or got married."[131]

The boardinghouse system had outlived its usefulness by the 1920s. A construction boom between 1900 and 1920 relieved the housing shortage. During that period 999 homes were built on the Hill, comprising 70 percent of the houses built there between 1900 and 1940; the next decade added another 321 units.[132] The national census of 1930 recorded virtually no boarders on the Hill.[133]

As the neighborhood grew three distinct housing patterns emerged. The first consisted of the single-family, three-room frame shanty. "We called them shotgun homes," laughed Carmelo Cacciatore, a Sicilian immigrant and carpenter-contractor who, better than anyone, knew their architectural simplicity. "If you fired a gun through the front door, it would pass straight through the back door," he explained.[134] Such homes were cheap yet durable. "The shanties are weather-beaten and worn," it was noted in 1916. "They are damp, even though the location of the cottage on the hillside causes the water to run off quickly."[135] Reformers, appalled at open sewers and dirt streets, mistook the dilapidation as a sign of resignation rather than the origins of hope.

The second architectural style, the two-story wooden tenement, served two families plus lodgers. The tenement was noticeably smaller than the downtown St. Louis or East Coast three- and four-story structures. For example, one quarter of the tenements in St. Louis's Little Italy served three or more families in 1930, while on the Hill fewer than 2 percent of the structures were inhabited by more than two families.[136] The wooden beams buttressing the tenements and cottages claimed illustrious lineage. Hill carpenters had requisitioned many timbers from the 1904 World's Fair. "When the World's Fair folded up," Roland DeGregorio explained, repeating an oft-told tale, "lumber was to be had for the taking—in a manner of speaking—so that's why so many homes on the Hill are made of lumber."[137]

The third housing style consisted of the single-family, one-story, four-room brick home. While wood characterized the uncertainty of the first years of the colony's existence, brick came to symbolize the permanence of the Hill. Appropriately, it had been the lure of the brickyards that had attracted the ambitious immigrants; by the 1920s a brick bungalow symbolized their dogged drive to acquire property. Brick was durable, as were these immigrants who had come to stay; it was cheap, especially if purloined from the district's ovens; and it was an unmistakable sign of affluence in an otherwise poor community.

The Hill's rise from immigrant ghetto to ethnic showcase paralleled the residents' unflagging determination to acquire even the most humble property. In 1900, 23 percent of St. Louis families owned their homes, but census takers found *no* Italian homeowners on the Hill, a situation that hardly improved in 1910.[138] By 1930, however, an incredible 59 percent of the 1,341 homes in the community were occupied by their owners, in contrast to a citywide rate of only 32 percent. In other words, 68 percent of the families in St. Louis lived as tenants, as opposed to only 41 percent of the families on the Hill.[139] Ten years of economic depression had only minimal impact on the community's housing market. The number of owner-occupied units fell only 6 percentage points between 1930 and 1940, a less severe decline than for the whole of St. Louis (down 7 percent).[140] On the eve of Pearl Harbor the Hill boasted a homeowner rate twice that of St. Louis.

When viewed from a broader perspective, property mobility cast an even more significant shadow. The plight of Little Italy can be viewed fundamentally as a residential crisis. Trapped in the inner city, living in crumbling tenements, caught in a crossfire between absentee landlords and escalating real estate prices, the Sicilian population was by 1940 a minority in a downtown settlement giving way to an encroaching black migration. St. Louis led the nation in substandard housing, and Little Italy was at the very heart of the slum tenement district. In 1908 the St. Louis Civic League had branded Little Italy as "the largest single area in which housing is conspicuously bad."[141] An Italian official who visited the colony in 1911 on a tour of midwestern cities pronounced Little Italy as the worst conglomeration of derelict housing she had seen. At least one-third of the tenements should have been destroyed by law, she believed.[142] Structural defects and the neglect of sanitation created debilitating living conditions, which worsened with overcrowding, poorly ventilated rooms, and standing water. Characterized by two- and three-story tenements, the colony's inhabitants had little reason or desire or chance to purchase their living quarters. In 1920 only 3 percent of the units in the neighborhood were owner-occupied (the Hill's rate was 53 percent). Moreover, 82 percent of the structures in Little Italy had been constructed before 1900, having once served as commercial buildings or having been abandoned by other ethnic groups, while only 1 percent of the homes on the Hill were of nineteenth-century vintage.[143] Finally, 19 percent of the structures in Little Italy stood vacant in 1940, indicative of their derelict condition and the fact that their owners simply had abandoned them; on the Hill, only 1 percent of the homes were uninhabited—the lowest rate in St. Louis and reflective of the community's residential desirability.[144]

In terms of property accumulation, the more geographically mobile foreign-born bought more expensive homes and paid higher rents than ghettoized Italians (see Table 6). Foreign-born Russian Jews, for example, paid an average of $8,770 for their homes in 1930, while the average Greek home was priced at $6,713. St. Louis Italians lived in homes appraised at $4,581, far less than the median price tag of the residences of other immigrants. The typical Hill home was valued at only

Table 6. Housing Costs for Foreign-born in St. Louis, 1930

Country of Birth	*Median Value of Home*	*Monthly Rent*
Germany	$6,215	$30.81
Greece	$6,713	$37.04
Hungary	$6,151	$25.68
Ireland	$6,116	$37.17
Italy	$4,581	$24.07
Italy—Hill	$3,100	N/A
Poland	$6,496	$24.69
Russia	$8,770	$42.08
Composite	$6,164	$31.12

Source: 15th Census of U.S., 1930, *Special Report on Foreign Born*, Table 23.

Table 7. Homeownership among Foreign-born Families in St. Louis, 1930

Country of Birth	*Percentage*
Italy (Hill only)	58.6
Germany	58.1
Ireland	56.7
Hungary	56.1
Italy	47.6
Poland	41.9
England	39.1
Russia	34.4
Greece	25.3
Composite	48.9

Source: *Federated Census for Metropolitan St. Louis, 1930,* Table 10.

$3,100, significantly lower than any other ethnic group in the city;[145] by 1940 the median-valued home in the community had fallen even further, to $2,571.[146]

The ability and willingness to pay higher mortgages did not necessarily mean higher levels of home ownership; indeed, there appeared to be an inverse relationship between the two variables. Greeks and Russian Jews seemed to be strikingly successful in their pursuit of expensive residences. However, that luxury was shared by few of their cohorts. In 1930 only 34 percent of the Russian Jews and 25 percent of the Greeks were homeowners, the lowest percentage among St. Louis foreign-born (see Table 7). In contrast, Hill Italians led immigrants in percentage of homeowners (59 percent), slightly ahead of the more established Germans (58 percent), Irish (57 percent), and Hungarians (56 percent).[147] It appeared that Greeks and Russian Jews preferred to invest their capital in their small business ventures rather than in residential property. Overall, Mound City immigrants were remarkably more property-oriented than native St. Louisans, a testimony to the strength of the immigrant dream. In 1930, 49 percent of the foreign-born families resided in their own homes, contrasted to only 29 percent of the locals.[148]

The property acquisitiveness on the Hill was shared by Italians in other cities. Across America, Sicilians and Lombards, Calabrians and Neapolitans, compiled high rates of homeownership. In 1930, for example, 69 percent of Philadelphia's Italians and 45 percent of Buffalo's Italians owned their own homes, although immigration historians have

Table 8. Homeownership among Foreign-born Families in Selected American Cities, 1930

Country of Birth	*City*	*Percentage*
Italy	Philadelphia	69
	St. Louis (Hill)	59
	Syracuse, N.Y.	52
	St. Louis	48
	San Francisco	47
	Buffalo, N.Y.	45
	Cleveland	42
	Chicago	41
	Boston	31
Russia	Syracuse, N.Y.	52
	Boston	44
	Cleveland	37
	St. Louis	35
	San Francisco	30
	Chicago	22
Greece	Syracuse, N.Y.	39
	San Francisco	25
	Boston	18

Source: 15th Census of U.S., 1930, *Special Report on Foreign Born*, Tables 20, 24.

been strangely silent in analyzing specific neighborhoods (see Table 8). The trend on the Hill appears to have been imitated in other urban, working-class districts. In Milwaukee peripheral areas appealed to blue-collar workers with large families and modest incomes. That city's Fourteenth Ward, composed of German and Polish-Americans, had high levels of homeownership and low housing costs.[149]

Property ownership takes on a cultural meaning only within the overall socioeconomic outlook of the ethnic community and family. From this perspective, how is it that Italian immigrants, generally recognized as the most impoverished and the least occupationally skilled, were so successful in the pursuit of property?

Economic survival and success in America depended on the combined wages of every adult (and often junior) member of the Italian family. The earning capacity of manual laborers promised so little, and upward occupational mobility was so difficult, that only through the investment of human capital were Hill Italians able to achieve the status of homeowners, even though this might mean leaving school early. Property mobility involved a trade-off. "I am now convinced that much of the uniqueness of this settlement was due to a sense of common purpose present in most of its [the Hill's] family units," observed Elmer Shorb Wood in 1973 as he reminisced about his involvement in the community in the 1930s: "Perhaps even more so was the depth of emotional commitment given to this common purpose. Because of several factors and certain amplifying events in the early 1930s, it was unusual to find a member of a family living on the 'Hill' who did not support the common cause—to establish a home—an Italian American home—and maintain it in this country of their adoption." In 1984, Wood reaffirmed his assessment: "Homeownership was one of the keys to the stability of that colony."[150]

A second explanation for the immigrants' seemingly disproportionate share of property was simply that ethnics, particularly Italians, eagerly started at the very bottom of the housing ladder. Italians preferred to invest their futures in property rather than career advancement. Low land values in a relatively unsettled area, cheap rents enabling Italians to accumulate savings, and inexpensively priced homes, all help to explain the impressive rates of property mobility.

When a promising catcher was asked by Branch Rickey, the legendary tight-fisted general manager of the St. Louis Cardinals, how much it would take to sign him, Joe Garagiola quickly replied, "Five hundred dollars." He later explained that the sum represented the amount left on the family mortgage. "My brother Mickey and I took the check to my father, who was then working at the kilns of Laclede-Christy. When he saw it, tears came to the poor man's eyes. The most he made in a week was something like fifty-five dollars."[151] "One of the chief objectives of the Italian in this country," observed Phyllis Williams in *South Italian Folkways* (1938), "is to own his own home."[152] By such a criterion Lombards and Sicilians in St. Louis succeeded beyond their wildest imaginations. But housing represented a means to an end, an investment for family in community. "My wife and I worked hard and we love our house," said Joe Palozzollo, a Sicilian immigrant, beaming with pride. "We would never sell it for any amount."[153]

Homeownership required the fantasies of the immigrant dream tempered by a working-class realism. Above all the workplace and urban setting demanded flexibility. The Volstead Act appalled some immigrants, amused others, and permitted a few to take advantage of the opportunities it afforded. By 1920 many homes on the Hill featured an unanticipated addition, a basement still. As we shall see, bootlegging added an unusual but socially important chapter to the community's history.

NOTES

1. Coleman, *Going to America*, 2.
2. "A Bit of Sunny Italy on a Hill," *Star-Times*, Apr. 3, 1936.
3. Interview with Antonio Ranciglio, May 29, 1975; information gleaned from naturalization petitions; interview with Robert DeMatti, Aug. 6, 1975.
4. Bodnar, "Immigration, Kinship, and Working-Class Realism," 48.
5. Aschemeyer, "Urban Geography," 82–83.
6. Interview with Antonio Ranciglio, May 29, 1975.
7. "Toilers of the Dark," *Globe-Democrat*, June 9, 1907, magazine.
8. Interview with Antonio Ranciglio, May 29, 1975.
9. Ibid.; *Thirteenth Census of the U.S.: 1910*, vol. 4, 597.
10. *Globe-Democrat*, June 9, 1907.
11. Interview with Antonio Ranciglio, May 29, 1975.
12. Interview with Robert DeMatti, Aug. 6, 1975.
13. Interviews with Louis Jean Gualdoni, Aug. 13, 1973, July 30, 1982.
14. Interview with Hugo Schoessel, July 10, 1973.
15. Crossland, "Immigrants in Industry," 17–18.
16. Interviews with Sam Chinicci, Aug. 8, Oct. 27, Dec. 19, 1975.
17. Interview with Antonio Cesare, July 11, 1973.
18. Interview with Lou Fuse, Aug. 12, 1973.
19. Quoted in *Historical Review*, 93.
20. *Twelfth Census of the U.S.: 1900. Statistics of Occupations*, 708–9.
21. *Federal Census for Metropolitan St. Louis, 1930*, Table 8; Foster "Hill," 8.
22. Ibid.
23. Ibid.; *Il Pensiero*, Aug. 17, 1929, IV.
24. Thomas, "Sequence of Areal Occupance," 88.
25. *Federal Census for Metropolitan St. Louis, 1930*, Table 8; Fendelman, "St. Louis Shoe Manufacturing."
26. *U.S. Immigration Commission Report: Emigration Conditions in Europe*, 172.
27. "Strangers Within Our Gate," *Charities* 3 (Feb. 4, 1904): 453. English and German emigrants, by comparison, brought sixty-four and forty-eight dollars respectively.
28. *Post-Dispatch*, May 26, 1901; *Republic*, May 17, 1901, p. 5; Miscellaneous Documents of the House of Representatives, 1882–83, vol. 13, pt. 20, *Re-*

port on the Statistics of Wages in Manufacturing Industries (Washington, D.C., 1885), 44; *Special Reports of the Census Office, Mines and Quarries* (Washington, D.C., 1905), 859.

29. *Post-Dispatch*, Apr. 30, 1912, p. 12.

30. Crossland, "Immigrants in Industry," 19.

31. *U.S. Immigration Commission Report: Immigrants in Industries*, pt. 23, 104; ibid.: *Floating Immigrant Supply*, vol. 16, Table 14.

32. *Republic*, Mar. 12, 1917; *Post-Dispatch*, Mar. 4, 1917.

33. *Twelfth Census of the U.S.: 1900*, vol. 100, St. Louis; 1910 Manuscript Census.

34. Foster, "Hill," 8.

35. *Sixteenth Census of the U.S.: 1940. Population and Housing, Statistics for Census Tracts, St. Louis*, vol. 4, Table 3. Precincts 13B and 13C perfectly correlate with the physical boundaries of the colony, hence the danger of ecological fallacy is minimal. For instance in 1930, 1,216 of the 1,332 family heads were either foreign-born Italians or native whites of Italian-born heritage.

36. Ibid.

37. Ibid.

38. Barton, *Peasants and Strangers*, 94–96.

39. Thernstrom, *Other Bostonians*, 116.

40. Kessner, *Golden Door*, 51–60.

41. Crawford, *Immigrant in St. Louis*, 42.

42. Saloutos, *Greeks in the United States;* Fairchild, *Greek Immigration.* For an excellent account of Greek life at the turn of the century see Christowe, *This is My Country;* see also Binsse, "Mr. Phasoulias"; Fay, "Greek Community"; Balk, "Economic Contributions of Greeks."

43. Crawford, *Immigrant in St. Louis*, 42.

44. Interview with Sam Lisitano, June 30, 1973; interviews with Anthony D'Ippolito (Aug. 6, 1975) and Charles Rancilio (June 28, July 14, 1973) confirmed the background opportunities in the old country.

45. Interview with Charles Palmisano, July 2, 1973; *Gould's St. Louis Red-Blue Book 1918.*

46. Garagiola, *Baseball Is a Funny Game*, 13.

47. *St. Louis Italian Societies and Business Directory for 1931*, 20–21.

48. *Star-Times*, Apr. 3, 1936.

49. Interview with Lino Gambaro, Aug. 29, 1973.

50. Wood, "Fairmont Heights," 35.

51. Interviews with Bishop Charles Koester, July 9, 1973, Feb. 16, 1976.

52. Naturalization petition, Louis Merlo, 1918; "Louis Merlo: A Legend in His Time," *Hill 2000*, Apr. 1972, 4.

53. *Post-Dispatch*, May 26, 1901, magazine; *St. Louis Italian-American Business Directory* (St. Louis, 1931).

54. The Hill—An Unwalled Inner City," *Globe-Democrat*, Aug. 4, 1967, p. N1; Garagiola, *Baseball Is a Funny Game*, 3.

55. Interview with Jo Anne Arpiani, Aug. 29, 1973.

56. *Star*, Jan. 30, 1910, IV, p. 1.

57. *Fifteenth Census of U.S.: 1930. Manufacturers, Reports by Industries*, vol. 3, 166–67; *St. Louis Italian-American Business Directory*.

58. Ibid. See also "Food Store, Last of Little Italy, Leaving Downtown for the Hill," *Post-Dispatch*, Apr. 8, 1976, p. C1.

59. Interview with Alphonse Ravarino, Aug. 8, 1975.

60. Ibid.; Schiavo, *Italians in Missouri*, 100; *Il Pensiero*, Aug. 17, 1929.

61. Ibid.

62. Ibid.

63. Barton, *Peasants and Strangers*, 93.

64. Foster, "Hill," 9; letter from David Rau to the author, Mar. 11, 1974.

65. Sullivan, "Hyphenism in St. Louis."

66. *Star*, May 3, 1924.

67. *Post-Dispatch*, Dec. 8, 1908.

68. *Post-Dispatch*, Feb. 13, 1908, p. 4.

69. *Star*, Jan. 28, 1921, p. 12. For other examples see *Star*, Aug. 26, 1927, p. 14, Sept. 25, 1927, Oct. 30, 1910, p. 4; *Post-Dispatch*, May 25, 1911, Mar. 4, 1911, p. 4, Feb. 16, 1911, Mar. 29, 1911; *La Lega*, Nov. 20, 1914, p. 2.

70. *Revolutionary Radicalism*, vol. 3, pt. 2, pp. 3770–71; Higham, *Strangers in the Land;* Hartman, *Movement to Americanize;* Mormino, "Over Here."

71. *Globe-Democrat*, June 8, 1915.

72. *Republic*, Oct. 29, 1918.

73. Sowell, *Ethnic America*, 290–94.

74. Thomas, "Decline of St. Louis," 124; Primm, *Lion of the Valley*, 467; Gendleman, "St. Louis Shoe Manufacturing."

75. Ets, *Rosa*; personal interviews in St. Louis, 1973–76. The 1901 Italian census depicts the rural character of the Lombard villages whence the Hill was populated: Arconate, 1,972; Boffalora Ticino, 1,971; Castano Primo, 4,831; Cuggiono, 3,636; Inveruno, 3,728; Marcallo, 2,350; Ossona, 1,561 *(Istituto Centrale)*.

76. Gambino, *Blood of My Blood*, 84.

77. *Social Statistics of St. Louis by Census Tracts* (St. Louis: Washington University School of Public Administration, 1935), 45.

78. *Fifteenth Census of the U.S.: 1930. Population*, II, Table 16.

79. Thernstrom, *Other Bostonians*, 162.

80. *Post-Dispatch*, May 26, 1901.

81. *Globe-Democrat*, May 7, 1901, p. 14.

82. *Post-Dispatch*, May 7, 1901, p. 2; *Missouri Socialist*, May 11, 1901, p. 3.

83. *Globe-Democrat*, May 8, 1901, p. 3.

84. *Post-Dispatch*, May 7, 1901, p. 2.

85. Ibid.

86. Ibid., Apr. 30, 1912, p. 12.

87. Ibid., May 24, 1912, p. 10.

88. *La Lega*, Mar. 9, 1917, p. 1; *Star*, Mar. 15, 1917, p. 2; *Globe-Democrat*, Mar. 3, 1917, p. 5; *Republic*, Mar. 12, 1917; *Post-Dispatch*, Mar. 4, 1917.

89. *La Lega*, Mar. 9, 1917, p. 1.

90. Ibid.

91. *Twelfth Census of the U.S.: 1900. Statistics of Occupations*, Table 43; *Thirteenth Census of the U.S.: 1910. Statistics of Occupations*, Table 17; *Fourteenth Census of the U.S.: 1920. Occupations*, Table 30; *Federated Census for Metropolitan St. Louis, 1930*, Table 8.

92. Ibid.

93. *Fifteenth Census of the U.S.: 1930. Unemployment*, vol. 1, Table 9.

94. Wood, "Fairmount Heights," 48.

95. Edwin Fenton and Samuel Baily both contend that Italian immigrants made few union inroads in the United States. See Fenton, "Immigrants and Unions"; Baily, "Italians and Organized Labor." Italians actively participated in the Argentine labor movement; 40 percent of the organized laborers there were Italian immigrants. For another perspective see Pozzetta, *Pane e Lavoro;* Mormino, "We Worked Hard"; Bodnar, "Immigration, Kinship, and Working-Class Realism"; Vecoli, "Italian American Workers."

96. Bodnar, *Workers' World.*

97. "This Man Would Limit the Number of Children," *Republic*, Dec. 4, 1910, magazine.

98. Rumbold, *Housing Conditions in St. Louis*, 84.

99. *Fifteenth Census of the U.S.: 1930. Special Report on Foreign-Born White Families*, supplement to vol. 6, Table 24; *Federal Census for Metropolitan St. Louis, 1930*, Table 12; Foster, "Hill," 10; *Social Statistics of St. Louis by Census Tracts*, Table 14.

100. Ibid.

101. Interviews with Sam Chinicci, Aug. 8, Oct. 27, Dec. 19, 1975.

102. *Social Statistics of St. Louis by Census Tracts*, 9–14.

103. *Sixteenth Census of the U.S.: 1940. Population and Housing*, Table 3; Ravitch, *Great School Wars*, 178; Gambino, *Blood of My Blood*, 256.

104. Ibid.

105. Yans-McLaughlin, *Family and Community*, 180; Schiavo, *Italians in Missouri*, 71. Schiavo reported an "extremely high number of work permits" granted to Italian-American children.

106. *Globe-Democrat*, June 9, 1907.

107. Wood, "Fairmount Heights," 32–33.

108. Interview with Isidore Oldani, Jr., Sept. 10, 1973.

109. *Thirteenth Census of the U.S.: 1910. Population and Occupational Statistics*, vol. 6, Table 8; quoted in Covello, *Social Background*, 229.

110. Crawford, *Immigrant in St. Louis*, 44–45.

111. IHRC, St. Louis International Institute Papers, Box 6, 1932.

112. Yans-McLaughlin, *Family and Community; Federal Census for Metropolitan St. Louis*, 1930, Table 8, "Gainful Workers 10 Years of Age and Older, By Industry Groups and Sex"; 1900 Manuscript Census, St. Louis; Primm, *Lion of the Valley*, 463–64; Bernardy, "L'Emigrazione," 39; interview with Angelina Merlo, Aug. 6, 1975.

113. Crawford, *Immigrant in St. Louis*, 44–45; Schiavo, *Italians in Missouri*, 60.

114. Keating, "A Study of Americanization," 40–41; see also, *Report on the Statistics of Wages in Manufacturing Industries*, 1886, 44.

115. Crawford, *Immigrant in St. Louis*, 45–46.

116. Wood, "Fairmount Heights," 49–50.

117. Interviews with Sam Chinicci, Aug. 8, Oct. 27, Dec. 19, 1975.

118. Interview with Paul Berra, July 31, 1973.

119. Smith, "Immigrant Social Aspirations."

120. Briggs, *Italian Passage*, 274.

121. Stolarik, "Immigration, Education, and Social Mobility," 112.

122. Breton, "Institutional Completeness of Ethnic Communities."

123. Wirth, *Ghetto*, 241–44.

124. *Star-Times*, Apr. 3, 1936.

125. Serpieri, *La Guerra*, 114–15.

126. Covello, *Social Background*, 257.

127. Schiavo, *Italians in Missouri*, 159.

128. Crawford, *Challenge of St. Louis*, 56.

129. Ets, *Rosa*, 160, 174.

130. *Thirteenth Census of the U.S.: 1910*, 5123 Pattison Ave., St. Louis.

131. Interviews with Sam Chinicci, Aug. 8, Oct. 27, Dec. 19, 1975.

132. *Sixteenth Census of the U.S.: 1940. Population and Housing*, Table 2.

133. *Fifteenth Census of the U.S.: 1930. Special Report on Foreign-Born*, Table 26.

134. Interview with Carmelo Cacciatore, Aug. 7, 1975.

135. Crawford, *Challenge of St. Louis*, 21.

136. *Federated Census for Metropolitan St. Louis*, 1930, Table 11.

137. Interview with Roland DeGregorio, Aug. 18, 1973.

138. *Twelfth Census of the U.S.: 1900*, St. Louis, vol. 100; *Thirteenth Census of the U.S.: 1910*; Primm, *Lion of the Valley*, 358. In Buffalo 2 percent of Italian households owned their homes in 1900; Yans-McLaughlin, *Family and Community*, 175.

139. *Federated Census for Metropolitan St. Louis*, 1930, Table 10; Primm, *Lion of the Valley*, 473.

140. *Sixteenth Census of the U.S.: 1940. Population and Housing*, Table 5.

141. Rumbold, *Housing Conditions in St. Louis*, 7.

142. Bernardy, "Condizioni di Vita," 59–60.

143. *Sixteenth Census of the U.S.: 1940. Population and Housing*, Tables 5, 6; *Social Statistics of St. Louis by Census Tracts*, 10–28. Little Italy lay in the most densely populated district in St. Louis; in 1930 there were 1,956 persons per 100,000 sq. ft. living there, as opposed to only 425 persons per 100,000 sq. ft. on the Hill.

144. Ibid., Table 2, "Characteristics of Housing by Census Tracts."

145. *Federated Census for Metropolitan St. Louis*, 1930, Tables 10, 23.

146. *Sixteenth Census of the U.S.: 1940. Population and Housing*, Table 5.

147. *Federated Census for Metropolitan St. Louis*, 1930, Table 10. It is impossible to compare individual immigrant neighborhoods because only the Hill comprised a homogeneously ethnic community in St. Louis.

148. *Special Report on Foreign-Born White Families*, Table 20; *Federated Census for Metropolitan St. Louis*, 1930, Table 10.

149. Simon, "Housing and Services."

150. Letter from Elmer Shorb Wood to the author, Aug. 22, 1973; interview with Wood, May 17, 1984.

151. Interviews with Joe Garagiola, June 19, Sept. 8, 1984.

152. Williams, *South Italian Folkways*, 6.

153. Interview with Joe Palozzollo, July 14, 1972.

Top: An eighteenth-century customs house crumbling on the bank of the Ticino River near Boffalora, in Italy. Olmi's *The Tree of the Wooden Clog* was filmed along this watery highway. Photo by the author. *Bottom:* "America." 1880 Census, Archivo Comunale, Cuggiono.

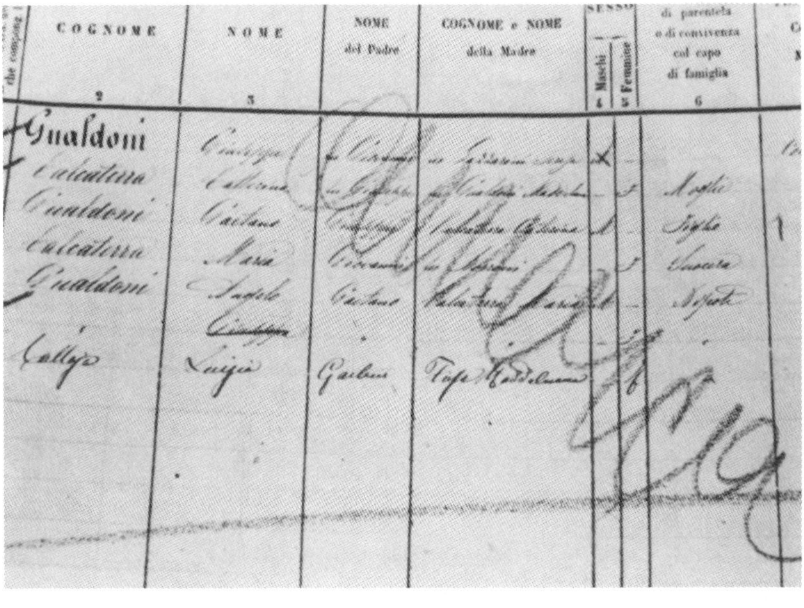

COGNOME 2	NOME 3	NOME del Padre	COGNOME e NOME della Madre	SESSO Maschi 4	Femmine 5	di parentela o di convivenza col capo di famiglia 6
Gualdoni	Giuseppe	Giovanni	[illegible]	×		
Calcaterra	Caterina	Giuseppe	Gualdoni [illegible]		[illegible]	Moglie
Gualdoni	Gaetano	Giuseppe	Calcaterra Caterina	[illegible]		Figlio
Calcaterra	Maria	Giovanni	[illegible]		[illegible]	Suocera
Gualdoni	Angelo	Gaetano	Calcaterra Maria	[illegible]		Nipote
[illegible]	Luigia	[illegible]	[illegible] Maddalena			

“He who crosses the ocean, buys his own house.” One of the first “shot-gun” homes on the Hill, ca. 1900. Archivo Comunale, Cuggiono.

Top: Lombard emigrants gather around the ubiquitous accordion, ca. 1900. Archivo Comunale, Cuggiono. *Bottom:* A 1901 portrait of the North Italy America Club, popularly known as "Big Club Hall." *St. Louis Post-Dispatch*, May 26, 1901.

Top: Beehive kilns, used in the manufacture of refractory brick, dot the industrial valley on the eve of World War II. Photo courtesy of the Lou Fuse family. *Bottom:* Italian and black miners probe the rich clay veins beneath the Hill. *St. Louis Globe-Democrat*, June 9, 1907.

ST. LOUIS STAR-TIMES

ROMANESQUE---A Bit of Sunny Italy on a Hill in St. Loui

LAUGHTER, WINE, SALAMI AND SPAGHETTI IN ABUNDANCE

Above, "Papa" Eugene Arpiani with a handful of Italian delicacies from his bakery. Right, John Volpi inspects his fine Italian sausage which has won him many a prize. Lower left, a lamplighter heralds the approaching night on "The Hill."

Self-reliant, opinionated, and indomitable, Regina Pozza was for decades a tavern keeper on the Hill. Photo courtesy of Geno Mariani.

Moonshine stills broken up by the police. *St. Louis Post-Dispatch*, ca. 1920s.

Father Peter Barabino, "The Flying Priest," with St. Ambrose students and sisters, ca. 1930. St. Ambrose Church Archives.

From a simple, wood-framed structure in 1902 to a splendrous replica of a Lombard Romanesque cathedral, St. Ambrose Church exemplifies the distance traveled by the Hill's inhabitants. St. Ambrose Church Archives.

Top: Louis Jean Gualdoni (behind the man with the placard) leads the St. Louis Twenty-fourth Ward faithful at the 1932 Democratic National Convention. *Bottom:* The Fairmount Democratic Soccer Club, 1926 state champions of the Municipal Soccer Leagues of Missouri. Gualdoni is third from the right, top row. Photos courtesy of the Louis Jean Gualdoni family.

Top: The St. Ambrose team, winner of the Parochial School Soccer League Championship in 1938, coached by Father Palumbo. Paul Berra, currently city treasurer, is in the center, top row; Joe Garagiola is in the center, third row. From an unknown newspaper clipping dated December 15, 1938, in the St. Ambrose Church Archives. *Right:* Hill residents Joe Garagiola and Yogi Berra meet at spring training, 1947. N.Y. *Daily News* Photo.

A *Post-Dispatch* photographer captures the moment in 1942 when seventy-nine-year-old Calogero Parino (*left*) explains to ninety-year-old Paolo Pedroli that the U.S. government no longer considers them "enemy aliens." Parino had lived in America since 1901; Pedroli immigrated to St. Louis in 1893.

The altar of St. Ambrose Church, ablaze with the martial spirit of World War II. The statue is of St. Sebastian, himself a soldier. Service flags are emblazoned with stars, sewn on by mothers whose sons are in the service. *St. Louis Star-Times*, 1943.

Top: The strains of war give way to demonstrations of relief as Hill patrons celebrate Italy's surrender in 1943. *Bottom:* V-E Day, 1945, sees sixteen Italian-American societies parade through the streets of the Hill. From undated clippings, *St. Louis Post-Dispatch.*

"The Italian Immigrants," by Rudolph Torrini, stands in front of St. Ambrose Church. Photo by Glenn S. Hensley, Missouri Historical Society.

Right: Tony Bossi, a tenor, croons to a Hill Day crowd, August 1973. Photo courtesy of Agino Mariani. *Bottom:* A quiet street on the Hill, 1975. Note the ornate terrazzo "fence." Photo by the author.

5 A Still on the Hill: Prohibition and Cottage Industry

Happy Days are here again
The skies above are clear again
We'll all have St. Louis Beer again
Happy Days are here again.

Jack Ryan, *Happy Days Are Here Again*

The setting is a dingy tenement in north St. Louis in the 1920s, still more than a memory for Tennessee Williams. A beleaguered Tom Wingfield stalks out of his apartment, leaving his crippled sister doomed to a life of loneliness amid her glass menagerie and a mother trapped in a dreamlit, lost civilization. "I'm going to the opium dens," Tom announces. "Yes, opium dens, dens of vice and criminals' hang-outs, Mother. I've joined the Hogan Gang. I'm a hired assassin. I carry a tommy gun in a violin case! I run a string of cathouses in the Valley! They call me Killer, Killer Wingfield. I'm leading a double life, a simple honest worker by day, by night a dynamic czar of the underground."[1]

Broadway and Hollywood hold a special place for that peculiarly American character, the gangster, a creature half admired and half feared. Along with jazz-era gin, gangland funerals, and G-Men, the scar-faced mobster has become a standard backdrop for the Roaring Twenties. A curious American public has been treated to an avalanche of literature dealing with organized crime, ranging from the officious Wickersham Report to the sensational Sunday confessionals.[2]

The voluminous literature dealing with urban crime in general and the phenomenon of the 1920s in particular suffers from tabloidism.[3] Too often such studies focus on the romantic, episodic careers of individuals while neglecting the broader dimensions of social history, or they concentrate on the experiences in particular cities—generally New York and Chicago—and then generalize about the whole country.[4] If, as scholars insist, to understand the Italian-American experience one must explore the contours of the neighborhood, then the study of urban crime has been written as if immigrants lived in a social vacuum. Inexplicably, Yans-McLaughlin, Briggs, and Cinel all ignore the phenomenon of Prohibition and the immigrant community. Aside from Humbert Nelli's *The Business of Crime* and John Kobler's biography of Al Capone, few scholars have addressed themselves to the problem of integrating ethnic crime and the neighborhood, the real world and the underworld.

Understandably, academics have ignored the topic of crime. First, much of the primary material is of dubious quality, inspired by nativist sentiments or tailored to mollify an enraged public. Second, underworld characters, unlike presidents or reform commissioners, seldom wrote letters or left their memoirs to local historical societies. If *mafiosi* did not kill reporters, neither did they converse with historians.[5] The reputed lord of the St. Louis Mafia, Anthony Giordano, told this author when an interview was humbly requested: "Hey son, if you know what's good for you, stick to your [expletive deleted] books!"[6] Don Giordano notwithstanding, most Italian-Americans expressed a surprising willingness to reminisce about Prohibition. Their recollections, supplemented by newspaper accounts and demographic data, provide a more realistic, if less violent and sensational, account of the relationship between the Eighteenth Amendment and an ethnic neighborhood.

THE NOBLE EXPERIMENT

To rural Missourians, St. Louis and Kansas City must have loomed as the modern Sodom and Gomorrah. While the state consistently voted dry, the two gateway cities staunchly opted wet.[7] St. Louis proudly flaunted the fact that 2,152 of the Show-Me State's 3,504 saloons were located within the city, which prompted a Missouri Central Baptist to call it "that beer-soaked and brewery-ridden den."[8] In 1890, sixteen million dollars worth of beer was manufactured in St. Louis. "Had I a son," swore the pious priestess of the WCTU, Helen Bullock, "I would rather see him bound to the rails before an approaching train than to see him at a bar of a St. Louis saloon."[9]

The temperance movement gathered strength during periods of social stress. Social scientists postulate that in periods of social flux, political reform becomes a means whereby traditional elites attempt to ensure status and social dominance. Thus the noble experiment, buffeted by winds of nativism, radicalism, labor unrest, and anxiety, was a device for imposing the rural-oriented, middle-class mores of waspish America on urban, lower-class European Catholics.[10] Speaking at the Tyler Place Presbyterian Church in 1901, a missionary expressed his anxieties. "They are strange to us," the speaker admitted, referring to the country's foreign-born. "The American saloon keeper is often the only human being with whom the immigrant comes into contact."[11]

The Eighteenth Amendment, for all the right or wrong reasons, became the law of the land in June 1919. "Prohibition is a kind of compulsion," sneered *La Lega*, a St. Louis Italian-American weekly, "a compulsion that differs only in form from that of the bayonet."[12] One of the most outspoken wets was the irascible Father Timothy Dempsey, the "Labor Priest" and minister to the working class. "The Prohibition—it's terrible, terrible," grumbled Father Tim from St. Patrick's parish near Little Italy. "It would a bin far better for the counthry if instead of the Pilgrim fathers landing on Plymouth Rock, Plymouth Rock had landed on the Pilgrim fathers. . . . There ushed to be a shaloon on every corner, but now there's a shtill in every cellar and a shpakeasy in ivry store. . . . Take Tony the Eyetalian. Tony got into trouble through shellin' his shtuff. . . ."[13]

Among the supreme ironies of the dry crusade was the monetary gain made by Italians, one of the very groups the zealots sought to protect from demon rum. While bootlegging was scarcely limited to practitioners with names ending in vowels, Italians certainly pursued the art with more zest than other contemporaries.[14] Moreover, Prohibition enabled some Italian-Americans to branch into other lucrative areas of organized crime, such as labor racketeering and narcotics. "It should be noted," observed Luciano Iorizzo, "that the Italians entered organized crime where it existed, such as in Chicago, but failed to establish large-scale underworld combines where they did not already thrive, such as in Oswego."[15] How does one explain this Italian gravitation toward bootlegging and the vastly different attitudes toward crime among ethnics in St. Louis and elsewhere in urban America?

BACKGROUNDS AND OPPORTUNITIES

Philosophically and culturally, both northern and southern Italians abhorred the puritanical restraints imposed by the Eighteenth Amendment. To hardworking immigrants the neighborhood saloon served as a social refuge, a place to which laborers gravitated after a long day's work to enjoy the friendship of *paesani*.[16] "The taverns on the Hill—and I've heard it said that there are almost a hundred of them—are strictly Italian," remembered Lawrence ("Yogi") Berra. "They're really more like neighborhood clubs than places of business. Take the one I've always hung out in since I got big enough, Grassi's. It's a plain place . . . and the fixtures haven't changed since old man Grassi opened it forty-two years ago [1919]. Rose, his daughter, says there are plenty of fancy cocktail lounges around, and they want their place to look like a real man's saloon. They even have a old-fashioned *bocce* alley in the backyard."[17]

The tavern served as the poor man's social center. In her 1911 visit to the Hill Amy Bernardy noted eighteen saloons, where "an incredible amount of beer is consumed." Each Sunday, she commented, Hill parishioners flocked to the Big Club Hall saloon to imbibe several kegs of beer and wine, a custom that brought the community to public attention since the practice violated the city's Lid Law.[18] In 1918, for example, Carlo Miriani, the manager of the North Italy Mercantile Company, was arrested for violating the city's Sunday Blue Law. Drinking on the Hill was not a social problem symptomatic of urban anomie; rather, it embraced social custom. "There wasn't a night those old timers didn't go to the corner tavern for a game of cards or bocce," remembered Mike Gioia. Alcoholism was nonexistent.[19]

Italian-Americans who enjoyed the camaraderie of the neighborhood pub also indulged in another old-world pastime: the fine art of distilling spirits. "See, the southern Italians had a knack, a knack for making moonshine," Roland DeGregorio explained. "They had an ancestral background on how to make different kinds of wine and turn the wines into hard liquor or mash."[20] "The Sicilians were from the little villages in the mountains," recalled an old-timer. "Shall we say that they were outside the law, that they didn't think too much of the law, even in the old country?"[21] When social mores collided with American law, especially something as repugnant as the Volstead Act, Italians were inclined to ignore the law. "You know how Prohibition was," responded Lou Berra, an elderly Lombard. "Everybody thought it was silly. If you made a few bucks selling booze—good for you!"[22]

Northern Italians shared with their southern brethren a contempt for the Volstead Act and an appreciation of the talent for transforming corn mash into hard whiskey. Rosa Cassettari recalled a story about her father, who worked in a Lombard factory that manufactured whiskey stills. "In that way," she explained, "he learned how whiskey was made and started to make it himself and sell it in the *osteria* [pub]." Since this activity was unlawful, Rosa's mother sought spiritual guidance from the village priest. "Don Domenic didn't scold," Rosa pointed out. "He said to watch out that she didn't get caught, that's all!"[23]

In St. Louis, priests such as Father Dempsey expressed their opinion of such lawlessness in different ways:

> Tony is an Eyetalian. What can you expect of an Eyetalian? What do they know about the law? Notin'. If they know a law and it doesn't suit 'em, it is no law to 'em. They are born that way. The only redaimin' feature of the Eyetalian is that the Pope is an Eyetalian. . . .
>
> I talked shtrong to the Prohibition agent. "Tony," I said, "has bin makin' that shtuff since infancy; it's like bakin' bread to 'im, and if he makes too much for himself and in the ginorosity of his heart lets his neighbors have som, kin ye arriest a man for ginorosity?" . . . Well, ye know I don't drink, but to protect me parishioner, I took a drink of the shtuff and the Prohibition agent took one. And then, to encourage and commend the Prohibition agent, I took another and he took another. . . . That Prohibition agent left me shtudy a better man than he had ever bin before.[24]

The height of church-congregation complicity occurred in January 1921 when St. Ambrose Church on the Hill burned to the ground. According to many elderly residents the fire began when a vat of moonshine exploded in the church rectory. Even if the story is apocryphal, the fact that so many people believe it is true authenticates the legend.

Moonshine found fertile soil in the labyrinthine cellars, garages, mines, and even churches of the Hill. Immigrants brought not only their family distilling secrets but a heritage of craftsmanship that aided the construction of elaborate stills. Coppersmiths, carpenters, and masons found a new outlet for their skills. Prohibition agents were dazzled by the maze of stills within the colony. "You know what they'd do?" asked a former revenue agent. "They'd take a basement and put cement all around it, make it leak-proof, and then they'd fill the basement up and put mash in it and ferment the mash in there. And then on the outside they'd have coils. Oh, they were something!"[25]

A successful bootlegging operation required many ingredients: raw materials, craftsmanship, brewing skills, and police protection. But these assets would have been wasted without the essential ingredient of cooperation among the residents. Not all Italian neighborhoods maintained harmony during Prohibition. In Oswego, New York, for example, fierce competition among bootleggers hindered the effectiveness of the operations. "Everyone that bootlegged or made liquor was too stupid to realize this [syndication]," remarked one immigrant from Oswego. "If they did organize . . . the profits would have been ten times greater."[26] Chicago Italians, by contrast, produced prodigious amounts of alcohol, not entirely because of neighborhood solidarity but rather because of the strong-arm tactics of the Genna brothers, Al Capone, and the syndicate.[27]

One might suspect that Prohibition intensified the schism between Hill Lombards and Sicilians, since the latter gained more notoriety in the moonshine trade. Ironically, Prohibition functioned as a strange matchmaker, bringing together Lombards and Sicilians in a symbiotic relationship. The Eighteenth Amendment, coming at a time when old-world antagonisms were eroding, actually strengthened ethnic relations, since bootlegging necessitated cooperation between the two factions, in the guise of *omertà* (silence), *onore* (honor), and *furberia* (cleverness). Moreover, the indiscriminate, nativist attacks against the colony helped solidify Italians. Profits also helped to dissolve regional rivalries. While Sicilians monopolized the actual manufacture of the product, Lombards participated in other phases. "There was a lot of money made on the Hill in them days," remarked Joe Correnti. "A lot of money. Sicilians would make the hooch and the Lombards who owned restaurants and taverns would retail it!"[28] Isidore Oldani, Jr., confirmed this relationship. "Yes, I think us Lombards were more in the retail line than manufacturing," he recollected.[29] Cinel observed in San Francisco that northern Italians succeeded in farming because agriculture "required cooperation and marketing skills that the individualistic Southerners were unlikely to possess."[30] The Prohibition era in St. Louis calls this generalization into question.

Insular and homogenous, secretive and protective, the Hill offered a haven for bootleggers. The social worker Elmer Shorb Wood confessed that he personally knew of "several hundred families, both Lombard and Sicilian," who participated in the various stages of bootlegging. Wood recalled the embarrassment of arriving at his office in the St. Louis Provident Association and noticing several boxes of wine and whiskey on his desk, a less than discreet thank-you from his Hill clients. "I'll tell you one thing," he remembered, "there was a big alcohol trade in those days." He added, "The men were employed part of the time each week at the brickyards" and at night they engaged in a branch of bootlegging activity. "Some hauled sugar, others had teams and dug cellars for stills or hauled equipment from place to place." Wood estimated that "about ninety percent of the men were engaged in some phase of it during prosperous times (1920–30)."[31] Moonshine served as both a cause and an effect of the ethnic rapprochement of the 1920s. "The Hill had equal opportunity moonshine," quipped Joe Garagiola. "Everybody made it."[32]

Prohibition functioned as an important agent of the 1920s neighborhood economy. Community grocers supplied the necessary raw materials: sugar, cornmeal, and yeast; businessmen bankrolled operations and loaned warehouse space; saloon keepers and soft drink vendors provided a ready outlet for the finished product; and St. Louis policemen conveniently looked the other way during business hours. "Oh, we Italians were shrewd," laughed Gino Mariani. The elderly immigrant gleefully recalled the story of a famous Hill bootlegger who brought such tremendous quantities of chicken feed from Ralston Purina that the firm invited the entrepreneur to an agronomy lecture on advanced methods of pullet production. Another grocer, he reminisced, was nicknamed the "Sugar Baroness" because she convinced suppliers that the tons of sugar she ordered each month were used to make candy.[33]

Isidore Oldani, Jr., vividly remembers his Lombard-born father assisting errant neighbors who seemed always one step ahead of the authorities. The elder Oldani, who was president of the St. Ambrose Church Building Committee, operated the Blue Ridge Soda Company, an establishment given an unexpected boost by the Volstead Act. "Whenever there was going to be a problem, a raid," Oldani recalled, "friends would warn us, and without asking, they would store their supplies in our garage and basement. I don't think the Hill knew of a lock then. It was nothing for us to come home from work and find our garage full of sugar or a basement with thirty, forty cans of moonshine."[34]

Bootleg whiskey required a commercial outlet, and on the Hill the neighborhood tavern admirably served the role. The saloon had been an important institution for the Italian immigrant before the Eighteenth Amendment. Socially it served as an oasis for the working man; economically it was one of the few enterprises in which an immigrant brickmaker with a few hundred dollars could invest and become a white-collar proprietor. Mound City brewers provided the major financial backing for the saloon keeper, paying the rent, license fee, and bond, and supplying the fixtures and beer, while the owner paid an initial fee ($200 in 1915) and agreed to sell only the brewer's beer and return a rebate.[35] "Every corner that didn't have a grocery store had a tavern," recollected Lino Gambaro.[36] Lombards dominated the Hill saloon trade before and after 1919. *Gould's*

Red-Blue Book, 1918 lists sixteen drinking establishments on the Hill, fourteen operated by Lombards. A glance at naturalization records during the period 1906–36 reveals thirty-eight Hill saloon keepers, all but two of whom were Lombards. How had Prohibition affected such individuals? Had reformers succeeded in the elimination of the saloon?

The Eighteenth Amendment wrought disaster on the St. Louis brewers, and along with the beer barons thousands of local saloons were forced to close shop. According to government documents Hill publicans experienced similar downward mobility because of the economic dislocation of Prohibition. Paolo Battista, for example, had just opened a saloon in 1918, but by 1921 he was working as a cook.[37] The fortunes of Paolo Garavaglia reflected the vicissitudes of the age. In 1911 the Lombard was employed as a bartender, graduating to saloon keeper by 1916; then in 1921 he changed the establishment's fare from draft beer to ice cream, in effect becoming a confectioner.[38] Seemingly, Prohibition devastated, or at least redirected, the small businesses on the hill.

An obvious credibility gap exists between the occupational information gleaned from government citizenship papers and oral histories, however. The latter indicate that many taverns continued to dispense whiskey and cheer through the guise of a soft drink parlor or candy store. The case of Cesare Regna typifies this delicate transition. Born in Lombardy, Regna labored at the brickyards until he had saved enough money to purchase a small saloon in 1917. Quicker than one could say "Volstead Act," Regna discreetly rearranged the fixtures to resemble a respectable soft drink parlor, all the while quietly serving adult customers in the rear of the store.[39] Another Lombard, Frank ("Papa Prost") Gianella, candidly admitted opening his first tavern in 1921, an unconventional year to enter the saloon business. In 1975 his establishment still retained a touch of Prohibition mystique by continuing to sell the nickel grab bags for children in the back room. "Only [back] then," the engaging taverner laughed, "we used to sell hooch in the back!" Mrs. Gianella coyly interrupted the conversation to remark, "You see, sometimes you have to cheat a bit to get along!"[40] By 1931 seventeen soft drink parlors and eighteen confectioneries operated on the Hill.[41] Before Prohibition there had been only a handful of such establishments.

The "noble experiment" thus brought about well-rehearsed socioeconomic patterns: Sicilians working part-time at the brickyards and full-time in their copper-coiled basements; Lombards exercising their mercantile talents as versatile confectioners; outsiders who had never visited the Hill frequenting the ever-popular soft drink parlors; and policemen showing a newfound interest in the welfare of ethnic businessmen. "The Hill was full of stills and it was nothing unusual to see a cop on the beat carrying a sack of sugar to a still," reminisced an elderly Lombard. "We used to load these vats down in the basement. To load the vats you had to have a truckload of sugar. The people in on it—those who had shares in it—they'd get together with the police and load the sugar and work it into the mash."[42]

St. Louis's finest were clearly on the take. "I remember the bagman," sneered Robert DeMattei. "They didn't give a damn about you making moonshine as long as they got their gravy, that's all."[43] St. Louis firemen also benefited in the trickle-down economy. "I'll tell you something personal. *Real* personal," hushed Roland DeGregorio.

> My father was connected with the biggest whiskey-making group that there was here. On the Hill. I was probably in the fourth grade and he told me, "Don't let no kids in this house!" So what did I do? I let a couple of kids in . . . they got in the shed and turned on the spigot and started drinkin' the moonshine. Ohhh, they got plowed. In fact, they got sick . . . the mother of one of the kids called the fire department. They came down and pumped the kid out. My dad, I remember he told me in later life that it cost him two five-gallon cans as a hush. Now you talk about moonshine—I know![44]

If the Hill claimed no *paesani* on the city's police or fire forces, it nurtured clout in an even more strategic area, the Internal Revenue Service. In the history of the Hill Jean Gualdoni ranks as one of the giants, the man who put the neighborhood on the political map. Few of the younger generation realize that Gualdoni, early in his career, worked as a Prohibition agent. In 1920 the twenty-seven-year-old Gualdoni was appointed to the Internal Revenue Service, Division of Alcohol and Firearms. "You know, it's a funny thing," the nonagenarian reminisced in 1982. "I'd go out on a job with a search warrant, and the first thing you know, I'd run across one of my friends operating a still. What could I do?"[45] Others candidly answered the question for Gualdoni. "Ohhh, Jean was on the revenue squad," smiled Lou Berra, "and on occasion he'd get notice that there's a raid coming on and he'd tell the bootleggers to be careful."[46] Gualdoni resigned from the department in August 1923, when he refused a transfer to Minneapolis.[47] For the Hill it was a landmark decision, since Gualdoni then began to collect his favors and embarked on a most remarkable political career. For bootleggers the decision was not as fortunate, since the community's watchdog now monitored votes rather than stills.

Revenue raids were so frequent in the 1920s that they became a social occasion on the Hill. Residents generally act bewildered when asked whether they remembered the police raids. "On the Hill! On the Hill!" an incredulous Joe Correnti laughed.[48] "Every Saturday night a still was raided," reminisced Les Garanzini, adding righteously, "mostly Sicilian."[49] The colony held the dubious distinction of harboring one of the first stills raided in the city (Nov. 1919), as well as claiming the first residents prosecuted for the manufacture of illicit whiskey.[50] "God, I must have seen at least a hundred stills busted," sighed Sam Chinicci.[51] "You know what I remember most?" asked the popular barber, Charles Rancilio. "When the agents busted a still, the residue slop flowed into the gutters. Chickens would eat the mash and weave away drunk after the meal!"[52]

Eliot Ness protégés, after years of ferreting out bootleggers, discovered an unfailing pattern—only Sicilians manned the illicit distilleries. "One day the federal men came down Wilson Avenue and were raiding homes," recalled Roland DeGregorio, the son of Sicilian immigrants. "Now they would go to the door. If the person talked in Lombard, they wouldn't bother going in. But if they talked Sicilian, they would raid the house, go in and find a still. That day, 5200 Wilson, our gutters were full of moonshine! So by the time they get to the Consolino's, my mother came out and started talking in Lombard to them. She says, 'Come on in; ohh, got a lot of stuff I want you to see.' They didn't come in and little did they know that the biggest still on the block was there."[53]

Other Sicilians demonstrated neither the linguistic talent nor the good fortune of Mrs. DeGregorio. Headlines such as "5000 Gallons of Alcohol Seized by U.S. Agents in Southside Garage," and "Dry Raids Here Trap Men of Alien Names," were commonplace.[54] In December 1921 agents interrupted the operations of a massive still at 5225 Bischoff, seizing 5,000 gallons of alcohol and the still itself, which produced 125 gallons per day.[55] One of the biggest busts in St. Louis history occurred in 1925 when revenue officials surprised a small group of Sicilians on the Hill. Agents confiscated 40,000 gallons of white lightning plus a prodigious unit capable of delivering 250 gallons a day.[56]

If Sicilians familiarized themselves with revenue agents, Lombards acquired an unsavory reputation among judges who prosecuted liquor violators. This proved particularly evident when Italian immigrants attempted to acquire citizenship in the 1920s. During that decade thirty-three Lombards and twenty-five Sicilians from the Hill were denied citizenship, the majority for "liquor violations" and "bad moral character."[57] For example, a judge vilified Giuseppe Zola as "a man unfit for citizenship because of bad moral character," since the Lombard had trafficked moonshine from his Hill candy store.[58] From the city dockets and front pages St. Louisans stamped Italians with the mark of lawlessness.[59]

In April 1927, for instance, Judge William Farris complained to the press that over 50 percent of the bootleggers on his docket were Italians. Claudio Delitalia, editor of the weekly *La Stampa Italiana*, answered the judge with this slightly sarcastic riposte: "I regret that since the enactment of prohibition, Judge Farris has found it necessary to familiarize himself with the pronunciation of Italian names. But I find reason to rejoice in the fact that despite the innumerable holdups that occur in our great city, we are very seldom confronted with an Italian name. Perhaps they are too busy violating the Volstead Act? Remember, every bootlegger must necessarily have a good number of customers to carry on successfully in his business."[60]

LITTLE ITALY

Judicial and editorial barbs stung mildly when compared to the penalties imposed by interlopers and warring factions. Spiralling profits (in 1920 alcohol sold for seventy-five dollars a gallon) and the growing number of stills (Nelli estimates that sixty-three million gallons of moonshine were manufactured in 1929) attracted the attention not only of judges and revenue agents but also of organized crime.[61] These entrepreneurs eliminated their rivals with a ruthlessness that would have embarrassed John D. Rockefeller. Tragically, a half-dozen moonshine-related murders occurred on the Hill during the 1920s, a record that paled compared to the unremitting gang wars in Little Italy during that period.

Internecine violence was scarcely new to the Hill or to Little Italy. The Black Hand, an amorphous band of extortionists, plagued Italian colonies from the turn of the century to the First World War.[62] Black Hand artists relied on fear and extortion, and the numerous bombings and killings reinforced Sicilians' fears of the dread *Mano Nera*. The Hill received its share of night callers. During one period, 1910–12, six murders were attributed to the reign of the Black Hand. "Dago Hill has become known in the police department as one of the bloodiest sections in the city," wrote a *Star* reporter following a 1911 bombing that left two dead.[63]

The stiletto and time-bomb of the Black Hand era were replaced by the sawed-off shotgun and Thompson submachine gun of the Roaring Twenties. On the night of February 22, 1922, the slaying of Sal Patti sensationalized St. Louis. Gun-wielding mobsters mowed down Patti outside his Hill home. A familiar name in bootlegging circles, Patti had bailed many colleagues out of jail.[64] Eight months later Patti's close friend John Coco, a Sicilian, was ambushed at the wheel of his Chandler roadster. According to police Coco was a "promoter," setting up *paesani* to run the stills and supplying the necessary supplies. He had been arrested in the first raid on the Hill in 1919.[65]

One of the most gruesome murders in St. Louis history occurred on the Hill in September 1923. Angelo Pastori, a Lombard immigrant, worked as a cook at Garavelli's Restaurant. Pastori, according to crime reporter Harry Brundidge, was approached by a group of Italian toughs and told to purchase meat from a preferred organization. The Lombard unwisely refused their offer. Returning home one evening, Pastori encountered two men as he walked across the Kingshighway viaduct. "Don't kill me," he pleaded as the thugs drove a dagger into his heart and pummeled him with baseball bats. Screaming in anguish he was then hurled over the viaduct onto the concrete pavement in front of Sala's Restaurant. The grisly episode qualified for Reid's *The Grim Reapers*.[66]

In the fall of 1930 residents noticed that each afternoon two outsiders pulled up to Oldani's Grocery and went into the establishment. Unbeknownst to the men, they had been spied on for months by unidentified men across the street. On the afternoon of November 21, 1930, Lester Barth and Dewey Goebbel, laden with bread and pasta, entered their flashy roadster and pulled away from the grocery. From a passing car came a fusillade of bullets, killing the two men. "In volume of fire, the attack on the gangsters has probably never been equalled in St. Louis history," an awed reporter wrote, viewing the battle scene. Barth and Goebbel were no ordinary tourists. Using underworld sources reporters speculated that the men were to have met a Sicilian bootlegger who had agreed to pay them $1,000 in protection money. Instead, the bootlegger had daringly invested his funds in hitmen. Six months later Mike Oldani, the Lombard grocer the slain men had visited daily, was shot while in his store.[67]

A distinctive pattern emerged from the violence of 1920–30. First, none of the murderers were ever brought to trial. Italians continued to obey the ancient law of *omertà*, that of complete silence. Second, there is strong evidence that the motivation as well as the muscle behind the killing originated in Little Italy, not on the Hill. John Coco and Sal Patti had refused to rebate part of their bootlegging profits to the Green Ones, a downtown Italian gang.[68] Similarly, Angelo Pastori had ignored demands from the same organization that he purchase meat from a preferred Sicilian firm. His murder served as a grim warning to other recalcitrant butchers.[69] Lester Barth and Dewey Goebbel were victims of a gang war between downtown rivals, the Green Ones and the Cuckoos.[70]

THE LINEUP

"St. Louis gangsters do not depend on printers' ink for advertising," observed a *Post-Dispatch* editorialist, "they say it with guns! There may be, and probably are, gangs in other cities but it is doubtful if anywhere in the civilized world the gang has reached the perfection of organization and has been as long-lived and tenacious as here in St. Louis . . . a dynasty. Gangdom, like the system at the other end of the social scale, has its 'first families'."[71] At the onset of Prohibition in 1919 four "families" jockeyed for power in St. Louis. The Hill lay on the periphery of this urban struggle, just as the community lay on the edge of the city. The most publicized organizations in 1919 were not Italian but Irish-American factions: Egan's Rats and the "Jellyroll" Hogan Gang. Both were archetypal of the gangster-politician symbiosis. William ("Constable") Egan had inherited the leadership of the gang from his brother Tom, whose saloon in the "Bloody Fourth" Ward housed a famous political center. Since the turn of the century Egan's Rats had battled the Hogan Gang for control of the city's vice interests.[72]

Prohibition intensified the friction between the two gangs. On Halloween night, 1921, William Egan was machine-gunned to death in front of a saloon at 1400 Franklin Avenue.[73] Leadership passed to the irascible William ("Dinty") Colbeck, who proceeded to declare war on the opposition. A truce brought about by Father Timothy Dempsey was short-lived and failed to stem the bloodletting. By April 1923 sixteen henchmen lay dead and the leaders of both factions had been expunged, imprisoned, or retired. "Jellyroll" Hogan, narrowly escaping assassination on several occasions, retired to the calmer world of Missouri politics, where he became a four-term state senator. "Dinty" Colbeck was dispatched to prison courtesy of a plea-bargaining aide. The colorful Irishman spent sixteen years behind bars, then in 1943 East St. Louis police discovered his bullet-ridden body outside a gambling dive. Ray Renard, Colbeck's Valachi, wisely left St. Louis for Hollywood, where he became a technical advisor for grade B gangster movies.[74]

The fate of Little Italy had been set in motion in 1910 when three youths left Palermo, Sicily. James Cipolla, Vito Giannola, and Alfonso Palazzollo were junior members of the *Stoppaglieri* faction (derived from the Sicilian word for "bottle stopper," meaning a youthful gang member). The triumvirate belonged to the class known as "the Green Ones," or "Green Onions," a phrase used to describe one faction on the feud-torn island. These young men were disenchanted with their criminal life-style, however, for as junior *mafiosi* they received only a slight share of the money they obtained from robbery and extortion; the chieftains of Palermo commanded the lion's share of the plunder. Vito told his friends that a *paesano* in St. Louis, Missouri, U.S.A., had written him about the golden opportunities available there to ambitious men such as themselves. *Mafiosi*, like *contadini*, were infected by the America fever. To finance their journey the trio held up a wealthy Palermo theater owner.[75]

Once in St. Louis, Palazzollo, Giannola, and Cipolla displayed a similar talent for extortion. Under the leadership of Cipolla the Green Ones terrorized merchants and small businessmen in Little Italy and occasionally on the Hill. The gang retained their name, the Green Onion faction, since Cipolla's name translates as "green onion." Prohibition opened new vistas for the organization, and they recruited new members to manufacture alcohol and collect protection money from Italians who dared bootleg without their seal of approval.

The tremendous profits reaped by bootlegging brought the Green Ones into deadly competition with their archrivals, the Cuckoos. Interestingly, the Italian factions never clashed with the city's Irish-American gangs, despite the close physical proximity. Their styles clearly differed. Whereas the Green Ones were headquartered at Little Italy's Santa Fara Club, the Cuckoos met at Russo's gas station; the Green Onions recruited only foreign-born Sicilians, while the Cuckoos comprised a mixed bag of Sicilians, southern Italians, and Irish-Americans. Even the choice of weaponry reflected cultural differences: the Green Ones preferred the effectiveness of the sawed-off shotgun; the Cuckoos perfected the tommy gun.[76]

The staccato roar of shotguns and machine guns left Italian blood on the streets of Little Italy, St. Louis County, and the Illinois east side. The murder of Cipolla in December 1921 triggered the first of many gang wars.[77] The *Globe-Democrat* headline of January 2, 1924, somberly told the story of the conflict: "Twenty-five Murders Remain Unsolved: St. Louis Gang Feud Took Heavy Toll During Past Year."[78] "Sometimes I can declare the truce of God between the gunmen," lamented Father Dempsey, "but in these bad Prohibition days, the truce is generally short."[79]

Within earshot of St. Patrick's Church in Little Italy gangsters blasted away at one another. The slaying of Cuckoo chieftain Tony Russo touched off the worst violence. The Cuckoos, losing their battle with the Green Ones, intervened in the "War of Sicilian Succession," a struggle among Chicago's first families of crime. According to Harry Brundidge, who claimed to have befriended gang members, Al Capone's rival Joseph Aiello offered to assist the Cuckoos. The price? Capone must be assassinated. Thus inspired, Tony Russo and his first lieutenant, Vincenzo Spicuzza, left for the Windy City to personally execute Capone.[80] John Kobler writes that Russo and Spicuzza were "free lance, out-of-town torpedoes," after $50,000 in cash promised by Aiello.[81] Whatever the motivation, both Russo and Spicuzza were found tommy-gunned to death, a nickel clutched in each hand, the signature of Jack McGurn. Capone sardonically sent $10,000 worth of flowers to the men's joint funeral. A reporter at the funeral observed a flashily dressed Italian youth who, walking away from the spectacular affair, turned to a friend and said, "That was a swell funeral them torpedoes got! Wonder what will happen next?"[82]

A bloodbath followed. On the night of September 9, 1927, Alphonse Palazzollo was lounging in front of a tombstone shop in the heart of Little Italy when four gunmen sprayed him with bullets, the signature of the Cuckoos.[83] In a three-month period following Palazzollo's murder ten other gang members were killed, and the warfare continued throughout 1928. The *Star-Times* observed in June 1928, "The slaying of two men last night in the home of Charles Spicuzza in the Sicilian gang feud reveals that a new chieftain has stepped into the leadership of the Green Ones, a gang of gunmen and extortionists which was all powerful until many of its members were slain by its enemies. One of the slain men was Dom Cataldi, known in the Italian quarter as the 'Sugar Man' because of his deals in that commodity and other bootlegger's supplies."[84]

The gang war became so fierce in the late 1920s that Archbishop John J.

Glennon forbade the granting of last rites to slain gangsters. However, families of fallen gunmen were known to persuade Father Dempsey to perform the services despite the archbishop's orders. "The next time I saw the archbishop he shook his long finger at me and said, 'Father Tim, don't do it again!' 'Why should I do it again?' Father Tim cracked. 'The poor boy was buried!'"[85]

By the early 1930s the gunsmoke had cleared. The gang warfare subsided for a number of reasons. First, the sheer volume of murders exacted a terrible toll on both organizations. During the period 1919–32 approximately sixty killings were attributed to the bootlegging wars. Second, Prohibition ended in 1933, removing a lucrative source of income from organized crime. Third, according to crime reporters Ted Link and Ed Reid, the most powerful members of the St. Louis Mafia left the Gateway City in the 1920s for Detroit, where Canadian liquor and racketeering offered greater opportunities. Peter Licavoli, the reputed head of Detroit's underworld and one-time member of the Purple Gang, had been born in St. Louis and earned his spurs with the Green Ones.[86]

THE BENEFITS OF PROHIBITION

Urban crime generated a myriad of opportunities which groups approached in different ways. Gangsters from Little Italy sought to maximize illicit profits and took their fight beyond the downtown colony. The inhabitants of the Hill, however, demonstrated less ambition and preferred the safety of their sheltered enclave. How does one explain these two very different attitudes toward crime in general and Prohibition in particular?

The Cuckoos and Green Ones were comprised for the most part of Sicilians whose parents had been born in the western and central provinces of the island, the traditional breeding grounds of the Mafia. By contrast, Sicilians on the Hill came from Augusta and Catania on the eastern coast of the island. In a report prepared for the 1876 Italian Parliament, Leopoldo Franscetti described eastern Sicily as "the tranquil provinces where it is possible to go around the countryside without fear of being killed or blackmailed."[87] But organized crime reflected more than geography and old-world traditions. As social scientists have pointed out, far more important to the makeup of organized crime was the environment of the host society.[88]

John Landesco contended in his acclaimed *Organized Crime in Chi-*

cago that the causes of criminal behavior lay rooted in the social organization and pressures of urban life, not in the individual ethnic traits of immigrant groups. His assertion that "the gangster is a product of his surroundings in the same way in which the good citizen is a product of his environment" was an intellectual breakthrough for criminologists.[89] Subsequent works, such as Clifford Shaw and Henry McKay's *Juvenile Delinquency and Urban Areas*, have reinforced Landesco's findings, pointing out that inner-city neighborhoods composed of recently arrived immigrants often experienced high delinquency rates, and high crime rates characterized each successive wave of new migrants.

Organized crime flourished in America long before the arrival of Italian immigrants. The late nineteenth- and early twentieth-century city, wrote Mark Haller in a seminal article, provided ambitious young men from the ghettos with many careers. Most immigrants spent their lives as "poor working stiffs." However, cities such as Chicago offered jobs in urban machine politics, labor unions, sports, the entertainment industry, and the organized underworld.[90] Chicago may not have been an equal opportunity employer, but it displayed an ingenious talent for inventive capitalism.

Italian immigrants on the Hill in 1919 faced diminishing opportunities: the community boasted few voters and certainly no political machine; few immigrants displayed any interest in sports; workers had attempted and failed to build a union base; and the entertainment industry consisted of some working-class saloons. Bootlegging became a sensible economic alternative. Moonshining, however, never provided the larger economic and social base that Haller and others have detailed—such as prostitution, nightclubs, and numbers—because the Hill was never part of that urban matrix. By the end of Prohibition in 1933 the community had created powerful political and social organizations in which to involve their children and invest their energies.

Environment played a tremendous role in the evolution of ethnic crime in St. Louis. On the Hill, the illegal foray into bootlegging radiated a civilizing influence; seemingly, the entire neighborhood participated in the venture in some way. The internecine violence, so prevalent in Little Italy, rarely happened on the Hill, for Little Italy was a far different urban creature. If the Hill was rooted, immobile, and homogeneous, Little Italy was rootless, mobile, and heterogeneous.

Crime offered a convenient, often alluring, avenue for upwardly mobile immigrants. Nelli observed that "many youngsters early realized that in the highly competitive, rootless society in which they lived, achievements measured in financial terms had high value, while the methods used to realize success received little attention or condemnation."[91] To young Italian-Americans running liquor for the Green Ones seemed more romantic and promising than peddling artichokes. Moreover, Italian mobsters were respected, even revered men in the community—witness the gala funeral of Tony Russo.

Prohibition meant handsome profits to the adventurous. The Genna brothers collected $350,000 every month from neighborhood stills in Chicago alone.[92] No one will ever know how many millions were realized from the illegal traffic, but the sum was surely staggering. Few studies, however, have examined the economic impact of Prohibition on the ethnic neighborhood. To the Hill, bootlegging served as an economic lifesaver. "I saw the first quart of alcohol sold on the Hill," exclaimed Sam Chinicci. "Twenty dollars! Then they started to expand! The product of alcohol became immense!"[93] Alky cooking became a cottage industry. In 1927 a quart of white lightning retailed for ten to fifteen dollars. Given the awesome size of some distilling units, many producing 250 gallons a day, bootlegging was a more profitable enterprise. But by 1930 profits had dropped dramatically because of oversupply, declining prices, and, according to Elmer Shorb Wood, "the increasing amounts which it was necessary to pay the law-enforcing officials for protection."[94]

Unlike Chicago or New York, the manufacture of domestic moonshine on the Hill was not dictated by an omnipresent Capone or Genna. It was conducted in a less competitive, less violent atmosphere: profit balanced by a sense of community and a dose of moderation. A former St. Louis chief of detectives stated in 1963 that the biggest problem with law enforcement on the Hill in the 1920s was not the residents but outsiders who attempted to interfere in the colony.[95] Almost every social index reported that the Hill was one of the healthiest and safest districts in St. Louis.[96] Hill Italians preferred to make a little money and stay healthy rather than compete with the Green Ones. Isidore Oldani, Jr., recalled an example of this discretion: "Once my dad ventured in with five other people into the moonshine business. They tried it . . . cooked it, and when it was ready for sale some red-hots from downtown came in and took it away from them. Dad didn't have the muscle or will, so that was that."[97] Few Hill Italians took the risks or paid the price to become *pezzenovante* (big shots). They perceived Prohibition not as an escape from their ethnic ghetto but rather as a means to uplift the neighborhood. Moonshine meant the difference between poverty and middle class.

Social scientists have pointed out the dramatic changes in the Hill community between 1919 and 1933. "The physical character of the district was the first change," Wood observed in 1935. "Small brick bungalows were built. Later, larger and more modern homes were erected along the edge of the settlement. Laborers, who always had walked to and from employment in the brickyards, now purchased automobiles. Clothes, the very latest and most classy, were bought regardless of price. . . . furniture dealers prospered equally well with their business colleagues, for seldom do you enter a home that you do not find expensive, overstuffed living room fixtures."[98] The social worker then cited one case where a young man employed as an orderly at a local hospital made many times his weekly pay selling liquor to the doctors and nurses. In fact, he so prospered that he bought a new home and his family (there were six children) took an extended trip to Italy. As one index of Prohibition prosperity, consider that fully 29 percent of the homes built in the neighborhood during the period 1900–1950 were constructed in the 1920s, as opposed to only 19 percent of the structures in metropolitan St. Louis.[99] Hill bootleggers, like their ethnic counterparts in Chicago, were also philanthropic. Wood speculated that some of the profits may have been directed toward "the erection of a quarter of a million dollar church, on which there is now only a debt of $12,000 [1935]."[100]

Daniel Bell, in a provocative assessment of ethnic crime, argues that each minority group has resorted to illegal tactics in its collective climb up the American socioeconomic ladder. Crime is as American as apple pie, he asserts, because criminals seek the same middle-class values that their host society pursues: a new home in suburbia, an affluent life-style.[101] Humbert Nelli similarly contends that second-generation Italian-American gangsters were assimilated into the American business ethos: "Part of their adjustment to American values became an effort to apply certain big business practices—such as efficiency, specialization and monopoly through the elimination of competitors—to the conduct of criminal activity."[102] Mark Haller writes, "Through organized crime, many members of those ethnic groups could achieve mobility out of the ethnic ghettoes and into the social world of crime, politics, ethnic business, sports, and entertainment."[103] These generalizations are inappropriate to describe the behavior of the Hill. Prohibition allowed the colony to acquire the trappings of the middle class, but it did not alter the value structure. Few local bootleggers paid the price for bigness and efficiency. No Mafia tyrannized the inhabitants. Prohibition infused money into the neighborhood economy; it did not take people out of the community. "Only a few [bootleggers] moved away from the Hill," observed a 1930s commentator.[104]

NOTES

1. Tennessee Williams, *The Glass Menagerie*, act 3, sc. 2.

2. U.S. Congress, *Enforcement of Prohibition Laws: Records of the National Commission on Law Enforcement*, House Document 722, 71st Cong., 3d Sess., 1931, 1–84.

3. See Colburn and Pozzetta, "Crime and Ethnic Minorities."

4. Nelli, *The Business of Crime*, ix.

5. An interesting exception to this rule is a book by the criminologist Francis Ianni, *Black Mafia*. The field research was conducted by blacks and Puerto Ricans who interviewed underworld figures.

6. Interview (of sorts!) with Anthony Giordano, July 2, 1973.

7. Renner, "Prohibition Comes to Missouri."

8. *Star*, Mar. 24, 1917, p. 2; *The Way and Word of the Central Baptists*, Nov. 6, 1916.

9. *Post-Dispatch*, Mar. 20, 1901, p. 1.

10. See Hofstadter, *Age of Reform;* Gusfield, *Symbolic Crusade;* Sinclair, *Prohibition.*

11. *Globe-Democrat*, Jan. 22, 1912, p. 4.

12. *La Lega*, Dec. 17, 1918, p. 1.

13. Interview, Fr. Timothy Dempsey with George Johns, n.d.

14. Southern and eastern European immigrants were well skilled in the fine art of bootlegging. In Wood River, Illinois, an industrial suburb of St. Louis inhabited by various ethnic groups, the most frequent violators of the Volstead Act were Croatians and Serbians rather than Sicilians. *Wood River Journal*, 1920–25; interview with Lou Cavic, a long-time resident of Wood River, July 3, 1973.

15. Iorizzo and Mondello, "Origins of Italian-American Criminality," 231.

16. Kingsdale, "'Poor Man's' Club"; Haller, "Organized Crime in Urban Society"; Suttles, *Social Order of the Slum.*

17. Berra and Fitzgerald, *Yogi*, 50.

18. Bernardy, "Sulle condizioni," 19; *Post-Dispatch*, Dec. 18, 1917, p. 1.

19. Naturalization petition, Carlo Miriani, 1917, 1918; interview with Mike Gioia, June 3, 1975.

20. Interview with Roland DeGregorio, Aug. 18, 1975.
21. Interviewee preferred anonymity.
22. Interview with Lou Berra, July 11, 1973.
23. Ets, *Rosa*, 24.
24. Interview, Fr. Timothy Dempsey with George Johns, n.d.
25. Interviews with Louis Jean Gualdoni, Aug. 13, 1973, July 30, 1982.
26. Quoted in McBride, "Prohibition in Oswego, New York," 62.
27. Kobler, *Capone*, 87–92.
28. Interview with Joe Correnti, Apr. 30, 1976.
29. Interview with Isidore Oldani, Jr., Sept. 10, 1973.
30. Cinel, *From Italy to San Francisco*, 151.
31. Letter from Elmer Shorb Wood to the author, Aug. 22, 1973; interview with Wood, May 17, 1984.
32. Interview with Joe Garagiola, Sept. 8, 1984.
33. Interview with Gino Mariani, Aug. 2, 1973.
34. Interview with Isidore Oldani, Jr., Sept. 10, 1973.
35. *Post-Dispatch*, Aug. 1, 1920, p. 1; Kingsdale, "'Poor Man's' Club," 272–92.
36. Interview with Lino Gambaro, Aug. 29, 1973.
37. Naturalization petition, Paolo Battista, 1921.
38. Naturalization petition, Paolo Garavaglia, 1921.
39. Naturalization petition, Cesare Regna, 1921. The subject, incidentally, was denied citizenship because of several liquor violations. The surname used here is a pseudonym, at the request of the family.
40. Interview with Frank and Rose Gianella, Aug. 1, 1975.
41. *St. Louis Italian Business Directory, 1931*. The stereotype of the candy store fronting as a speakeasy was widely circulated. See Wilson, "Ice Cream Joints," 63–66.
42. Interview with Lou Berra, July 11, 1973.
43. Interview with Robert DeMatti, Aug. 6, 1975.
44. Interview with Roland DeGregorio, Aug. 18, 1973.
45. Interviews with Louis Jean Gualdoni, Aug. 13, 1973, July 30, 1982.
46. Interview with Lou Berra, July 11, 1973.
47. Undated newspaper clippings, Gualdoni papers, in the possession of Louis Jean Gualdoni.
48. Interview with Joe Correnti, Apr. 30, 1976.
49. Interview with Les Garanzini, Aug. 7, 1975.
50. *Post-Dispatch*, Oct. 22, 1920, p. 1; *Globe-Democrat*, Nov. 9, 1919, p. 1.
51. Interview with Sam Chinicci, Oct. 27, 1975.
52. Interview with Charles Rancilio, June 28, 1973.
53. Interview with Roland DeGregorio, Aug. 18, 1973.
54. *Globe-Democrat*, Apr. 8, 1925, p. 2; *Star*, July 29, 1920, p. 1.

55. *Star*, Dec. 10, 1921, p. 8.

56. *Globe-Democrat*, Apr. 27, 1925, p. 1.

57. Naturalization petitions, 1919–30.

58. Naturalization petition, Giuseppe Zola, 1925. The name has been changed at the request of the family.

59. *Star*, Jan. 26, 1921, p. 1, July 19, 1920, p. 3, May 3, 1924, p. 8, Dec. 27, 1921, p. 1; *Post-Dispatch*, May 17, 1924, p. 1.

60. *Post-Dispatch*, Apr. 28, 1927, p. 24; see also the autobiography of another prominent judge, Dyer, *Autobiography of Reminiscences*, 271; *Globe-Democrat*, Apr. 30, 1924, II, p. 1.

61. Nelli, *Business of Crime*, 159.

62. Nelli, *Italians in Chicago*, 124–50; Nelli, *Business of Crime*, 75–110.

63. *Star*, Aug. 11, 1911, p. 1. For other Black Hand stories see *Globe-Democrat*, Jan. 22, 1912, p. 1, Oct. 20, 1911, p. 1, March 6, 1908, p. 1, Aug. 12, 1911, p. 2; *Post-Dispatch*, June 23, 1911, II, p. 1, May 5, 1907, magazine, June 12, 1915, p. 1, Jan. 27, 1911, p. 1; *Republic*, July 22, 1906, IV, p. 1.

64. *Globe-Democrat*, Feb. 3, 1922, p. 1.

65. *Post-Dispatch*, Oct. 6, 1922, p. 1; *Star-Times*, Oct. 5, 1922, p. 1; *Star*, July 29, 1920, p. 1.

66. *Post-Dispatch*, Sept. 17, 1923, p. 1; *Star-Times*, Sept. 17, 1923, p. 2. Reid, *Grim Reapers*, 73–74.

67. *Post-Dispatch*, Nov. 22, 1930, p. 1; *Star-Times*, Nov. 22, 1930, p. 1. *Post-Dispatch*, June 25, 1931, p. 1.

68. *Globe-Democrat*, Feb. 3, 1922.

69. *Star-Times*, Sept. 17, 1923; Reid, *Grim Reapers*, 73–74.

70. *Post-Dispatch*, Nov. 22, 1930, p. 1.

71. Ibid., Mar. 2, 1924, p. 12.

72. Ibid., Aug. 16, 1963.

73. Ibid., Nov. 1, 1921, p. 1.

74. Ibid., Aug. 16, 1963.

75. Brundidge, "Black Hand," 1. This was the first of a series of articles dealing with organized crime in St. Louis. Brundidge, a reliable reporter, claimed to have interviewed many of the participants.

76. *Post-Dispatch*, Aug. 18, 1963; *Star-Times*, Nov. 21, 1927, p. 1.

77. *Star-Times*, Dec. 29, 1921, p. 1; *Post-Dispatch*, Dec. 29, 1921, p. 1.

78. *Globe-Democrat*, Jan. 2, 1924, p. 1.

79. Interview, Fr. Timothy Dempsey with George Johns, n.d.

80. *Star-Times*, Aug. 9, 1916, p. 1.

81. Kobler, *Capone*, 205.

82. *Star-Times*, Aug. 16, 1927, p. 4.

83. *Post-Dispatch*, Sept. 10, 1927, p. 1.

84. *Star-Times*, June 20, 1928, p. 1.

85. Interview, Fr. Timothy Dempsey with George Johns, n.d.

86. Reid, *Grim Reapers*, 294; *Post-Dispatch*, Apr. 25, 1956; Walsh, "Detroit Hoods," 1.

87. Franchetti, *La Sicilia nel 1876*, 125.

88. Nelli, *Business of Crime*, 138.

89. Landesco, *Organized Crime in Chicago*, 123.

90. Haller, "Organized Crime," 210–33.

91. Nelli, *Italians of Chicago*, 144.

92. Kobler, *Capone*, 90.

93. Interviews with Sam Chinicci, Aug. 8, Oct. 27, Dec. 19, 1975.

94. Wood, "Fairmount Heights," 24–25. Wood writes that he based his information on "several years of listening to casual conversations in the community."

95. *Globe-Democrat*, June 23, 1963.

96. *Social Statistics of St. Louis by Census Tracts, 1930.*

97. Interview with Isidore Oldani, Jr., Sept. 10, 1973.

98. Wood, "Fairmount Heights," 23.

99. *Seventeenth Census of the U.S.: 1950. Census Tract Statistics of St. Louis*, Table 3.

100. Wood, "Fairmount Heights," 25.

101. Bell, *End of Ideology*.

102. Nelli, *Business of Crime*, 139.

103. Haller, "Organized Crime," 228.

104. Wood, "Fairmount Heights," 25.

6 The Church

Like people, like priest.
Hos. 4:9

The setting envelopes an industrial neighborhood of St. Louis in the early 1930s. Each home in the compact ethnic community shines; well-scrubbed and freshly painted exteriors are festooned with gaily colored red, white, and green banners. Brass bands trumpet the celebration of Saint Sebastian's Day. Hundreds of young girls in First Communion dresses lead the long procession through the winding streets of the Hill. The resplendent statue of San Sebastiano, laden with dollar bills, commands the scene. Situated on the reviewing stand, or more accurately seated on three chairs near the entrance of St. Ambrose Church, is the Irish triumvirate of Archbishop John J. Glennon, Monsignor Timothy Dempsey, and Father James Johnston. As the procession enters the portals of St. Ambrose, the husky crew carrying the statue miscalculates the clearance and the alabaster head of San Sebastiano unceremoniously bounces down the steps. The Hibernian prelates gasp in horror. The jocular Monsignor Dempsey finally quips, "How stupid. If it had been Saint Patrick, he would have ducked!"[1]

The comic event strikingly capsulizes the difficulties inherent in interpreting the Catholic church in urban America. However apocryphal, the episode might be seen as a clash between self-righteous, overzealous Irish Catholics and unassimilable, pagan Italians. In reality the Irishmen—intimate guests and old friends of the Italian community—had graciously agreed to preside at the *festa* as an expression of their deep feelings for fellow Catholics. Given the cultural predilections of the Gaelic trio, it is not inconceivable to imagine that the evening ended in the church rectory, with the gathered faithful savoring ravioli and Dago Red.

The fraternal interchange on the Hill contrasts sharply with the cacophony in the American Catholic church. Few American institutions underwent such tumult and confronted such awesome and unprecedented problems. A bewildering variety of ethnic groups left the Old World to reemerge as strangers in the new land with only religious affiliation in common. Largely composed of illiterate peasant stock, this new influx pressed the startled and unprepared Irish-German hierarchy for secular and spiritual relief. The American Catholic church had skyrocketed from 650,000 members in 1840 to more than 12 million constituents in 1910. In 1860 New York City numbered thirty-two parishes; by 1910 sixty Italian parishes alone had been established![2]

The sheer breadth and immensity of the immigrant church stands unchallenged, though historians register less certainty when evaluating the efficacy of the Catholic church in assisting Italians in this milieu. An earlier generation of scholars praised the church as the great Americanizer, a forceful agent of democracy;[3] revisionists have challenged not only the conclusions but the assumptions as well. Italian peasants, contended Rudolph Vecoli, the most strident revisionist critic, brought to America a distrust of the Church of Rome fueled by centuries of neglect and corruption. In America the predominant Irish clergy overtly browbeat and covertly despised the "folk Catholicism of the Italian immigrant."[4] Those few Italian priests who accompanied their flocks across the ocean could expect indifference, contempt, and even physical violence—especially among northern Italians, whom Vecoli summarized as "extremely anticlerical."[5] "Not a few left Italy," suggested Vecoli, "because of some indiscretion or scandal."[6] In sum, according to the revisionists Italian immigrants proved to be poor church builders and troublesome churchgoers in America.

The St. Louis religious experience amplified the debate between supporters and critics of the Catholic church. Italians participated on a variety of levels in the church, and their successes and failures must be evaluated within the dynamics of time and place. Their behavior demonstrated the difficulty in generalizing about the diverse religious patterns of three million Italian immigrants. To clarify the debate, historians must sharpen their focus on what Richard Niebuhr has called "the foundational unit of American denominations," the local parish.[7] From this perspective congregations are deemed a more important source than archbishops, parish archives more revealing than nativist ravings, and forces within the immigrant colony more significant in shaping ethnic identity than those outside.[8]

THE GENOAN EXPERIMENT, 1880–1900

Beginning in the period after the Civil War, several hundred Genoans settled in St. Louis and quickly found success at the vegetable and fruit stalls of Produce Row. These Genoans wished to salute their successes with an Italian church. Their demands produced results when, in 1868, Father Muhlsiepen—"the Apostle of the Germans" and vicar-general of the city's foreign-born—assisted them in the creation of an Italian parish. Guided by the Black Franciscans, the church was dedicated under the appellation of Saint Bonaventure.[9]

The Italian parish foundered and closed in 1883. A number of factors contributed to the demise of St. Bonaventure: the church was located several blocks from the Italian enclave, which itself was in a state of flux; a mixed congregation of Germans, Poles, and Italians made strange churchfellows; an undercurrent of hostility agitated the Genoan parishioners and Irish-German clergy; and finally, the very successes achieved by the Genoans removed their families from the inner city to the more affluent midtown.[10] St. Bonaventure, like hundreds of big-city churches, was left to newer immigrants.

By 1890 the nature and composition of the city's Italian population had changed dramatically, but not so the attitude of church leaders. In 1889 Scalabrinian priests—a brotherhood that ministered to Italian immigrants—attempted to establish an Italian mission in St. Louis, but they were rebuffed by Archbishop Peter Kenrick. "It seems the Archbishop was very old and had had many bad experiences with the Italians," wrote the Scalabrinian Francesco Zaboglio. "When I began talk about the Italians, he literally shut himself in silence. The subject was dropped."[11]

The Italian problem was rekindled by Pietro Bulfamante, known as the "Sicilian Lay Brother," in 1896. "An emergency situation" existed in St. Louis, wrote Bulfamante in a letter to the Missionaries of Saint Charles Borromeo.[12] In Hammontown, New Jersey, Father Cesare Spigardi alerted the Scalabrinians of the problem. "At St. Louis there are 18,000 Italians left by themselves because they have no mission," Spigardi declared.[13] The Scalabrinian order dispatched Father Giacomo Gambera to St. Louis in 1896, but he too failed to persuade the church hierarchy of the need for an Italian mission. Archbishop Kain reprimanded the priest, pointing out that the Jesuits provided adequate spiritual nourishment to the Italians.[14] In 1899 Father Beccherini reported, "In St. Louis there are 18,000 Italians totally abandoned. The Archbishop has Mass celebrated for them in the basement of three American churches, where some American priest says some words in Italian, and everything stops there."[15]

In December 1899 Cesare Spigardi arrived to battle the church hierarchy. A remarkable cleric, he succeeded where others had failed. On the threshold of a brilliant tenure in St. Louis, Father Spigardi galvanized the Italians by a combination of talent, charm, and timing.

CESARE SPIGARDI, THE ITALIAN PRIEST

The son of Angela and Pietro Spigardi, Cesare was born at Pomponesco, in the province of Mantua, on August 31, 1859. As a young boy he had hoped to become a tailor but was persuaded to enter the diocesan school of Cremona. During the next quarter-century the young student came under the tutelage of some extraordinary teachers in his native Lombardy.

A region rich in ecclesiastical tradition, Lombardy was steeped in the legends of Saints Ambrose and Charles Borromeo of Milan. At the historic towns of Como, Cremona, Piacenza, and Mantua, Spigardi was guided by his mentors, Bishops Bonomelli and Scalabrini, and later by Cardinal Sarto, who would become Pope Pius X. Spigardi possessed a special feeling for his native Lombardy, a relationship shared by Bishop Scalabrini, who wrote, "Among my parishioners, I had hundreds of silkworkers, weavers. . . . I was able to see firsthand the miserable conditions under which the people worked. . . ."[16]

After his ordination in 1884 Father Spigardi served the industrial workers of Casalbuttano, where he helped erect a hospital for the poor. During the bitter winter of 1890 he observed Bishop Sarto auctioning church relics to feed the poor. He never forgot those memories, even when he was elevated to monsignor in 1894, a title he ignored, once remarking, "My people would be afraid to come to me were I decked out in purple."[17] Like millions of his countrymen the new monsignor chose to cast his fortune in America. On January 7, 1895, he set sail for New

York; among his companions in steerage were Lombards from Cuggiono. After five years of missionary work in parts of New Jersey and in Boston, Philadelphia, and Kansas City, Cesare Spigardi was reunited with his *paesani* in December 1899 in St. Louis.

The St. Louis milieu must have daunted even this energetic priest. Italians in the city were geographically, culturally, and economically fragmented. The spur of St. Bonaventure still rankled with Catholic officials, and no Italian parish was in sight. Father Spigardi, soon dubbed "the Italian Priest," arranged an interview with a reporter from the *Republic* in April 1900. "I built one [a church] in Kansas City, where there are not more than 2,000 Italians," he emphasized. "There are more than 10,000 Italians in this city, 6,000 of whom cannot speak English. I mean to try and lift them above their squalid surroundings and give them a church. . . . I will establish a school where the young of those poor Italians may be educated. We have many Catholic churches here, true, but they are attended by well-dressed peoples, and the poor Italians who have no fine feathers with which to bedeck themselves do not care to mingle with them."[18]

The indomitable monsignor quickly brought his pledge to fruition. By the end of the first year Our Lady of Hopes (soon to be renamed St. Charles Borromeo) had been dedicated. Located in midtown St. Louis at Nineteenth and Morgan, Our Lady of Hopes served the Genoans and more affluent Italians. In 1902 he purchased an abandoned church, which was refurbished and dedicated to Our Lady Help of Christians. Located at Tenth and Wash, it served the Sicilians of Little Italy.[19]

Time has since ravaged the Italian priest's early legacies. After his death in 1931 St. Charles Borromeo fell into disuse. Today the church is surrounded by a ghetto, and except for a plaque dedicated to Cesare Spigardi there is nothing to indicate the presence of an Italian congregation. The fate of Our Lady Help of Christians has been more final. That church served two generations of Sicilians, but after World War II, the parish and colony inherited insoluble problems. White flight, a burgeoning black population, deteriorating housing, and rising land values spelled the end for Little Italy and her parish. In 1975 Our Lady Help of Christians was demolished, and four years later Father Edward Filipiak, its revered pastor, was killed in the rectory at the nearby Shrine of St. Joseph.

The heinous crime against Edward Filipiak shocked St. Louisans. Nowhere were cries of injustice heard louder than at St. Ambrose, the third church constructed by Cesare Spigardi. Many of the religious relics from the downtown church were salvaged by Hill Italians, who seemed to realize that history had been kinder to their own Italian colony. Father Filipiak's brutal murder and the desecration of a church were inconceivable on the Hill, in no small part because of the awesome presence and influence of Father Spigardi's greatest legacy, St. Ambrose.

SANT' AMBROGIO, THE FORMATIVE YEARS, 1903–21

In 1902 Lombards had lived on the Hill some twenty years, but still the colony lacked a church. When the spirit yearned—and that seemed infrequently—Italians walked six blocks to St. Aloysius for religious sustenance. Fathers Holweck and Long ministered to a predominantly German congregation, but they agreed to preach for their Italian neighbors as well. Italians grumbled over their second-class treatment, a feeling reciprocated by Father John Long, who in the 1930s remarked to a young divinity student that Italians came to church three times in their lives: for baptism, marriage, and burial.[20]

Spearheaded by Cesare Spigardi's vigorous leadership the Hill constructed a modest, wood-framed church in 1903 on the corner of Cooper and Wilson avenues.[21] Dedicated to the first bishop of Milan and a champion of Lombardy, Sant' Ambrogio (St. Ambrose) symbolized the emerging community. The 1903 St. Ambrose paled in comparison to its twelfth-century namesake in Milan, but the structure signaled a beginning for Hill Italians. "The Church," reported the *Globe-Democrat*, "is a new frame structure . . . built at a cost of $10,000. The building and nearly all the houses in the neighborhood were tastefully decorated with the National and Papal colors. . . ."[22] Members of the North Italy American Club and Anita Garibaldi Society, 700 strong, welcomed Archbishop John Glennon and Father Spigardi to the Hill.[23]

From its inception St. Ambrose lacked the status of a separate parish; rather, it functioned as a missionary station for the first few years. A shortage of Italian priests and a lack of housing on the Hill forced Father Spigardi to direct operations from his headquarters at St. Charles Borromeo. Each Saturday he and/or his assistants traveled to the colony to hear confessions; then, after preaching two Masses and Catechism on

Sundays they returned to their home parish. This arrangement lasted until 1905, when Father Luciano Carotti was appointed resident pastor at St. Ambrose; the church was recognized as a separate Italian parish in 1907.[24]

Born in Cremona, Lombardy, in 1865, Luciano Carotti took his religious vows in 1897, two years after his *paesano* and mentor Cesare Spigardi left for America. Choosing the life of a Capuchin missionary, Father Carotti labored among the poor of Lombardy before setting sail for America in 1903, where he worked with New York City Italians prior to joining Father Spigardi in St. Louis in May 1905.[25] He lived austerely, having pledged himself to a life of poverty, and once on the hardscrabble Hill his life-style did not materially improve. He had not only inherited a new church but a host of problems as well.

The disruptive ethnic bickering between the churlish Lombards and Sicilians threatened the future of the colony in general and St. Ambrose in particular. In the first decades of the century the Milanese commanded every advantage, both in and out of the church. Numerically, northern Italians outnumbered southern Italians; economically, Lombards were more successful as small businessmen than were Sicilians; and organizationally, the North Italy America Club was far better equipped to compete in an urban society than the regionally divided Sicilian mutual aid societies. Spiritually, Fathers Spigardi and Carotti were kindred Lombards. The very naming of St. Ambrose underscored privilege. New-world conditions, coupled with old-world animosities toward organized religion, caused Sicilians to back away from religious involvement on the Hill. The suspicion that St. Ambrose was a tool of northern Italians, and resentment that church fathers were Lombards first and men of God second, enjoyed widespread popularity among southern Italians. "Well," snorted one Sicilian, "the Lombards used to say that the church was *theirs!* Sometimes I would say 'I'm going to *the* church' because if you said *our* church, they'd resent it!"[26] A social worker wrote, "Remarks are made, especially by Sicilians, that as long as you contribute to the church, you are a welcome member. The women are not so outspoken. . . ."[27]

Religious events such as the *feste* precipitated group conflict rather than harmony from 1903 through the 1920s. When Cuggionesi honored their patron saint, Our Lady of Mount Carmine, Sicilians either ignored the event altogether or mocked the procession. Similarly, Lombards gasped at what they considered irreverent pageantry when Sicilians flaunted their patroness, Santa Rosalia. "It was at the *festa*," noted an observer, "that friction between folk from other villages reached the fever point."[28]

St. Louis social workers sneered at the ethnic bickering and the organizational efforts of St. Ambrose. They found local clerical leadership "second rate." In 1915 reformers surveyed the neighborhood in hopes of establishing a settlement house. The colony, according to one staff member, "was overripe for such work."[29] Louis F. Bedenz, a settlement house worker, discussed the matter with Father Carotti, who initially seemed pleased with the project. But Bedenz cautioned reformers about approaching the Italian priest: "We cannot count on him too much, however, not because of any unwillingness on his part, but because he has no conception of how to proceed in organized work."[30] The settlement house was stillborn. Father Carotti felt the Italian immigrants were not ready for a settlement house and, even more serious, that reformers would impose their middle-class values on the colony.

Critics who doubted the priest's organizational abilities also questioned his talents for fiscal management. If financial solvency served as a yardstick by which to measure parish success, Father Carotti was not a likely candidate for clerical elevation. There were seats for only 500 in the church. Even with three Sunday Masses, fewer than one-fifth of the community attended services. The faithful who did attend Mass regularly were either unable or unwilling to support the church financially. In 1916, for example, the congregation donated a total of $1,009.20, a decrease from the 1909 offerings of $1,903.10. Only picnics and raffles saved the mortgage. More dollars were collected through bazaars than through the collection plate.[31] Hill Italians, like their brethren elsewhere, were notoriously poor contributors to the church coffers during the era 1900–1920.[32]

On the evening of January 19, 1921, huddled in the tiny rectory of St. Ambrose, fifty-six-year-old Luciano Carotti fired the antiquated stove, which some still believe was a moonshine still. The stove overheated and the wood-framed church turned tinderbox and burned to the ground. The ominous firebell tolled a haunting question: Was St. Ambrose worth rebuilding? In January 1921, when a northern Italian dared not marry a southern Italian, would a Sicilian help a Lombard rebuild what the Sicilian considered an irrelevant church? Ironically, the very night the flames of St. Ambrose scorched the neighborhood, the editor of *La Lega Italiana* criticized the ethnic bickering that plagued the Hill. "The spirit of *campanilismo* that reigns among Italians on the Hill is deplorable," thundered the ethnic weekly, which was located in Little Italy. "If a Sicilian comes up with an idea, then the northerner will reject it. This disunity and discord is our ruin and we ought to combat it."[33]

The very future of St. Ambrose and the colony hung in a delicate balance between ethnic tension and institutional development. The key to the success of both the community and the church lay not in the hands of quarrelsome Italians but rather in those of second-generation Italian-Americans. If St. Ambrose was to be rebuilt, would the new chapel be frequented only by elderly immigrants clutching their old-world rosaries and new-world disappointments? Or even worse, would the parish be surrendered to the newest wave of urban dwellers—the young Italian-Americans who were swiftly assimilating into mainstream America?

TO BUILD A CHURCH: OLD WINE IN NEW BOTTLES

The small German church on Shaw Avenue where Hill Italians assembled after the fire seemed cold and naked compared to the comforting confines of St. Ambrose. Gone were the familiar statues of San Sebastiano, Santa Rosalia, La Madonna del Carmine, and Santa Teresa. Father Carotti stepped to the pulpit and somberly announced, "Last Thursday, January 20th, 1921, the Lord wished to try our Faith and good will." Thus he began the sermon of his life: "He permitted that our parish church, our Mother Sant' Ambrogio Church, should be destroyed by fire. It was His will, and therefore we as humble servants must say, 'Thy will be done.' However, it is necessary that we unite with one strong determination to erect a new church!"[34] He went on to trace a brief history of the Hill, its evolution from a mining camp to a prosperous colony. If it could progress from a collection of wooden shacks to row after row of well-kept bungalows, might not the parish "erect a new church, this time not of wood, but of bricks?"[35] To realize this dream organization and cooperation would be imperative. The first step in the unfolding drama was taken by the priest. "Whatever be your status," he exhorted, "rich man, laborer, businessman or property owner, Tuesday and Wednesday evenings, January 26th and 27th at 8:00 P.M., we shall hold a grand reunion at the club house at 5200 Shaw Avenue to discuss matters regarding a new church. A special committee will be established. Help your desolate Mother Church, St. Ambrose!"[36]

Big Club Hall, previously an exclusive Lombard haunt, opened its doors to the greater colony for discussion of the future church. Father Carotti, fully cognizant of the historic ethnic tensions, maximized the rivalries to the church's advantage. The St. Ambrose Building Committee reflected this new-sought ethnic balance. Isidoro Oldani, born in Lombardy in 1881, was elected president of the committee; since his arrival on the Hill in 1902 he had been a leading force in community affairs.[37] A Sicilian, Calogero Mugavero, was elected vice-president; he had settled on the Hill in the early 1890s, becoming one of the first southern Italians to be accepted by the Lombard majority.[38] The position of secretary went to Giovanni Gioia, a prosperous businessman–saloon keeper who had left Cuggiono in 1886 to join a handful of pioneers on *la Montagna.*[39] Ignazio Riggio, called "the King of the Sicilians," was elected treasurer. "Save Luciano Carotti," wrote Giovanni Schiavo in *The Italians in Missouri*, "no individual commanded more respect in the community than Riggio."[40] The St. Ambrose Building Committee was fortified by an ethnic balance necessary to ensure colonywide success. The four men, two Sicilians and two Lombards, pillars of the community, each articulated the potential benefits of unity. It was now the task of the committee to channel Hill dollars and energies into a new church building.

The challenge to create and build with distinction captivated the community's imagination. The Vincenzo Bellini Dramatic Club, disbanded since the First World War, reorganized purposely to aid the new church. In 1921 a rival theatrical troupe, composed of recent immigrants, was persuaded to consolidate with the older society so as to strengthen their collective efforts.[41] Elsewhere an army of volunteers canvassed the neighborhood to solicit funds for the cause. Each family was asked to pledge sixty dollars, a dollar a month for five years (not an easy task for a laborer who earned only twenty-five cents an hour in 1920).[42]

It was plain to even the most unabashed booster that St. Ambrose faced a Herculean struggle. In February 1921 the parish still owed $13,082 on the original church.[43] How could an immigrant community, one of the poorest in St. Louis, fulfill the dream that planners were dreaming? Yet barely had the ashes cooled from that January fire when architect Angelo Corrubia swaggered through the portals of Big Club Hall, his arms laden with stacks of drawings feverishly sketched at the request of his intimate friends, Fathers Spigardi and Carotti. The new edifice, as envisioned by the renowned architect, would not only bear the name of Sant' Ambrogio but would also embody the style of that historic Milan church. As Corrubia drew back the curtain revealing the long graceful arches and beautiful basilica of the new St. Ambrose, many could only mutter, "*Dio Mio!*"

If the new church required financial sacrifices it also exacted human charges. "Your beloved pastor, Fr. Carotti will soon undertake a trip to Italy to regain his health," a stunned congregation was told in June 1922.[44] The crisis threatened to paralyze the movement. Luciano Carotti had been the "Pioneer Priest," the embodiment of St. Ambrose for twenty years. But in April 1923 he was succeeded by a man who would equally earn his epithet, the "Brick and Mortar Priest."[45]

Father Julius Giovannini, at six feet tall and two hundred and fifty pounds, was a giant of a man both physically and spiritually. For him, the road to St. Louis had been a tortuous one. Born in the Piedmont of northern Italy in 1873, at age eighteen he entered the Seminary of Mondovi. Twice his studies were interrupted by military service; first in the war with Abyssinia and then in the Milan riots of 1898. In 1900 he was finally consecrated in the Society of Francis de Sales. After six years of missionary work in Lombardy and Piedmont the Salesian missionary departed for America where he ministered to the Italians of New York and New Jersey. In 1914 he was called to assist Cesare Spigardi in St. Louis, where he served in Little Italy until his calling in 1923.[46] The sagacious Father Spigardi had selected the right man for the job. Soon after his arrival the self-assured Giovannini boldly promised parishioners that with their cooperation he would erase the existing debt, break new ground, and complete the building of the new church, all within three years' time.

The "Brick and Mortar Priest" modernized the church administration but in the process angered some individuals by his scorn for tradition. In January 1925 he instituted the controversial monthly envelope system, ostensibly to streamline the treasury but also to allow an intimate look into congregational pocketbooks. Occasionally St. Ambrose Church published a directory, which listed to the penny the annual amount donated by each parishioner. Even more unpopular, especially among the Sicilians, was Father Giovannini's usurpation of the *feste*. Since the inception of St. Ambrose, groups outside the church had organized the feast days, celebrations that raised huge sums of money. The daring priest's gambit now transferred control to the church, a strategy that nearly produced catastrophic results.

On the evening of October 16, 1925, Father Giovannini received a rather unusual visit. Angered by his power play, three Sicilian immigrants threatened his life if the policy were not changed. Clearly shaken, the man of the cloth wrote a last will, scribbling that the *banditi* had given him fifteen days to leave town or pay the consequences. "I forgive them for their insane act," he wrote, "and I thank them for the opportunity to let me die as a martyr. . . ." He then pledged all his earthly assets to St. Ambrose.[47] The drama spilled onto the altar of the church. "One Sunday morning," remembered seventy-year-old Carolina Borghi, "he [Giovannini] got up on the [pulpit] and said, 'Well, I'm ready. If anyone wants to kill me, they got their chance now!' Finally he said that carrying a saint out of the church is more or less mockery. . . . If you want to make a donation, you should do it in church and help the church."[48]

The unscathed priest, perceptively recognizing the potential of the colony's young people, quickly tapped into their resourcefulness, a move that coincided with the efforts of Joe Causino of the YMCA and Louis Jean Gualdoni of the Fairmount Democratic Club to harness this vast reservoir of raw energy. Father Giovannini boldly asked the young to sacrifice a much-prized dime a week for the crusade, and to further the movement he encouraged them to peddle bricks to generate still more money and zeal. "I remember the priests used to give us a pile of bricks and we'd go out and sell 'em," chuckled Mike Gioia.[49] The Italian cleric's unbounded faith in the younger generation was vindicated. In 1925 they invited him to a mass meeting where they presented him with $500—in dimes![50]

While adolescents hawked red-clay bricks for pennies, their parents contributed in an equally innovative and meaningful fashion. Like the citizenry of France during the construction of Chartres, or in the spirit of a frontier American barn raising, Hill Italians scaled the scaffolds of St. Ambrose to assist in the work. "Every member of the parish felt it his duty to offer assistance towards the advancement of this noble work. Some men donated not one day but several."[51] While the men laid bricks the women spent many hours at the flouring board, rolling ravioli for countless benefit suppers. "Everybody worked hard for the church," remembered Carolina Borghi. "We women cooked, donated prizes."[52]

Throughout 1925 and 1926 the walls of St. Ambrose, fired from the local clay that burned to an enchanting red brick, dwarfed the tiny neighborhood homes. "When you see a big structure like that going up," exulted Mike Gioia, "it lightens you up. Our parents never took us anywhere, so it was really something!"[53] The sight of such a monumental undertaking was dizzying, a physical realization of the quantum leap emigrants had made from their hovels in Lombardy and Sicily. In their seasonal migrations up the alluvial plain of the Po and the Adige, many had made a special pilgrimage to the magnificent cathedrals of northern Italy, such as Santa Maria Maggiore at Como and San Petronio at Bologna. The Church of Sant' Ambrogio, where kings and German emperors were lionized with the Iron Crown of Lombardy, was considered one of the jewels of Romanesque architecture. A part of twelfth-century Italy was brought across the ocean with the 1926 completion of St. Ambrose in St. Louis, a stunning example of the transference of culture. From their majestic belfries housing the parish bells to their richly carved interiors, which prepare the visitor for the great bays of rib vaults, the two churches are remarkably similar.[54] St. Ambrose on the Hill deviates in one characteristic exception: its ceiling is studded with thousands of silver stars—like the tomb of Galla Placidia in Ravenna—another idea by the master fundraiser Julius Giovannini. Bishop Charles Koester, marveled, "Giovannini sold the stars in the ceiling. He even sold the bricks . . . anything!"[55]

As masons capped the last Hill-fired terra-cotta tiles on the roof, St. Ambrose Church presented a stunning profile. But Father Giovannini was worried that the interior might not be embellished in the same grand style. The diplomatic priest dipped into the wellspring of creativity to solve the problem. He gleefully announced that the community's voluntary associations would be responsible for the interior furnishings. Deftly he had pitted the colony's social clubs against each other. Proud Cuggionesi could never tolerate Augustini providing a more generous setting for their patron saint. A new race had begun; once again the conversion of ethnic rivalry into ethnic creativity had become the leitmotif.

The financing of the church bells also illustrated the competitive nature of the community. The faithful of Cuggiono subscribed a bell to La Madonna del Carmine, matched by those of Inveruno who dedicated their chimes to Santa Teresa. The patrons of Marcallo enshrined their bell to San Nazario, while the loyalists of Casteltermini (Sicily) honored San Vincenzo Ferreri.[56] Contributions to enhance old-world saints and new-world associations poured in from other sources. Sicilians from Catania dedicated the altar to their patron saint, San Sebastiano, a figure who would acquire ominous significance during the dark days of World War II. Sicilians from Augusta insisted that their saint, the Archangel San Michele, be prominently housed in the new church. The altarpieces of San Luigi and Sant' Agnese were conferred by societies of their namesakes. The workingmen of the colony dedicated a statue to St. Joseph.

St. Ambrose Church was, above all, a rare monument to St. Louis's disparate Italian population. The stamp of Italian-American creativity and accomplishment could be seen in every phase of the grand project, from the architectural design to the artistic frescoes; from the mining of the clay to the making of the bricks that graced the structure. The architect, Angelo Corrubia, a graduate of the Massachusetts Institute of Technology, was regarded as one of the finest designers in St. Louis.[57] The brickwork and terra-cotta adorning St. Ambrose was the work of the Rallo-Brugnone Construction Company. A Sicilian emigrant, Calogero Rallo had nearly starved during the depression of 1908, reduced to shelling pecans at a downtown sweatshop. By the 1920s his firm was one of the leading construction companies in the city and would grow to become one of the largest in the Midwest.[58] The skilled marble and tile work was performed by the Venetian Mosaic Company, while the scagliola columns were the responsibility of R. Paolinelli. The Art Mosaic and Tile Company finished the terrazzo handiwork, and the marble detailing was handled by the Guidici Marble Company. Vincent Borghesi, manager of the Roman Art Company, donated the lighting fixtures. Local artists Albert Matteuzi and John Pisani lent their expertise to the paintings and frescoes. The concrete and hardware were furnished by Herman Pieri Construction and the Ponciroli Mercantile Company respectively. Brick and ornamental tile had been supplied by two Cheltenham firms, the St. Louis Terra Cotta Company and the Hydraulic Brick Company.[59] Many of the aforementioned Italian businessmen and craftsmen had been attracted to St. Louis by the 1904 World's Fair.

As the Hill awaited the grand unveiling of St. Ambrose eight carefully wrapped boxes arrived from Torino, Italy. They contained furnishings for the church: a splendid ostensorium, a golden chalice, gilded silver pyxes, candelabra, chandeliers, and flowers for the altar. Also included were sacred vestments and flag standards for the church societies. The exquisite vestments were of inestimable value, having been hand-embroidered in silk, gold, and silver by the renowned Clement Trappi works in Turin. The gifts had been donated by Father Julius Giovannini, who had sacrificed his savings from twenty-five years in the priesthood to show his appreciation for the parish.[60]

The bells of St. Ambrose, complete with dedicatory inscriptions, rang out on the morning of June 26, 1926. It was the Hill's day in the sun.

Every flower was cut and every home scrubbed for the arrival of Archbishop Palica of Rome, Archbishop Glennon and Monsignor Spigardi of St. Louis. A litany of praise spilled forth that Sunday, but none was more meaningful than the tributes given by the "Brick and Mortar Priest." "When I assured my people in May, 1923, that if they would cooperate with me, the church of Sant' Ambrogio would be built in three years, no one believed me," said Father Giovannini. "By my own efforts, I could not have accomplished this work, neither could my parishioners have achieved it if they had worked alone. However, we shared our difficulties, our sacrifices, our labors. May this be the beginning of great and noble enterprises which the united Italian peoples can accomplish in the future of the good of their name."[61]

The human and financial costs of the new St. Ambrose Church were staggering. Father Carotti had succumbed to illness in 1922, and although only he realized it Father Giovannini was deathly ill. The church itself had cost over a quarter-million dollars; to be precise, $278,525.80.[62] Panegyrized *Church Progress*, "This monument of Italian art represents a feat of achievement rarely if ever equalled by a congregation of working people."[63] Hill Italians were the least educated and most blue-collared of any group in St. Louis in the 1920s. How and why did the community erect such a monument, particularly during a period in which capital might have been diverted toward educational, economic, and familial concerns?

St. Ambrose was a product of the interweaving of religious motivations, neighborhood aspirations, and economic realities, and timing was critical to the success of the enterprise. The old St. Ambrose burned in 1921, a watershed period for Italian-Americans. Prior to that time resources had been dissipated by familial necessities and the fraternal orders. But by the 1920s private insurance firms underwrote family needs as membership in the mutual aid societies declined. Congress, meanwhile, shut off the supply of new immigrants with the Draconian legislation of 1921 and 1924. For a quarter-century Italy had exchanged American dollars for new emigrants. Steamship tickets were necessities, a brick church a luxury. The restrictive legislation fortuitously released large sums of money that might have gone to aid the Cunard steamship line rather than the ethnic colony. Moreover, immigrant neighborhoods had generated a small, albeit significant, class of merchants, saloon keepers, and grocers. Each member of the St. Ambrose Building Committee, for example, was a small businessman. A large number of Hill

Lombards and Sicilians also earned handsome profits from the clandestine moonshine trade. Considerable profits from bootlegging, speculated a social worker, may have helped to reduce the new St. Ambrose debt to only $12,000 by 1935.[64]

The permanence of the Hill underscored the creation and success of the new St. Ambrose. The uncertainties of urban life during the colony's settlement had contributed to the ineffectiveness of the first church. "It is a widely held thesis among parish priests in the big cities," observed Joseph Fichter, "that the mobility of their parishioners not only makes the pastoral function more difficult but also interferes with both religious practices and social participation."[65] By the 1920s the Hill had become one of the most stable settlements in America, characterized by an impressive rate of homeownership (over 50 percent of Hill families). This permanence contrasted sharply with the experience in other cities, which partly explains the travail of Catholicism in the twentieth century.

Leadership within the church also ensured the success of St. Ambrose. The Virginian William Byrd once remarked that "America is free from the three great scourges of mankind—priests, lawyers, and physicians." Not so on the Hill, where men of the cloth flocked to work in the dynamic community and were in turn beloved. The colony had been blessed and, reciprocally, nurtured forthright, outstanding clerics during the twentieth century. "Priests were the sparkplugs of the community," said Bishop Charles Koester. "We spoke to more people than any other person on the Hill."[66]

Priests mirrored the stability of the Hill, particularly after the 1920s. Beginning with Cesare Spigardi the colony received a number of clerics who had spent peripatetic careers among the nation's ethnic enclaves. Father Spigardi, after laboring in New York, New Jersey, and Missouri, never left St. Louis after his arrival in 1906. Similarly, Fathers Carotti, Barabino, Giovannini, and Lupo served out their spiritual careers at St. Ambrose after years of colony-hopping. Peter Barabino, a Scalabrinian missionary from Genoa, arrived in America in 1906. His spiritual travels took him to Bleeker Street in New York City and to the ethnic enclaves of Cincinnati and Chicago. In 1920 he came to the Hill and remained there until tuberculosis took his life in 1939. Fiorenzo Lupo, a Lombard, had labored in the missionary fields of South America until the revolution in Mexico forced him into exile in the early 1920s. In 1926 he joined Monsignor Spigardi in St. Louis and served as his assistant until his appointment to St. Ambrose in 1934. Father Lupo remained on the Hill until his death in 1948.[67] In studying immigrant church history it is difficult to measure "success" beyond a number count of parishioners and churches. By a yardstick of clerical permanence, St. Ambrose prospered under the tutelage of some remarkable priests.

The inspiration of the Hill, like the genius of American politics, lay in its ability to transmute rivalry into creativity. Leaders perceived the reinvigorated church as a community crucible, where Lombard and Sicilian, Democrat and Republican, young and old, could meet to debate and solve public problems. The church provided a social crucible from which their competitive tendencies were tempered for the common welfare.

St. Ambrose Church embodied the will of its people. It is impossible to distinguish between the church and the Hill; after 1926 the two were intimately intertwined in a symbiotic relationship. The church lived up to its great expectations. By the eve of the Great Depression St. Ambrose had become the social linchpin of the community, an institution of incalculable influence. This experience contrasted sharply with patterns found by Harvey Zorbaugh in Chicago's "Little Hell." "There are no organizations, nor individuals," wrote the sociologist in 1929, "that have an effective influence through the colony. The church retains little effective control in the colony."[68] That same year Giovanni Schiavo wrote that on the Hill "the center for all activities is St. Ambrose. The priest indeed directs most of the activities of this section, and it is only rarely [*sic*] that something is done without his advice. A religious event on Fairmount Heights assumes the importance of a national event."[69] The church on the Hill was envisioned as something more than just expensive brick and stained glass—it was to be a settlement house, social center, and sanctuary for the neighborhood residents. "The key is the unity of the Hill," explained a former pastor. "Families know each other. People turned out for weddings, for funerals, turned out for confirmations, first communions, war celebrations, war bond sales, any kind of community enterprise."[70]

The period between the completion of St. Ambrose and the Japanese attack on Pearl Harbor saw the church expand its social plans of action, broaden its youth-oriented programs, and continue to groom outstanding leaders. The key to the success of St. Ambrose involved the relationship between parish priest and the colony's young. Increasingly after 1926 the church sought to make inroads among the Hill youth, particularly by the recruitment of dynamic clerics who appealed to this generation. Prior to the 1930s the community had been ministered to by priests such as Fathers Spigardi, Carotti, and Giovannini, men who had been fifty years of age or older by the time of their coming to the parish. However, after the 1930s four priests under the age of thirty-five arrived on the scene. Interestingly, two of the new church fathers were American-born, reflecting the changing sensitivities of the colony.

One of the first youth-oriented priests was Father Peter Barabino, who appealed to the colony's young on a different level—from an airplane. "He had this airplane," remembered Lou Berra. "It was held together with baling wire and God knows what else!"[71] Perhaps the most popular priest ever on the Hill, Father Peter and his Sunday excursions are still fondly recalled. "Well, he has to be a Saint!" swears Charles Oldani. "It would snow and he'd drag thirty or forty sleds behind his car."[72] Under the direction of the "Flying Priest" the St. Ambrose Men's Sodality was organized in 1930, followed by the founding of the Young Christian Mother's Sodality, Mary Help of Christian's Society, and the St. Ambrose Alumni Society, in 1932.[73]

The arrival of Father John Wieberg in 1931 ensured the success of the youth program. Born in the German settlement of Koelztown, Missouri, and a student at the American College in Rome, Wieberg became the first non-Italian priest to make a dramatic impact in the enclave. Father John, as he was affectionately called, proved a tireless worker among the young, organizing the popular parish athletic club, The Crusaders, and the first Boy Scout troop. Tragically, he died in an automobile crash in 1936 at the age of thirty-one. His love for his adopted people was evident in his will: "I bequeath and devise my estate as follows: To the Reverend Pastor at St. Ambrose, $100 for the repose of my soul. To Cardinal Glennon the rest of my estate to be used and applied to the Catholic School of St. Ambrose Church."[74]

Father Anthony Palumbo was next to inherit the Hill constituency. Born in southern Italy in 1904 he was brought by his parents to St. Louis in 1914, where he grew up on the edge of the Hill. After his ordination in 1932 he was assigned to St. Ambrose. He recalled, "The church at that time was the center of not only the spiritual activities of the colony, but the social activities gravitated around the church and parish. Italians [sought] social outlets in and around the parish confines and made for a very closely knit community and closely knit parish."[75] Father Palumbo and Joe Causino of the Southside YMCA were instrumental in organizing area youth into an athletic federation. "No problem was so big that Father Palumbo couldn't figure it out," reminisced Joe Garagiola, one of the more successful alumni of the parish athletic program.[76] "On the history of soccer on the Hill," observed Robert Burnes, sports editor of the *Globe-Democrat*, "no one did more to start it [soccer] than Father Palumbo."[77]

The careful grooming of the colony's younger generation on parish athletic fields was carried over into the parish classrooms. In 1906 St. Ambrose opened the first Italian parochial school in St. Louis. The Hill's modest one-story frame schoolhouse, even with extensive improvements in 1916, was a meager achievement. Given the availability of free public schooling and the impoverished condition of the first generation, few immigrants were prepared to sacrifice family funds for such a luxury as a private school. "It must be mentioned," confessed a church historian, "that the development of the school was not as flourishing as that of the parish [during the 1920s]. While 300 children annually had registered at the parochial school, thousands were forced to attend the public school."[78] In 1935 the St. Ambrose School Building Committee was formed, and by 1942 nearly $50,000 had been collected to erect a school, which would be completed after the war.[79]

St. Ambrosians embarked on an ambitious campaign to erect a much needed convent, kindergarten, and day nursery in 1935. The community pledged over half a million dollars and the stunning three-story Sacred Heart Villa, designed by Corrubia, was dedicated on May 12, 1940, "in a very beautiful and colorful procession," *Il Pensiero* noted, "made doubly so by the brilliant-hued costumes of the marchers and the multitude of tall and stately American and Italian flags and banners, proudly borne aloft by members of the Italian societies, five thousand men, women and children in an eight-block long procession. The homes throughout the entire community of Fairmount were gaily decorated with American and Italian flags."[80] In 1940, 35 percent of the community's women worked for wages, and the Villa's nursery assisted these mothers; in 1900 hardly any Italian mothers had worked for wages outside the home. Few things reflected more the changing attitudes on the Hill.[81] In 1940, for the first time in the community's history, there were also more women than men on the Hill.

Indicative of the new attitudes instilled since the 1920s was the revival of the religious festivals. The religious *feste* during the period 1900–1920 often degenerated into ethnic disharmony and were discontinued in the early 1920s. Ethnic factionalism calmed during the hiatus, and religious celebrations were resumed in the 1930s. Ethnoreligious zealousness, once a source of divisiveness, now served as a competitive yardstick by which the new church encouraged participants to funnel energies and dollars into the coffers of St. Ambrose. The nature of competition, however, had changed. The two factions now shared a consensual stake in the church and the community. Sicilians no longer thought Lombard patron saints were irreverent or unimportant; rather, the two groups now competed to see which of them might attract larger crowds, build more elaborate floats, and conduct a more spectacular fireworks display.

Spurred by the competition, Lombards and Sicilians hurled themselves into religious gamesmanship. "Santa Rosalia and San Sebastiano," a nostalgic Roland DeGregorio reminisced. "Now those were the religious celebrations that started off at church at the morning and then the Saint was put on a carriage and eight men in front and eight men in the back would carry the carriage through the streets and they'd have singing and musicians. They were all dressed gaily in red, white and green and then at night they'd start in the churchyard and sell beer and wine and end up with the fireworks display. I mean big!"[82] Carolina Borghi, a northern Italian, fondly recalled the pageantry of the Feast of San Sebastiano, the patron saint of Catania, Sicily. "San Sebastiano's Feast," she exclaimed, "they used to carry the statues around—the old-fashioned type and they'd have a procession. Everyone who was sick and couldn't get well could walk the street barefooted and people used to pin dollar bills on the Saint to receive a miracle."[83]

To hardworking Italian families mired in the Great Depression the festivals represented a combination state fair, Fourth of July, and evangelical revival. "It was fascinating to go there as a little boy," recollected Sam Chinicci, "to see the raffling off of chickens, live chickens, lambs. This man came here—Mr. Parisi, a Catanesi—he would go around for this special affair. This was his business. He would roast the chick peas, roast the seeds for *passatempi* [literally pastime, snacks]. Just like the old country!"[84] A staff member of the International Institute observed the Festival of St. Sebastian in August 1935 and noted, "When you witness an Italian celebration you forget that you are living in times of depression."[85]

No *festa* could begin without the brassy Italian band. "Professor Azzolino came from New York and with the help of Luciano Van Cardo opened a music store on Shaw Avenue," wrote Silvio Pucci in his autobiography. "They played at the Corpus Christi celebrations and night concerts and festivals of Santa Rosalia and San Domenico."[86] Pucci's son, Sylvio, Jr., today a professional musician, earned his musical spurs on the *festa* circuit. "On Saturday night we'd play at sponsors' homes," he warmly recalled. "We'd be invited inside for Italian bread and wine. Sicilian wine was powerful! Next morning we'd meet at the church and would play for the people entering the church. When the bells began, *The Italian March* would be played. Afterwards, we'd play Sousa marches. After supper there would be a concert and a church bazaar. Then a bomb—the fireworks! Fireworks you wouldn't believe! All this for three bucks for both days."[87] Joe Garagiola vividly remembers his father patiently soliciting contributions for the Festa di Santa Teresa. "For sheer entertainment," Garagiola confessed, "the Sicilians had it—Santa Rosalia. It was like the siege of Normandy."[88]

"It is difficult to determine whether the pulse beat of *la Montagna* is to be found at St. Ambrosio's Church or down the street at the 'Big Club,'" wrote Harry Brundidge in 1936. This was because the affairs of the two were so tightly interwoven; those that began in the church wound up at the club, and those that had their inception at the club wound up at the church.[89] Isidore Oldani, Jr., expressed this feeling of interrelatedness in a slightly different manner when he exclaimed that "the Big Club Hall and St. Ambrose—they were the two hubs—from the beginning of time."[90] But Oldani, still a young boy in 1926, viewed the Hill's history through rose-colored glasses. St. Ambrose had come a long way from its start as a tiny frame church in 1903 to a majestic house of worship in 1926 to a well-organized parish in 1941.

If St. Ambrose Church was the focal point of the Hill, the local political machine surely measured the focus with the keenest eye. During the dedication of the church a gift of two angels nestling a band of holy water was offered by the Fairmount Democratic Club. Boss Plunkitt, a Tammany ward heeler, would have approved of both the gift and the machine that had developed on the Hill. Sixty years following the birth of the Fairmount Democratic Club the parish church still exerts an awesome amount of political awareness. "There's something you have to understand about the Hill," explained Robert Ruggeri, Democratic alderman in 1981. "The power of the Roman collar in an ethnic neighborhood is enormous. Without the church the triangle would have a hard time standing upright."[91]

NOTES

1. Interview with Msgr. James Johnston, July 17, 1973.
2. Ellis, *American Catholicism*, 123; *The Immigrant Church*, 78.
3. Commager, *American Mind*, 232; Herberg, *Protestant-Catholic-Jew*, 88–102.
4. Vecoli, "Cult and Occult," 37.
5. Vecoli, "Prelates and Peasants," 235–36.
6. Ibid., 241; see also Nelli, *Italians in Chicago*, 181–82.
7. Niebuhr, *Social Sources of Denominationalism*, 26.
8. See Greene, "For God and Country."
9. *Western Watchman*, Apr. 27, 1872; Galus, "History of Catholic Italians."
10. *Western Watchman*, Dec. 16, 1871; Galus, "History of Catholic Italians," 79.
11. Rome, Centro Studi Emigrazione, Missionari di S. Carlo Scalabriniani, MS, Francesco Zaboglio to Bishop Scalabrini, 1889, St. Louis.
12. Ibid., Fr. Gambera to Bishop Scalabrini, 1896, St. Louis.
13. Ibid., Fr. Spigardi to Bishop Scalabrini, 1897, New Jersey.
14. Ibid., Fr. Gambera to Bishop Scalabrini, 1896, St. Louis.
15. Ibid., Fr. Beccherini to Fr. Gambera, Feb. 25, 1899, St. Louis.
16. Quoted in Felici, *Father to the Immigrants*, 25.
17. Naturalization petition, Cesare Spigardi, 1907; Galus, "History of Catholic Italians," 63–107; *Il Pensiero*, May 16, 1931, p. 3; *Globe-Democrat*, Aug. 5, 1903, p. 2; *Post-Dispatch*, Dec. 15, 1901, p. 1.
18. *Republic*, Apr. 7, 1900, p. 7.
19. Galus, "History of Catholic Italians," 79.
20. Interview with Fr. Walter John Galus, Aug. 8, 1973. Galus wrote his master's thesis on the history of the Italian Catholics in St. Louis.
21. *Nuova Chiesa Italiana*, 3–7.
22. *Globe-Democrat*, Aug. 3, 1903, p. 2.
23. *Republic*, Aug. 3, 1903, p. 9.
24. *Nuova Chiesa Italiana*, 5.
25. Naturalization petition, Luciano Carotti, 1911.
26. Interview with Filomena Cacciatore, May 28, 1975.
27. Wood, "Fairmount Heights," 41–42.
28. Ibid.
29. *Central Blatt and Social Justice*, Aug. 1915, p. 126.
30. Ibid.
31. *Nuova Chiesa Italiana*, 74.
32. Vecoli, "Prelates and Peasants," 235.
33. *La Lega*, Jan. 20, 1921, p. 1.
34. *Historical Review*, 14.

35. Ibid.

36. Ibid.

37. Interview with Charles Oldani and Isidore Oldani, Jr., Sept. 10, 1973; Naturalization petition, Isidoro Oldani, 1910.

38. Interview with Blase Mugavero, Sept. 2, 1973; "Calogero Mugavero: Patriarch of the Hill," *Hill 2000* 3 (Mar. 1973).

39. Interview with Joseph Gioia, Jr., June 3, 1973; interview with Mike Gioia, June 3, 1975; *La Stampa*, Aug. 19, 1927, p. 2.

40. "The Riggio Family," *Hill 2000* 2 (Mar. 1972); interview with Mrs. Ignazio Riggio, July 2, 1973; Schiavo, *Italians in Missouri*, 60.

41. Cunetto, "Italian Language Clubs," 13–14.

42. *Historical Review*, 14–15.

43. Ibid.

44. Ibid.

45. Interview with Fr. Anthony Palumbo, Aug. 3, 1975.

46. Naturalization petition, Julius Giovannini, 1914.

47. Letter from Fr. Julius Giovannini, Priest File, St. Louis Archdiocese, Chancery Archives. The letter was written in Italian.

48. Interview with Carolina Borghi, May 29, 1975.

49. Interview with Mike Gioia, June 3, 1975.

50. *Historical Review*, 16.

51. *Nuova Chiesa Italiana*, 7.

52. Interview with Carolina Borghi, May 29, 1975.

53. Interview with Mike Gioia, June 3, 1975.

54. Alsopp, *Romanesque Architecture*, 143–45; Conant, *Carolingian and Romanesque Architecture*, 128–49. Interestingly, the Lombard community of Herrin, Illinois, also made a significant contribution to American Romanesque architecture. In 1925 the Lombards constructed St. Mary's Church, a beautiful rendering of thirteenth-century Romanesque architecture.

55. Interview with Bishop Charles Koester, Feb. 16, 1976.

56. *Nuova Chiesa Italiana*, 25–27; *Il Pensiero*, Aug. 17, 1929; *La Stampa*, Aug. 19, 1929.

57. Schiavo, *Italians in Missouri*, 87–88.

58. Rallo and Hulbert, *Rallo Family*, 107.

59. *Nuova Chiesa Italiana*, 20–21; *Il Pensiero*, Aug. 17, 1929; "Pisani's Decorative Painting Spans Half Century," *Hill 2000* 2 (Nov. 1972); Schiavo, *Italians in Missouri*, 98–117.

60. *Historical Review*, 20.

61. Ibid.

62. Ibid., 24.

63. *Church Progress*, June 1926, 13.

64. Wood, "Fairmount Heights," 23–24.

65. Fichter, *Social Relations*, 95.

66. Interviews with Bishop Charles Koester, July 9, 1973, Feb. 16, 1976.

67. Naturalization petitions, Cesare Spigardi (1907), Peter Barabino (1924), Julius Giovannini (1914), St. Louis Diocesan Archives, Priest Files.

68. Zorbaugh, *Gold Coast and Slum*, 177.

69. Schiavo, *Italians in Missouri*, 60.

70. Interviews with Bishop Charles Koester, July 9, 1973, Feb. 16, 1976.

71. Interview with Lou Berra, July 11, 1973.

72. Interview with Charles Oldani, Sept. 10, 1973.

73. *Historical Review*, 25.

74. St. Louis Archdiocese, Chancery Archives, Priest File; *Historical Review*, 41–43.

75. Interview with Fr. Anthony Palumbo, Aug. 3, 1973.

76. Garagiola, *Baseball Is a Funny Game*, 13.

77. Letter from Robert Burnes to the author, Jan. 22, 1976.

78. *Historical Review*, 27.

79. Ibid.; Owens, *Loretto in Missouri*, 196–99.

80. *Il Pensiero*, June 16, 1939, p. 1.

81. *Sixteenth Census of the U.S.: 1940. Population and Housing*, IV, Table 3, "Years of School Completed, Employment Status, Class of Workers, Major Occupation Group."

82. Interview with Roland DeGregorio, Aug. 18, 1973.

83. Interview with Carolina Borghi, May 29, 1975.

84. Interviews with Sam Chinicci, Aug. 8, Oct. 27, Dec. 19, 1975.

85. IHRC, St. Louis International Institute, Aug. 27, 1935, Box 6.

86. Pucci, "My Memories of the Hill."

87. Interview with Sylvio Pucci, Jr., Aug. 30, 1973.

88. Interviews with Joe Garagiola, June 19, Sept. 8, 1984.

89. "Romanesque—A Bit of Italy on a Hill," *Star-Times*, Apr. 3, 1936, p. 19.

90. Interview with Isidore Oldani, Jr., Sept. 10, 1973.

91. Undated *Post-Dispatch* clipping, 1981, St. Ambrose rectory.

7 A Political Coming of Age

If you want to get anywhere, you got to unite.
Louis Jean Gualdoni

Mississippi's venerable John Sharp Williams once harangued his colleagues on what in 1915 bordered on a national migraine: immigration restriction. The xenophobic southern gentleman illustrated the immigrants' corruption of American politics with a colorful tale. "Fred Talbot used to tell a story about a political convention," Williams crackled:

> Somebody got up after awhile and addressed the Chairman. "Mr. Chairman, I want to nominate for Alderman of the First Ward the great German-American, Mr. Fritz Hefner." Mr. Hefner was nominated. Somebody else said, "Mr. Chairman, I want to put into nomination for Alderman of the Second Ward Mr. O'Kelly." Mr. O'Kelly was nominated. . . . Another got up and said, "Mr. Chairman, I want to nominate for Alderman of the Fourth Ward Mr. John Smith. I am sorry that I cannot say he is Irish-American, or a German-American, or Swiss-American, or an Italian-American. He would have been if he could have been, but it is his misfortune to have been born here, and it is his misfortune that his grandfather and great-grandfather were even born here." Then somebody with a foreign accent hollered out from the back benches, "That know-nothing son of a sea cook, put him out!"[1]

Williams was neither the first nor the last to cite the preponderant influence of ethnicity on the turbulent world of American politics. In recent years historians have suggested that a primordial factor in shaping American voting behavior was the prevalence and intensity of ethnocultural conflict at the grassroots level.[2] The political history of the Hill thus reflects the changing perceptions and priorities of Italian-Americans as well as the changing context of local, state, and federal relations. Paralleling the development of the parish church and athletic clubs, the Hill's political ascendancy resulted from gradual structural changes, quickened by spasms of opportunity.

Local self-government had sparkled as a gemstone of democracy during much of the nineteenth century, yet by 1890 most commentators agreed with Lord Bryce's charge that city government conspicuously tainted the American experiment.[3] St. Louis, in the grip of Boss Butler, provided a textbook from which muckrakers examined the political cancer. "When I set out to describe the corrupt systems," confessed Lincoln Steffens, "I meant to show simply how the people were deceived. . . . But in the very first study—St. Louis—the startling truth lay bare that corruption was not merely political, it was financial, commercial, social; the ramifications of the boodle were so complex . . . the mind could hardly grasp them."[4]

America's cities, products of a half-century of rampant urban growth, reflected the prevailing value system of privatism and local control. Governmental agencies, pressed by a burgeoning population and increased demands for public services, responded ineffectively. Cities such as St. Louis willingly permitted private utility companies to provide public services such as mass transit and electricity. Into the void of political leadership stepped a peculiarly American (although usually Irish) character, "the Boss."

Standing securely under the chestnut trees of St. Louis was Edward ("the Village Blacksmith") Butler. Aided by loyal chieftains such as Thomas ("the Snake") Kinney, Butler controlled St. Louis politics like no one before or since.[5] Like his counterparts across the nation, Butler's reign was the product of escalating problems associated with immigration, industrialization, and urbanization. Corruption was rampant as "Butler's Indians" terrorized unfriendly precincts and patronized friendly corporations. "The Village Blacksmith is now tasting the sweets of power," pronounced the *Post-Dispatch* in 1882. "He is Ward Warwick of St. Louis. He makes Constables, Aldermen, Judges, Legislators, Governors, etc., and occasionally looks after slop contracts and city charters."[6] Theodore Dreiser, then a cub reporter, felt humbled by Butler's presence. "What force in the man! What innate gentility of manner and speech. He seemed like a prince disguised as a blacksmith."[7]

The conventional wisdom holds that bosses provided essential services for immigrants, cutting through the red tape of city hall and rocking the cradle of urban liberalism. The sparsely documented record indicates that during the formative stage of political development, 1880–1920, neither the Democratic bosses nor Republican mayors provided any services for Hill Italians. Except for financial benefits to one individual, the Hill existed in the political and metropolitan backwaters, lacking sewers, paved streets, trolley connections, and naturalized citizens. A handful of short-run pragmatists and long-term optimists maneuvered to manipulate local political opportunities, envisioning Italians voting as a bloc, co-opting the enclave's ethnic strength.

Political clout involved some rather elementary principles at the turn of the century. Individuals and precincts were rewarded by the number of votes they mustered, but in order to vote in St. Louis immigrants had to first initiate naturalization proceedings. Moreover, citizenship demanded a commitment: a trip to the courthouse, red tape, and a steep $2.50 fee.[8] Not surprisingly, Hill Italians displayed little interest in the franchise, a privilege few had ever enjoyed in the old country and few understood here. The 1898 List of Registered Voters for the Ninth Precinct, Twenty-fourth Ward (the Hill) reveals near total apathy among the Italians; of 180 registered voters—the majority of whom were of German descent—only 3 Italians are listed.[9] The St. Louis Democratic party was about to remedy this situation.

The turn of the century marked the golden age of political corruption in St. Louis. Boss Butler, aided by his overzealous "Indians," masterminded a series of election victories. "Election day in 1900 came and it was indeed an eventful day in St. Louis," observed the *Globe-Democrat:* "A livery company sent a band wagon to Jim Cronin's saloon. . . . These wagons were loaded with 'Indians.' They drove from ward to ward, precinct to precinct. Their work was open and notorious. . . . [They] visited more than twenty precincts on that election day and they voted from five to eight times in each precinct."[10] Congressman Richard Bartholdt remembered "registration lists padded with hundreds of fraudulent names. . . ."[11] Sneered Congressman William W. Rucker, "The shameful conditions so long existing is due to the fact that the community there [St. Louis] has been and is blighted by the political boss, and is populated by a lot of miserable underlings who are subservient to the will of the boss."[12] St. Louis, declared embattled reformer Lee Meriwether, was "as devoid of self-government as Moscow."[13]

In the fall of 1902 John Dolan, an Irish-American leader of the Twenty-fourth Ward and chairman of the Democratic party, approached

Giovanni Barbaglia, who was then president of the North Italy American Society, to explain how he could ease Barbaglia's countrymen through the naturalization maze and make it worth Barbaglia's effort. With the help of Thomas Barrett, a marshal of the U.S. Court, Dolan arranged special evening sessions for Barbaglia's *paesani*. On three occasions in early October 1902 Barbaglia marshaled large numbers of Lombards to City Hall, and there the machine, courtesy of Dolan, treated the prospective citizens to several rounds of drink. "We drinks 'em and we votes 'em," was a popular slogan of the stormy Twenty-fourth Ward Democrats. The grateful Lombards then marched to court, where Barrett processed the group en masse.[14]

Lombards had not realized that citizenship could be so effortless, and Barbaglia was soon hounded by other countrymen who were eager to become naturalized. Although the deadline for the November election had passed, Dolan suggested that Barbaglia discreetly bring him a list of Lombard allies. This accomplished, he then delivered the list to Barrett, who had purloined a sufficient number of naturalization certificates. Patrolman John Murphy delivered the documents to Barbaglia's residence and helped to forge more than ninety certificates.[15] The naturalized citizens then quickly exercised their newly won franchise.

The Democratic primary on October 7, 1902, ranked as one of the most spirited in St. Louis history. "Riot and bloodshed, repeaters and police interference were the most prominent features of the Democratic primary yesterday," reported the *Globe-Democrat*.[16] Years later an old-timer told a social worker that he had voted under seven different names.[17] St. Louis papers casually noted the extra-heavy voter turnout in the Twenty-fourth Ward.[18] Journalists investigated the story and in January 1903 the scandal broke. By the end of the month a half-dozen Hill Lombards were arrested "for aiding and abetting the commission of frauds in connection with naturalization." The government's star witness, Giovanni Barbaglia, was granted immunity for his evidence against Dolan and Barrett, both of whom served time in prison for the affair. The trial in the fall of 1903 brought the Hill torrents of unsavory publicity.[19]

The naturalization scandals had far-reaching implications. First, the affair stigmatized Hill Italians and effectively removed them from city politics for twenty years. Residents who voted between 1903 and 1920—and they were few—supported the Republican ticket. Second, the investigation, coinciding with Joseph Folk's cause célèbre, the prosecution of Boss Butler, dismantled the last great political machine in St. Louis.[20]

Henceforth Mound City politics played on a theme of fragmentation and decentralization. No Pendergasts emerged in St. Louis in the twentieth century; instead, political power shifted to the wards. When the Hill reentered the political arena in the 1920s it was able to accomplish far more because of local clout. Third, Italian immigrants who wished to vote faced stiffer requirements after 1906, ironically related to abuses on the Hill. Two landmark cases evolved from the St. Louis naturalization trials: *Dolan* v. *U.S.* (1903), and *Janke* v. *U.S.* (1903). Evidence taken from these cases was forwarded to the Justice Department and called to the attention of President Theodore Roosevelt, who appointed a commission to study the matter. The result was the Naturalization Act of June 29, 1906, the first revision in the country's naturalization law in more than a century, which demanded exacting literacy and character qualifications from immigrants seeking citizenship.[21] "It will be easier for the proverbial camel to go through the eye of a needle than for an alien to become a citizen of the United States," swore a St. Louis court official.[22]

The substantive changes introduced by the legislation presented a severe challenge to the political aspirations of Hill Italians. Illiteracy prevented many Lombards and Sicilians from acquiring citizenship; as late as 1930, 35 percent of the colony's foreign-born residents were illiterate. Immigrants in the state of Missouri could secure the franchise provided they met a rigid test of qualification. The criteria remained fairly standard between 1899 and the 1930s: an immigrant male, twenty-one years of age or older, could vote if he had resided in the state one year and declared his intention to become a citizen of the United States. A declaration of intention—the first of two steps necessary for naturalization—required the filing of first papers, which cost five dollars. An immigrant could become a citizen after at least one and not more than five years. In addition, the prospective citizen-voter was required to bring along two character witnesses. In all, citizenship and franchise qualifications imposed a burden on impoverished immigrant communities and a near impossible goal on transient laborers. Clearly the process needed institutional support, which would eventually come in the 1920s.[23]

Other factors contributed to the subsequent political apathy on the Hill. The imprisonment of John P. Dolan, the area's political mentor, removed a trusted friend and confidant. David Patterson Dyer further complicated matters for Hill immigrants. After his celebrated role as U.S. Attorney in the naturalization fraud, Dyer was appointed to a federal judgeship by President Theodore Roosevelt. One of his important functions was to grant or deny citizenship to immigrants. Judge Dyer, who witnessed the Lincoln-Douglas debates, served as a Union Army officer, and prosecuted the Whiskey Ring, openly clashed with the Italians in the courtroom. From 1906 until his death in 1924 at age eighty-six Dyer was a thorn in the side of Hill immigrants. He denied scores of Italians citizenship for reasons most commonly dismissed with the cryptic note, "Denied—immoral character." Bootlegging convictions, in particular, angered him. Dyer's mistrust of Italian aliens epitomized the battle over Immigration Restriction, which pitted old-line Americans against "new" immigrants.[24] In addition, his chief assistant, Monroe Bevington, was an outspoken nativist. "Election frauds, rioting, Bolshevism, and every sort of social disease go hand in hand with the masses of undigested immigrants about us," Bevington warned in 1921. "If immigration is to continue unchecked, this nation should adopt radical treatment for the immigrants who herd into the foreign quarters of our great cities, making them the breeding grounds for anarchy and radicalism of the most unbalanced sort."[25]

The nature of Italian-American political life during the formative period 1890–1920 remains largely unexamined by immigration historians; or else historians relegate political development to the periphery of the more important issues of mobility and community. In part this treatment reflects a general consensus that Italian immigrants were politically impotent, preferring to dedicate their energies to the welter of family and work. The paucity of Italian-American political studies also reflects the preponderance of community studies dealing with the period in question. According to Yans-McLaughlin, attempts by Buffalo (N.Y.) Italians to participate in the political arena ended in frustration.[26] Briggs has concluded that the colonies of Kansas City and New York's Rochester and Utica "were slow in developing an Italian-American power base. . . ."[27] Italians remained shut out of Boston politics until 1939.[28] Zorbaugh, in his pioneering *The Gold Coast and the Slum*, contended that Chicago Italians were "utterly unable or unwilling to participate in the [city's] political life,"[29] a contention countered by Humbert Nelli, who has made a claim for significant Italian immigrant participation early in their Chicago experience. Chicago's Italians quickly adapted to the Windy City's ward politics, a theme paralleling Nelli's view of a larger pattern of social and economic accommodation. According to Nelli, "By 1920 Italians had effectively adjusted to politics in the various parts of the city where they live."[30]

If the rank-and-file Italian immigrant appeared on the whole unconcerned with American politics, the same cannot be said about the *prominenti*, the elites who served as ethnic brokers to the outside world. In particular, the editors of the immigrant press devoted considerable energy to encouraging Italian political participation. It might be added that political advertisements and contributions constituted a significant portion of press income. In general, however, Italians expressed skepticism toward the elite. Since most immigrants neither read the editorials in the original nor cared to understand the translations, one should be wary of the flowery prose flowing from the editors' pens. The immigrant press in St. Louis scorned the behavior of the unlettered masses. *La Lega Italiana* mocked the behavior of one Hill Italian who, when asked by the naturalization examiner to recite the national anthem, proceeded to sing *L'Inno di Garibaldi*. The editors ridiculed this political naivete as "*Ignoranza Grossa e Grassa.*"[31] A scanning of voter registration lists and electoral returns on the Hill between 1890 and 1920 leads to the conclusion that Italians regarded political participation as a fool's errand, a confusing and unrewarding venture.

For two decades following the voting scandals of 1902 Hill Italians chose to draw the community's political blinds. Italian immigrants ignored political issues, neither registering nor voting during the Progressive Era, an attitude paralleling the neighborhood's relationship with St. Louis social agencies. The ethnic enclave's utter inability to attract urban amenities such as city sewers, paved roads, and trolley service were partly attributable to the colony's political isolation. Mass political apathy did not discourage urban leaders from courting the ethnic vote, however. Republicans tapped Giuseppe Gioia in hopes the Lombard leader might deliver anticipated immigrant votes. Gioia performed the role of political intermediary between the Hill and St. Louis during the period 1904–20, but his talents and his countrymen's interest were found wanting.

Born in Cuggiono in 1880, Gioia left Lombardy in 1896, exchanging his sharecropper's *zappa* for a miner's shovel in St. Louis. He quickly rose to leadership in the North Italy America Club and shortly after 1900 purchased a tavern and acquired citizenship—a requirement for saloon keepers (in the 1910 census [under the misspelling Joia] he was listed as a liquor merchant). In addition to his proprietor status Gioia was also distinguished by having acquired citizenship, a rarity among Italian immigrants in 1910. He retained his allegiance to the GOP until his death in 1946, but he failed to convert Hill Lombards and Sicilians to the Republican standard. The marriage of ethnicity and politicization depends on an undefined combination of personality and timing, of local and national expectations and opportunities.[32]

The success of Italian political leaders required a symbiosis between Italian voters and St. Louis political leaders. Immigrants had not brought with their cultural baggage a tradition of political ethnicity—meaning not that Lombards or Sicilians arrived deracinated, but rather that ethnicity as a political resource originated from the interaction between the foreign enclave and host society. In the old country peasants were not expected to play a meaningful role in the formal political process. In 1860 less than 2 percent of the Italian population could vote. The voting reform act of 1882 increased the suffrage from 600,000 to 2 million males, but literacy requirements disfranchised most peasants and sharecroppers. It would not be until World War I that universal adult suffrage emerged in Italy.

The 1920s ushered in the first wave of political ethnicity on the Hill. A diffusion of political ethnicity can be traced to a confluence of factors: the demographics of the first and second generation, a rising economic standard of living, deference toward political leaders, and a feeling among immigrant men—and now women—that naturalization might confer jobs as well as citizenship. Ultimately, immigrants and their children realized that in a pluralist society ethnic differences afforded prospects of social and economic mobility.

COMING OF POLITICAL AGE, 1920–41

Two important publications appeared in 1929 and charted the progress made by St. Louis Italians in the arena of politics. "Political influence in the realistic game of politics is measured by the voting strength that a group can muster," wrote Merle Fainsod in his study of the city's ethnic groups, 1908–28; "and beyond this test, the local Italian community falls down."[33] Fainsod, who would become a prominent Kremlinologist, also charged that "the local Italian community has not developed any outstanding political leadership."[34] Giovanni Schiavo, in his study of *The Italians in Missouri*, noted that "the Italians of St. Louis have shown an incredible apathy towards local politics."[35] Ironically, at the very time the publications appeared, the Hill was coming of political age and was on the threshold of a remarkable political transformation.

The earliest sign of the reawakening occurred in the summer of 1924. For the first time since 1902 immigrants from the Hill were flocking to the courts to become citizens legally. Between June 10, 1924, and September 26, 1924, 6 percent of those granted citizenship in St. Louis came from the Hill, a figure far out of proportion to the colony's numbers.[36] In July a burly Lombard nailed a sign above the window at 1920 Cooper Avenue: "Fairmount Democratic Club." The neighborhood would never be the same.

Carlo Gualdoni had left feudal Lombardy in 1886 to join a handful of *paesani* in the austere labor camp in southwest St. Louis. He soon sent for his bride, Angelina Calcaterra, who gave birth to Louis Jean, the first of their twelve children, on December 4, 1892. These early pioneers had little time for politicking, as evidenced by the fact that Carlo Gualdoni did not bother to become a citizen until 1925, when he was fifty-nine years old.[37] He labored in the clay mines; his sons were afforded more of an opportunity to choose an occupation. Louis Jean Gualdoni began his apprenticeship in the mines, starting work at age thirteen. "I quit school to help support all those children my mother and father had," he explained. He soon learned a memorable political lesson when hired as a grocery clerk and butcher by the North Italian American Society Cooperative Store. "The way you got a job," he recounted in a voice that belied his ninety years, "was that you had to be elected at this meeting. . . ."[38]

With the outbreak of the First World War Gualdoni traded his butcher's apron for the nattier look of army khaki, serving in Company G of the 354th Infantry. Because of his proportions—he stood six feet tall and weighed over 200 pounds—he gained fame as a boxer in the service, losing only one decision, to a pugilist by the name of Garrison. "Actually, he was really an Italian," laughed Gualdoni. "He had changed his name. Before the fight he whispered to me, '*Paesano*, we're Italian, so let's not hurt one another, okay?' So the first punch, he nearly tears my head off! I said to myself, 'I'm going back to the Hill where a man's word is something.'"[39]

Gualdoni returned to civilian life in 1919 to resettle on the Hill and resume his calling at the meat counter. The butcher shop where he worked sported a saloon in the rear, and there he fatefully met James B. Conroy, an active labor leader and politician in the Twenty-fourth Ward. Conroy's brother was a priest with many friends at St. Ambrose. A job was discussed sometime in 1920, and eventually Conroy accompanied

Gualdoni to the office of John Dolan, the reemerged political boss of south St. Louis and an old friend of those on the Hill. Gualdoni was then introduced to John H. Whitmore, Democratic committeeman, and Whitmore and Dolan agreed to nominate him for the potentially powerful position of Internal Revenue Agent. Whitmore also appointed him a precinct captain. The germ of the Hill's political machine was born that afternoon. "Jean," the veteran politicos advised him, "you build that Italian vote up out there and you'll have every Democratic politician after you. They'll want your friendship and support, and they'll do anything they can for you." Gualdoni recalled saying to himself, "You better get busy!"[40]

His position as a revenue agent placed Gualdoni in one of the most sensitive jobs imaginable, a predicament not unappreciated by ward politicians. Oral recollections leave little doubt that the aspiring politician contracted an acute case of myopia during certain raids on the Hill and that this discretion was highly valued by residents. By 1923 Gualdoni grew tired of defending his stormy reputation at headquarters and resigned when asked to transfer to Minneapolis. One year later he was herding still operators into a formidable political machine.[41]

The first medium from which he sought to reach *paesani* was the Fairmount Democratic Club. "I had money and I spent it to open this headquarters at 1920 Cooper [Ave.] and we met there all the time," Gualdoni remembered.[42] His keen political sense told him that the future of Hill politics pointed toward the large numbers of young men and teenagers in the community. "Jean came down and gave us young men a pep talk," recalled Lou Berra, who was eighteen in 1924. "'Look,' Jean told us, 'I'll pay your rent, I'll buy your coal, and all you got to do is talk Democrat. Just build it up. Come election time, work for the Democratic Party.'" Berra mused, "Jean was the first Democrat. He started the Fairmount Democratic Club. I believe that everybody on the Hill my age, even anyone over forty-five, at one time or another belonged to the Fairmount Democratic Club. I mean, if you didn't belong, something was wrong with you. He converted the whole damn neighborhood!"[43] Lou Cerutti was also a charter member of the Fairmount Democrats. "Jean took teenagers like myself, figuring in a few years they'll vote!" Cerutti, a furniture dealer, reminisced. "The club was real social. It was a place to keep off the streets. . . . there were two-three pool tables. . . . he'd take us out to the soccer games, no matter how cold."[44]

Soccer offered more appeal to young Italian-Americans than discussion of tariff reform or good government. Philosophically, Gualdoni disdained ideological platforms and provided personal favors for his constituents instead. "I'll tell you something," he whispered with a twinkle in his eye—the mark of a man of experience—"It's only human nature that a person, whether he's Italian or not, he goes along with the guy who does the most things for him. And that's what the Italians did . . . and what I did. I put myself out, you know, to help these people, and I spent quite a lot of my own money! I never took a dime from 'em either. I took their votes though! . . . whenever I promised to do something, I did it. . . . That was the secret of my political activities. . . ."[45] Gualdoni carefully groomed a cadre of young, hardworking precinct captains. "I'd get a precinct captain who was real active in his precinct," he explained. "Whoever could deliver the best was in the spot. I made a lot of changes, a lot of changes. Because they would be in a powerful spot, they could do a lot of things for their people . . . like getting jobs, favors, things like that. They'd want to be in there and hold on, and the only way to hold on was to be active. . . ."[46]

In 1926 Gualdoni tapped a young Italian-American, Lou ("Midge") Berra, to help organize the Hill. Emiglio Berra had left his native Lombardy in 1901 to start a new life. Finding steady work at the brickyards, he and his wife reared seven children, the third one—Lou—born in March 1906.[47] Like most of his contemporaries Lou Berra grew tired of schooling and found employment at Evens and Howard Tile Factory in the early 1920s. His amicability and leadership impressed factory officials and soon he became a foreman. But the gregarious Berra preferred counting Democrats to counting sewer tiles. The pioneering work accomplished by Gualdoni attracted the young Italian-American, and his mentor appointed him political coordinator in 1926.[48] From then until his death in 1964 Midge Berra devoted his life to Hill politics. Indeed, he died in 1964 arguing politics at a convention.[49] "His whole life, I would say, from the 1920s on," recollected Father Anthony Palumbo, a contemporary, "was completely devoted to helping others through politics. . . . I can truthfully say his whole life was given to his people."[50]

In their 1926 evaluation of the Hill's voting bloc, both Gualdoni and Berra recognized an acute problem that hamstrung efforts to build an effective machine. Until sufficient numbers of second-generation Italian-Americans had reached the voting age, the Hill political machine necessarily comprised immigrants. But the colony had shown little interest in naturalization proceedings since the affair in 1903. Between 1906 and

1920 only seventy-nine Hill immigrants became citizens.[51] The two politicos thus embarked on a major effort to expand the voting rolls of the community's foreign-born.

To tutor immigrants Gualdoni hired Ed Tobin, a clerk from the U.S. District Court. "That was the beginning; after that other Italians here got in on it," Gualdoni boasted.[52] "My Dad became a citizen," reminisced Roland DeGregorio. "He became a citizen, like others became citizens, because they studied their questions and answers like 'Our Fathers.' In other words, if you would say to 'em, 'Who was the first President of the United States?' he not only knew the answer to that question but he also knew the answer to the next question and the next. Now if—and it happened many times—if the judge asked the question and then skipped one, he would give the wrong answer. But they learned it like a prayer."[53] Gualdoni and Berra personally accompanied hundreds of foreign-born Lombards and Sicilians to the courthouse to bear witness for the prospective citizen-voters. "One of my duties as leader of the Hill was to help with citizenship papers," Midge Berra told a reporter in 1962. "The federal government investigated me once because there were 1800 people with my name on their citizenship papers! The government thought maybe I was selling papers, but I wasn't. It was just part of the services we gave."[54]

The struggle to persuade Italian immigrants that their naturalization would benefit the community was no easy task. In 1920 only 25.7 percent of St. Louis's foreign-born Italian women and 28.2 percent of the men had become citizens, as opposed to 80 percent of the German men, 78 percent of the German women, and 46 percent of the Russian Jews (men and women); only Greek immigrants had established a poorer record in seeking naturalization.[55] Although the figure for the Hill was not given in census calculations, it was probably lower than 25 percent since there was little incentive to acquire citizenship before the 1920s. But by 1930, 40 percent of the city's foreign-born Italian men and 32 percent of the women had become citizens; and significantly, another 18.3 percent had taken out their first papers, an indication that the machine's cogs were in motion. In spite of the impressive gains achieved during the 1920s, Italian immigrants still ranked last when compared to other St. Louis foreign-born residents, an indication that many Italian immigrants continued to spurn Americanizing efforts of politicization. Evidence exists that Hill Italians accepted the tenets of this politicizing but perceived politics through the lens of ethnic power.[56] During a two-year period monitored by the International Institute, 1936–38, a remarkable one-quarter of the applicants securing citizenship were Italian—most of them derived from the Hill, according to director reports—a tribute to the efforts of the Hill machine.[57] By 1940 fully 48 percent of the Hill's immigrants had become citizens and another 11 percent had taken out their first papers.[58]

Immigrants were reminded by watchful ward heelers that their vote was a vote for community power. As further inducement patronage jobs were lavishly distributed among the Democratic faithful. A tale by Elmer Shorb Wood exemplifies the strength of patronage. Wood had carefully prepared an elderly Italian for his citizenship test. After the immigrant successfully passed the exam, Wood asked how it felt to be an American. "Without even answering the first question," Wood insisted, "the first thing the man said to me was, 'How do I get to Midge Berra's house? He promised me a job!'"[59] The rise of the Hill machine meant patronage power, and Berra and Gualdoni kept the organization well oiled with a plethora of jobs. So many Hill Italians were placed on the city payroll, reported one authority, that many Democrats began to complain about the colony's clout.[60] Gualdoni funneled patronage through his position as state Democratic committeeman, 1926–46; street commissioner, 1936–41; Democratic committeeman from the Twenty-fourth Ward, the largest in the city, 1936–44; and manager of Kiel Auditorium, 1951–63. In 1932 a political columnist labeled Gualdoni the second most influential Democrat in the state, after Tom Pendergast. In the 1930s Gualdoni directly controlled almost 200 jobs, a figure made more impressive when added to his associate's growing power. Between 1929 and 1962 Lou Berra held one of the most lucrative patronage jobs in the city, that of revenue collector. In addition, he was elected to the board of aldermen, 1938–54, where he chaired the powerful ways and means committee. In 1954 he was also elected constable.[61]

The New Deal and its pluralist coalition dramatically increased the leverage of Hill Democrats. Lyle Dorsett, among others, has pointed out that while the New Deal may have generated the source of jobs in the federal government, it did not alter the "all important function of local distribution of such services."[62] Moreover, the Hill's heavily working-class constituency gratefully accepted many menial city jobs in the 1930s and 1940s, positions less attractive to more prosperous groups. Gualdoni repeatedly told the story of his philosophy toward patronage. "The night after Barney Dickmann was elected Mayor in 1933," he recalled, "Barney put me on the patronage committee. . . . One day the chairman of the committee gave me cards, I think nineteen or twenty different jobs, in the sewer department which I wanted. I wanted small jobs; you take a big job and you might not be able to get three or four smaller jobs. I wanted smaller jobs to be able to take care of more people. . . . when I brought them to the club that night, oh what a scramble!"[63] Berra followed the same practice. "Midge was more of a guy who would rather have fifteen real jobs than a couple of boss jobs," explained a political associate.[64]

The Fairmount Democratic Club naturally exercised a strong influence on the local economy, as Gualdoni and Berra helped with permits and applications. Many residents laud Berra and Gualdoni for opening up the area economy to Hill Italians. "Ohh, it was hard for Italians to get jobs at Quick Meal and McQuay-Norris [local factories] in the 1920s," contended Roland DeGregorio, the local mailman. "Up to that time, it was mainly Germans working there. Finally Midge broke the ice somehow, and if you wanted a job before and after the war, he got you a job. See? These men would try and get their people jobs. They worked for their people. I remember going to Midge Berra, and he got me a job at Quick Meal after the war in '45."[65]

While patronage greased the machine's political gears, personal service ensured a smooth and successful operation. The Gualdoni-Berra machine was foremost a community-based affair; politics of the personal favor was no mere campaign rhetoric. "Most politicians when elected forget about the people," sneered Charles Pozza. "Not these!"[66] Tales of the machine's helping hand are as common as ward heelers frequenting funeral parlors. "Midge worked in politics twenty-four hours a day," exclaimed Paul Berra, former St. Louis City treasurer, now the city comptroller, and Midge's long-time colleague. "Midge would do anything and everything for anyone in his ward," he marveled.[67] Hill Italians appreciated such concern.

"They was wonderful," swore saloon keeper Frank Gianella.[68] Charles Rancilio, who barbers near the Fairmount Democratic Club, delights in retelling Midge Berra tales. "I've seen Midge pay guys' fines," he whispered. "And I mean some of them fines were heavy. When he died, he had a stack of parking tickets like this," laughed Rancilio, his fingers spread two inches apart.[69] The Hill politico was the community's benevolent protector and spokesman. "Midge Berra wasn't the greatest literary expert," chuckled Bishop Charles Koester, "but he could say the words that meant what he said. He made a tremendous impression."[70] Few enemies dared to antagonize Berra on his home turf. "If there was anything he didn't like," reminisced Charles Rancilio, "he'd go down to city hall and raise hell!"[71]

No activity on the Hill escaped the omnipresent bosses, whose appointment calendars rivaled Plunkitt of Tammany Hall. Between funerals and political appointments, wrote a *Globe-Democrat* reporter, it was nearly impossible to interview the hustling bosses of the Hill.[72] "I remember a variety of visitors," recalled Lou Berra, Jr., Midge's son, who in 1973 served as assistant to Mayor John Poelker and continues to serve in urban affairs: "My mother's and father's house was like Grand Central Station. Any time of the morning or evening, people would come and go needing favors from my Dad. My Dad spent countless hours at the police station, straightening out kids and getting 'em out of trouble. . . . Police would call my Dad first, then their parents . . . that's why he was called 'The King of the Hill.' He helped everyone . . . the elderly immigrants used to call him President Berra."[73]

For the machine's twenty-four-hour, year-round services the Hill electorate richly rewarded Democratic candidates on polling day. Beginning in the 1920s and climaxing in the quarter-century after the New Deal, but continuing through the 1980s, the Fairmount Democratic Club compiled an awesome political record. In 1970 the *Globe-Democrat* labeled the colony as the most consistent delivery ward in St. Louis during the previous half-century.[74]

How had the Hill ascended the political ladder so quickly? The enclave's ecological characteristics—a homogeneous population, a blue-collar constituency, and overlapping neighborhood-precinct boundary lines—buttressed the colony's political foundation. Furthermore, the lack of a centralized machine resulted in a centrifugal power structure in St. Louis, causing wards to become, in Glen Holt's phrase, "a satrapy of competing interests."[75] The Hill also anchored the powerful Twenty-fourth Ward, the largest in the city, with 29,687 registered voters in 1937.[76] Although the Hill controlled only a half-dozen of the ward's seventy-two precincts, the enclave's remarkable triumphs at the ballot box, and growing influence in patronage and power, generated clout.[77] "It's not the percentage that counts so much," contended the political architect Gualdoni, "as it is where there is a certain group that stands as a bloc, a bloc that votes together. That's what made the Italians!"[78] As Kerry Patch and the southside German wards diminished in strength each year, the Hill grew more powerful. Most importantly, the community accentuated stability, cohesiveness, and mutual courtesies, nurturents for an ethnopolitical hothouse.

Timing also underpinned the Hill's political successes. The Fairmount Democratic Club was primed precisely at the moment local, state, and federal power passed from the Republicans to the Democrats. Gualdoni possessed a remarkable instinct for backing the right candidate, sometimes at great risk to his own career. In 1932, for instance, one might have expected the veteran to go along with the Missouri delegation's support of favorite son Jim Reed at the Democratic Convention, especially considering that Tom Pendergast, Kansas City's powerful boss, vigorously backed Reed. Gualdoni, however, bolted from the flock in support of Franklin Roosevelt, so angering Pendergast that the two burly politicans squared off in fisticuffs. The rest of the Missouri delegation quickly followed Gualdoni's lead in backing FDR.[79]

If Gualdoni's decision to support Roosevelt in 1932 required political acumen, his brassy backing of Judge Harry Truman for senator in 1934 took sheer courage. He was the only St. Louis politician of note to support the Pendergast-backed Truman, who ran against St. Louis Congressman John Cochran. A historical chasm separated St. Louis and Kansas City politicians, and Gualdoni's lack of urban loyalty must have smacked of apostasy to many veterans. Truman received only 3,737 votes in St. Louis, but almost half of those came from Gualdoni's ward.[80] Truman needed Gualdoni even more in 1940 when he again narrowly escaped defeat. Truman's refusal to disavow his friendship with the now-disgraced Pendergast Machine cost him dearly in St. Louis.[81] His opponent was Lloyd Stark, the ambitious Missouri governor who relentlessly pressed the campaign. But Gualdoni stuck with his friend from Independence, to the amazement of St. Louis editorialists and Democrats.

Truman won the August 6, 1940, U.S. senatorial primary by a mere 7,000 votes, precisely the number of votes Gualdoni's ward garnered for him. In seven key Hill precincts Truman had outpolled Stark, 4,925 votes to 450.[82] Gualdoni received a telegram the morning following the election: "I sincerely appreciate all you did for me in St. Louis. . . . When I come to St. Louis, I want to meet you personally. [signed] Harry S. Truman."[83] A quarter-century later Truman's aides vividly recalled Gualdoni's instrumental role in the 1940 campaign. "Gene [*sic*] Gualdoni was the typical ward boss and he carried Harry Truman's ward," remembered General Harry Vaughn. "I mean he carried his ward for Harry. I'm not sure, but there were probably more votes than there were people in the ward!"[84] Mildred Lee Dryden, Truman's personal secretary, related that Gualdoni was the only political leader in St. Louis who came out for Truman. "We should always be grateful for Jean Gualdoni."[85]

The awesome pluralities turned out by the Fairmount Democratic Club attracted reform-minded journalists who hoped to scoop a scandal-ridden, boss-corrupt organization. Marsh Clark, political editor of the *Globe-Democrat* during the 1950s, recalled his feeble efforts to investigate the Hill in 1954: "We spent an entire day looking and didn't find anything except an old-fashioned, thorough political organization."[86] Roland DeGregorio recalled the time when the *Star-Times* released a story under the headline, "There's Graft on the Hill!":

> Dago Hill's got graft! The election comes out and there's only nine Republican votes out of the eight precincts! . . . There must be graft. The *Star-Times* reporter comes out and Midge Berra says to the reporter, "Shut your mouth. Just a minute! Shut up! Shut your goddamn mouth! Before you go through the ballot boxes I will name you the nine Republicans." And he went right down the list, "Pucci, Donati, Ferrara, Gioia, . . ." Then he told the reporter, "And not that we hate those men or anything. Those men are respected for what they do. But don't say we stuff the boxes. It's just the way it is!" And that's the way Midge could deliver 2,500 votes. That poor reporter went away mumbling to himself.[87]

Paul Berra recalled another episode that infuriated reformers: "When the old-timers who couldn't speak too much English would come to vote, they would say, 'Give me Midge, me want Midge's ticket.' Well, the poor judges didn't know what to do!"[88]

The evolution of the Hill political organization involved three distinct stages, roughly paralleling the maturation of the colony. During the first stage, 1900–1920, immigrants saw little relevance in political participation, and political benefits rewarded only the colony's elite. The second stage of development, 1924–41, witnessed aroused political consciousness among both the first- and second-generation elements. Political concerns became community issues, and group voting translated into tangible returns: increased patronage, police protection, New Deal programs, and recognition. During the third stage of development, from the end of World War II to the present, the neighborhood's continued political finesse has guaranteed efficient city services, Great Society block grants, and the obligatory Columbus Day oration.[89]

In perspective, what has political success meant to the Hill? Would the community have suffered without the presence of Gualdoni, Berra, and the Fairmount Democratic Club? How were boss politics beneficial to the colony? Robert Merton's description of the classic political machine and its functions fits the Hill milieu in many respects.[90] The local Democratic party provided services desperately needed by Lombards and Sicilians: Gualdoni and Berra helped immigrants find jobs, open doors, and acquire citizenship, as well as turkeys at Christmas. Bosses penetrated the imposing bureaucracy, providing a buffer in an alien world. "You know, in a community like this, you gotta have somebody to keep control of things," explained eighty-year-old Carolina Borghi. "A lot of us old-timers didn't know what the score was till Midge and Jean told us."[91]

Boss politics aided in the maintenance of community and ethnic pride. "Politics was a great unifying factor for the Hill," reflected Bishop Charles Koester, a priest of such legendary reputation that even today his portrait can be found on many walls, alongside the Pope and John F. Kennedy. "The relationship between the party headquarters and the church was a very close one. Anything that the community needed, as we priests saw it, all we had to do was call up Jean Gualdoni or Midge Berra. They stood by their people. . . . It was a constant interchange of ideas and things of public concern between party headquarters and the church. . . ."[92] The Catholic church also worked closely with Democratic leaders in the implementation of policy. "I would say that without *any* exaggeration, I could run into Midge Berra seven to ten times a week. . . . They were involved in it and so were you. And you ran to see them about something rather than call them up. Just down the street. Or you just stopped by to see what was going on. Your whole life on the Hill revolved around a succession of meetings and people."[93]

Yet party involvement also retarded assimilation, accentuating class and ethnic tensions. In the 1920s Italians clearly saw the advantage of a powerful political liaison to protect bootlegging cells, in effect, privileged sanctuaries. In the 1930s Democratic leaders appealed to Hill voters as Italian-Americans, raising the bloody shirt of ethnicity.[94] In 1938 Mayor Dickmann eagerly cut the ribbon to formally rename Cooper Avenue as Marconi Avenue.[95] A 1957 Ford Foundation study reported that nationality no longer played a significant role in voting in St. Louis, except on the Hill.[96]

Overall, in both manifest and latent forms, Hill bosses got things done. But were they necessary to accomplish such things?[97] Would the

Hill have fared better under a more progressive city government whereby residents acquired efficient transportation systems and urban services? Neighboring precincts have recently complained that the Hill received political favors in the awarding of city services. As late as the 1950s, for instance, the Hill still lacked a community park. In an age of political cynicism—note that many of the interviews for this study were conducted during the era of Watergate, which might partly explain the halcyon view of the good old days—Hill residents expressed an overwhelming vote of confidence for their past political leaders. If personal life-styles are any indication, the Hill's politicians live and lived quite humbly, in the style of Chicago's Richard Daley.

The political history of the Hill mirrored the colony's rise from an isolated ethnic settlement in 1900 to a well-organized community since the 1920s. The Robert Park assimilationist school of thought contended that once the immigrant base disappeared, so would the political boss. The history of the Hill, as well as other Italian-American studies, reveal the complexities of the ethnic experience. Ironically, among Italian-Americans on the Hill, the harnessing of the first generation, coinciding with the emergence of the second generation, signaled the rise of the community as a powerful political force. Italian-Americans developed a sense of political-ethnic awareness as a result of interacting with the urban network. Politics, while it delivered jobs to needy applicants, protected bootlegging quarries, and promoted ethnic identity, on the whole has failed to redistribute power or fundamentally affect social mobility. In the long run, the Hill was and is better off because of effective politicking and accommodation. Politics in pluralist America is, after all, the art of the possible, not the art of the desirable. It is rarely an arena of morals, but more often an arena of interests.

The changing perceptions of Italian-Americans, as well as the changing structural context of urban America and local politics, are reflected by the political history of the Hill. Italian-Americans accommodated the political establishment and in the process acculturated to the values of Americanism (naturalization and war) and pluralism (voting and patronage). Political accommodation drew Italians into the mainstream, but at the same time it rewarded ethnic behavior: bloc voting, celebrating Italian heroes, and rewarding local political bosses.

Ever since Italian immigrants and their children first tasted the fruits of machine politics in the early 1920s, the Hill community has sustained loyalty and maintained support for the neighborhood Democratic party.

That the community inaugurated a love affair with organized sports precisely at the moment immigrants discovered organized politics is more than a coincidence. Immigrants such as Giovanni Garagiola may not have grasped the mutuality between Americanism and sport, but others did. During the darkest hours of the First World War and its aftermath, Americans shuddered at the ignoble Black Sox scandal. "[We are] impressed with the fact that baseball is an index to our national genius and moral character," the grand jury foreman declaimed. "The American principle of merit and fair play must prevail. . . ."[98] Baseball prevailed, to the fortune of immigrant sons such as Joe Garagiola, the all-American boy from Elizabeth Avenue in St. Louis. The gregarious Garagiola traded the tools of ignorance for a microphone and has since made a successful career promoting baseball, Detroit cars, and at various times presidential candidates.

NOTES

1. U.S. Congress, Senate, Senator Williams speaking, 62nd Cong., 2d Sess., Apr. 18, 1915, *Congressional Record*, vol. 47, pt. 5, 4974–75.

2. Swieranga, "Ethno-cultural Political Analysis"; Kleppner, *Cross of Culture;* Jensen, *Winning of the Midwest;* see also Leubke, *Immigrants and Politics;* Holt, *Forging a Majority;* Allswang, *House for All Peoples.*

3. Bryce, *American Commonwealth.*

4. Steffens, *Shame of the Cities*, 2; see also Meriwether, "Reign of Boodle," 46.

5. *Post-Dispatch*, May 3, 1903, IV, p. 1; see also *Post-Dispatch*, Apr. 20, 1904, p. 5, May 15, 1912, p. 1, Mar. 1, 1913, p. 2, Sept. 11, 1882; *Republic*, June 14, 1908, V., p. 1.

6. *Post-Dispatch*, Sept. 11, 1882, p. 1.

7. Dreiser, *Book about Myself*, 109–10.

8. Crawford, *Immigrant in St. Louis*, 66–67.

9. Gualdoni Papers, Missouri Historical Society, MS.

10. *Globe-Democrat*, Jan. 27, 1912, p. 6.

11. Richard Bartholdt Papers, Missouri Historical Society, MSS, speech, "Political Corruption in St. Louis," June 27, 1902.

12. U.S. Congress, House, Representative Rucker speaking, 63rd Cong., 2d Sess., June 19, 1914, *Congressional Record*, 51, 19741.

13. Meriwether, "Reign of Boodle," 46.

14. *Post-Dispatch*, Nov. 14, 1903, p. 1, Nov. 12, 1903, p. 1, Nov. 9, 1903, Nov. 7, 1903, p. 1; St. Louis Voter Registration Lists, St. Louis Archives, City

Hall, 1900–1902, Ward 24, Precinct 9; Dyer, *Autobiography and Reminiscences*, 272–90.

15. Ibid.; *Dolan* v. *U.S.*, in *Federal Reporter*, vol. 133 (1903).

16. *Globe-Democrat*, Oct. 8, 1902, p. 13.

17. Wood, "Fairmount Heights," 47.

18. *Globe-Democrat*, Oct. 8, 1902, p. 13.

19. *Post-Dispatch*, Jan. 24, 1903, p. 1, Nov. 7, 9, 12, 14, 1909; *Globe-Democrat*, Nov. 27, 1903.

20. Geiger, *Joseph W. Folk*.

21. Dyer, *Autobiography and Reminiscences*, 272.

22. *Republic*, Aug. 27, 1906, p. 12.

23. *Social Statistics of St. Louis by Census Tracts*, 1935, 45; Dyer, *Autobiography and Reminiscences*, 273; Crawford, *Immigrant in St. Louis*, 66–67; *Revised Statutes of Missouri 1899*, chap. 102, art. 8, sect. 7232; *Revised Statutes of Missouri 1909*, chap. 43, art. 14, sect. 6109; *Revised Statutes of Missouri 1919*, chap. 30, art. 2, sect. 4748; *Revised Statutes of Missouri 1929*, chap. 61, art. 2, sect. 10178.

24. See naturalization petitions, 1906–20.

25. *Globe-Democrat*, Apr. 21, 1921, p. 1.

26. Yans-McLaughlin, *Family and Community*, 121–23.

27. Briggs, *Italian Passage*, 172.

28. Trout, *Boston*, 278.

29. Zorbaugh, *Gold Coast and the Slum*, 175.

30. Nelli, *Italians in Chicago*, 123.

31. *La Lega*, Nov. 24, 1916, Mar. 9, 1917.

32. Interviews with Joe Gioia, Jr., June 3, 1975, and Mike Gioia, June 3, 1975; U.S. Manuscript Census, St. Louis, 1910, Daggett Ave.

33. Fainsod, "Influence of Racial and Ethnic Groups," 361.

34. Ibid., 374.

35. Schiavo, *Italians in Missouri*, 90.

36. U.S. naturalization papers, vol. 99, 1924. The dates June-September 1924 correspond to vol. 99.

37. Naturalization petition, Carlo Gualdoni, 1925; "Louis J. Gualdoni Prospers on Hard and Fast Politics," *Star-Times*, May 16, 1938.

38. Interviews with Jean Gualdoni, Aug. 13, 1973, July 30, 1982.

39. Ibid.

40. Ibid.

41. Ibid.; *Star-Times*, May 16, 1938. Did Gualdoni collect payoffs from bootleggers? The federal government claimed the politician had earned $79,000 during the period 1923–25 and had failed to pay adequate income taxes for those years, a charge Gualdoni denied. The two sides eventually settled for an added tax of $2,177. See *Star-Times*, May 16, 1938.

42. The Hill had originally been called Fairmount Heights, hence the derivation of the name. Interviews with Jean Gualdoni, Aug. 13, 1973, July 30, 1982.

43. Interview with Lou Berra, July 11, 1973.

44. Interview with Lou Cerutti, Aug. 7, 1975.

45. Interviews with Jean Gualdoni, Aug. 13, 1973, July 30, 1982.

46. Ibid.

47. Naturalization petition, Emiglio Berra, 1926. Berra is a very common Lombard surname, and more than eighty Berras are listed in the St. Louis phone book.

48. "Midge Berra: Myth and Mystery," *Globe-Democrat*, Apr. 22, 1962, p. 6D.

49. *Post-Dispatch*, May 19, 1964, p. 9.

50. Interview with Fr. Anthony Palumbo, Aug. 3, 1973.

51. Naturalization papers, 1906–20.

52. Interview with Jean Gualdoni, Aug. 13, 1973, July 30, 1982.

53. Interview with Roland DeGregorio, Aug. 18, 1973.

54. *Globe-Democrat*, Apr. 22, 1962. Naturalization petitions listed the names and addresses of the applicant's witnesses.

55. *Fourteenth Census of the U.S.: 1920. Population*, vol. 2, 851.

56. *Federal Census for Metropolitan St. Louis, 1930*, Table 24, 476.

57. IHRC, International Institute, St. Louis, "Distribution by sex of 1571 declarants for citizenship between March, 1936 and March 1938 at the U.S. District Clerk's office." During the two-year period 378 Italian males and 32 Italian females applied for citizenship, indicative of the continuing male power structure on the Hill. It should be added, however, that a woman became eligible to vote upon her spouse's naturalization.

58. *Sixteenth Census of the U.S.: 1940. Population and Housing*, vol. 6, Table 3.

59. Wood, "Fairmount Heights," 60–61.

60. Ibid.; interview with Elmer Shorb Wood, May 17, 1984.

61. Interviews with Jean Gualdoni, Aug. 18, 1973, July 30, 1982; Missouri Historical Society, MS; *Star-Times*, July 10, 1936; *Post-Dispatch*, July 17, 1935; *Globe-Democrat*, Aug. 26, 1931, July 9, 1936, Apr. 18, 1941, May 23, 1941, Aug. 26, 1942, Nov. 2, 1946, Oct. 29, 1946; *Globe-Democrat*, May 18, 1964; Washington University, Urban Archives, Raymond R. Tucker Papers, series 1, box 2.

62. Dorsett and Dorsett, *Pendergast Machine*, 102–13.

63. Interviews with Jean Gualdoni, Aug. 18, 1973, July 30, 1982.

64. Interview with Paul Berra, the city comptroller for St. Louis, July 31, 1973.

65. Interview with Roland DeGregorio, Aug. 18, 1973.

66. Interview with Charles Pozza, Aug. 6, 1975.

67. Interview with Paul Berra, July 31, 1973.
68. Interview with Frank Gianella, Aug. 1, 1975.
69. Interview with Charles Rancilio, June 28, 1973.
70. Interviews with Bishop Charles Koester, July 9, 1973, Feb. 16, 1976.
71. Interviews with Charles Rancilio, June 28, July 14, 1973.
72. *Globe-Democrat*, Apr. 22, 1962.
73. Interview with Lou Berra, Jr., Aug. 17, 1973
74. *Globe-Democrat*, Dec. 12, 1970.
75. Holt, "Future of St. Louis," 213; see also Dorsett and Dorsett, *Pendergast Machine*, 92; Mitchell, *Embattled Democracy*, 8; Muraskin, "Municipal Reform," 223–24.
76. *Star-Times*, May 16, 1938; Gualdoni Papers.
77. Election returns, St. Louis Archives, City Hall, 1925–40.
78. Interviews with Jean Gualdoni, Aug. 13, 1973, July 30, 1982.
79. Gualdoni Papers; Mitchell, *Embattled Democracy*, 146; *Post-Dispatch*, July 1, 1932, p. 4a, June 27, 1932, p. 2a; *Missouri Democrat*, July 27, 1934.
80. "Is It the Same Gualdoni?" *Post-Dispatch*, July 16, 1934; *Post-Dispatch*, Aug. 29, 1934, p. 1c, Aug. 8, 1934.
81. *Globe-Democrat*, Aug. 3, 1940.
82. Ibid.; *Post-Dispatch*, Aug. 7, 1940; abstract of votes, Board of Election Commissioners, Aug. 6, 1940, DA-824.
83. Gualdoni Papers, MS, letter.
84. Harry S. Truman Library, Independence, Mo., oral history interview with General Harry Vaughn by Charles Morrissey, Jan. 14, 16, 1963, Alexandria, Va.
85. Ibid., oral history interview with Mildred Lee Dryden by Charles Morrissey, Sept. 26, 1963; see also interview with Harry Easley.
86. *Globe-Democrat*, Apr. 22, 1964.
87. Interview with Roland DeGregorio, Aug. 18, 1973. To improve the Hill's rapport with the press Jean Gualdoni claimed in an interview to have hosted "lobster and clam" parties once a month for the fourth estate.
88. Interview with Paul Berra, July 31, 1973.
89. Litt, *Beyond Pluralism*, 18–28; *Globe-Democrat*, Mar. 28, 1972.
90. Merton, "Latent Functions of the Machine," 27–62.
91. Interview with Carolina Borghi, May 29, 1975.
92. Interviews with Bishop Charles Koester, July 9, 1973, Feb. 16, 1976.
93. Ibid.
94. Meister, "Ethnics, Blacks, and Machine Politics," 110.
95. *Globe-Democrat*, Dec. 1, 1938, p. 1
96. *Paths of Progress*, 15.
97. Lotchin, "Power and Policy," 1–50.
98. Quoted in Guttmann, *From Ritual to Record*, 96.

8 The Playing Fields of St. Louis

A Day for Toil
An Hour for Sport
Ralph Waldo Emerson, *Merlin's Song*

Old-timers cannot recall a bigger or more emotional gathering ever. Over 800 Italian-Americans came together to reminisce, laugh, and dream on the evening of April 25, 1981; several hundred others were turned away, in disappointment, from the Teamsters' Council House. The event they celebrated was a reunion of the old athletic clubs of the Hill; more precisely, the evening memorialized Joe Causino, a youth counselor who organized the community a half-century earlier. His alumni included Joe Garagiola, who flew there directly from a baseball engagement to wax nostalgically about "Uncle Joe" Causino, "the Hill's Guardian, Godfather, and Overseer."[1]

Sport played a role in the lives of Italian-Americans that was far more lasting than any athletic anecdote. It was galvanic in the acculturation of ethnic youth, whose athletic voluntary associations underpinned neighborhood foundations in the 1920s and 1930s. Sport channeled forces that had historically divided Lombards and Sicilians and harnessed these divisive energies into creative participation. The emergence of a neighborhood athletic federation also provided a powerful symbol of ethnic group identity. Recreational enterprise performed a dual purpose: it accentuated the Italianate character of the colony while allowing athletes to become Americanized and acculturated into a larger urban society through participation on intracity teams.[2] Sport encouraged not only the preservation of an ethnic subculture but the preservation of the community itself.

Several forces helped to solidify Italian-Americans gathered on the

Hill into a cohesive ethnic community. These factors—geographic isolation, the local economy and limited occupational prospects, the Catholic church, the neighborhood school, and the urban gangs—also contributed to and were affected by the phenomenon of sport. No-nonsense Italian immigrants had come to St. Louis to work: no work, no dignity. Yet the demands of work and the necessities of family survival exacted harsh sacrifices. Having endured a rigid social economy that treated peasants like slaves, Lombards and Sicilians viewed leisure as a playtime for the *prominenti* (the elite). "A cane, work, and bread make for beautiful children," counseled a Sicilian proverb. Another adage cautioned parents, "Stupid and contemptible is he who makes his children better than himself."[3]

Giovanni Schiavo, a pioneering historian writing about the St. Louis Italian community, observed in 1929: "It is well known that as a whole the Italian immigrant has not brought with him any traditions of national games. . . . the only pastime for which the immigrant is noted is apparently *bocce* (an Italian game resembling lawn bowling). National American games do not appeal to the average Italian."[4] Schiavo pointed out, however, that the sons of these immigrants were attracted by the lure of sport. "Their leisure," he wrote, "is more a sign of their own particular environment, rather than the influence of national trends." Yet precisely at the moment Schiavo penned those words (1929), Hill Italian-Americans were poised at a pivotal crossroads, as national and local forces were reshaping the values and institutions of ethnic America.

The 1920s witnessed a transformation of American sport and the rise of the athlete as hero. The proliferation of radio and the urban tabloid penetrated ethnic America, even once-isolated colonies such as the Hill. Italian-Americans were swept into the sporting vortex both as spectators and participants. Whereas no Italians were represented in baseball's major leagues between 1901 and 1906, and only 2 Italian rookies broke into the circuit in 1920 (out of a total of 133 rookies), by 1941 fully 8 percent of big league baseball rosters counted Italians, more than double their share of the white professional ball-playing population.[5] The individual exploits of Tony Lazzeri, Ernie Lombardi, and Joe DiMaggio popularized baseball in Italian communities. The boxing ring also served as a springboard for ethnics. By the 1930s Italian-Americans boasted more champions than any other ethnic cohort.[6] These idols became significant role models for second-generation ethnics who, importantly, now had the time to indulge in leisure recreations.

The first waves of Italian immigrants possessed neither the time nor inclination to play soccer or join an athletic club. "With me," quipped Joe Garagiola, "they could put the ball players in the Litany of Saints, but Papa Garagiola couldn't go for it, so asking him for equipment was out." By the mid-1920s, however, industrial laborers received one-and-a-half-days' rest per week and some paid holidays. Moreover, the young remained in school longer and began work at a later age than their immigrant fathers. The depression reinforced these characteristics. An area social worker noted that in 1933, 60 Italian students were enrolled at the local Wade School; by 1936 that number had increased to 175.[7]

Youth would be served. Italian parents, unconcerned with birth control, produced large families, thus supporting the swelling ranks of the second generation, who were susceptible to the lure of athletics. During the decade of the 1920s more than 700 men aged fifteen to thirty matured on the Hill. A thousand more joined the demographic ranks in the 1930s. The under-thirties age group was now in the majority.[8] Significantly, these young men were second-generation Italian-Americans, aggressively "new world" in social outlook. In sociological terms this group was becoming acculturated, acquiring America's language, aspirations, and ideas. Boys were rebelling against the patriarchal domination of old-world fathers, reported social worker Elmer Shorb Wood in 1936; many "were ashamed of their parents."[9]

Contemporaries often mistakenly associated youth gangs with family breakdown, urban decay, and moral laxity. But the Hill was never an ethnic ghetto disintegrating under social pressures. The Italian family survived the passage of immigration and the rigors of industrialization in remarkably good health. The 1930 census offers a demographic profile of this stable Italian-American community (Table 9). Census takers discovered a total of 2,219 married persons, the greatest numbers belonging to the Italian-born (1,825). In addition, 569 persons over age fifteen lived in the colony; however, only 208 of the singles were foreign-born, indicating the popularity of marriage among Italian immigrants. A total of 181 widows and widowers lived in the community in 1930, the majority belonging to the foreign-born (162), the greatest number of them widows (114). Divorce was exceedingly rare; only 4 divorced men (0.16 percent)—all foreign-born—lived in the colony out of a total of 2,400 adults, married or widowed.

"A large family brings prosperity to the parents," a Sicilian proverb promised. Italian immigrants in St. Louis had not struck prosperity, but

Table 9. Italian-American Family Profile: Hill Population Age Fifteen and Older, 1930

	Foreign-born		*Native White of Foreign Parentage*		*Total*
	male	*female*	*male*	*female*	
Single	117	91	206	155	569
Married	993	832	129	265	2,219
Widowed	48	114	4	15	181
Divorced	4	0	0	0	4
Total	1,162	1,037	339	435	2,973

Source: *Federal Census for Metropolitan St. Louis, 1930*, Table 7 (Washington, D.C., 1932).

their dedication to family and commitment to community created and sustained a culture of community stressing integrity, decency, and honor. Social indices confirm the Hill's reputation as a bulwark of communal health. Its rates of venereal disease, child welfare cases, and frequency of welfare rank among the lowest in St. Louis.[10] How the children of the Hill interpreted these values and adapted to American institutions would become clear.

The neighborhood school, another powerful Americanizing and organizing influence, served both as a laboratory for democracy and a cauldron of socioeconomic conflict. Italian parents looked on the American school with suspicion. Unlettered immigrants (in 1930 illiteracy rates for foreign-born adults on the Hill approached 40 percent) perceived the institution as a threat to parental influence.[11] Compromised by the growing needs of the family and pressing economic realities, Hill Italian-Americans made limited educational gains. Educational prospects improved in the 1930s but the outlook still remained bleak. "Most of the Italian children have difficulty in school because of their language handicaps and poor home training," wrote a social worker in 1936.[12] Appallingly, in 1940 only eleven Italian-American males over age twenty-five claimed a high school diploma, making them the least-educated group in metropolitan St. Louis. Blue-collar workers flourished in a community where strong personal association mattered more than achievement orientation.

Inside P.S. 101 children learned world geography; outside the cloistered halls they quickly assimilated the essentials of ethnophysical geography. "Well, let's give you a little geography," chuckled Lou Berra, obviously delighted in his role as teacher: "Kingshighway . . . the creek . . . railroad tracks . . . that was *our* boundary! . . . Up the Hill we had the Blue Ridge Gang—Irish. To the northwest we had the Cheltenham Gang—a mixture of Germans and more or less natives. East of Kingshighway was the Tower Grove Gang, what most of us refer to as Hoosiers, people up from small towns . . . then the Dog Town Gang to the west. . . . You go beyond that and you get your ass kicked around, so you stayed within your limits."[13]

The rude confrontation with a hostile outside world presented a difficult transition to some, a challenging proposition to others. "In school they taught me all about democracy," remembered Sam Chinicci, a Sicilian immigrant. "Then you would come outside and find these antagonisms and would have to fight for all the things they taught you in school. We used to have these fights."[14] To outsiders there was no mistaking the Hill's ethnic boundaries; to insiders, once Italian-Americans left the colony, "Krauts," "Micks," and "Hoosiers" lurked in the shadows. "If you got caught on the other side of Southwest Avenue," reminisced Lou Cerutti, who attended school during the 1920s, "you got the heck kicked out of you!"[15]

Like urban teenagers across the country Hill Italian-Americans clustered into their street-corner societies. "Every kid on the Hill belonged to a gang or club," remembered Joe Garagiola. "You either belonged or were out of the action." The Hawks, Falcons, Ravens, Little Caesars, and Stags proliferated throughout the 1920s and 1930s, climaxing in 1941 when nearly fifty neighborhood clubs boasted about 1,000 neighborhood members.[16] Whereas the spirit of *campanilismo* (old-world localism) governed the selection and membership of the mutual aid societies among the first-generation arrivals, second-generation club members relied on block-territorial imperatives, regardless of their parent's old-world ties. "All the kids around my age who lived on Elizabeth Avenue made up a sports club," recollected Yogi Berra.[17]

In urban enclaves across the nation gang members coalesced around territorial loyalties. "There is a definite geographical basis for the play group . . . ," contended Frederick Thrasher in his classic study. "The gang . . . is characterized by the following types of behavior: meeting face-to-face, milling, movement through space as a unit, conflict and planning. The results of this collective behavior is the development of tradition, unreflective internal structure, *esprit de corps*, morale, group awareness and attachment to local territory."[18] In *Street Corner Society* the participant observer William Foote Whyte reported the raucous and colorful life-style of Cornerville. Like Cornerville's gangs, Hill athletic clubs mapped out territories, sponsored clubhouses, respected intricate internal hierarchies, participated in local politics, and bootlegged moonshine.

The Hill claimed its own William Foote Whyte in the character of Elmer Shorb Wood. A social worker and graduate student, Wood became a confidant to the colony, reflecting later, "I doubt if there was another person who had been in more homes and had the pleasure of knowing and observing family life on the Hill to a greater degree than I [1930s]."[19] The young sociology student became fascinated by the gang phenomenon, whose characteristics bore great similarity to other working-class, bachelor subcultures. He wrote: "Boys and young men between ages 16–25 have . . . established gangs, or what they term athletic clubs, where they spend their unoccupied time. . . . A few years ago when the easy money was available [Prohibition era] and the community gave them a free rein, the activities of these gangs became anything but moral. One or more prostitutes from outside the Hill would be imported."[20] Wood further reported that at one school the teachers complained that "Italian boys are not trustworthy, especially on the playgrounds, and always have to be watched, as they delight in hurting someone." The lament was a familiar one on the Hill. In 1915 a local teacher had complained of "continual indulgence in alcohol" by the youth, as well as the lack of "legitimate amusements."[21]

Clearly, Italian "toughs" threatened the future direction of the community. Organized sport helped transform the raw, undisciplined energies of young Italian-Americans into constructive outlets for societal-approved violence. In sport as in life there is a fine line between keen and healthy rivalry and rancorous, self-destructive competition. Sport polarized the clubs in the early 1920s: "We had soccer teams nobody could beat," boasted a proud Roland DeGregorio. "But then," he said, his voice slipping noticeably, "we used to fight among ourselves."[22]

The man who directed the Hill's athletic fortunes arrived in 1925. Joseph Causino, a social worker, walked into St. Ambrose Church in 1925, eager to proselytize sport and brotherhood. A new breed of social worker, he had been formally trained as a recreation director and was employed by the St. Louis Southside YMCA. Despite the Italianate sound of his name, Causino was a third-generation Bohemian whose family (originally named Kacena) had prospered in St. Louis. Reared a Catholic, he later converted to Lutheranism. Having graduated with a fine arts degree from Washington University, Causino was forced to cut short a promising artistic career when his family suffered a severe economic setback. He found a career with the Young Men's Christian Association.[23]

Nationally, the YMCA had made an extensive effort to counsel America's burgeoning adolescent population. Social work and sociology in the 1920s focused on Americanization, disorganization of the family, youth problems, juvenile delinquency, social integration, and playgrounds. The social unrest accompanying the First World War profoundly shook American reformers. The Lusk Committee Report (1920) applauded the work of the St. Louis YMCA "among Italians west of Kingshighway—ill-named as 'Dago Hill.'" The YMCA constructed a playground at Shaw Avenue, described as a "character building enterprise." By 1920 the organization had erected over 1,000 buildings, valued at ninety-six million dollars. Locally, the YMCA, which had begun in St. Louis in the 1850s, had established a southside branch to serve the distant Hill by the 1920s.[24]

Joe Causino discovered in the Hill an enclave in need of formal direction. The area lacked a recreational center, or even a playing field. Causino represented the ethos of the YMCA—an appeal for citizenship, the Protestant work/play ethic, the creed of Americanization—and he appealed to the youth on their own grounds. "When Causino and I first went to the Hill in the 1920s," reflected Harold Keltner, the former director of the Southside YMCA and today a ninety-two-year-old retiree who lives one block from his old office, "we discovered the boys were engaged in moonshine, but we quickly forgot that. The boys were just trying to help their families."[25] "He kept us out of jail," volunteered one of his many converts, who added, "It took a guy like Joe Causino to see that we were headed for trouble. . . . We let off steam that way [with sports]. And that's why a lot of guys will tell you that, by the grace of God and Uncle Joe Causino, we were all cleancut kids."[26] "You call me Uncle Joe," he admonished gang members. "Don't ever call me Mr. Causino." A quarter of a century later, shortly before his death in 1969, he recollected, "Like a lot of people, I had the idea that there was something unfriendly about this place. But they treated me wonderfully."[27]

Causino, who learned to speak Italian, fully expected opposition from immigrant parents. "My father never liked my playing ball," remembered Yogi Berra. "He always got sore if I came home dirty and he would smack me for sure if my pants were torn!"[28] Soon after Causino's arrival an angry parent cornered the youth worker and demanded that he state his intentions. "I want to bring in an organized recreational program," the undaunted Causino replied—in fluent Italian. "I want to make them better citizens, good Americans." The immigrant smiled, satisfied with the answer. "That's what we want," he said, "we want our boys to be good Americans."[29] Sport accelerated the process of Americanization.

But how does one explain this acceptance of sport, given the general distrust shown for educators? Resistance to education stemmed from conflict between the cultural values of the family, the community, and the Americanizing influence of the schools. But Italians—and Causino was a surrogate Italian—controlled sport. In other words, control of education rested beyond the Hill, but sport and recreation could be controlled at the local level.

Countless huddles, rap sessions, and confrontations later, plenty of good Americans graduated from Uncle Joe's school. Grown men forcefully swear to Causino's decisive impact on their lives and the Hill's future. "The greatest who ever lived. Dynamite!" declared Phil Verga. "If you needed dough, he gave you money. If you needed a job, he'd help you find a job." Les Garanzini concurred: "He was concerned with us young kids on the Hill. . . . He was for clean living, good people. . . . He got us sponsors for each club . . . ours was the Fawns . . . then he had this clubhouse—he'd let us use the clubhouse for the whole weekend—30, 40 boys. Go camping, hiking. A clean life. Lead a clean life. Be active in sports to raise a good, clean body. He was very concerned with the young people."[30] "It finally got to the point," exclaimed Lou Berra, "where Uncle Joe got us working together. One of the things that welded us together was sports."[31]

Uncle Joe packaged pride, character, unity, and the strenuous life through the appeal of baseball and soccer. Few denied that Causino's techniques and programs were a roaring success. His recreational programs dovetailed with the ambitious St. Ambrose Church youth movement and created an effective hold on the colony's young people, leaving little room or inclination for deviation. St. Louisans lauded his efforts, and the St. Louis Community Council designated the Hill in the later 1920s as "the healthiest district in the city," with *no* cases of juvenile delinquency. Causino's reputation spread beyond the Hill, and in 1945

Hollywood offered the social worker a contract to depict his story on film, an arrangement never consummated.[32]

Soccer and baseball served as a recreational antidote for the depression-strapped Hill. The city opened its first public playground on the Hill in 1924, located at Shaw School. Attendance figures dramatically indicate the increasing popularity of recreation—as well as the rising number of young people: in 1924, 59 residents used the playground daily; by 1934 the figure approached 1,000.[33] And beyond the colony Americans continued to indulge in leisure activities with even greater enthusiasm than before.[34] For St. Louisans free entertainment was offered each Sunday throughout the 1920s and 1930s, as millions of soccer, baseball, and softball fans crowded into urban parks. In 1927–28, for example, over a million St. Louisans attended soccer matches at a cost to the city of only $1,985, or $0.0018 per capita.[35] Sport received a federal boost in the 1930s as New Deal programs sought to involve urban youth. "I was thirteen years old [in 1939] and just as juvenile as our juvenile delinquents of today," reminisced Joe Garagiola. "That was the reason for this league, a project undertaken by the WPA to keep us juveniles off the streets."[36]

The blistering competitiveness, channeled into a communitywide spirit, proved unbeatable on the diamond and the soccer field. The Hill's athletic *risorgimento* upset the balance of power in St. Louis soccer, hitherto dominated by the German Sports Club, the Spanish Society, and the Irish Catholic League. "The Hill had some of the city's most fantastic kickers," contended Bill Kerch, veteran reporter for the *Globe-Democrat*. "They were simply outstanding . . . very well disciplined . . . not vicious, . . . the best in the city."[37] Trouncing Germans and Irishmen added a new dimension to ethnic rivalry, proving far more popular than belting the *paesano* next door.

Sport offered an acceptable outlet for the free-spirited Italian-Americans. Soccer matches in particular were impassioned affairs. During the 1929–30 Municipal Soccer League season, fifty-one players were suspended for roughness and fighting.[38] A typical match in 1934 involving southside rivals Dog Town and Dago Hill nearly ended in a riot before 3,500 not-so-sedate fans. "The game was tough all the way through," complained Coach Norman of Carlstrom's Dog Town. "This is nothing new with our games with St. Ambrose," he continued, scowling. "I couldn't stand such conduct so I took my team off the field."[39] But the violence and ill feelings were short-lived. Soccer collisions were a mild form of cathartic release, an acceptable outlet for socially approved violence. "To individuals too ready to follow some subversive drummer," suggested Eugen Weber, "games offered opportunities for self-assertion and sometimes for indulging in competitive violence."[40]

The spirited play exhibited in the 1930s made St. Louis the capital of American soccer, with the Hill shining as one of its brightest jewels. "The Hill was an important breeding ground for soccer players," wrote sport historian James Robinson. "Since 1929 the Hill has been an outstanding center for soccer activity in the St. Louis area."[41] The 1928–29 season was the first in which Hill athletes competed under one banner. That year soccer players rallied under the banner of Calcaterra Undertakers, winning the title in the city's Foundry League.[42] In a remarkably brief period Hill Italians had successfully perfected the team demands of soccer. In 1924 Louis Jean Gualdoni, a Democratic politician, could find no local Italian youths to play on his Fairmount soccer team. "No one. None," laughed Gualdoni, today in his nineties. "There was none of 'em who could qualify. This was before Joe Causino and Father Palumbo. What I wanted was a winner . . . eventually we got lots of Italians on the team."[43]

The popularity of soccer on the Hill must be evaluated in terms of the St. Louis environment. German immigrants had introduced the turnverein and soccer in the nineteenth century, and the popularity of the game persists today. Moreover, since the Hill's geographic and ethnic neighbors, the Irish and Germans, played soccer, it was only natural that the community's youth would embrace the sport. Soccer remained a second- and third-generation phenomenon; Italian immigrants had neither played nor understood *calcio* in the Old Country.

After 1930 Hill athletes vied for supremacy in nearly every sport. In the early 1930s the gangs were formally organized into an overarching federation, calling themselves the Royal Knights of Italy (later changed to Fairmount Athletic Union because of antifascist publicity).[44] The federation, brainchild of Sam Chinicci, a volunteer, promoted tournaments and intramural competition. "I used to organize parades to motivate the boys," said Chinicci, then a gas station operator. "I organized the federation with the help of the National Youth Administration."[45]

Like everything else sport after 1930 tended to revolve around St. Ambrose, reinforcing the parish as the unquestioned social center of the community. "On Sunday morning, everybody in our neighborhood went to church," reminisced Yogi Berra. "There was never any questions about it if you were going. We went unless we were flat on our backs . . . and it didn't pay to fake. If you were too sick to go to Mass in the morning, you can bet your life you were going to be too sick to go out and play ball in the afternoon."[46] When Yogi quit school after the eighth grade a concerned Papa Berra asked Joe Causino and Father Charles Koester of St. Ambrose to guide the errant young man.

Sport, like politics and the brown derby, flourished in urban Catholic America. Sons of Irishmen, Poles, and Italians took to baseball and basketball, football and soccer. Frank Deford described the phenomenon: "In the palmy days of yore, when order reigned over innocent games, sport was uplifting, and a glorious celebration, like the Mass. Sport and the church both stood for authority. . . . Heroes were larger than life, canonized as athletic saints, a comforting adjunct to the church's own hagiology. The Roman Church has always been perturbed by sex, and for its male adolescents, joining a team was considered the next best thing to a vow of celibacy."[47]

Deford's portrayal of the Catholic church as the bastion of conservatism and the nexus between church and sport fits the well-ordered Hill. Yogi Berra explained: "Another thing that helped in our neighborhood was the church. St. Ambrose's was the big institution on the Hill, and we could count on catching it from the old man if we forgot to go to confession on Saturday afternoon on our way to take a shower at the 'Y.' So we didn't dare do anything too bad during the week because we knew we'd have to tell the priest about it in the confessional on Saturday."[48] Joe Correnti remembered: "Juvenile delinquency! Hell no! And if we didn't watch ourselves, our fathers would beat our asses. . . . And if they didn't, Joe Causino would tan our butts. And if Uncle Joe missed us, the priests would haul us in the rectory for a 'conference.'"[49] "Stay up to eleven and you saw the priest," Mickey Garagiola recalled. "No problem was so big that Father Palumbo couldn't figure it out," reminisced Mickey's brother Joe. When Garagiola was asked to try out for the St. Louis Cardinals, he began to search for a catcher's mitt. "None of our guys had one," he wrote. "The only one we knew of belonged to Louis Cassani. He wasn't one of the boys, but Father Palumbo said that our Johnny Colombo knew Gino Pariani who knew Louie Cassani. The network began operation and we got our mitt."[50]

The Hill had completed a remarkable athletic transformation in a span of less than twenty years. When in the early 1920s local politicians attempted to organize a soccer team they could find no qualified Italians with which to man the team and thereby attract Democratic voters. By 1929 the first organized Hill soccer team had won the divisional championship, and by 1940 St. Ambrose climaxed the prewar successes with the Missouri Ozark Amateur Championship. The fiery leader of that team, Joe Numi, would return after the war to lead area soccer teams to new heights. Coach Numi was guaranteed quality players since his farm team, St. Ambrose, won the Sublette Park Parish School League title twelve consecutive years, 1934–45.[51]

One the eve of Pearl Harbor the Hill stood poised on the threshold of highly publicized local successes. Its era of national recognition would come after World War II. Until Joe Garagiola and Yogi Berra came along, few local youths had dreamed of being paid to play baseball. Sport had certainly not provided an economic springboard out of the ethnic ghetto for Hill youth prior to 1941, and athletic scholarships would await another generation. Berra dropped out of school at age fourteen, and only his spirited play in the American Legion League allowed him to escape the neighborhood. Signed in 1943 by the Yankees, the five-foot-seven, 190-pound catcher reminded Larry McPhail of "the bottom man of an unemployed acrobatic team," but he could hit baseballs. Garagiola had signed with the St. Louis Cardinals in 1941, for a bonus of $500.[52]

Sport had a catalytic impact on the Hill, an effect measured far beyond tarnished trophies. Potentially the greatest threat to community stability had been the gang; if the Hill could not win the affections of its young, the neighborhood was doomed. "If the gang does not become conventionalized in some way into the structure of the community as its members grow older," Frederic Thrasher ominously warned readers in 1927, "it often drifts into habitual crime and becomes completely delinquent."[53] The assorted gangs on the Hill were tamed and energized by Joe Causino, the Catholic church, and immigrant fathers. So great a transformation had occurred by 1934 that Harold Keltner published a YMCA guide ironically entitled *Gangs: An Asset to the City of St. Louis.* Keltner described an encounter on the Hill: "Good sportsmanship is one result of the direction of athletics. The Little Caesars, for instance, last year played several ineligible men on their baseball team. This they did unwittingly and, when they discovered it, wrote a special letter of apology to all the clubs and voluntarily forfeited all of the games."[54]

A handmaiden for solidarity, sport became a vehicle that helped transform factional conflict into creative competition. By 1941 the Hill had become, partly through the medium of sport, an ethnic phalanx. Young and old, Lombard and Sicilian, old-world mustachioed Petes and new world Yogis passionately identified themselves with the Hill, with St. Ambrose, with neighborhood teams. "What impressed me the most about the kids from the Hill," insisted Father Anthony Palumbo, priest and soccer coach at St. Ambrose (1932–48), "was that they were willing to make a lot of sacrifices to play on the team . . . they were willing to sacrifice for the Hill."[55] Joe Garagiola distinctly recalled being approached by an elderly immigrant, who said, "Hey Joey, you the first boy what comes from the Hill, witha name ends a,e,i,o, who getta name in the paper, and no killa somebody."[56]

That sport played such a critical role among Hill youth can be attributed to the ecological characteristics of the locale. These structural factors also reinforced the ethnic dimension of the sport network. Historically, ethnic identification is likely to intersect with territorial commonality whenever ethnic residential patterns converge with a working-class population. The Hill is a striking case in point. Boston's Italian West End, a much studied neighborhood, also exhibited similar characteristics: a strong identification with territorial space, high investments in interpersonal relationships, and strong personal association rather than achievement orientation.[57]

Sport not only crystallized Italian-American feelings within the colony but also provided a public forum for St. Louisans, and in a broader sense Americans, to judge the neighborhood from a perspective other than busted stills and ethnic caricatures. A St. Louis columnist rhapsodized in 1949: "All is not spaghetti, macaroni and choice wine on the Hill, that famed neighborhood in Southwest St. Louis. The principal occupation is sports and the main export nationally is known athletes. Many people think that it is baseball . . . but almost every other sport has produced a similar quota of great stars."[58] Observed a reporter from the prestigious *Post-Dispatch* in 1941: "The Hill is a neighborhood of some 10,000 first-, second- and third-generation Italians. It boasts its own factories and stores, its schools and churches. But best of all, it boasts of being a neighborhood with the lowest juvenile delinquency rate of the city."[59]

Organized athletics had distinctly altered local perception of the Hill and its Italian inhabitants. But what role had sport played in retarding or encouraging the acculturation of Italian-Americans? Had athletics promoted assimilation into a greater urban society?

Sport played a complex, often conflicting role in the formation of urban-ethnic values. On the one hand, athletics fostered acculturation to American ways of life by mixing nationalities in team play. "Sports was a tremendous thing for us Italians," exclaimed Joe Correnti, a dry cleaner who helped organize local soccer teams. "You must remember we were almost a closed community. Sports was an outlet for us."[60] Athletic competition forced Hill players to go outside the sheltered neighborhood and encouraged immigrant parents to observe the spectacle of American sport. In his book *City People*, Gunther Barth described how the urban ballpark helped acculturate polyglot city dwellers in the late nineteenth and early twentieth centuries. The introduction and intricacies of sport turned immigrants into true spectators, "who not only saw the events on the field but also could sense their significance for everyday life."[61] So too did baseball and soccer widen the vistas of the provincial Hill.

On the other hand, organized recreation promoted ethnoreligious identity through competition and the preservation of parish-colony teams. Ironically, the high-water mark of Hill athletic competition occurred during a period in which two forces, the mass media and the automobile, were making important inroads into the colony. But the Ford Coupe and the Gateway Trolley, the *Post-Dispatch* and the Zenith radio, while widening the social vistas of the community, also served to make Hill Italians more conscious of their uniqueness. Urban journalists, eager for unusual copy, accentuated the Italian character of the Hill and the Latin flavor of its athletes, such as Dino Restelli's recipe for his mother's spaghetti.[62]

The 1920s marked the chrysalis of the Hill. Willing prisoners of their own cocoon, the first generation accepted the boundaries imposed by geography and erected by themselves. The 1920s changed forever the relationship between the community and city. Successive challenges to the ethnic colony came in the form of the Immigration Restriction Act of 1924, which thrust the future into the hands of the second generation. Confronted by the Americanizing appeals of the neighborhood schools, the exigencies of demography, the anxieties of the family, and the socializing message of the YMCA, Italian-Americans saw sport as a means to group dignity, communal pride, and local control. Sport offered, however illusory, a springboard to upward mobility and a socially approved safety valve; it generated a galaxy of local and national role models and an effective dialogue with the rest of St. Louis.

Athletics also served the needs and anchored the values of the host society. Historically, baseball and soccer were perceived and in turn promoted as approved sports for the laboring classes. Organized recreation, with its socializing ethos of the acceptance of authority, helped prepare working-class youth for the rhythms of the brickyards and assembly lines. Youngsters preoccupied with relief pitching, and Tinkers to Evers to Chance, were less likely to be propagandized by the surplus theory of labor and the troika of Marx, Engels, and Lenin. Sport, in its regimented demands on obedience, subordination, authority, teamwork, and violence, had also bred an intense belief system that valued patriotism. And this intense sense of patriotism, converging with the collective maturation of several thousand Italian-Americans determined to prove their loyalty to America, unleased a flood of human energies with the call to arms in 1941.

The organizing impulse of recreation and community served as a reservoir of strength during the Hill's greatest challenges: the depression and World War II. The war stripped the enclave of its manhood and threatened to dissolve the bonds of community. It should come as no surprise that it was a young priest, doubling as soccer coach and editor of a rag-tag newspaper (named after a parish athletic club), who orchestrated the community's efforts during these crises.

NOTES

1. *Hill 2000*, Apr.–June, 1981; interviews with Gerald Rupert, director of the St. Louis Southside YMCA, July 30, 1982, and Joe Garagiola, June 19, Sept. 8, 1984.
2. See Rader, "Quest for Subcommunities"; Pooley, "Ethnic Soccer Clubs in Milwaukee"; Sorrell, "Sports and Franco-Americans in Woonsocket"; Spreitzer, "Sociology of Sport"; Somers, *Rise of Sports;* Child, *Italian or American.*
3. Quoted in Covello, *Social Background*, 257, 272.
4. Schiavo, *Italians in Missouri*, 81.
5. Riess, *Touching Base;* 188–92.
6. Riess, "Race and Ethnicity," 45.
7. Interviews with Joe Garagiola, June 19, Sept. 8, 1984; Wood, "Fairmount Heights," 42–45; interviews with spokesmen from area industries, July 14, 1975; Bernstein, *Lean Years*, 66–74; *Globe-Democrat*, Sept. 26, 1926, p. 1.
8. *Federal Census for Metropolitan St. Louis Tabulated by Enumeration Districts and Census Tracts*, 1930, 85–87; Foster, "Hill."
9. Wood, "Fairmount Heights," 45.
10. *Social Statistics of St. Louis by Census Tracts*, Tables 12, 13, 19, 21.

11. *Federal Census for Metropolitan St. Louis*, 1930, Table 6.

12. Wood, "Fairmount Heights," 45.

13. Interview with Lou Berra, July 11, 1973.

14. Interviews with Sam Chinicci, Aug. 8, Oct. 27, Dec. 19, 1975.

15. Interview with Lou Cerutti, Aug. 7, 1975.

16. Garagiola, *Baseball Is a Funny Game*, 15; *Post-Dispatch*, July 23, 1941, p. 2.

17. Berra and Fitzgerald, *Yogi*, 35.

18. Thrasher, *Gang*, 25.

19. Letter from Elmer Shorb Wood to the author, Aug. 22, 1973.

20. Wood, "Fairmount Heights," 35–36.

21. Budenz, "Conditions in 'Dago Hill,'" 126.

22. Interview with Roland DeGregorio, Aug. 18, 1973.

23. Information provided by Causino's daughter, Beverly Estes, Cape Girardeau, Mo.

24. Betts, *America's Sporting Heritage*, 176; Starbird, *Story of the YMCA; Revolutionary Radicalism*, vol. 3, pt. 2, p. 3770.

25. Interview with Harold Keltner, July 30, 1982.

26. Interview with Roland DeGregorio, Aug. 18, 1973.

27. *Shot: the Soccer Paper*, Dec. 1947, 1; *Post-Dispatch*, Mar. 1, 1953; clipping, undated (ca. 1967), St. Louis Public Library, St. Louis.

28. Berra and Fitzgerald, *Yogi*, 35.

29. *Post-Dispatch*, Mar. 1, 1953.

30. Interviews with Phil Verga, Aug. 6, 1975, and Les Garanzini, Aug. 7, 1975.

31. Interview with Lou Berra, July 11, 1975.

32. Minutes, Board of Managers, Southside YMCA, Dec. 12, 1944, Feb. 14, 1945; St. Louis Community Council *Report* (1928), 16.

33. Board of Education Records, 1924–36, St. Louis Public Library.

34. Dulles, *America Learns to Play*, 365–74.

35. Robinson, "History of Soccer," 177–78.

36. Garagiola, *Baseball Is a Funny Game*, 11.

37. Robinson, "History of Soccer," 185; letter from Bill Kerch to the author, Apr. 28, 1976.

38. Robinson, "History of Soccer," 177.

39. *Post-Dispatch*, Nov. 12, 1934.

40. Weber, "Gymnastics and Sports," 96. The idea of the social safety valve was introduced by Paxson in his seminal article on "The Rise of Sport." An increasing number of social scientists have rejected the idea of sport acting as a safety valve. "There is . . . good reason to believe that competitive sports often evoke and worsen the aggressiveness of the competitors," writes Montagu, *Nature of Human Aggression*, 281.

41. Robinson, "History of Soccer," 190; interview with James Robinson, Aug. 7, 1973; Glanville, *Book of Soccer*, 124.

42. Ibid., 191.

43. Interviews with Jean Gualdoni, Aug. 13, 1973, July 30, 1982.

44. Wood, "Fairmount Heights," 36.

45. Interviews with Sam Chinicci, Aug. 8, Oct. 27, Dec. 19, 1975.

46. Berra and Fitzgerald, *Yogi*, 44.

47. Deford, "Religion in Sport," 97.

48. Berra and Fitzgerald, *Yogi*, 44–45.

49. Interview with Joe Correnti, Apr. 30, 1976.

50. Garagiola, *Baseball Is a Funny Game*, 13, 17; Deford, "Religion in Sport," 134.

51. Robinson, "History of Soccer," 192; *Crusader Clarion*, Nov. 30, 1944, p. 2.

52. Deford, "Religion in Sport"; Blount, "Yogi."

53. Thrasher, *Gang*, 54.

54. Keltner, *Gangs*, 8.

55. Interview with Fr. Anthony Palumbo, Aug. 8, 1973.

56. Garagiola, *Baseball Is a Funny Game*, 16.

57. Gans, *Urban Villagers;* Fried, *Urban Working Class*.

58. *Star-Times*, Aug. 8, 1949.

59. *Post-Dispatch*, May 9, 1941.

60. Interview with Joe Correnti, Apr. 30, 1976.

61. Barth, *City People*, 149.

62. *Star-Times*, Aug. 8, 1949; *Post-Dispatch*, Apr. 30, 1976; letter from Bill Kerch to the author, Apr. 28, 1976.

9 Over Here: A Neighborhood Survives the War, 1941–45

War is the health of the state.
Randolph Bourne

Great struggles elicit great responses. Or great failures. The life histories of first-generation founders of the Hill orbited the act of emigration and settlement. They were pioneers, and in conversation and action they never let their children forget that they were present at the creation. It was a generational experience, a single set of values and bonds that pervaded a society, much as the Civil War had for another age and section. To second-generation Italian-Americans on the Hill, economic depression and war crystallized their emotions and fixed their mind-sets.

Sadly, few immigration historians have focused their attentions on the ethnic neighborhood. One must balance local-ethnic themes with overarching generalizations, such as Eric Amfitheatrof's contention, "In the grimmest months of the Depression, some Italian-Americans began having second thoughts about the decision they or their parents had made in leaving Italy. . . . Everywhere there was hunger or the threat of civil disorder."[1]

The depression ravaged the Hill economy, a locale already strapped by the stagnating St. Louis industrial climate. The clay mines had already begun to play out, and by 1930 the Cheltenham brick and tile factories employed 20 percent fewer men than in 1920.[2] Increasingly, salaries of women who worked at Ligget and Myers—cigarettes were a depression-proof industry—supplemented the family income. Because of the depression, noted sociologist Grace Keating, who studied the Hill during the early 1930s, "most of the living for the families has been secured through the earnings of the women and girls . . . employed in the stemming department of the [tobacco] . . . factory, . . . [who would] earn from $5 to $10 a week."[3] According to the 1930 census, 78 percent of the colony's males over the age of ten and 23 percent of the females over ten were gainfully employed. Only a handful of the city's 125 census precincts reported a lower percentage of its male work force employed, although one must remember both the unreported employees of bootleggers and the fact that statistics for 1930 do not adequately reflect the full concussion resulting from the depression. The percentage of Hill women employed was only slightly lower than citywide.[4]

In 1930 the Hill looked desperately to a local economy that would never again sustain families as the immigrant generation had known. A new economy, built on restaurants and services, would replace the industrial base but would not evolve until the 1950s and 1960s. In 1930, 63 percent of the male work force still labored in traditional lines, such as the brick and clay complex, iron foundries, shoe factories, and building industries.[5] The repeal of the Volstead Act in 1933 ended the lucrative underground economy of bootlegging.

The 1930s depression, coinciding with the rise of the second generation, a transportation revolution, and the building of communal institutions, broadened the vistas of the Hill. Whereas an earlier generation shielded the community from the purview of interfering outside agencies, the depression forced the neighborhood to look beyond its boundaries. The Fairmount Democratic Club, the pilothouse for local bosses, engineered the linkage between colony and city. Already by 1930 almost 3 percent of the local work force was employed by the St. Louis Street Department, indicative of patronage payoffs.[6]

Part of the local mythology sustains the idea that the Hill refused aid during the depression. "The Hill fared fine," snapped Lou Berra when asked about the 1930s. "I don't think we had one relief case on the Hill." Another resident emphasized, "I know for a fact, people who went on relief you could count on your right hand."[7] In truth, a number of local families did obtain relief, albeit on a small scale. Elmer Shorb Wood was a social worker for the St. Louis Provident Association between 1930 and 1933, and his district included the Hill. He reported that "the ratio of Social Service Exchange was lower than would be expected in an immigrant colony." He calculated that 15 percent of the Hill's families obtained some form of relief, as compared to the citywide average of 25 percent.[8]

Relief must be seen in a context stripped of raw statistics, however. Wood painted a fascinating portrait of a community desperately struggling to maintain dignity in spite of adversity. "They were proud people," he recalled a half-century later, "so proud that I was forced to be inventive in order to get them to accept help." He continued: "I seen more men who were unemployed who refused to accept help than I did who demanded help. These men simply did not want help . . . as soon as they got a job they told me. . . . the church provided lots of help, but simply couldn't take care of all of 'em . . . and even the liquor trade couldn't take care of all of 'em. Nor the political bosses. . . ."[9] Wood utilized neighborhood institutions to coordinate help to destitute families. Frances Leotta, a Sicilian immigrant who worked at her family grocery until her death in 1975, outlined the operation. "Then there was this man, Mr. Wood," she recalled. "Well, he used to bring my husband tickets, welfare tickets . . . he was trying to get some relief for the people here. Mr. Wood would give the ticket to us, a ticket for food," she explained. "Mr. Wood had a lot of respect for the Italian people. We helped a lot of people with food. We never said nothing about this here relief. . . . We kept it quiet."[10]

The depression challenged the community, and the Hill responded with resilience and cooperation. "Honey, this is the Hill," eighty-year-old Carolina Borghi responded when asked about the depression. "Like one family the husband would run out of work and another family would pitch in and bring food—only if it was a pot of spaghetti."[11] "All members of the community accepted some responsibility for the crisis," observed Wood. "Grocery stores extended credit to the amount of 200–300 dollars. Furniture stores waived payments for their merchandise for months and sometimes for years. Friends made loans, sometimes to the point of self sacrifice, and those who were employed, spoke so often to their employers about a job for some friend, that their own were sometimes jeopardized. . . . individuals with political influence placed so many of their countrymen on city jobs that there was resentment throughout the city. . . ."[12]

Jo Anne Arpiani remembered "St. Anthony's barrel," placed behind the family's bakery. "All the stale bread my uncles would throw in those two or three barrels," she wistfully recalled. "Anybody who asked for anything would get it. Most would ask, 'Is there anything I can do for a loaf of bread?'"[13] Exclaimed Mary Ronzio, "The grocery stores! They would let you stretch your bills for months and months. . . . We never had to beg. Because we had community."[14] "You see," explained Isidore Oldani, Jr., "no one suffered on the Hill because everyone helped one another. You always had a relative, a friend who would carry you for awhile. The grocers . . . and Jean Gualdoni [the boss], he used to give coal and groceries."[15] Remembered Tony D'Ippolito: "Yeah, in a sense it was depression, but people got by. . . . there was a family here who used to have grocery stores, the Di Martinos—they support a lot of families. Leotta family. They support a lot of families. 'Go ahead,' they would say. 'Put it in the basket, don't worry about it.' That's why I love the Hill."[16] Father Anthony Palumbo explained the phenomenon very simply: "People were willing to help one another because they knew one another."[17]

Interestingly, many of the elderly people I interviewed saw the depression as a difficult time but in perspective not a traumatic one. "The Depression was really not that bad," believed Maria Griffero. "In the old country I used to work in the *filanda*, silk work. In Italia, everybody was poor."[18] "I didn't have no Depression," grinned Angelina Merlo. "My husband was a cook. Sometimes I give food to my neighbors."[19] Recalled Father Jaspar Chiodini: "We had enough to eat, we had homes, we had church and school. . . . My memories of the Depression are pretty happy ones."[20] Geno Mariani recollected, "I think Italians survived . . . because economically we were already poor." City Comptroller Paul Berra felt the Italian diet helped ward off the worst aspects of the depression. "The main dish was spaghetti, so there was no real problem with food," he remembered.[21]

When asked about the depression Roland DeGregorio roared, "My brother, my sister, and I were the fattest kids on the block! Because dad worked in the spaghetti factory and he brought it home every day . . . so we had it morning, noon, and—no lie—without being a liar, I can say that I had spaghetti every day of my life from 1929 until about 1932. . . . Italians ate pretty good. They went to work and didn't expect handouts and they went out and worked."[22] For Les Garanzini, depression staples consisted of "Soup! Soup! Soup! . . . Yeah, cold winters and not enough heat. . . . Mom and Dad felt real sorry for us children. . . . But I'll tell you one thing. The food in those days, the mothers could take nothing and make something out of it. . . . They made something out of nothing. Polenta, *rostida* [stew]."[23]

The oral histories of the Great Depression sound more like *Good Times* than *Hard Times*. In part the interviews may have served as a sounding board for the elderly who were confused by the culture shock of the 1960s and 1970s. The human psyche scarred by the bad times remains more invisible, as in this description by Elmer Shorb Wood: "I wouldn't want to live through what I lived through with those families," he sighed. After a painfully long pause he spoke in barely audible tones: "And I guess I wouldn't want this country to—[crying] I wouldn't want to sit down with Joe Crespi anymore at his kitchen table to hear him cry—because he had been a worker—and he didn't know where to turn, didn't know this country. . . ."[24]

The depression tested the fibre of the Hill as a community. The failure of a radical movement to take root can be attributed to a number of factors. Lombards and Sicilians had not emerged from radical origins, nor had they articulated a critique of the capitalist order. Immigrants to the Hill fully accepted the tenets of capitalism and molded their community around the reality of the factory system, small businesses, and the possibility of failure. What troubled many Americans about the depression was the steady erosion of individual control, the realization that in a modern industrial society, distant, impersonal forces had usurped power and control from local autonomous institutions that sustained community life. The proliferation of chain stores during the depression wrested business from neighborhood groceries. But on the Hill—and in many other neighborhoods where mom-and-pop stores carried customers through hard times—no A&P's or Piggly Wigglies appeared. The smaller institutions epitomized the strength and resiliency of community enterprise.

World War II, not the New Deal, ended the Great Depression. If the latter tested the viability of local institutions in the face of economic crisis, the former clouded the very future of the community. In this struggle a community could very well win the war but lose the peace. The most explosive, destructive forces civilization had yet seen were unleashed during World War II, which served to parade history on a grand stage: the Machiavellian geopolitical intrigue at Yalta and the sweep of armies across sea and land sealed the fate of nations and people. But the war involved more than battles and diplomacy. It also intertwined the destiny of thousands of neighborhoods, such as the Hill, whose history has largely gone unwritten.

Italian-American involvement in World War II inexorably intertwined the fortunes of the motherland and Mussolini. To immigrants confounded by the seeming bankruptcy of capitalism on the right and the specter of bolshevism on the left, fascist Italy radiated the charm of strength. Strutting with out-thrust chin, Mussolini with his braggadocio delighted a generation of hero-worshipers, ranging from unlettered emigrants to Walter Lippmann and William Randolph Hearst.[25] Inspired by the stirring stanzas of *Giovanezza*, Mussolini's Italy sought to capture the hearts and minds, if not the pocketbooks, of Italian-Americans. "My order is that an Italian citizen must remain an Italian citizen," asserted Il Duce, "no matter what land he lives, unto the seventh generation."[26]

Today few immigrants will confess to having admired Mussolini, but there is evidence that in the mid-1930s the Hill defended and supported fascist Italy. "Mussolini was important to the older people," explained Sam Chinicci, one of the leaders of the local antifascist movement. "They thought him another Julius Caesar."[27] In 1936, for example, 450 women on the Hill donated their gold wedding bands to the "New Rome," and in appreciation the Italian government sent the patriots steel bands forged from a World War I cannon, each inscribed, "They gave their gold to the Fatherland."[28] The Catholic church also became an ardent supporter of the Concordat between the Pope and fascism. Father Fiorenzo Lupo accepted a medal from Mussolini in 1932 for his missionary efforts in the American vineyard.[29] Efforts to delineate a more precise relationship between the Hill and fascism were ineffective, however. Few interviewees wished to discuss this chapter of the colony's history, and little documentation exists in printed form.

The golden era of the New Rome faded as the paper empire crumbled. World opinion sided with the victims when Italian troops massacred Ethiopians. Admiration for Mussolini dropped further when he courted Nazi Germany in the late 1930s. In St. Louis an Anti-Fascist Society was formed in 1937. "I saw what Mussolini and his government were doing to the Italian people," remarked Sam Chinicci. "The Italian people wanted the same liberties that Garibaldi and Mazzini fought for!"[30] When Il Duce strained diplomatic relations with the United States following Italy's declaration of war against England and France, local feelings were aptly summarized by the *Globe-Democrat* headline of June 11, 1940: "BLUE MONDAY FOR ST. LOUIS ITALIANS."[31] The colony expressed its mood in a variety of ways. "If this country should go to war against Germany and Italy," growled Frank Tommaso, "it will be my pleasure to fight those guys who joined Hitler." Mariano Marchi, the Italian consul in St. Louis, fancifully boasted that American *paesani* would soon goose-step for the fatherland.[32] The Hill's resident intellectual and leading antifascist, Dr. Nino Caradonna, wrote, "Italy is not acting in sincerity! Humanitarianism is not her motive. Like a vulture, she casts an even blacker shadow over the stark tragedy being enacted in the theatre of war. Let us not forget the fact that we are American, that the heritage of this great country is ours. Above everything, we are American citizens."[33]

Life on the Hill entered a new era on a cold, crisp December afternoon in 1941. Families had departed from St. Ambrose Church in anticipation of that sacred institution, the Sunday meal: women huddled in cramped basement kitchens, generously ladling polenta and ravioli; in living rooms mustachioed men drank lavish toasts of vintage 1941 Dago Red. "Our house was full of people all the time, especially after church on Sunday," recalled Isidore Oldani, Jr. "Wine flowed free—*ciquats*—shots of whiskey—flowed free. . . . There was so many places like that. I guess we were so close to each other."[34] But on that certain Sunday a grim news bulletin pierced the gaiety and closeness. "Japanese forces have attacked the American installation at Pearl Harbor," John Daly laconically announced. Shock, disbelief, and fear swept the neighborhood. Pearl Harbor, like the Hill, was once a smug island of security. On the evening of December 7, 1941, tears flowed freely with Dago Red.

War meant different things to different people. To the parents of Mario Bazzetta, Pearl Harbor spelled tragedy, since their son had been stationed aboard the *Arizona*. To the parents of the 1,500 sons born between 1918 and 1926, values such as duty and honor were suddenly wrested from the family and usurped by the government.[35] What would happen to the enclave suddenly shorn of its youth? And what of several hundred Italian citizens, their alien status now an issue? While the Hill manifested an intensely American spirit, fully one-third of the community's foreign-born had not been naturalized by 1940. Would these immigrants be branded "enemy aliens," as were German-Americans in 1917? Memories still lingered of the painful campaign to Americanize immigrants during the First World War. Italian-Americans were about to take the loyalty test.

Attorney General Francis Biddle confirmed the worst fears of Hill immigrants. The government stamped the stigma of "enemy alien" on the 600,000 Italians and 264,000 German immigrants who had refused to become citizens and secure naturalization. Federal officials confiscated potential contraband materials: firearms, ammunition, maps, cameras, and radios. Aliens were required to register and notify the government if they moved or traveled. Officials, aware of the patriotic attitude on the Hill, tempered such orders, and Italian-Americans never endured the appalling conditions that Japanese-Americans did.[36] There would be no

Italian Manzanars. Wartime hatred was directed against Hitler and Mussolini rather than the German and Italian people. Moreover, in 1917 one of every three Americans had been an immigrant or child of an immigrant. The Americanizing efforts by the public schools and the closing of the immigration gates assured most citizens that few German- or Italian-Americans held divided allegiances during World War II.

During World War I, the initiative behind 100 percent Americanism had originated within governmental agencies such as the Committee for Public Information. During the second war, however, ethnic communities such as the Hill became forges of patriotism. Few battles were fought with as much intensity and pride as the Hill's homefront effort to win this war. But unlike 1917 immigrants were not cajoled or coerced into battle; rather, the people of the Hill were among the first to volunteer. "American society has never really faced up to the implications of its own dynamism," wrote Lowell Carr and James Stermer in *Willow Run*, their classic study of war.[37] The Hill was a microcosm of America, a source of untapped and unrealized strength, ready to exploit the moral equivalent of war.

Piqued, excited, impassioned (perhaps bored by the parochial environment), Italian youth stampeded to induction centers in herds, an unexpected by-product of large families. Lures of swaying palm trees and a patriotic calling intoxicated teenagers who had rarely ventured beyond Kingshighway. "When World War II broke out," remembered Mario Puzo, then living in Hell's Kitchen in New York, "I was delivered. There is no other word, terrible as it may sound. . . . what an escape it was."[38] For the first time in the colony's history large numbers took the Vandeventer bus, not to "Dollar Day" at the Famous-Barr store but to the unfamiliarly grim confines of Fort Leonard Wood. More than one son conned immigrant parents into signing consent papers with the airtight logic of young Roland DeGregorio. "Dad," pleaded the young man to his Sicilian father, "the Marines are fighting in the Pacific and I won't fight against your brother and cousins in Italy." "So, that's why you'll find a lot of Italians on the Hill who went into the Marines and Navy," DeGregorio explained later.[39] Other parents displayed less compassion for their ancestral homeland, and a small number of area men enlisted in the Army.

Few neighborhoods contributed more to the ranks than the Hill. From a total population of 6,300 over 1,100 men enlisted or were drafted into the armed services.[40] One particular enclave, the 5200 block of Wilson Avenue, sent more than 40 men overseas; the Passanise family of Bischoff

Avenue gave six sons.[41] Characteristic of the community's fighting spirit, nearly every able-bodied young man aged eighteen to thirty rallied to battle standard. "There was no cowardice here," one veteran explained.[42] It was a time for American patriotism, across the United States.

A close-knit enclave, minus 1,100 young men, pondered the awful present and distant future. How would the neighborhood keep in touch with the boys? Would soldiers, once they had seen the world, return home to the old-fashioned colony? Would the community be a home fit for heroes? America might well win the war, but the Hill might lose the battle for community. The initial step toward the preservation of the neighborhood was taken soon after the first men shipped out in early 1942: a local newspaper was launched.

The fourth estate had never flourished on the Hill. In 1941 the community tolerated, but scarcely supported, two papers: *Il Pensiero* and *The Fairmount News*. Dr. Cesare Avigni, a cousin of Father Cesare Spigardi, had assumed editorship of *Il Pensiero* in 1917. Avigni, who held a doctorate in ceramic engineering, nursed the financially plagued paper from his office in Little Italy, until he moved the press to the more secure Hill in the 1930s. His fortunes continued to sag, and more than one friend swore that Avigni actually starved to death in 1953.[43]

Dr. Nino Caradonna fared little better in terms of public appreciation and financial remuneration. A native of Alcamo, Sicily, he received several college degrees before he volunteered for duty during the First World War. Nursing an ear injury that aggravated him throughout his life, Caradonna immigrated to Cleveland following the war. In Ohio he edited several newspapers and acquired a reputation for his antifascist writings and poems. Caradonna moved to the Hill in the 1930s and reestablished his newspapers and literary magazines. In an effort to win the allegiance of the second generation he printed large portions of his paper in English. The paper had little impact, and only his tenacity—he not only wrote and edited *The Fairmount News* and *La Zotta* but also printed the papers in his basement—sustained their meager existence.[44] "Impact?" mocked Joe Correnti, who in the late 1930s worked for Caradonna. "No, it had no impact at all. . . . the second generation wasn't interested in an Italian paper. . . . my father and three uncles, none of 'em knew how to read the Italian newspaper."[45] Wartime demands for conformity and Americanism severely hurt the foreign-language press; 165 such publications folded during the war.

Given this background of journalistic and literary indifference, how did a twenty-six-year-old German-American priest succeed with a popular, community newspaper? The European catastrophe had driven this young priest from Rome to St. Louis. In 1936 Charles Koester was a student at the American College in Rome; in March 1942 he received his first priestly assignment: St. Ambrose parish on the Hill. Thirty-four years later he reminisced about his trepidation prior to arriving in St. Louis: "I had read in the paper about all the raids and moonshine on the Hill." Father Koester's youthful drive, sincerity, and fluent Italian quickly endeared him to the St. Ambrose congregation. He came away from his first appearance before the parish with at least two vivid impressions: first, the "tremendous enthusiasm of the school children—the warmth they always had for the priests"; and second, the "desperate need to supply local servicemen with news from the home front."[46] The established papers were simply not "youth oriented . . . life completely evolved around the Hill's youth . . . it was natural that things evolve around the parish church."[47] The *Crusader Clarion*—named after the first parish athletic club—was conceived by Father Koester as a marriage between church, youth, and community.

The printed medium had rarely witnessed such an unlikely combination for success. Headquarters resembled an underground press and the staff consisted of energetic but inexperienced young people. The German-American cleric was no neophyte to journalism, however; his father had been a newspaper editor in Jefferson City, Missouri. The first edition of the *Crusader Clarion* rolled off a crude mimeograph machine in November 1942. The staff underestimated the appeal of the inaugural issue, since only sixty copies had been printed. "It was a great contribution to many parents," explained the priest/editor. "Many of their parents couldn't write a letter . . . and simply could not supply the information we could."[48] By 1945 the *Crusader Clarion* boasted 4,600 subscribers. Accounting procedures were disregarded; copies were mailed gratis to servicemen. Residents had only to walk as far as the nearest grocery to pick up the latest issue. To the Hill, Father Koester had become an Ernie Pyle dressed in black.

Lonely servicemen, hopelessly heart-sick for the things they "ain't got," were overjoyed to receive the *Crusader Clarion*. "Your old Crusader buddies are not forgetting you," a scribe promised them in the first issue. "All the news you ever wanted to hear that you were always interested in. The bulletin will give as complete coverage as the *Star-Times* gives to ALL the scandals on the Hill."[49] "As I read the paper my heart overflowed with happiness," exulted Charlie Ferrario, recalling receipt of his first copy. "For the rest of the day I talked and bragged so much about our club [Crusaders] that the gang got tired of hearing me!"[50] The tabloid became a cohesive force in the war-fragmented community. "That paper is what really kept us together," mused Roland DeGregorio. "You go back and ask, 'What kept the Hill together?' That paper is what kept us together. It was like a letter from your buddy. In that paper was letters, names, everybody knew where and what your friends were doing. . . . And really, that paper is what kept the spirit going. Like myself, I'd go to Honolulu and run into five guys from the Hill. And we got together and we had a ball and that was put into the paper and everybody all over the world knew that the five of us were together. See, when we grew up on the Hill, everybody knew everybody."[51]

Heroic deeds and comic relief, reunions and homecomings, all peppered the columns of the *Crusader Clarion.* No fiery editorials, no opinion-editorial page nor divisive topics crept into this neighborhood gazette. "It was the best thing I could have got," swore Lou Cerutti, who had entered the service at age thirty-two. "Good clean literature that didn't bother any of our boys," he insisted. "The only thing I didn't like about it—well—being a Brownie rooter [he brags that he has never seen a Cardinal game]—I'm overseas and dammit if the Cards and Browns don't get in the World Series!"[52] Mickey Garagiola wrote to the paper: "You fellows don't know how much your paper helps. It sure makes a fellow feel good."[53]

While patrons anxiously awaited victory in the Pacific, the home front found reason to rejoice. The first occurred not on the island of Midway but rather in the quicksand world of politics and diplomacy. Within months of each other in late 1942 two events raised the spirits of the Hill: the reclassification of non-naturalized Italians, and the denunciation of Mussolini.

The Roosevelt administration had never felt that Italian aliens posed a national security threat, when compared to the image of the potentially menacing German immigrant. "I don't care so much about the Italians," President Roosevelt once said to Attorney General Francis Biddle. "They are a lot of opera singers, but the Germans are different, they may be dangerous." Ever mindful of the Italian-American vote, Roosevelt instructed Biddle to announce on Columbus Day 1942 that Italian immigrants would no longer be regarded as "enemy aliens" and therefore were exempt from regulation. In New York renowned conductor Arturo

Toscanini, on hearing the announcement, burst into tears.[54] In St. Louis Italians rallied on the Hill at the North Italian Big Club Hall. Lombard and Sicilian differences now seemed trivial. The colony's political leader, Jean Gualdoni, exhorted the gathering that America was a land worth dying for. "Let it never be said," he pleaded, "that in this country that when the test came, we of Italian extraction were found wanting in any degree. . . . We of Italian extraction must aid the war effort. We must buy bonds. We must roll bandages. We must help in the USO." An elderly immigrant asked if he could express his dissent in Italian. He was denied.[55] For Italian-Americans, John Diggins commented, "war was the fuel of the melting pot."[56]

The St. Louis press applauded the Hill's jingoism. "ITALIANS HERE CALL MUSSOLINI DEMON," the *Globe-Democrat* gleefully reported.[57] "If anyone questioned the loyalty of Italo-Americans," the *Post-Dispatch* noted, "such doubts must have been resolved yesterday when St. Louisans of Italian background crowded into the public hall to denounce Mussolini. . . . In almost every report of heroic exploits on the fighting fronts, on casualty lists and in civilian war activities, there are names which bear the sign of Italian-Americans. They represent loyal Americans willing to fight and die for the freedom and opportunity which they found under the Stars and Stripes."[58] The paper concluded, "Mussolini couldn't carry a precinct on the Hill!"

The fires of patriotism burned even hotter when natives learned in September 1943 that Il Duce had fallen from power. Community spokesman Henry Ruggeri denounced the fallen dictator as "the darkest demon from the lowest depths of Hell."[59] The morning headlines of St. Louis dailies revealed the local sentiment: "ITALIAN-AMERICANS HAIL SURRENDER WITH PARADE AND TOASTS," and "HILL JUBILANT OVER MUSSOLINI'S DISMISSAL."[60] The drums were soon muffled and the cheering stopped, however, for Germany and Japan remained unbeaten. The *Crusader Clarion* brought the war home in a vivid manner. "It was the biggest thrill of my life," wrote Charlie Ferrario, reporting on his clandestine paratrooper descent over Sicily. "It brought me back to the Hill as I remembered it: fireworks set off in the churchyard, hot tamales sold by traveling cooks and prized-baked hams raffled off at five cents a chance. The tracers flashing across the sky and enemy aircraft explosions illuminated the eerie night. . . ."[61]

Local soldiers paid the price for their heroism. Thousands of men never returned from the rotting jungles of New Guinea, including Charlie

Gualdoni, one of twenty-four Hill residents who died during the war. Ironically, the young Gualdoni had been named after his uncle, who had fallen at Caporetto.[62] New Guinea also claimed the life of Angelo Calcaterra. "Only recently it had been announced," reported the *Crusader Clarion*, "that he had been decorated with the Distinguished Flying Cross for his fifty missions over the South Pacific."[63] Calcaterra's brother Frank wrote to the home folk: "I would like to ask you Crusaders especially to remember my brother Angelo in your prayers and mass communions. My brother was killed when both the motors of his plane went dead. I know that this is war and it's something we all must face. . . . It was God's will."[64] The unenviable task of delivering letters to the families of fallen servicemen rested with John Anthony. As the community mailman, Anthony personally delivered all twenty-four such letters during the war. "It was very sad, very sad," he reminisced. "Mothers with sons overseas would stop me and hand me their letters . . . no one read English. Oh, it was so sad."[65]

The melancholic Abe Lincoln once quipped during the darkest days of the Civil War that without the ability to laugh he might as well forfeit the will to live. In the same vein laughter lifted the pall of tragedy that enveloped the Hill. Father Adrian Dwyer left the rectory of St. Ambrose in 1940 for an assignment with the Leathernecks. He promised the faithful that someday he would return with a smile, "cussin' like any other good Marine!"[66] John Tapella informed the curious that "French beer tastes like weak home brew!"[67] Reared within the sheltered enclave, touring servicemen delighted the home folks with tales of the exotic and ribald. "The French girls in North Africa are alright," confessed Dan Puricelli, then admitted, "I like it better at home where they are more plentiful and I can understand them better!"[68] Having endured insufferable agonies at boot camp, Leo Ferranto reassured friends that "these Southern belles are teaching me the proper accent!"[69] Hawaii failed to impress Vic Mancuso, who hoped "to get back to the best place in the world—the Hill."[70]

Others returned to their roots. As American armies liberated Sicily they were hailed as conquering heroes. None were more welcome than soldiers united with old-world relatives. "I saw the place Papa was born and the place where he played hide-and-seek," wrote Sam Therina from Sicily. "Your sisters told me that never in their life did they think they would see one of your sons, and boy, were they glad to see me!"[71] Sgt. Joe Pastorello met his grandmother for the first time. "I had a long talk with her and asked her if she would come to the States when this is all over," he revealed. "She said she would."[72] While some local boys found their Italian kin, others longed for a reunion with American relatives. Nick Nicoletti, a P.O.W. in Germany, instructed his fiancee to be "waiting at the church. I intend to keep our date!"[73] She waited, and the Hill waited, but not quietly.

Countless communities such as the Hill actively participated in the civilian dimension during the war. St. Ambrose became the community cockpit. "One of the things that strikes my mind," recalled Father Anthony Palumbo, "was the tremendous outpouring of the people in anything that had to do with the spiritual welfare of the boys."[74] St. Ambrose reflected this spiritual intensity, its altar ablaze in religious and military symbolism. Mothers with sons in the military patiently sewed service stars on the altar's flags. Father Fiorenzo Lupo, interviewed by a reporter in 1942, pointed out several women performing such service. "They're saying a prayer for all those boys, that they'll come back," he explained. "Neither has been naturalized, but they pray for their neighbors' sons who are fighting for their homes."[75] Bathed in the mellow refractions of the votive candles and stained glass of St. Ambrose stood the imposing statute of St. Sebastian. An officer in the Roman Imperial Army, Sebastian was executed by the Emperor Diocletian for his refusal to deny Christ. Arrows piercing his side, he became the patron saint of the soldier.

While activities were most visible within the church, every neighborhood cell buzzed with war-related duties. Civilians on the Hill, as across America, received a vicarious sense of participation in the myriad drives to salvage grease and collect aluminum. If the purpose of the programs was to instill a high level of community integration, it worked.[76] But the Hill already was an integrated community. "We have the will to win," a local hero reminded home folk. "All we ask is that you people back home back us up."[77] The Hill needed no further reminder. Elderly immigrants stammered out verbs at citizenship classes filled to capacity. Over 600 area women rolled bandages for the Red Cross.[78] Secretary of the Treasury Henry Morgenthau utilized bond drives to "make the country war-minded," and as few Italian-Americans wished to be branded "slacker," financial contributions poured forth in local torrents: $78,000 in 1943, a figure topped in the subsequent bond drive. In 1943 the Hill became the first neighborhood in St. Louis to exceed its war chest quota.[79] Perhaps the most deeply felt sacrifice came when zealous patriots converted the *bocce* court at Rose's Tavern into a victory garden. Eggplant and chicory, war staples, basked in the sun where legendary *bocce* games had been played with intensity.[80]

The colony's youth, not to be outdone, also participated in the war effort. Boy Scout Troop 212 sold over $20,000 in war bonds in 1944, in addition to sponsoring countless scrap metal, paper, rubber, and aluminum drives.[81] The children also grasped the importance of public relations. Reporters summoned to the neighborhood in 1941 discovered "hundreds of youngsters belonging to the various clubs . . . staging their own defense demonstration." Spokesman Richard Severino, flanked by a poster proclaiming "Hitler Can't Get Our Goat," eloquently sermonized on the theme, "I Am An American": "My father and mother was born in Italy and because they did not have a chance to get to be the thing they wanted to be, they decided to come to a nation they had read about as a land where people could be anything they wanted to be and go to any kind of church they wanted to and stay home if they wanted to."[82] While across America officials noticed an extraordinary increase in juvenile delinquency during the war years—juvenile workers attributed it to the lack of customary restraints and the collapse of morality during wartime[83]—no such problem existed on the Hill. Italian-American youth continued to unleash their frustrations and energies through traditional outlets such as parish/city athletic teams and church-related activities.

Youth rallies, bond drives and the success of the *Crusader Clarion* helped preserve the morale of the Hill during the period 1941–45. When the men returned the community was ready for their homecoming. V-J Day must have been the happiest day in the colony's history. Tears or smiles, sometimes both, instantly appear whenever the magic phrase "V-J Day" is mentioned. An orgy of grief and spontaneous joy erupted that September night in 1945 when Johnny began marching home. "Out on the Hill, where people really know how to celebrate," the *Post-Dispatch* reported, "strings of cans were attached to autos . . . musical instruments appeared, and the strains of 'Santa Lucia' and 'O Sole Mio' were heard, as Tojo was hanged in effigy."[84] "All the people dancing, singing, the bands playing," recalled Angelina Merlo. "Ohhh, my goodness!"[85] "Well, let me tell you about me," smiled Roland DeGregorio. "I got hurt and was discharged the day before the war was over . . . was out in front of Ruggeri's at 6:00 o'clock that night when the news was announced. I began directing traffic, a bottle of whiskey in one hand and a quart of beer in the other, and everybody who passed got a drink. Then Mr. Ruggeri about that time opened his saloon and opened it to the house, open bar, and the street was closed off and we were dancing in front . . . and then about 10:30 that night the street came up and hit me in the face. . . . *That* was a beautiful day!"[86]

The Hill for one brief moment resembled Times Square. "It was a riot!" reminisced Charles Rancilio, who still barbered at the same shop in 1984 as he did in 1945. "Everybody out in the street, singing. Italians do it in a big way! All the saloons open—all you can drink!"[87] Tony D'Ippolito, also a barber, confirmed the picture. "When the war was over we got trucks and blocked Daggett Avenue . . . and went around with Mike Coco's trucks and had music until 5:00 o'clock in the morning. This is truth, honest to God's truth!"[88] Husbands, sons, and brothers all tramped home, all heroes in the eyes of the Hill. The community even organized groups to welcome the men back. "An official welcome home," Bishop Charles Koester recalled. "I've never heard of any neighborhood that did this on their own—spontaneously!" Leaning back in his chair he fondly summarized his thoughts about war and community. "Those were great memories," he said, tears running down his face. "And there is no question about it, they were *stirring events* that we'll never see again. Especially the great enthusiasm and unity that existed among these people. Such a strong, wholesome unity!"[89]

One would like to believe that war brought out the very best in American society, that the struggle acted as a social catharsis, draining off internal social antagonisms. As Randolph Bourne observed, "war is essentially the health of the State."[90] In April 1942 thousands of flag-waving citizens posed for news-hungry journalists in city after city; the next morning Americans opened their newspapers to read about the spontaneous demonstration of patriotism.[91] But it seems that the patriotism was at times only a thin veneer that obscured a deeper layer of discontent and despair. The 1942 town meetings were staged by the Office for Civilian Defense for the benefit of public relations.[92] The OCD could not stem the undercurrent of dissatisfaction elsewhere, however.

"From the barber who wouldn't shave bomber-workers, to Ford Motor Company executives who so bitterly fought government and union plans for housing them," wrote Lowell Carr in his study of one wartime community, "from top to bottom at Willow Run, nobody deliberately and openly opposed the war effort. Not at all. All they ever did, all anybody ever did, was merely to fight—inwardly, outwardly, psychologically, politically, socially, stubbornly, persistently to the end—every impact of the war effort that threatened their own precious little areas of security. . . ."[93] Willow Run in the early months of 1940 had been a stand of trees near Detroit, Michigan. By the summer of 1945 more than a quarter of a million people had moved into the four-county region surrounding the military complex. Chaos reigned. "The net result was inescapable," observed Carr. "Inadequate housing, inadequate community services, inadequate everything threw the major burdens of the bomber upheaval squarely on the shoulders of the men and women needed so desperately to get the bombers rolling. The armed services were going all-out, no doubt about that. But civilian America never did."[94]

Uncontrolled expansion and federal payoffs carried a price: increasing governmental interference in every sector of the local economy. In Seneca, Illinois, the government provided two out of every three houses in the city, all of which resembled one another in cost, style, and quality. Efforts by the Federal Housing Administration to promote a feeling of community in the housing projects met with indifference and contempt. "A newsletter to keep tenants informed about their common interests and problems was undertaken," wrote Robert Havighurst, "but it was discontinued after the first issue. . . . Residents seem never to have thought of themselves as making up a single social group."[95] Overall, observed a team of sociologists, the wide disparities in economic, social, and moral behavior prevented war homes from integrating into a successful community.[96]

The American social fabric was ripped apart during the war years. Richard Polenberg observed that "the disruption of family life, the sense of impermanence, the absence of traditional attachments, the competition for scarce facilities—all increased the tension between newcomers and oldtimers and made for anything but social cohesion."[97] The war, while healing certain divisions, left America a society divided along class, ethnic, and racial lines. The Hill, compared to other communities, seemed remarkably free from the dissonant tensions and strains of the war. Just how had it retained such community strength during the upheaval? The Hill, unlike Willow Run, Seneca, Charleston, San Diego, Hampton Roads, and a score of other cities, was not victimized by war-generated, urban implosion. Rather, the enclave remained stable throughout the conflict, thus spared the acute housing and public service problems that wracked war-boom towns.

The Hill's population, which remained settled and homogeneous, was another factor. "Next to loneliness," observed Bill Moyers in *Listening to America*, "the national disease is homesickness; just about everyone in

America is from somewhere else."[98] World War II certainly fed the mobile instincts of Americans. The war years witnessed migration on an unprecedented scale: twelve million men and women joined the armed forces and another fifteen million civilians moved across county lines to seek work.[99] Before the war, for example, 89 percent of the Japanese-Americans lived on the West Coast; by 1950 only 58 percent resided there.[100] Black Americans continued in their great migration, clustering in northern ghettos after the war, and rural families moved to the cities in increasing numbers. The roots of the Sunbelt can be traced to the dynamics of the war.[101]

The urban church also played an important role in the preservation of traditional values. Prewar America instinctively looked to that institution as a source of strength and a bellwether of change. "The churches met the individual spiritual needs of their people," wrote Robert Havighurst. "They [churches] brought people together for all kinds of friendly face-to-face sociability that made Seneca a community, a place where people lived a common life. . . . How did the war boom affect churches? What role did these churches play in New Seneca? Did churches discover new things to do—human needs to meet that had not existed in Seneca before the war?"[102] Indeed, war brought social cleavage to the churches, as it had to the greater society. One newcomer lamented that when she attempted to attend church "nobody ever spoke to me or looked at me."[103] But on the Hill the church exerted a powerful Americanizing and unifying force. Moreover, by transcending a strictly religious role St. Ambrose acted as an integrating force for the parish. Through the competitiveness of the land war effort (such as parish bond drives and athletic competition), St. Ambrose was drawn further into the pluralist urban society.

The war had been won; now it remained to be seen whether the Hill could survive the peace. The period following World War II proved to be one of unrelenting economic prosperity, but alas, for ethnic communities from Boston to San Francisco, the very successes bred by the Age of Affluence generated powerful tendencies toward change and disintegration. Thousands of Little Italies and Chinatowns went the way of urban renewal and communal atrophy.

NOTES

1. Amfitheatrof, *Children of Columbus*, 285.
2. *Fifteenth Census of the U.S.: 1930. Population and Housing*, Table 8.
3. Keating, "Americanization of the Italian Immigrant," 40.
4. *Social Statistics of St. Louis by Census Tracts*, Tables 31, 32.
5. *Fifteenth Census of the U.S.: 1930. Population and Housing.*
6. Ibid.
7. Interviews with Lou Berra, July 11, 1973, and Mary Ronzio, July 9, 1973.
8. Wood, "Fairmount Heights," 56.
9. Interview with Elmer Shorb Wood, May 17, 1984.
10. Interview with Frances Leotta, May 29, 1973.
11. Interview with Carolina Borghi, May 29, 1975.
12. Wood, "Fairmount Heights," 26.
13. Interview with Jo Anne Arpiani, Aug. 29, 1973.
14. Interview with Mary Ronzio, July 9, 1973.
15. Interview with Isidore Oldani, Jr., Sept. 10, 1973.
16. Interview with Tony D'Ippolito, Aug. 6, 1975.
17. Interview with Fr. Anthony Palumbo, Aug. 3, 1973.
18. Interviews with Maria Griffero, July 25, 1973, Oct. 27, 1975.
19. Interview with Angelina Merlo, Aug. 6, 1975.
20. Interview with Fr. Jaspar Chiodini, Sept. 13, 1973.
21. Interviews with Agino Mariani, Aug. 2, 1973, and Paul Berra, July 31, 1973.
22. Interview with Roland DeGregorio, Aug. 18, 1973.
23. Interview with Les Garanzini, Aug. 7, 1975.
24. Interview with Elmer Shorb Wood, May 17, 1984.
25. Diggins, *Mussolini and Fascism*, 12–67.
26. Quoted in "Mussolini and Italian-Americans," *New Republic* 52 (Sept. 14, 1927): 89.
27. Interviews with Sam Chinicci, Aug. 8, Oct. 27, Dec. 19, 1975.
28. *Post-Dispatch*, Mar. 20, 1936, p. 18; see also *Post-Dispatch*, May 7, 1927, letter to the editor from A. J. Freschi, a prominent businessman who supported Mussolini.
29. *Post-Dispatch*, Sept. 12, 1941, p. 12. Agino Mariani exiled from Italy by the fascists, helped organize an antifascist society in St. Louis. Interview with Agino Mariani, Aug. 2, 1973.
30. Interviews with Sam Chinicci, Aug. 8, Oct. 27, Dec. 19, 1975.
31. *Globe-Democrat*, June 11, 1940, p. 1.
32. Ibid.
33. *Fairmount News*, June 1940, p. 3.
34. Interview with Isidore Oldani, Jr., Sept. 10, 1973.

35. *Sixteenth Census of the U.S.: 1940. Population and Housing*, Table 3.
36. *Post-Dispatch*, Dec. 9, 1941, p. 3, Apr. 13, 1944, p. 2, Jan. 6, 1942.
37. Carr and Stermer, *Willow Run*, 6.
38. Puzo, "Choosing a Dream," 34.
39. Interview with Roland DeGregorio, Aug. 18, 1973.
40. *Fifteenth Census of the U.S.: 1930. Population Bulletin, Families of Missouri*, 36–37. As a comparison, George Kelly has noted that in St. Monica's Parish, New York City, 750 men volunteered for the services out of a parish population of 25,000 (*St. Monica's Parish*, 78).
41. Interviews with Bishop Charles Koester, July 9, 1973, Feb. 16, 1976.
42. Interview with Roland DeGregorio, Aug. 18, 1973.
43. *Il Pensiero*, Aug. 17, 1929; interviews with Agino Mariani, Aug. 2, 1973, and Joe Correnti, Apr. 30, 1976.
44. Interview with Nino Caradonna, June 30, 1973; IHRC, Caradonna Papers; *Post-Dispatch*, Sept. 18, 1955.
45. Interview with Joe Correnti, Apr. 30, 1976.
46. Interviews with Bishop Charles Koester, July 9, 1973, Feb. 16, 1976.
47. Ibid.
48. Ibid.; interviews with Maria and Gloria Griffero (July 25, 1973, Oct. 27, 1975), who worked on the staff of *Crusader Clarion* and loaned the author a copy of their paper.
49. *Crusader Clarion*, Nov. 1942.
50. Ibid., Jan. 11, 1943.
51. Interview with Roland DeGregorio, Aug. 18, 1973.
52. Interview with Lou Cerutti, Aug. 7, 1975.
53. *Crusader Clarion*, Jan. 11, 1943.
54. Biddle, *In Brief Authority*, 230–31.
55. Missouri Historical Society, Gualdoni Papers, MS; *Post-Dispatch*, Jan. 4, 1943.
56. Diggins, *Mussolini and Fascism*, 352.
57. *Globe-Democrat*, Jan. 4, 1943, p. 1.
58. *Post-Dispatch*, Jan. 4, 1943, editorial.
59. *Star-Times*, Sept. 8, 1943.
60. *Globe-Democrat*, Sept. 8, 1943, p. 1; *Post-Dispatch*, Sept. 8, 1943, p. 1.
61. *Crusader Clarion*, Jan. 25, 1944.
62. Interviews with Louis Jean Gualdoni, Aug. 13, 1973, July 30, 1982.
63. *Crusader Clarion*, July 19, 1944.
64. Ibid., Jan. 25, 1944.
65. Interview with John Anthony, Aug. 8, 1975.
66. *Crusader Clarion*, Mar. 15, 1943.
67. Ibid., May 25, 1943.
68. Ibid., Dec. 31, 1943.

69. Ibid., Dec. 31, 1947.
70. Ibid., May 25, 1943.
71. Clipping ca. 1943 from scrapbook of Maria and Gloria Griffero.
72. Ibid.
73. *Crusader Clarion*, Mar. 31, 1944.
74. Interview with Fr. Anthony Palumbo, Aug. 3, 1973.
75. *Star-Times*, Oct. 24, 1942.
76. Polenberg, *One Nation Divisible*, 47–48.
77. *Crusader Clarion*, May 25, 1943.
78. *Fairmount News*, June 1942; *Crusader Clarion*, July 19, 1944.
79. *Post-Dispatch*, Oct. 19, 1944, p. 10. Hill war committees chose to work independently of the International Institute. MS, IHRC, box 8.
80. Interview with Rose Grassi, June 29, 1973.
81. *Crusader Clarion*, Feb. 15, 1943, Oct. 11, 1944; "Enemy Aliens in Name Only," *Post-Dispatch*, Aug. 21, 1942, p. 3D.
82. *Post-Dispatch*, July 25, 1941, p. 2.
83. Abbott, "Youth in Wartime"; Slawson, "World at War," 534.
84. *Post-Dispatch*, Sept. 14, 1945, p. 1.
85. Interview with Angelina Merlo, Aug. 6, 1975.
86. Interview with Roland DeGregorio, Aug. 18, 1973.
87. Interviews with Charles Rancilio, June 28, July 14, 1973.
88. Interviews with Tony D'Ippolito, Aug. 6, 1975.
89. Interviews with Bishop Charles Koester, July 9, 1973, Feb. 16, 1976.
90. Bourne, *War and the Intellectuals*, 69.
91. Polenberg, *America at War*, 11.
92. Ibid.
93. Carr, *Willow Run*, 312.
94. Ibid.
95. Havighurst and Morgan, *Social History*, 79.
96. Ibid., 81.
97. Polenberg, *War and Society*, 144.
98. Moyers, *Listening to America*, 309.
99. Polenberg, *One Nation Divisible*, 54.
100. Daniels, *Concentration Camps, USA*, 166.
101. Bernard and Rice, *Sunbelt Cities*.
102. Havighurst, *Social History*, 153.
103. Ibid., 154.

Epilogue:
The Salvation of a Community, 1945–82

"It seems very pretty," Alice said when she had finished it, "but it's rather hard to understand."

Lewis Carroll, *Through the Looking-Glass*

Fleeced by the quartermaster and kissed in Times Square, GI Joe trekked home to exchange his battle chevrons for a new life-style. For millions of immigrants and their descendants V-J Day signified not only a good-bye to the military but also the denouement of the old ethnic neighborhood. Hundreds of Little Italies and Slovak Hollows came crashing down, some by the force of the wrecking ball, others by the weight of inertia, and others by the silent anguished parting of elderly immigrants.

Few individuals comprehended the changing realities as did Father William H. Reeves, pastor at Our Lady Help of Christians in Little Italy. The war tolled the death knell of the colony, in deep trouble before Pearl Harbor. Once the home of thousands of Sicilians, it had long since lost the original residents and been taken over by trucking companies and an encroaching black proletariat. One family that chose to resist fashion was the Polizzi clan, whose fourteen-year-old son Salvatore would witness the death of one Italian colony and help breathe life into another.

Vast social and economic forces were at work in 1945, none more turbulent than the expansive powers emanating from the federal government. With the power to destroy and create—sometimes confusing the two—Washington had become a full-fledged partner in urban America. "Urban renewal" buzzed in the air in 1945, as evidenced in a poignant letter from Father Reeves to Archbishop Cody, the latter about to attend a conference dealing with proposed changes for north St. Louis. The priest asked His Eminence to "bear in mind the welfare of this parish," and went on to prophesy that "unless some improvements are made in this neighborhood, there will be few if any Italian people here in a short time. In the past few years, possibly 600 of 700 Italian families have moved from where they were formerly within reasonable walking distance from this church."[1]

Father Reeves's plaintive plea went unheeded, and a litany of change engulfed near north St. Louis between 1945 and 1980: the erection of high-rise, low-income tenements, the proximity of an interstate highway, a rising crime rate, the destruction of Our Lady Help of Christians, and the construction of the Cervantes Civic Center. Urban renewal has seldom if ever been so complete. The doxology is no longer heard at the immigrant church; rather, union bosses and civic leaders sing the praises of successful redevelopment. The Civic Center represents St. Louis's effort to project a modern image, while the townhouses help lure young professionals back to the center city. Economically, urban renewal appears to have worked. The complex is sanitary and efficient, but few mistake it for a neighborhood.

On the other side of St. Louis a neighborhood sparkles, but the Hill might well have gone the path of Ybor City in Tampa, the Valley in Chicago, or the West End of Boston, immigrant quarters that shared the plight of Little Italy.[2] Why and how had the Hill succeeded? The reasons tell us as much about the community after World War II as its history before.

Marriage patterns suggest how a society interacts with other cultures. Church records after the 1930s offer an index of acculturation, but not all residents belonged to St. Ambrose or were married in the community. However, between 1943 and 1950 the *Crusader Clarion* published every marriage involving at least one Hill resident. Over 400 marriages occurred during that period, 43 percent of which involved a Hill Italian-American and a non-Italian mate, in marked contrast to the pre-1930 period in which marriage to a non-Italian was rare. Between 1943 and 1950 almost half the marriages (46.5 percent) involved mates of whom both were of Italian extraction *and* living on the Hill. Another 10 percent of the marriages consisted of one partner who was a Hill Italian and the other an Italian-American, though not one living in the immediate neighborhood. Whereas an earlier generation frowned on unions between northern and southern Italians, this custom had clearly broken down after Pearl Harbor. Still, over 56 percent of Hill marriages involved endogamous unions.[3]

Sport continued to accentuate the ethnic vitality of the Hill since Pearl Harbor. Nothing has dramatized and publicized the community more than the individual successes of Joe Garagiola and Yogi Berra, who have made Elizabeth Avenue one of the most famous sandlots in America. Since the 1940s the Hill has spawned four major league baseball players and a half-dozen minor leaguers, a remarkable achievement considering the size of the neighborhood. In addition to Garagiola and Berra, Dino Restelli and Jimmy Pisoni made it for brief periods to the majors. Garagiola, who has made a career out of ridiculing his playing days, which in retrospect were quite respectable, was the first to achieve acclaim, batting .316 during the 1946 World Series.[4]

The Hill also achieved considerable post–World War II fame in soccer. Local teams captured the National Collegiate Club Championship in 1947–48 and again in 1949–50. Joe Correnti, one of the organizers of the teams, recalled the experience. "The real battles were played at Sportsman's Park . . . and before good-paying crowds where the familiar chant throughout the stands at every game was, 'Send those foreigners back to Italy!'" In 1950 local athletes Gino Pariani, Charley Colombo, Frank Wallace, Frank Borghi, and Johnny Barrale starred as members of the U.S. World Cup Team that upset England 1–0 before 100,000 fans in Brazil. The 5400 block of Daggett Avenue has produced six professional soccer players; most recently, Jeff Cacciatore has reaped success at the collegiate and professional ranks.[5]

While sports has served as a familiar reference point for the Hill, organized recreations have not functioned as springboards to economic success for more than a handful of individual athletes. Critics such as Harry Edwards correctly argue that modern sports is the opiate of the masses, offering the illusion of riches while in reality holding back individuals who spend wasted hours on the sandlot rather than in the classroom. But organized recreation also provides noneconomic returns such as the instillment of ethnic pride, publicity of neighborhood fame, and foci for alumni, as well as communal awareness. Spokesmen like Garagiola argue that sport broadened the horizons of Hill youth. As he notes, he had never worn pajamas or seen a formal living room until he toured the minor leagues.

Perhaps the single most dramatic change in the lives of Hill Americans following the war was their new relationship with the federal government. Two generations of Italian-Americans had lived in isolation (although economic and immigration patterns tied them to larger movements). Suddenly Washington affected the way the community educated its children, financed its homes, and interrelated with the rest of St. Louis. The New Deal and the Fair Deal revolutionized the urban polity. Future leaders might debate the level of federal participation but not the basic premise of social security, low-income housing, the GI Bill, and later Medicare. A government that fought a depression and waged global war now subscribed to the tenets of activist liberalism. Such a government, resolved as it was to recast cities and underwrite suburbia, upset the equilibrium of the ethnic neighborhood. Immigrant communities became pawns in a flurry of federal projects that undermined the physical and social foundations of some areas, while paving a path to the middle class for others. Urban renewal meant promise to some, tragedy to others, generating an ongoing debate over the rights of individuals versus those of communities.

Returning veterans were promised a GI Bill of Rights, an act of far-reaching design for American society. Between 1945 and 1950 over two million veterans attended college under the generous benefits of that bill.[6] The Hill, an educational backwater before the war, only slightly improved its academic profile. In 1940, 25 residents claimed a high school diploma; by 1950 that number had climbed to 225. In 1940 the median grade completed by a Hill Italian-American was 5.3, the worst in a city that averaged 8.2; by 1970 the Hill's median years of schooling had risen to over 8.5, though it still lagged behind the city's 9.6 average, and even further behind if the county residents were included at 12.3. In 1970 only 1 percent of the community had graduated from college.[7]

What appears as a persistent unwillingness of individuals and groups to invest in education is in part a reflection of the rigidity of the statistical source. The census does not allow us to discover the educational attainment of those who left the neighborhood. Clearly, the residents who remained in the community had been rejected or had themselves rejected education as a means of upward mobility. One suspects, however, that returning veterans who took advantage of the GI Bill left the old neighborhood upon recognizing its restrictive economic opportunities. "I think the Hill began to break up after World War Two," reflected Father Jasper Chiodini. "Younger kids started going to high school, to college." In fact, St. Louis—a historic victim of the state legislature—offered few public educational opportunities relative to other urban areas, and collegiate aspirants generally had to leave the city to seek a higher education. Educational success, with its rising expectations and increased mobility, meant the Hill would be populated by a residential residue older, poorer, and less mobile. But the community had prospered under poverty; now the postwar years tested its ability to cope with success.

A distinctive Italian subculture dominated the Italian-American family in the postwar years, continuing to direct energies away from careers highly rewarded in our capitalist society. "There was no doubt that I was the 'bad' child because I wanted to finish school," a reflective Mary Ann Favini admitted. "When I was young, I didn't want to be Italian, I wanted no part of the Hill." Like the character in *A Cup of the Sun* who wants to be a writer but knows that if she goes away she will have nothing to return to, Favini reluctantly chose education and career over community and family.[8]

Ambitious sons and daughters like Favini left the Hill following the war in part because of the rigidity of the community, in part because of the local economy. Blue collars predominated in the postwar work force, and as late as 1970 two-thirds of the positions held by neighborhood residents were classified as blue collar. In 1950 the median income of the Hill family stood at $3,333, a figure still comparatively low but indicative of the steady gains made by the working classes.[9] Following the war several of the previously important employers, such as Magic Chef, McQuay Norris, and Marlo-Coil, closed or relocated. Increasingly, food retailing and restaurant work provided the major sources of area employment.

For many Hill residents missed educational chances as well as limited economic opportunities constricted them to the old neighborhood following the war. The commitment to stay remained an individual and familial decision; meanwhile, policies made in Washington forced others to contemplate the price of community. If Italian-Americans' refusal to take advantage of educational benefits retarded economic mobility, then the federal government's resolution not to become a partner to housing rehabilitation nearly wrecked the neighborhood in the 1950s.

The Italian passion for property is well documented. Before World War II Italians maintained the highest levels of homeownership in St. Louis. This drive, however, included a costly trade-off: a forced mortgage on their children's future economic prospects. Homes on the Hill may have been owner-occupied, but they comprised the most inexpensive housing found in St. Louis.[10] The existence of so many older homes—in 1940 the great majority of units predated 1920—spelled future problems in terms of maintenance and improvement. In 1940 fewer than two-thirds of Hill homes possessed both a flush toilet and a private bath. In 1950 the average price of a house on the Hill was $7,000, compared to a citywide average of $9,600.[11]

Returning servicemen found a federal government prepared to infuse billions of dollars into a depressed housing market—for *new* homes. The Veterans' Administration and Federal Housing Administration denied funds for the rehabilitation of older homes, a decision of incalculable harm to immigrant communities. A government that financed the construction of ranch houses in Clayton further smoothed the road to suburbia with massive subsidies: the completion of high-speed freeways and interstate highways, construction of new schools, and the relocation of factories. Most younger Americans eagerly embraced or aspired to the suburban life-style and its creature comforts.

Compared to St. Louis suburbs such as Normandy, Affton, and Maplewood, the Hill received virtually no postwar housing subsidies or advantages. Moreover, the neighborhood—with the completion of Berra Court in the early 1950s—had no place to build new homes. Many veterans wished to return to the Hill, but the homes for sale proved to be inadequate or insufficient in number; in 1950 fewer than 1 percent of the structures on the Hill were vacant.[12] The community was saturated, and many sons and daughters were forced to move to the surrounding neighborhoods.

The Hill thus lost a significant number of people after World War II. But most alarming to community leaders was not the absolute loss of population; rather, it was those key elements forced to leave the neighborhood: young, middle-class Italian-Americans. The colony was becoming smaller and grayer. Between 1930 and 1950 the Hill population declined from 6,089 to 5,353; more telling, however, was the percentage drop in the population under age 25, from 57 in 1930 to 36 some twenty years later, and the increase in population over age 55, from 5 to 18 percent.[13]

A community can withstand a loss of population, but it cannot survive the loss of communal values and institutions. A combination of factors gravely threatened the neighborhood in the 1950s and 1960s, crises never faced before nor even imagined by the pioneers of the 1880s. Urban America had become integrated into a national system of subsidies, dependencies, and exchanges. Internally, modern transportation facilities, the media, and government linked neighborhoods and locales into the city-state. It was increasingly difficult to live independently within the metropolis. Once the geographic isolation of the Hill allowed its inhabitants to live apart from the city, but by the 1950s the locale had been engulfed by St. Louisans in an ever expanding move westward and southward. The Hill no longer was even a hill; tall buildings and smokestacks had long dwarfed the physical properties of the community.

New faces and ethnic groups had taken the place of former city residents. Blacks, who had long competed for low-paying jobs at the brickyards but who did not live on the Hill, now competed for vacant housing in south St. Louis. The federally financed Mill Creek Valley slum clearance project, dubbed "Hiroshima Flats," pushed thousands of blacks into a nervous southside housing market. Coinciding with the Mill Creek project came a number of Supreme Court decisions liberalizing housing restrictions and minority rights. The historic failure of St. Louis to attract large numbers of southern and eastern European immigrants accentuated the city's black-white dichotomy and attracted media attention on the Hill as an ethnic test case. Urban blight descended over south St. Louis as tens of thousands of whites fled to the county or the burgeoning Sunbelt.[14] Tax rolls decreased and urban amenities declined as the newer residents required more services, forcing more of the middle class to move in a now-familiar chain reaction. More Afro-Americans lived in poverty in St. Louis than in any other comparably sized city in the United States.[15] The Hill braced in fear, in part an irrational response since no blacks lived there, in part a rational defense considering the ominous and inexorable push of the black ghetto and its devastating consequences.

The timing of the black migration caught the Hill at its weakest moment since the 1880s. First, the spirit of Italian nationalistic pride had evaporated in the backlash of World War II. Mussolini and fascism tarnished Italian pride. "We don't give a damn for Italy," scowled a young resident in the 1940s, "we're living for America." An incident at the St. Ambrose School in April 1941 epitomized these new values. The 267 pupils at the school "went on strike" because the church pastor, Father Fiorenzo Lupo, replaced the American-born teachers at the academy with an Italian order of nuns. "We want to be taught by Americans," protested one student.[16] The war experience besmirched Italian culture. By 1950 the Italian-language periodicals *La Zotta, America*, and the *Fairmount News* had dissolved, and Alfred Pini, editor of *Il Pensiero*, confessed to a reporter in 1955, "When the old generation is gone from the Hill, the paper will go too."[17] On May 28, 1950, the Vincenzo Bellini

Dramatic Society presented the organization's last play, ironically entitled *Terra Lontana* (The Distant Land).[18] Indeed, Italy was fading from relevance. The church felt the postwar tremors as well. So many former residents had moved to the contiguous neighborhoods that two of the most popular pastors at St. Ambrose, Fathers Anthony Palumbo and Charles Koester, were reassigned to the neighboring parishes. The archdiocese formally redefined the status of St. Ambrose in 1955, changing it from a national to a territorial parish.[19]

Other institutions also hoped to redesign the Hill in the 1950s and 1960s. Three ominous developments shocked the community. In the 1950s rumors first circulated that an interstate highway would dissect the neighborhood. Confident that their politicans could fix anything, residents ignored the situation. Whether politicians "sold out" the Hill, as more than one critic has suggested, or whether bureaucrats selected the community as the path of least resistance, Interstate 44 moved steadily toward the densely populated Hill. The highway department purchased scores of marked homes in the area, and according to a student of the project the bureaucrats "without scruples rented property to anyone—and I say this judiciously—to people who did not care for their property, since it was not theirs."[20] Residents remember scornfully "the Hoosiers and *farmioli* [rural whites]" who rented property in the 1950s.

A second threat materialized in 1965 when residents discovered that an alderman had approved construction of a drive-in movie theater on Macklind Avenue, on the western edge of the Hill. Finally, in 1970 the National Lead Company, with encouragement from the Metropolitan Sewer District, began to pump 40,000 gallons of polluted effluent daily into abandoned clay mines under the Hill.[21] Confronted by aggressive bureaucratic and corporate interests, and uncertain of the viability and resiliency of traditional local institutions, the people responded to the neighborhood threats by creating new organizations. The times demanded new tactics, and for these the Hill looked to the man dressed in black, the "Guerrilla Priest."

Father Salvatore Polizzi, with extraordinary mastery of group dynamics, reawakened the Hill. The son of Sicilian immigrants, Polizzi was born in Little Italy in 1931. He holds bittersweet memories of the old neighborhood, sweet in the closeness of the families, bitter because of the brutal eradication of the colony. Polizzi left Little Italy for a calling to the priesthood, one day to minister to Italians on the Hill. On his arrival in 1956 he detected a void in leadership, an institutional breakdown in the structures that had worked so effectively in the past. The Hill needed a stimulus, an infusion of energy, and Father Polizzi chose to promote the Hill to the rest of St. Louis. August 15, 1965, inaugurated Hill Day, an ethnic festival expected to draw 5,000 spectators; instead it attracted 80,000 St. Louisans, most of them newcomers to the alien neighborhood.

The day before Hill Day I, news of the planned drive-in filtered through the rectory. Father Polizzi recalls, "I went to the university and asked them how do we go about this?" Soon he traded in his frock for an academic gown and acquired a master's degree in urban studies, to obtain a familiarity with the labyrinthine regulations of city/federal policy. "When I went to seminary, who knew about zoning laws, or Meals on Wheels or Section Eight housing?" he reflected. "The [critics] say it isn't church work, but I'm not sure what church work is today!"[22] He masterminded the founding of neighborhood improvement groups, such as the Hill Improvement Association and Hill 2000, community organizations that operate within the framework of conventional networks, such as St. Ambrose Church and the Fairmount Democratic Club. "What we have here is what I call the triangle—the Church, the elected officials and the people of the neighborhood, all working together."

After successfully scuttling the drive-in theater and halting the pumping of sewage under the neighborhood, Father Polizzi spearheaded a coalition of politicians (including Paul Berra, city treasurer of St. Louis) and Hill 2000 and chose to tangle with the highway interests. Interstate 44 had been built, destroying scores of Hill homes in the process. Even worse, the highway's concrete corridor stranded an island of 450 residents on one side, with the closest overpass a mile away. "The Highway took ninety-eight families," remembered mailman Roland DeGregorio, "ninety-eight homes they took because it was my route. A few died. They were so heartbroken they died. They came to this country and that was their first house. . . . Taveggi's wife—she died. Taveggi's wife, mother, grandmother—his father who was born and raised here—they died."[23]

Hill representatives asked city, state, and federal officials to rectify the problem by constructing a new overpass. A committee from the Hill went to the capitol in Jefferson City, Missouri, in September 1971 for a hearing. Polizzi recalled the affair: "When we went there, Paul Berra stood up and said, 'The highway cuts the people off from their church.' Then Al Giufridda [alderman] stood up and said, 'It cuts the people off from their church.' And then I stood up and one of the highway commissioners asked, 'Isn't there a Methodist Church on the Hill?' I said, 'There had been one but it was torn down by another highway project.'"[24] In vain Father Polizzi scolded and informed the state highway commissioners: "These people all shop in the area. It is one of the few areas left in the city where the local neighborhood grocery stores still exist. . . . The idea today is identity . . . trying to get people back to a community." The commission refused the Hill's request, whereupon they chose to take their crusade to Governor Warren Hearnes. In October 1971 Father Polizzi, along with a local political triumvirate, met with the governor, but he too denied their request. "We discovered that when the fight gets ugly, you just have to get mad, and get the people behind you," said the priest. "We can mobilize 500 people for a meeting within a few hours."[25]

Rebuffed by rural-dominated officials at the state level, the Hill took the fight to Washington, where the neighborhood discovered it had some powerful friends. Paul Berra contacted Thomas Gioia, a prominent St. Louis lawyer, to arrange a meeting with Secretary of Transportation John A. Volpe. Meanwhile the neighborhood called on native son Joe Garagiola, in 1971 a national celebrity, to help in the fight. "The fact that I was hosting the *Today Show* didn't hurt our cause," admitted Garagiola. He contacted Rhode Island Senator John Pastore, America's first senator of Italian extraction, to assist in the lobbying effort. (Garagiola would later become politically active assisting Gerald Ford's 1976 campaign.) Other Italian-American organizations, such as Boys Town of Italy, and the Italian-American Chamber of Commerce of Michigan, were contacted to argue in behalf of the neighborhood.[26]

The Nixon administration and the Department of Transportation were besiged by lobbyists for the Hill. "I called him [Secretary Volpe—who incidentally is of Italian background] and explained that this is the way things are on the Hill," remembered Joe Garagiola, "that people like my mother could be trapped on the other side. The Hill must be helped. If those ladies are cut off from going to church, from the store, they will die." The Hill lobby made its point. One final strategy was undertaken, as Father Polizzi offered $50,000 if the Department of Transportation would construct the overpass, knowing full-well that officials would not or could not accept the money. The check represented a symbol of neighborhood power readily recognized by the media.[27]

In November 1971 a delegation from the Hill left for Washington to meet with the Secretary of Transportation and officials from the Federal

Highway Department. The delegation included an official from the St. Louis Urban Institute, a sign of greater awareness to the bureaucratic society of which they were a part. In Washington they huddled with Senator Symington and Congresswoman Sullivan. Confronted by ethnic pressure points, the Nixon administration pledged its full support for an overpass for the Hill. The *Post-Dispatch* editorialized, only half-jokingly, that perhaps the Transportation Department could build a model of the Ponte Vecchio as a bridge over the hill.[28] On November 18, 1971, official word came from Washington that the Hill would get its overpass. "Church bells rang on the Hill last night to celebrate that an overpass would be built over Interstate 44," reported the *Globe-Democrat*. "It [the ringing of bells] was a sign of joy. The people knew what it was. We are sure this came down from Volpe," explained Father Polizzi.[29]

The new ethnicity is a form of historical consciousness; and for the Hill the battle for the overpass forged such a consensus and consciousness. It took a national fight to show residents the uniqueness and vibrancy of the neighborhood. What an irony, for a community that during most of its history defiantly refused to look beyond its local borders, to discover in the 1970s that it possessed national visibility and a sudden desirability. The Hill had become the darling of the media. Soon Secretary of Transportation Volpe, about to become Ambassador to Italy, visited the community and discussed with Father Polizzi—in Italian—the state of the neighborhood. "It was just a beautiful scene to see so many people enjoying themselves without rowdiness," the ambassador remembered.[30]

Father Polizzi's success can be attributed to his tapping of key elements in the community (the elderly, businessmen, politicians) and the crystallization of awareness over the direction of the neighborhood. In particular he articulated a powerful message to the elderly, who by 1970 constituted nearly one-third of the population. For his myriad efforts the priest emerged as a celebrated figure, a Saul Alinsky of the cloth. "Sal runs what amounts to a guerrilla government on the Hill," an urban anthropologist once remarked. "It's a kind of human cooperative."[31] Selected as one of America's fifty most promising young leaders by *Time* magazine in 1974, Father Polizzi, during his tenure at St. Ambrose (1961–81), fought relentlessly to uplift and resolidify the Hill. When local youths deviated from the law, police customarily delivered the boys to the priest for creative counseling.[32] When the Great Society offered its largesse to inner cities, Father Polizzi, along with Monsignor Adrian

Dwyer—who has been intimately associated with the St. Ambrose parish since 1934—mastered the arcane science of grantsmanship. For decades the Hill and Washington had been estranged, either because of the neighborhood's commission or the government's omission, but by the late 1960s federal dollars paid for area cleanups, the planting of trees, entitlement programs and meals for the elderly, and ethnic heritage awareness.[33]

Sometime in the turbulent period of the late 1960s a movement was noted by trend spotters that *Time* magazine called "The Rise of the Ethnics." Michael Novak popularized the idea in his angry *The Rise of the Unmeltable Ethnics* (1971), asking the irresistible question, "How American are you if your grandparents came from Serbia in 1888?" Other analysts suggest that the white ethnic movement did not pick up steam until the televised version of Alex Haley's *Roots* bolted millions of viewers to their couches in January 1977.[34] Haley, of course, had not really caused the roots phenomenon, but he did provide an endearing vehicle for its popularization. Corporate America only too happily packaged the product for consumers, with the same sensitivity as frozen ravioli and *frijoles negros*. *Roots* and ethnic pride appealed to a white ethnic America ridiculed by television and lampooned by degrading images, such as *The Untouchables*, popularly called "Cops and Wops," "the Fonz," *Mean Streets*, *Godfather*, *Paradise Alley*, *Baretta*, "Ratzo" Rizzo in *Midnight Cowboy*, and Tony Manero's *Saturday Night Fever*. Movies and the media portrayed Italian-Americans as lazy, violent, emotional, criminal, sociopathological, nonintellectual, libertine, and selfish. The white ethnic movement offered second- and third-generation Italian-Americans a salve to soothe their collective hurts and an elixir from which to drink with newfound pride.

The immigration historian Marcus Hansen once remarked that what the second generation wishes to forget the third generation wishes to remember. Perhaps the white ethnic movement would have naturally occurred, but a number of precipitating events forced the idea into the breach. The philosophy of white ethnic solidarity sounded an edifying note to ethnic-starved and psychologically insecure Italian-Americans. Paradoxically, an American culture that once glorified individualism now preached the balkanization of ethnic separatism. Millions of third-generation ethnics who had long since left the old neighborhood could now indulge in the symbolic trappings of ethnicity without actually belonging to an ethnic group in the traditional sense (i.e., a mutual aid society, church, or neighborhood). Retailers quickly capitalized on the market: "KISS ME, I'M ITALIAN" buttons became a recognizable fad. Mary Ann Favini, "the bad daughter" because she rejected the Hill for a career, confessed that when she "went home to Italy, I thought, my God, this is what I really am and I loved it!"[35]

Residents of the Hill grasped those symbols of ethnic America (the old country, regional foods, collective pride) and translated them into a cohesive urban policy (pluralist participation, neighborhood studies, public policy statements). A reawakening of ethnic consciousness became a handmaiden to the rejuvenated Hill, as Italian pride symbolized unity, continuity, and utility. Evidence of filiopiety appeared on a number of levels, beginning in the late 1960s and cresting in the 1970s: local schools began offering Italian-language courses to eager students; Hill Day grew more successful and at times riotous; fire hydrants sparkled in tri-color shades of green, white, and red; the community erected a statue by Rudy Torrini of "The Italian Immigrants"; after forty years, Il Teatro Italiano was revived; journalists from *Time* magazine and the *Christian Science Monitor* joined city officials in lauding the distinctiveness of the colony; Hill 2000 published a monthly newsletter filled with recipes, urban survival lessons, occasional interviews with old-timers; new ethnic politicians arose, including Paul Mario Berra, who found the middle name now an asset; and scores of new *ristoranti* began, emphasizing not the generic attractions of Italian food but rather the regional appeal of *risotto milanese* or *pasta catanesa*. The local ethnic revival was solidified by 150 new Italian immigrants who settled on the Hill after 1950.

The structural basis of the Hill strongly influenced the ethnic resurgence. Peter Venturelli, a student of Chicago's Tuscan community, has concluded that an ethnic neighborhood's social, commercial, and religious establishments, "in addition to providing important goods and services, these institutions, whose genre is essentially ethnic, give meaning to content and structure to form."[36] Within these institutions residents continually redefine their relationships with one another and sense the weight of tradition and continuity. An example of such tradition and consensus: in 1982, 1,200 of the community's 1,400 families belonged to St. Ambrose parish.[37]

The rekindled ethnic awareness on the Hill may also be attributed to real or perceived threats to the community's class and racial makeup. "With a person of the same social class but of a different ethnic group," notes Milton Gordon in his classic study of *Assimilation in American*

Life, "one shares behavioral similarities but not a sense of peoplehood. With those of the same ethnic group but of a different social class, one shares a sense of peoplehood but not behavioral similarities. The only group which meets both of these criteria are the people of the same ethnic group and same class."[38] As late as 1970 two-thirds of the Hill work force still wore blue collars, including increasing numbers of women who found employment in the area's restaurant and food retail businesses, although male waiters are still the rule at the more expensive establishments. The popularity of the neighborhood restaurant has created a cottage industry for many women, who make thousands of homemade ravioli and meatballs in their kitchen workshops. In 1930 women constituted 20 percent of the Hill labor force, a figure that grew to 43 percent in 1970.[39] Hill families, hounded by inflation, found a second paycheck necessary to stem the mounting pressures of the 1960s and 1970s.

The post-1960 anxieties shared by Hill residents reflected the structural changes affecting St. Louis. Resurgent ethnicity coincided with the Hill's perception of downward mobility (real and imagined) and racial influx (black and omnipresent). Sociologists Richard Juliani and William Yancey have explored this issue of emergent ethnicity, probing the question, "What social forces promote the crystallization and development of ethnic solidarity and identification?" They contend that new forms of dynamic ethnicity cannot be explained by traditional assimilationist and pluralistic perspectives, which emphasize the cultural origins of ethnic groups. "Rather than viewing ethnicity or ascribed status generally as being inevitably doomed by the processes of modernization," the authors suggest "that ethnic groups have been produced by structural conditions which are intimately linked to the changing technology of industrial production and transportation." Moreover, they point to the importance of common occupational ties, residential stability, and institutional dependencies as ecological determinants for emergent ethnicity.[40]

For Hill Italians the concentration of working-class families living in a densely populated, geographically contained neighborhood, drawing on common traditions of history, language, and culture, created a powerful ethos for resurgent ethnicity. Ethnicity assumed a myriad of forms and functions, serving as an idiom for neighborhood maintenance, blue-collar pride, and a protective cloak against racial change. Above all else ethnicity became intertwined with territorial imperatives. Since the late 1960s the clearly defined neighborhood has provided a varied format for insiders and outsiders. The Hill offers a colorful ethnic atmosphere where St. Louisans play *bocce* under grape arbors and sample panettone and canolli in one of the many mom-and-pop grocery stores. The neighborhood has become a cultural mecca, an asylum where outside Italian Americans may walk the streets, testing their traditions and ethnicity through the spectrum of living history. The Hill has become an ethnic Williamsburg, a living laboratory and a time warp enshrining elements of modernity and community. Incredibly, in a nation dedicated to novelty and newness, the Hill has retained the essential vestiges of its ancestors: the neighborhood remains working class *and* Italian. Its greatest threat is not isolation but overexposure, the danger of ethnic chic, of becoming the trendy attraction for the urban gentry. But that hasn't happened . . . not yet at least.

The community has changed in subtle ways since the 1970s. As late as 1973 dozens of mom-and-pop grocery stores and bakeries still catered to a local clientele; one recognized neighbors and heard Italian spoken over the counter. Discovered in the 1970s and popularized in the 1980s, the Hill has been deluged by outsiders, its narrow streets swamped by a curious public eager to make a pilgrimage to Joe Garagiola's birthplace, play *bocce* at Rose's Tavern, or find hearth-baked bread. In 1973 one could still buy *gelato* (ice cream) from an elderly immigrant who sold the homemade delicacy from her back porch. In 1983 the first *gelateria* in Missouri opened across the street from St. Ambrose. Its shining brass antique bar, capuccino machine, and tutti-frutti flavors speak to the new prosperity on the Hill, an elegance matched in the proliferation of swank restaurants in the neighborhood. Daily, streams of outsiders wait in line at Amighetti's Bakery to consume 600 loaves of bread and submarine sandwiches.

The rise of the ethnic food emporium constitutes an important chapter in local economic opportunities and changing public attitudes. The Italian restaurant, today perhaps the most identifiable symbol of the ethnic enterprise and a synonym for the Hill, was not always such an avenue for mobility. Prior to 1940 only a handful of restaurants and lunchrooms existed on the Hill, most of them located on Kingshighway or Manchester Boulevard, indicating that they catered to an American audience. Few Italians could afford to frequent restaurants, and Italian food had not yet acquired its savory reputation. The 1950s saw the rise of the *ristorante*, as returning veterans sought the delicacies they had first sampled in Europe. The affluence of the 1950s and well-known personalities like Perry Como, Frank Sinatra, and Dean Martin popularized Italian food. Neighborhood taverns and soft drink parlors, which for decades had served lunch for customers, evolved into full-service restaurants.

The Sala family offers an example of such mobility. In 1860 Antonio Sala joined Garibaldi's Red Shirts, earning his revolutionary laurels as a cook. After the unification of Italy he exchanged his military rewards for a coveted tobacco and food license. It was at the Ristorante di Sala that nephew Angelo learned the rudiments of the culinary craft. An apprentice restaurateur and tobacconist, Sala left for America in 1904 with his uncles' blessing and financing. In St. Louis, Angelo Sala hauled sewer tile until he accumulated enough to open a saloon. St. Louis brewmaster Josef Griesedieck guaranteed the investment, with the agreement that Sala purchase Griesedick's beer. The typical 1914 saloon included the ubiquitous free-lunch table, and soon the lunches became as popular as the pails of beer children carried to their fathers at the end of each working day.

Sala's original clientele in the 1920s came from the city's southside German neighborhoods. "Italians were lining up at my door to work, not eat out!" Because the patriarchal Germans preferred to leave their wives and daughters in their cars while they indulged inside, Sala came up with a novel idea: curb service for women. By the 1950s Sala's was one of a dozen first-class restaurants on the Hill, most having evolved from working-class saloons. Many of the establishments, such as Ruggeri's, featured third-generation owners and waiters averaging thirty-five years of experience.[41] Sadly, Sala's and Ruggeri's closed their doors in 1976 and 1981 respectively, victims of location, retirements, and the "new" Italian cuisine. In their places dozens of smaller and more expensive restaurants and other pizza parlors and sandwich shops now dot the Hill.

Also closing its doors in 1982 was the Blue Ridge Bottling Company, another business that could not adjust to modern demands. Founder Isidoro Oldani had immigrated to the Hill from Marcello in 1902. Penniless, he labored in the brickyards until he too accumulated enough to purchase a lunchroom-saloon. That venture ended in failure. "Dad said that if he got everything for nothing," his son Isidore, Jr., recalled, "he still couldn't make a profit in them days. Beer for a nickel and you'd get a bowl of soup and a free sandwich." Oldani then worked for several southside bottling firms, Mayer-Meinhardt and Enno Sanders Mineral

Water Company. There he received his apprenticeship in beverage making and his baptism to the outside world. "He got a horse and wagon and peddled soda," his son remembered. "He said it was terrible because people were real clannish in them days and he worked the southside where there was lots of German people."[42] Convinced that the colony could support a beverage maker and equipped with the necessary cash, Oldani persuaded *paesano* Luigi Venegoni to assist in organizing the Blue Ridge Bottling Company. When Blue Ridge began mixing the sugar and carbonated waters in 1914 it was only one of more than a thousand nationwide. "Our Roman Club Ginger Ale and Lemon-lime was fabulous. We used only the finest ingredients, real oil of lemon from Messina," explained Isidore Oldani, Jr.

If some Hill merchants profited from the illegal fruits of the "noble experiment," Oldani and Venegoni profitted from the legal ramifications of Prohibition. In 1914 the firm sold only 4,000 cases of soda water; by 1929 Blue Ridge was producing 140,000 cases of soda and mineral waters (plus a lucrative sideline in sugar!). The success of the company crested during World War II when brisk business necessitated the use of twenty delivery trucks and the employment of dozens of persons to deliver 650,000 cases of soda. Oldani's two sons, Isidore, Jr., and Charles, inherited a prosperous business, albeit one increasingly threatened by the maw of big business. The big five soda conglomerates—Coca-Cola, Pepsi-Cola, Seven-up, Dr. Pepper, and R.C. Cola—waged a ruthless campaign in the 1950s to expand and dominate the chaotic soft drink market. Simultaneously, thousands of local bakeries, macaroni companies, and beer firms were being devoured by Wonder Bread, the R&F Macaroni Company, and Budweiser. In the 1970s the Blue Ridge Bottling Company was St. Louis's last, purely local beverage firm still in operation, and it existed only marginally. No regular deliveries were made and a thirty-year-old bottling machine produced only several thousand cases a year.[43]

The Blue Ridge Bottling company closed its doors in February 1982. The firm, forced to move in the 1960s because of the interstate highway, stopped manufacturing soda in 1975 but continued to wholesale beverages the last few years. Inside the company's warehouse was an 1893 bottling machine, a legacy of earlier, more prosperous times. One wonders how the fortunes of Blue Ridge might have been different. Had there been an aggressive advertising policy, might Roman Club Ginger

Ale today be the uncola? One can also speculate whether the competition and cost would have been worth it.

If Blue Ridge was a firm that could not compete in an international corporate world, the Ravarino and Freschi Macaroni Company epitomized the success story of small business made good. Like Blue Ridge and the beverage business, the macaroni business was intensely competitive. In 1919 there were 557 pasta factories in the United States. Ravarino and Freschi bought out several local pasta companies on the Hill and has thrived since relocating in the neighborhood. Alphonse Ravarino, on graduating from the Notre Dame School of Business in 1935, reluctantly agreed to join the family enterprise. He remains a driving force behind the company fifty years later and is credited with having succeeded in the business with new marketing and advertising techniques. Today the company operates four factories and, from their corporate headquarters and factory on the Hill, employs many local workers and recent Italian immigrants.[44]

Like Richard Daley's Bridgeport, the Hill has become celebrated as a place that works. Neighborhood institutions, rooted in intense personal contact, continue to perform effectively, from the Fairmount Democratic officials, who can no longer provide jobs but who still help with city stickers and red tape, to St. Ambrose priests, who no longer can "index" books but who still command powerful respect and provide important social services.

The future augurs brightly for the fifty-two-block capsule in southwest St. Louis, in spite of a population decline from 6,089 in 1930 to 4,257 in 1970. Community leaders, frankly worried about the impact of the elderly in the area, who in the 1980 census constituted over one-third of the population, openly encourage the young to return to the neighborhood. Spearheaded by the Hill 2000 corporation, which purchases property to resell to attractive buyers, demand for neighborhood property has outstripped supply of housing stock. "If I had fifty three-bedroom houses, I could sell them by nine o'clock tomorrow morning," Salvatore Polizzi told a journalist in 1980.[45] Hill 2000 has buttressed the material improvements in the community, subsidizing by $1,000 any homeowner who added an extra room and providing rebates of $500 for exterior improvements. Property values underscore the remarkable upward mobility registered by the neighborhood. In 1940 homes sold on the Hill for $2,500, cheaper than practically anywhere in St. Louis; by 1980 the typical remodeled shotgun home sold for $29,000, which was $5,000 more than the average St. Louis house.[46] One resident told a reporter why she spurned the suburban crabgrass for the Hill: "I didn't buy a house, I bought the neighborhood."[47] In 1982 only three single-family detached houses were built in the city of St. Louis, one of which was constructed on the Hill by the Caputa family. "This is home for me," said Sam Caputa. "Our friends and family are all here."[48]

In an age of cultural blandness the Hill offers a refreshing contrast. "An architect would take one look at it [the Hill] and predict that the whole thing will become a slum," notes Norton Long, a professor of urban affairs at the University of Missouri, St. Louis.[49] Explains George Wendel, director of the St. Louis University Center for Urban Programs: "The Hill is a rare mix of little bits, a magic combination you won't find very often these days. . . . For instance, it violates every law known to city planners. Planners hate the kind of mixed usage you find on the Hill. They go crazy over things like having a saloon on one corner, a grocery store on another, an auto repair shop on the third, and a residence on the fourth."[50] In 1971 Missouri Senator Tom Eagleton described the Hill as "the finest neighborhood in St. Louis."[51]

A feeling for community continues to intertwine the lives of Hill inhabitants, just as it had fifty years earlier. In 1935 Jessie Bernhard concluded, in a doctoral study aimed at measuring neighborhood anxieties, that the Hill demonstrated a higher degree of community interrelationships than any district in St. Louis.[52] In 1969, amid the maelstrom of Vietnam and social unrest, a team of Washington University researchers distributed a questionnaire among Hill residents. To the question, "Is there a strong feeling of community on the Hill?" 92 percent of the respondents answered affirmatively; another 71 percent felt that there was no other place in St. Louis they would rather live.[53] In the late 1970s Washington University sociologists again questioned Hill residents' depth of feeling regarding their neighborhood. Over 80 percent of the respondents (6 percent of the entire population participated in the survey) expressed a high degree of satisfaction in the neighborhood; 90 percent maintained a strong feeling of community; 75 percent never considered moving; and 75 percent had lived in their homes for over ten years.[54] The author Martin Mayer extolled the virtues of the Hill as a model neighborhood in his 1978 book, *The Builders*. In 1971 Congresswoman Leonor K. Sullivan, who lives near the Hill, described the neighborhood as "a true family area. There is nothing to touch it anywhere."[55]

The success of the Hill, in addition to attracting national exposure, appears to have inspired other neighborhoods to emulate its example. "Hooray for the people of the Hill," exulted Mary Eckert in a 1971 letter to the *Post-Dispatch*. "I live in Webster Groves, where the highway department has completely shut some people out of the old orchard shopping district."[56] St. Louis historian Neal Primm points to the Hill's role as an inspiration for redevelopment movements in Carondolet and Soulard. Moreover, the Committee for the Survival of the Near South Side owed its existence to the Hill's fight for neighborhood solidarity. "A new dimension had been added locally to the concept of ethnic awareness," Primm concluded, "at a time when multi-million dollar housing schemes and renewal projects were failing, one small community was bucking the tide and winning. . . . the Hill became a showcase. . . ."[57]

In early 1981 the Hill registered shock when news broke that Archbishop John L. May wished to reassign Father Salvatore Polizzi to St. Roch's parish. The disappointed priest accepted the transfer, much to the delight of the St. Roch parishioners, who hoped he would be able to rejuvenate the Skinker-DeBaliviere west-end neighborhood. While he has been sorely missed—"It was like the Pope leaving Rome"—the Hill community has adjusted smoothly. His replacement, the vivacious Father Vincent Bommarito, ironically a neighbor of the Polizzi family in Little Italy, has displayed impressive leadership qualities.[58] Monsignor Adrian Dwyer still leads the parish, adding continuity and integrity.

SOME CONCLUDING REMARKS

Sociologists Richard Juliani and William Yancey have postulated the thesis of emergent, dynamic ethnicity, contrasting the phenomenon to traditional interpretations of assimilation over time. They stress the importance of structural conditions in the promotion of ethnic solidarity and identification. Ethnic groups become interest groups, whose persistence is attributable to salient economic and political issues, not merely quaint symbols of the past.[59]

The Hill's postwar behavior conforms to the patterns suggested by the structural model but also suggests compatibility with the traditional pluralist model, which stresses the importance of culture. Pluralist scholars such as Harold Abramson, Nathan Glazer, and Andrew Greeley hold that ethnic groups resisted assimilation, drawing instead on the wellspring of their cultural heritages. The structural realities imposed on the Hill after

1945—race, geography, and ecology—acted as a precipitant for group-colony behavior. Such behavior, however, cannot be understood without looking at the relationship to the community's occupational strata, institutional development, and residential stability over the previous half-century.

The postindustrial revolution has spawned a school of thought that diagnoses the social ailment of the land as a deficiency of community life. Threatened by energy shortages, alienated by the homogeneity of the shopping mall, and eviscerated by the decline of the family, many Americans see a return to small communities as a bedrock of stability and order. "The Hill is a good example of what positive instrument Italians can make of their kind of living, their way of living here, " explained Mario Montecalvo, the Italian consul in St. Louis in 1973. "I don't say that the Hill will save urban America . . . but still it's a good example. Downtowns are going to hell, but little downtowns like the Hill are helping . . . [in the] return to urban life."[60]

Communities like the Hill pose an unsettling problem for urban planners, however. In a pluralist society, should the colony's example be one of emulation or judication? How does one balance the heritage of an ethnically homogeneous neighborhood with the liberal tenets of busing and desegregation? The embattled nature of the ethnic neighborhood has given rise to a number of fiery and controversial "spokesmen," such as former mayor Frank Rizzo of Philadelphia and Newark's Anthony Imperiale. "There is no program that the government can ever set up that can duplicate a neighborhood, with its responsibilities, its communications, [and] the feelings of belonging that it imparts," believes Newark's Stephen Adubato.[61] It would be wrong, however, to interpret the neo-ethnic revival on the Hill since the 1960s as simply a defensive political protest. Far more powerful than the ecological restraints imposed on the neighborhood are internal motivations, the products of three generations of history.

The success of the Hill has predictably attracted commentators who see the community's history as a vindication of laissez-faire capitalism, as an example of immigrants pulling themselves up by their collective bootstraps. "In the squabble over integration-segregation, school busing and other race mixing, the law collides with human nature," Paul Harvey, America's most listened-to radio personality in 1971, stated. "You can see what I'm trying to say from the top of a Hill in St. Louis,

Missouri. Most all people, given a chance, segregate themselves. . . . Americans of whatever ethnic origin prefer to segregate themselves. They just don't want anybody telling them what to do."[62]

It is true that for most of the community's history families looked to themselves, not St. Louis or Jefferson City or Washington, for help or advice. Children took care of elderly parents, who preferred to stay in the neighborhood rather than move to Sun City. When a father and mother were out of work the neighbors or family saw that there was food on the table. When Tony broke the law the priest and the father belted him in the head and then made recompense. But here also is a community that has learned to change, to accommodate New Deal–Great Society liberalism. Local political bosses secured patronage plums for the party faithful; priests cut through the bureaucracy to secure needy parishioners meals-on-wheels and energy insulation—all accomplished without a loss of dignity or community. A community must be, above all, flexible.

In witness of the disintegration of so many ethnic communities since World War II, how can one explain the regenerative powers of the Hill? Yans-McLaughlin asks the pertinent question, "Are some ethnic groups more successful than others in maintaining old-world traditions?" Few would deny the persistence of Italian-Americans in hanging on to the old neighborhood, but this fact does not explain why the Hill survived and Little Italy did not. I believe that Italian-American history is ultimately local history, the story of how specific individuals from specific old-world villages settled in specific new-world settings. Until we explore the nuances of this local experience, generalizations about immigrant militancy, anticlericalism, and regional environmentalism will be incomplete.

Hill settlement patterns have diverged sharply from conventional notions of ethnic residential development. Recent scholarship in the new social history maintains that three major themes emerged during the development of the immigrant urban ghetto: inner-city location; small-scale clustering and absence of a single dominant ethnic group; and rapid-intensive geographic mobility. Much of the Hill's divergent behavior can be attributed to the colony's atypical development: extensive-high clustering; physical and social isolation; and deep roots with limited geographic-occupational mobility.

The survival of the Hill depended on a combination of urban, class, and ethnic variables. The ecological reality of the Hill isolated Lombards and Sicilians miles from the congestion and commotion of urban St. Louis. The colony's inhabitants arrived with a sense of security, knowing that the enclave was stable and *paesani* were nearby. The structural reality of the colony allowed Lombards and Sicilians to experiment and create communal institutions. Some, such as the mutual aid societies, enterprises, and cooperative groceries, failed to change and meet the new needs of the next generation. But others, such as the church, recreational groups, and political organizations succeeded, and lasted several generations. Immigrants willingly experimented and adapted to changing structures. They were not inert. Timing was critical. A unique amalgam of local conditions and international settlers arrived at a certain point in St. Louis history to carve out a community.

Immigrants created institutions that mirrored community values, maximized ethnic concerns, and maintained working-class solidarity, preserving family honor at all costs. Families persisted in sustaining a cohesive network of support. Immigrants displayed deft control over their lives, breathing life into a community that ministered to their needs. But families and institutions were not static. They provided the flexibility to promote and participate in new economic patterns, educational changes, political involvement, recreational forums, religious institutions, the arena of war, urban renewal, the Great Society and New Deal, and the ethnic revolt. In essence, they survived because the alternative was loss of community, loss of family dignity. Individuals and families rejected the guiding lights of education, mobility, and suburbia for a commitment to the old neighborhood. *La via vecchia* (the old way), modernized with brick, sewers, and sidewalks, was best.

Will the Hill survive the last decades of the twentieth century? The answer lies within the community, not in Washington, D.C., or Jefferson City. "Civilisation," contended Kenneth Clark, "means something more than energy and will and creative power. How can I define it? Well, very shortly, a sense of permanence."[63] To assert self-determination a community must first undergo a rite of self-discovery and self-indentification. The preservation of folkways and recipes must also accompany the sense of shared struggle. If the Hill is to remain an ethnic showcase for the next generation it must impart to grandchildren the idea of who they are and where they came from. History can become a source of pride and power. "I know histhry isn't true Hinnessy, because it ain't like what I see ivry day in Halstead Sthreet," said Mr. Dooley many years ago, about another community. "If any wan comes along with a histhry iv Greece or Rome, that'll show me th' people fightin', gettin' drunk, makin' love, gettin' married, owin' the grocery man an' bein' without hard coal, I'll believe they was a Greece or Rome, but not befur'. I want to know what nations lived iv, not what they died iv!"

NOTES

1. St. Louis, St. Louis Archdiocesan Archives, MS, Chancery Parish File, Our Lady Help of Christians, letter from Fr. William H. Reeves to Archbishop J. Cody, Jan. 9,.1945.

2. Royko, *Boss;* Gans, *Urban Villagers;* see also Caro, *Power Broker,* 463–65; Nelli, "Myth of Urban Renewal."

3. *Crusader Clarion,* 1943–50.

4. *Globe-Democrat,* Aug. 27, 1947, p. 3C; *Star-Times,* May 20, 1947, Aug. 8, 1949.

5. Correnti, "Correnti's Soccer Team,"*Hill 2000,* Oct. 1974; Sorrell, "Sports and Franco-Americans in Woonsocket."

6. Goulden, *The Best Years,* 67.

7. *Sixteenth Census of the U.S.: 1940. Population and Housing,* Table 3, pp. 38–50; *Seventeenth Census of the U.S.: 1950. Population and Housing Statistics,* Table 1; O'Leary, "Ethnicity in Defense of Class," 234.

8. Waldo, *Cup of the Sun;* "View from the Hill," *Post Dispatch,* Aug. 18, 1974, magazine.

9. O'Leary, "Ethnicity in Defense of Class," 229–34; *Seventeenth Census of the U.S.: 1950. St. Louis and Adjacent Area,* Table 1, p. 11.

10. Little and Nourse, "Neighborhood Succession Process," 30.

11. *Sixteenth Census of the U.S.: 1940. Population and Housing,* Tables 2, 6; *Seventeenth Census of the U.S.: 1950. St. Louis and Adjacent Areas,* Table 2.

12. Ibid., Tables 4, 6; Little and Nourse, "Neighborhood Succession Process," 2–58; Williams, *St. Louis,* v; Polenberg, *One Nation Divisible,* 129–32; Mayer, *Builders,* 123–24, 161.

13. O'Leary, "Ethnicity in Defense of Class," 227.

14. Cervantes, *Mr. Mayor,* 68; Little and Leven, "Internal Migration," 13–24; *Urban Decay in St. Louis;* Mayer, *Builders,* 151–53; Primm, *Lion of the Valley,* 472–504.

15. Dubman, *Poverty in St. Louis,* 24.

16. "Enemy Aliens in Name Only," *Post-Dispatch,* Aug. 21, 1942, p. 3-D, Apr. 22, 1941.

17. Interview with Nino Caradonna, June 30, 1973; "Foreign Language Press in St. Louis," *Post-Dispatch,* Sept. 18, 1955.

18. Cunetto, "Italian Language Clubs in St. Louis," 23.

19. Interviews with Fr. Anthony Palumbo, Aug. 23, 1973, Bishop Charles

Koester, July 9, 1973, Feb. 16, 1976, and Msgr. Adrian Dwyer, Aug. 20, 1970, Apr. 10, 1976, July 30, 1982.

20. Interview with Fr. Salvatore Polizzi, Aug. 12, 1973.

21. Ibid.; "The Hill, St. Louis," *Christian Science Monitor*, Feb. 14, 1974, p. F-1; "1000 Pledge Fight Against 'Hill' Drive-In," *Globe-Democrat*, Aug. 26, 1965.

22. Interview with Fr. Salvatore Polizzi, Aug. 12, 1973; "A Goodbye to the Hill," *Post-Dispatch*, Mar. 1, 1981, p. 1-D; "St. Louis: Pride on 'the Hill,'" *Time*, Apr. 29, 1974, p. 27; letter from Fr. Salvatore Polizzi to the author, Aug. 18, 1984.

23. Interview with Roland DeGregorio, Aug. 18, 1973.

24. *Globe-Democrat*, Sept. 30, 1971; Polizzi, "Edwards Street Overpass Controversy."

25. Interviews with Fr. Salvatore Polizzi, Aug. 12, 1973, Msgr. Adrian Dwyer, Aug. 20, 1970, Apr. 10, 1976, July 30, 1982; clippings, St. Ambrose Church.

26. Interviews with Joe Garagiola, June 19, Sept. 8, 1984; Polizzi, "Edwards Street Overpass Controversy," 26–28.

27. Ibid.; "Hill's $50,000 Offer Stuns I–44 Officials," *Globe-Democrat*, Nov. 6–7, 1971.

28. *Post-Dispatch*, Nov. 14, 1971; Polizzi, "Edwards Street Overpass Controversy," 28–30.

29. *Globe-Democrat*, Nov. 20–21, 1971; *Post-Dispatch*, Nov. 19, 1971.

30. Letter from John A. Volpe to the author, Aug. 10, 1984.

31. *Post-Dispatch*, Mar. 1, 1981.

32. "The Hill Sticks Together," *Globe-Democrat*, Mar. 28, 1972, p. 4-B.

33. Horrigan and Feminella, "Little Italy Now," 65–69; see also "A Day on the Hill," *Post Dispatch*, Oct. 11, 1978, p. 1D.

34. Novak, *Rise of the Unmeltable Ethnics;* Novak, "How American Are You?"

35. *Post-Dispatch*, Aug. 18, 1974.

36. Venturelli, "Institutions in an Ethnic District," 35.

37. Interviews with Msgr. Adrian Dwyer, Aug. 20, 1970, Apr. 10, 1976, July 30, 1982.

38. Gordon, *Assimilation in American Life*, 53.

39. O'Leary, "Ethnicity in Defense of Class," 230.

40. Yancey and Juliani, "Emergent Ethnicity."

41. Interview with Theresa Sala, Aug. 7, 1975; letter from Angelo Sala to the author, Aug. 16, 1975; "Sala's Cafe Going the Way of the 15-cent Lunch," *Post-Dispatch*, Oct. 27, 1976; "Ruggeri's," *Globe-Democrat*, July 4, 1973.

42. Interview with Isidore Oldani, Jr., Sept. 10, 1973; naturalization petition, Isidoro Oldani, 1910; *Il Pensiero*, Aug. 17, 1929.

43. Ibid.; see also Parenti, "Blessings of Private Enterprise."

44. Interview with Alphonse Ravarino, Aug. 8, 1975.

45. *Attenzione*, 67.

46. *Census of Population and Housing, 1980, Missouri*, Tract numbers 1131, 1134, 1135 and St. Louis.

47. *Christian Science Monitor*, Feb. 13, 1974.

48. Undated clipping, *Post-Dispatch*, ca. 1983, St. Ambrose Church.

49. *Attenzione*, 1980.

50. Ibid.

51. Polizzi, "Edwards Street Overpass Controversy," notes.

52. Bernhard, "Measurement of Neighborhood," 29.

53. McCurdy and Smith, "Urban Design for the Hill," 152–59.

54. O'Leary, "Ethnicity in Defense of Class," 351.

55. *Globe-Democrat*, Nov. 6–7, 1971.

56. *Post-Dispatch*, Oct. 31, 1971.

57. Primm, *Lion of the Valley*, 444.

58. "A Goodbye to the Hill," *Post-Dispatch*, Mar. 1, 1981, p. 1D; interview with Fr. Vincent Bommarito, July 7, 1984; clippings, St. Ambrose Church.

59. Yancey and Juliani, "Emergent Ethnicity."

60. Interview with Mario Montecalvo, Sept. 10, 1973.

61. "An Act of Love," *I-AM* 1 (Aug., 1977): 29.

62. "View from the Hill in St. Louis, Mo.," Paul Harvey News, transcript, 1971.

63. Clark, *Civilisation*, 75.

A Note on Sources

In 1906 the Department of Commerce established the Bureau of Immigration and Naturalization to administer a new and comprehensive law addressing the thorny issue of citizenship. The naturalization process comprised three steps: the filing of a declaration of intention (first papers); the petitioning for naturalization under the applicant's signature (second papers); and a hearing which granted or denied citizenship. The declaration was to be submitted no less than two years and no more than seven before filing a petition.

Naturalization petitions (1906–36) provided a rich source of information for immigrants in St. Louis. To become American citzens after 1906 immigrants were required to provide precise life history data, including such things as place and date of birth of the applicant and his wife and children, place and date of marriage, date and port of embarkation and time of arrival, port of entry, and information on the period between immigration and naturalization. In addition, petitioners volunteered information about their occupation and address at the time of first application and at the eventual granting of citizenship, generally a period of three to five years. I studied the papers of every Italian immigrant seeking citizenship in St. Louis between 1906 and 1936. Altogether, this sample comprised 600 Italians who lived on the Hill and 300 who lived in Little Italy. In addition, several hundred petitions were sampled from Greek, Jewish, and Hungarian immigrants. Few Italian women applied for citizenship since they were naturalized as a result of their husband's status and displayed little interest in politics.

How representative are such documents? If immigrants were mobile and peripatetic, how could one expect them to remain in one place long enough to apply and wait for naturalization proceedings? Moreover, if Italian immigrants came to America as "birds of passage," seeking only a nest egg to return to the old-world village, why would such individuals waste the effort and money (five dollars) to become citizens of a country they would soon leave? Such factors were considered, but I believe they were not characteristic of the behavior of Hill Italians. As documented by city directories and school reports, the Hill was immobile, isolated, and homogeneous, uncommon traits for an immigrant colony. Elderly residents of Cuggiono cannot recall many *americani*, repatriated Italians who returned to the *paese* after earning their fortune in St. Louis. One might also argue that naturalized Italians represented the economic elite, immigrants who had made it and preferred to remain in America. Yet a survey of the 600 Italians on the Hill revealed that 83 percent were blue-collar workers, hardly an economic elite. By 1940, 76 percent of the Hill's male immigrants had been naturalized or had taken out their first papers. Thus, these petitions survey a broad spectrum of the colony.

Bibliography

I. INTERVIEWS

All interviews, unless otherwise indicated, were conducted in St. Louis by the author. Tapes are on deposit at the Southern Collection of the University of North Carolina, Chapel Hill, and at the Library of the University of Missouri, St. Louis.

Alagna, Paul, by Gayle Swiler, Nov. 13, 1973
Anthony, John, Aug. 8, 1975
Arpiani, Jo Anne and Dario, Aug. 29, 1973
Berra, Fannie, Aug. 6, 1975
Berra, Lou, July 11, 1973
Berra, Lou, Jr., Aug. 17, 1973
Berra, Paul Mario, July 31, 1973
Bianchi, Angelina, Aug. 28, 1973
Bommarito, Fr. Vincent, July 7, 1984
Borghi, Carolina, May 29, 1975
Borghi, Frank, July 18, 1973
Cacciatore, Carmelo and Filomena, May 28, 1975, Aug. 7, 1975
Caradonna, Nino, June 30, 1973
Cavagnaro, Greer, Sept. 4, 1973
Cavic, Lou, July 3, 1973
Cerutti, Lou, Aug. 7, 1975
Cesare, Antonio, July 11, 1973
Chinicci, Sam, Aug. 8, 1975, Oct. 27, 1975, Dec. 19, 1975
Chiodini, Fr. Jaspar, Sept. 13, 1973
Clavenna, Mary, Oct. 27, 1975

Coco, Mary, Sept. 13, 1973
Correnti, Joe, Apr. 30, 1976
Cusamano, Rose, July 30, 1973
DeGregorio, Roland, Aug. 18, 1973
DeMatti, Robert, Aug. 6, 1975
Dempsey, Fr. Timothy, by George Johns, n.d.
D'Ippolito, Anthony, Aug. 6, 1975
Dwyer, Msgr. Adrian, Aug. 20, 1970, April 10, 1976, July 30, 1982
Erutti, Leo, July 2, 1973, Aug. 1, 1973
Evola, Nick, July 29, 1973
Filipiak, Fr. Edward, Aug. 14, 1973
Fuse, Agatina, June 27, 1973
Fuse, Lou, Aug. 12, 1973
Galus, Fr. Walter John, Aug. 8, 1973
Gambaro, Lino, Aug. 29, 1973
Garagiola, Joe, June 19, 1984, Chicago; Sept. 8, 1984, Phoenix
Garanzini, Les, Aug. 7, 1975
Giacoma, Fred, Sept. 20, 1973
Giambalvo, Mariano, Aug. 31, 1970
Gianella, Frank and Rose, Aug. 1, 1975
Gioia, Joseph, Jr., June 3, 1975
Gioia, Michael, June 3, 1975
Giordano, Anthony, July 2, 1973
Grassi, Rose, June 29, 1973
Greco, Mary, Sept. 16, 1973
Griffero, Maria Imo, July 25, 1973, Oct. 27, 1975
Gualdoni, Louis Jean, Aug. 13, 1973, July 30, 1982
Hoagland, Elia, July 7, 1973
Johnston, Msgr. James, July 17, 1973
Keltner, Harold, July 30, 1982
Koester, Bishop Charles, July 9, 1973, Feb. 16, 1976
Leotta, Frances, May 29, 1973
Lisitano, Sam, June 30, 1973
Manfredini, Delores, Oct. 17, 1975
Mariani, Agino, Aug. 2, 1973
Mazzula, Annie Russo, Sept. 13, 1973
Merlo, Angelina Coco, Aug. 6, 1975
Mihanovich, Clement, Aug. 3, 1973
Monteclavo, Mario, Sept. 10, 1973
Mugavero, Blase, Sept. 2, 1973
Mugavero, Rose Gitto, Sept. 13, 1973
Oldani, Charles, Sept. 10, 1973

Oldani, Isidore, Jr., Sept. 10, 1973
Palmero, Jaspar and Mary, May 29, 1973
Palmisano, Charles, July 2, 1973
Palumbo, Anthony, Aug. 3, 1973
Palozzollo, Joe, July 14, 1972
Pedecrela, Charles, June 29, 1973
Peek, George, July 25, 1973
Pertici, Mario, Aug. 14, 1973
Poelker, Msgr. Carl, July 29, 1973
Polizzi, Fr. Salvatore, Aug. 12, 1973
Pozza, Charles, Aug. 6, 1975
Pucci, Sylvio, Jr., Aug. 30, 1973
Puricelli, Angelina, July 12, 1973
Ranciglio, Antonio, May 29, 1975
Rancilio, Charles, June 28, 1973, July 14, 1973
Ravarino, Alphonse, Aug. 8, 1975
Restivo, Anne, Aug. 6, 1975
Riggio, Mrs. Ignazio, July 2, 1973
Riggio, Mrs. Joseph, June 10, 1973
Robinson, James, Aug. 7, 1973
Rocco, Augustine, Sept. 16, 1973
Ronzio, Mary, July 9, 1973
Rupert, Gerald, July 30, 1982
Russo, Sam, Sept. 10, 1973
Sala, Theresa, Aug. 7, 1975
Schoessel, Hugo, July 10, 1973
Selvaggi, Julius, Aug. 15, 1973
Sullivan, Frances Garavaglia, Aug. 6, 1975
Torno, Maria, June 19, 1973
Travaglia, Theresa, Aug. 6, 1975
Vacaranzza, Victor, July 18, 1973
Venegoni, Lena, Aug. 6, 1975
Verga, Phillip, Aug. 6, 1975
Wood, Elmer Shorb, May 17, 1984, Naples, Fla.
Zucchero, Mary, Aug. 11, 1973

II. ARCHIVES

Archivio, la Chiesa di San Giorgio, Cuggiono, Italy.
Archivio Comunale, Cuggiono, Milano, Italy.
Bureau of Immigration. United States Naturalization Petitions. U.S. District Court, St. Louis, Mo.

Centro Studi Emigrazione. Missionari di S. Carlo Scalabriniani. Rome, Italy.
Immigration History Research Center. The Italian Collection; Rosa Casetteri Collection. University of Minnesota, Minneapolis.
Library of Congress. Woodrow Wilson Papers. Washington, D.C.
Missouri Historical Society. St. Louis, Mo.
St. Louis Archdiocesan Archives. St. Louis Cathedral. St. Louis, Mo.
St. Louis Public Library. St. Louis, Mo.
Sant' Ambrogio Archives. St. Ambrose Parish, St. Louis, Mo.
State Historical Society of Missouri. Columbia, Mo.
Truman Library. Independence, Mo.
Washington University. Raymond R. Tucker Papers. St. Louis, Mo.

III. GOVERNMENT DOCUMENTS, UNITED STATES AND ITALY

"Advisory Commission on Intergovernmental Relations." *Trends in Metropolitan America*, Washington, D.C.: U.S. Government Printing Office, 1977.
Annual Report of the Commissioner-General for Immigration. Washington, D.C.: U.S. Government Printing Office, 1907.
Bolletino dell'Emigrazione, Roma, 1910–23.
Censimento di Cuggiono. Archivio Storico di Milano.
Censimento di 1880. Archivio Storico di Cuggiono.
Istituto Centrale di Statistica Popolazione Residente dei Comuni al Censimenti (dal 1861 al 1961), Roma, 1961.
Eleventh Census of the United States: 1890. Population-Missouri. Washington, D.C.: U.S. Government Printing Office, 1890.
Fifteenth Census of the United States: 1930. Washington, D.C.: U.S. Government Printing Office, 1932.
Fourteenth Census of the United States: 1920. Population. Washington, D.C.: U.S. Government Printing Office, 1922.
Liber Baptizatorum Sancti Giorgi, Chiesa di San Giorgio, Cuggiono.
Liber Conjugatum Sanet, Chiesa di San Giorgio, Cuggiono.
Seventeenth Census of the United States: 1950. Population and Housing Statistics, vol. 6, Washington, D.C.: U.S. Government Printing Office, 1952.
Sixteenth Census of the United States: 1940. Populating and Housing, vol. 6. Washington, D.C.: U.S. Government Printing Office, 1942.
Sixth Census of the United States: 1850. Missouri. Washington, D.C.: U.S. Government Printing Office, 1853.
Social Statistics of St. Louis by Census Tracts. St. Louis: School of Business and Public Administration, Washington University, 1935.
Statistics of the Population of the United States at the Tenth Census, 1880. Washington, D.C.: U.S. Government Printing Office, 1883.

Stato delle Anime, 1860. Archivio Storico di Milano.
Thirteenth Census of the United States: 1910. Population and Occupational Statistics, vol 6. Washington, D.C.: U.S. Government Printing Office, 1914.
Twelfth Census of the United States: 1900. Statistics of Occupations. Washington, D.C.: U.S. Government Printing Office, 1914.
Twentieth Census of the United States: 1980. Census of Population and Housing, Missouri. Washington, D.C.: U.S. Government Printing Office, 1981.
U.S. Congress. Senate. *U.S. Immigration Commission Report. Emigration Conditions in Europe.* vol. 12. Washington, D.C.: U.S. Government Printing Office, 1911.
U.S. Congress. Senate. *U.S. Immigration Commission Report. Immigrants in Cities.* vol. 23. Washington, D.C.: U.S. Government Printing Office, 1911.
U.S. Congress. Senate. *U.S. Immigration Commission Report. Immigrants in Industries.* vol. 16. Washington, D.C.: U.S. Government Printing Office, 1911.

IV. BOOKS AND ARTICLES

Abbott, Grace. *Bulletin of the Immigrants' Commission*, no. 2. Springfield: State of Illinois, 1920.
Abbott, Josephine, "What of Youth in Wartime?" *Survey* 79 (Oct. 1943): 265–67.
Allswang, John. *A House for All Peoples: Ethnic Politics in Chicago.* Lexington: University Press of Kentucky, 1970.
Alsopp, Bruce. *Romanesque Architecture: The Romanesque Achievement.* New York: John Day Co., 1971.
Amfitheatrof, Erik. *The Children of Columbus: An Informal History of the Italians in the New World.* Boston: Little, Brown and Co., 1973.
Angle, Paul. *Bloody Williamson: A Chapter in American Lawlessness.* New York: Alfred Knopf, 1952.
Annoni, Antonio. *Cuggiono e Zone Vicine.* Marcallo: n.p., 1893.
Il Baco la Seta nella Storia di Cuggiono. Cuggiono, 1973.
Badi, Giuseppe. *Cuggiono: Brevi Notizie.* Busto Arsizio: Tipografia Orfanotrofio, 1950.
Baily, Samuel L. "The Adjustment of Italian Immigrants in Buenos Aires and New York, 1870–1914." *American Historical Review* 88 (April 1983): 281–306.
———. "The Italians and Organized Labor in the United States and Argentina, 1880–1910." *International Migration Review* 1 (Summer 1967): 56–66.
Baker, Paul R. *The Fortunate Pilgrims: Americans in Italy, 1800–1860.* Cambridge, Mass.: Harvard University Press, 1964.

Balk, Helen. "Economic Contributions of the Greeks to the United States." *Economic Geography* 19 (1943): 270–75.

Banfield, Edward. *The Moral Basis of a Backward Society*. Glencoe, Ill.: Free Press, 1958.

Barth, Gunther. *City People: The Rise of Modern City Culture in Nineteenth-Century America*. New York: Oxford University Press, 1980.

Barton, Josef. *Peasants and Strangers: Italians, Rumanians and Slovaks in an American City, 1890–1950*. Harvard Studies in Urban History. Cambridge, Mass.: Harvard University Press, 1975.

Bek, William G. "Gottfried Duden's Report, 1824–27." *Missouri Historical Review* 11 (July 1918): 258–70.

Belcher, Wyatt W. *The Economic Rivalry Between St. Louis and Chicago, 1850–80*. New York: Columbia University Press, 1947.

Bell, Daniel. *The End of Ideology*. New York: Free Press, 1962.

Bender, Thomas. *Community and Social Change in America*. New Brunswick, N.J.: Rutgers University Press, 1978.

Berkner, Lutz. "Recent Research on the Family in Western Europe." *Journal of Marriage and Family* 35 (1973): 395–406.

Bernard, Richard, and Bradley Rice, eds. *Sunbelt Cities: Politics and Growth Since World War II*. Austin: University of Texas Press, 1983.

Bernardy, Amy. "L'Emigrazione delle Donne e dei Fanciulli nel Nord America." *Bolletino dell' Emigrazione*, 1909, pp. 3–208.

———. "Sulle Condizioni delle Donne e dei Fanciulli Italiani negli Stati del Centro e dell' Ovest della Confederazione del Nord degli Stati Uniti." *Bolletino dell' Emigrazione*, 1911, pp. 3–170.

Bernstein, Irving. *The Lean Years*. Boston: Houghton-Mifflin, 1960.

Berra, Yogi, and Ed Fitzgerald. *Yogi: The Autobiography of a Professional Baseball Player*. Garden City, N.Y.: Doubleday and Co., 1961.

Berryman, Jack W. "From the Cradle to the Playing Fields: America's Emphasis on Highly Organized Competitive Sports for Preadolescent Boys." *Sport History* 2 (Fall 1975): 112–31.

Berthoff, Rowland. *An Unsettled People: Social Order and Disorder in American History*. New York: Harper and Row, 1971.

Betts, John Rickard. *America's Sporting Heritage*. Reading, Pa.: Addison Wesley Publishing Co., 1974.

Bianco, Carla. *The Two Rosetos*. Bloomington: Indiana University Press, 1974.

Biddle, Francis. *In Brief Authority*. New York: Doubleday, 1962.

Binsse, H. L. "Mr. Phasoulias: Eating in Greek Restaurants." *Commonweal* 33 (January 31, 1941): 366–68.

Blick, Doris, and H. Roger Grant. "French Icarians in St. Louis." Missouri Historical Society *Bulletin* 30 (October 1973): 3–28.

Blount, Roy, Jr. "Yogi." *Sports Illustrated* 60 (April 2, 1984): 84–97.

Bodnar, John. *Workers' World: Kinship, Community and Protest in Industrial Society, 1900–1940*. Baltimore, Md.: Johns Hopkins University Press, 1982.

———. "Immigration, Kinship and the Rise of Working-Class Realism in Industrial America." *Journal of Social History* 14 (1980): 45–67.

———. "Immigration and Modernization: The Case of Slavic Peasants in Industrial America." *Journal of Social History* 10 (1976): 44–71.

Bourne, Randolph. "Emerald Lake." *New Republic* 9 (January 16, 1917): 267–68.

Brackenridge, Henry. *Views of Louisiana: Together with a Journal of a Voyage Up the Missouri River in 1811*. Baltimore, Md.: Schaeffer and Maund, 1817.

Braudel, Fernand. *The Mediterranean and the Mediterranean World in the Age of Philip II*. 2 vols. New York: Harper and Row, 1966.

Brandenburg, Broughton. *Imported Americans: The Story of the Experience of a Disguised American and His Wife Studying the Immigrant Question*. New York: Stokes Co., 1904.

Breton, Raymond. "Institutional Completeness of Ethnic Communities." *American Journal of Sociology* 70 (1964): 193–205.

Briggs, John. *An Italian Passage: Immigrants to Three American Cities, 1890–1930*. New Haven, Conn.: Yale University Press, 1978.

Brooks, George. "Some Views of Old Cheltenham." Missouri Historical Society *Bulletin* 22 (October 1965): 32–35.

Brundidge, Harry. "How the Black Hand Came to St. Louis." *St. Louis Star-Times*, November 21, 1927.

Bryce, Lord. *American Commonwealth*. rev. ed. New York: Putnam, 1921.

Buber, Martin. *Paths in Utopia*. London: Routledge and Kegan Paul, 1949.

Budenz, Louis. "A Survey of Conditions in 'Dago Hill.'" *Central-Blatt and Social Justice* (August 1915).

Burke, Harry Rosencrans. *From the Day's Journey: A Book of the By-Paths and Eddies about St. Louis*. St. Louis: William Harvey Miner Co., 1923.

Caroli, Betty. *Italian Repatriation from the United States*. New York: Center for Migration Studies, 1973.

Carpi, Leone. *Delle Colonie e Dell' Emigrazione Italiana all' Estero*. 4 vols. Milan: Tipografica Editrice Lombardia, 1874.

Carr, Lowell, and James Stermer. *Willow Run: A Study of Industrialization and Cultural Inadequacy*. New York: Harper, 1952.

Caro, Robert. *The Power Broker: Robert Moses and the Fall of New York*. New York: Knopf, 1975.

Cassidy, Robert. "No Blues in St. Louis: A Trip Through St. Louis's Hill." *I-AM* 1 (1977): 30–37.

Cervantes, Alfonso J. *Mr. Mayor*. New York: Nash Publishing, 1975.

Child, Irwin. *Italian or American: Second Generation in Conflict*. New Haven, Conn.: Yale University Press, 1943.

Chudacoff, Howard. *Mobile Americans: Residential and Social Mobility in Omaha, 1800–1920*. Urban Life in America Series. New York: Oxford University Press, 1972.

Cinel, Dino. *From Italy to San Francisco: The Immigrant Experience*. Stanford, Calif.: Stanford University Press, 1982.

Cipolla, Carlo. *Cristofano and the Plague*. Berkeley: University of California Press, 1973.

Coleman, Terry. *Going to America*. New York: Pantheon Books, 1972.

Colburn, David, and George Pozzetta. "Crime and Ethnic Minorities in America." *The History Teacher* 7 (1974): 597–609.

Conzen, Kathleen Neils. *Immigrant Milwaukee, 1836–60*. Cambridge, Mass.: Harvard University Press, 1976.

———. "Immigrants, Immigrant Neighborhoods and Ethnic Identity: Historical Issues." *Journal of American History* 66 (December 1979): 603–15.

Commager, Henry Steele. *The American Mind*. New Haven, Conn.: Yale University Press, 1950.

Conant, Kenneth John. *Carolingian and Romanesque Architecture, 800–1200*. Pelican History of Art Series. Baltimore, Md.: Penguin Books, 1959.

Covello, Leonard. *The Social Background of the Italo-American School Child*. Leiden: E. J. Brill, 1967.

Crawford, Ruth. *The Immigrant in St. Louis*. Studies in Social Economics. St. Louis: n.p., 1916.

Crockett, Norman. "A Study of Confusion: Missouri's Immigration Program, 1865–1916." *Missouri Historical Review* 57 (April 1963): 248–60.

Cronin, Constance. *The Sting of Change: Sicilians in Sicily and Australia*. Chicago: University of Chicago Press, 1970.

Daniels, Roger. *Concentration Camps, USA: Japanese-Americans and World War Two*. New York: Holt, Rinehart and Winston, 1971.

Darst, Stephen. "Prufrock with a Baedeker: Only the Dead Know St. Louis." *Harpers* 248 (January 1974): 28–34.

Davis, Allen. *Spearheads for Reform: The Social Settlement and the Progressive Movement*. Urban Life in America Series. New York: Oxford University Press, 1967.

Deford, Frank. "Religion in Sport." *Sports Illustrated* 38 (April 16, 1976): 88–98.

———. "They Call It a Game." *Sports Illustrated* 38 (April 9, 1973): 116–20.

Diggins, John. *Mussolini and Fascism: The View from America*. Princeton, N.J.: Princeton University Press, 1972.

Dore, Grazia. "Some Social and Historical Aspects of Italian Emigration to America." *Journal of Social History* 2 (Winter 1968): 95–122.

Dolan, Jay P. *The Immigrant Church: New York's Irish and German Catholics, 1815–65*. Baltimore, Md.: Johns Hopkins University Press, 1975.

Dorsett, Lyle, and Mary Dorsett. "Rhetoric versus Reality: One-Hundred and Fifty Years of Missouri Boosterism." Missouri Historical Society *Bulletin* 28 (January 1972): 77–84.

———. *The Pendergast Machine*. Urban Life in America Series. New York: Oxford University Press, 1977.

Dreiser, Theodore. *A Book About Myself*. New York: Boni and Liveright, 1922.

Dubman, Sue. *Poverty in St. Louis*. St. Louis: Center for Metropolitan Studies, University of Missouri, 1973.

Dulles, Foster Rhea. *America Learns to Play: A History of Popular Recreation, 1607–1940*. New York: D. Appleton-Century Co., 1940.

Dunne, Thomas. *Ellis Island*. New York: W. W. Norton and Co., 1971.

Dyer, David Patterson. *Autobiography and Reminiscences*. St. Louis: William Harvey Miner Co., 1922.

Edwards, Bob. "The Italian Hill." National Public Radio, September 27, 1985.

Ellis, John Tracy. *American Catholicism*. Chicago History of American Civilization. Chicago: University of Chicago Press, 1956.

Ets, Marie Hall. *Rosa: The Life of an Italian Immigrant*. Foreword by Rudolph Vecoli. Minneapolis: University of Minnesota Press, 1970.

Fairchild, Henry Pratt. *Greek Immigration to the United States*. New Haven, Conn.: Yale University Press, 1911.

Fay, Sharon. "Greek Community: Strong Ties But No Ghetto." *Los Angeles Times*, January 28, 1969.

Featherstonaugh, George. *Excursion Through the Slave States*. 2 vols. London: Harper and Brothers, 1844.

Felici, Icilio. *Father to the Immigrants: John Baptiste Scalabrini*. trans. Carlo Chiesa. New York: P. J. Kennedy and Sons, 1955.

Fichter, Joseph. *Social Relations in an Urban Parish*. Chicago: University of Chicago Press, 1954.

Fletcher, Ralph, Harry Hornback, and Stuart Queen. *Social Statistics of St. Louis by Census Tracts*. St. Louis: Washington University, 1935.

Foley, William E., and David C. Rice. *The First Chouteaus: River Barons of Early St. Louis*. Urbana: University of Illinois Press, 1983.

Foerster, Robert F. *The Italian Emigration of Our Times*. Harvard Economic Studies. New York: Russel and Russel, 1919.

Franchetti, Leopoldo. *La Sicilia nel 1876*. Florence: Vallecchi, 1925.

Fried, Marc. *The World of the Urban Working Class*. Cambridge, Mass.: Harvard University Press, 1974.

Frisch, Michael. *Town into City: Springfield, Massachusetts, and the Meaning of Community, 1840–80*. Harvard Studies in Urban History. Cambridge, Mass.: Harvard University Press, 1972.

Gambino, Richard. *Blood of My Blood: The Dilemma of the Italian-American.* Garden City, N.J.: Doubleday, 1974.

Gans, Herbert. *The Urban Villagers: Group and Class in the Life of Italian-Americans*. New York: Free Press, 1962.

Garagiola, Joe. *Baseball Is a Funny Game*. Philadelphia: J. B. Lippincott, 1960.

Geiger, Louis C. *Joseph W. Folk of Missouri*. Columbia: University of Missouri Press, 1959.

Gilmore, Al-Tony. *Bad Nigger: The National Impact of Jack Johnson*. Port Washington, N.Y.: Kennikat Press, 1974.

Glaab, Charles, and Theodore Brown. *A History of Urban America*. New York: Macmillan, 1976.

Glanville, Brian. *A Book of Soccer*. New York: Oxford University Press, 1979.

Glazer, Nathan, and Daniel Patrick Moynihan. *Beyond the Melting Pot: Negros, Puerto Ricans, Jews, Italians and Irish of New York City*. Cambridge: Massachusetts Institute of Technology Press, 1963.

Gleason, Philip. *The Conservative Reformers: German-American Catholics and the Social Order*. Notre Dame, Ind.: University of Notre Dame Press, 1968.

Goldfield, David, and Blaine Brownell. *Urban America: From Downtown to No Town*. Boston: Houghton Mifflin Co., 1979.

Gordon, Milton. *Assimilation in American Life*. New York: Oxford University Press, 1964.

Goulden, Joseph. *The Best Years, 1945–50*. New York: Atheneum, 1976.

Greele, Ronald J. "Movement Without Aim: Methodological and Theoretical Problems in Oral History." In *Envelopes of Sound*. ed. Ronald J. Greele. Chicago: Precedent Publishing Co., 1975.

Greeley, Andrew M. *Why Can't They Be Like Us? America's White Ethnic Groups*. New York: E. P. Dutton Co., 1971.

Green, Constance McLaughlin. *American Cities in the Growth of the Nation*. New York: J. DeGraff, 1957.

Greene, Victor R. "For God and County: The Origins of Slavic Self-consciousness in America." *Church History* 35 (1966): 446–60.

Greenfield, Kent Roberts. *Economics and Liberalism in the Risorgimento: A Study of Nationalism in Lombardy, 1814–48*. rev. ed. Baltimore, Md.: Johns Hopkins University Press, 1965.

Gusfield, Joseph. *Symbolic Crusade: Status Politics and the American Temperance Movement*. Urbana: University of Illinois Press, 1963.

Gutman, Herbert G. *Work, Culture and Society in Industrializing America*. New York: Knopf, 1976.

Guttmann, Allen. *From Ritual to Record: The Nature of Modern Sports*. New York: Columbia University Press, 1978.

Hall, Stephen S. "Italian-Americans: Coming into Their Own." *New York Times Magazine*, May 15, 1983.

Haller, Mark. "Organized Crime in Urban Society: Chicago in the Twentieth Century." *Journal of Social History* 4 (Winter 1971–72): 210–34.

Handlin, Oscar. *The Uprooted*. New York: E. P. Dutton, 1951.

Hansen, James E. III. "Moonshine and Murder: Prohibition in Denver." *Colorado Magazine* 50 (Winter 1973): 1–24.

Hareven, Tamara. "Family Time and Industrial Time: Family and Work in a Planned Corporation Town, 1900–1924." *Journal of Urban History* 1 (May 1975): 365–90.

Hartmann, Edward George. *The Movement to Americanize the Immigrant*. Columbia University Studies in History. New York: Columbia University Press, 1948.

Havighurst, Robert, and H. G. Morgan. *The Social History of a War-Boom Community*. New York: Longmans, Green and Co., 1951.

Hays, Samuel P. "The Changing Political Structure of the City in Industrial America." *Journal of Urban History* 1 (November 1974): 6–58.

Headlam, Cecil. *Venetia and Northern Italy*. London: J. M. Dent and Co., 1908.

Herberg, Will. *Protestant-Catholic-Jew: An Essay in American Religious Sociology*. Garden City, N.Y.: Doubleday, 1955.

Higham, John. "Hanging Together: Divergent Unities in American History." *Journal of American History* 61 (1974): 5–28.

———. *Strangers in the Land*. New York: Atheneum, 1960.

Hillery, George A., Jr. "Definitions of Community: Areas of Agreement." *Rural Sociology* 20 (1955): 111–23.

Holli, Melvin, and Peter d'A. Jones, eds. *The Ethnic Frontier: Essays in the History of Group Survival in Chicago and the Midwest*. Grand Rapids, Mich.: Eerdmans Publishing Co., 1977.

Hoftstadter, Richard. *The Age of Reform*. New York: Knopf, 1955.

Holt, Glen E. "St. Louis's Transition Decade, 1819–30." *Missouri Historical Review* 76 (1982): 365–82.

Horrigan, Kevin, and Richard Feminella. "Little Italy Now: St. Louis." *Attenzione* 2 (December 1980): 65–69.

Holt, Michael. *Forging a Majority: Formation of a Republican Party in Pittsburgh, 1848–60*. New Haven, Conn.: Yale University Press, 1969.

Historical Review, Brief Sketches, and Data of Saint Ambrose Church. St. Louis: n.p., 1943.

Horowitz, David. *The Italian Labor Movement*. Cambridge, Mass.: Harvard University Press, 1963.

Hubbs, Barbara Burr. *Pioneer Folks and Places: An Historic Gazeteer of Williamson County*. Herrin, Ill.: Herrin Daily Journal, 1939.

Ianni, Francis. *Black Mafia*. New York: Simon and Schuster, 1974.

Iorizzo, Luciano, and Salvatore Mondello. *The Italian-Americans*. Boston: Twayne Publishers, 1971.

———. "Origins of Italian-American Criminality: From New Orleans Through Prohibition." *Italian-Americana* 1 (Spring 1975): 21–36.

Italo-American Cavalry Golden Jubilee Pamphlet. St. Louis: n.p., 1942.

Jackson, Kenneth T. "Metropolitan Government versus Political Autonomy: Politics on the Crabgrass Frontier." In *Cities in American History*. ed. Kenneth Jackson and Stanley Schultz. New York: Knopf, 1972.

Jensen, Richard. *The Winning of the Midwest: Social and Political Conflict, 1888–96*. Chicago: University of Chicago Press, 1971.

Juliani, Richard. "American Voices, Italian Accents: The Perception of Social Conditions and Personal Motives by Immigrants." *Italian-Americana* 1 (Autumn 1974): 1–26.

Kaufman, Harold R. "Toward an Interactional Conception of Community." In *Perspectives on the American Community*. ed. Roland Warren. Chicago: Rand McNally, 1966.

Kelly, George. *The Story of St. Monica's Parish, New York City, 1879–1954*. New York: St. Monica's Press, 1954.

Kennedy, Ruby Jo Reeves. "Single or Triple Melting Pot? Intermarriage in New Haven, 1870–1950." *American Journal of Sociology* 58 (1952–53): 56–60.

Kessner, Thomas. *The Golden Door: Italian and Jewish Immigrant Mobility in New York City, 1880–1915*. New York: Oxford University Press, 1977.

Ketner, Harold S. *Gangs: An Asset to the City of St. Louis*. New York: National Probation Association, 1934.

Kingsdale, John M. "The 'Poor Man's' Club: Social Functions of the Urban Working-Class Saloon." *American Quarterly* 25 (October 1973): 472–92.

Kirschten, Ernest. *Catfish and Crystal*. Garden City, N.Y.: Doubleday, 1965.

Kleppner, Paul. *The Cross of Culture: A Social Analysis of Midwestern Politics, 1850–1900*. New York: Free Press, 1970.

Konnyu, Leslie. "The Hungarians in Missouri." *Missouri Historical Review* 46 (April 1952): 257–61.

Kobler, John. *Capone*. New York: Putnam, 1971.

Kouwanhoven, John A. "Eads Bridge: The Celebration." Missouri Historical Society *Bulletin* 30 (April 1974): 759–81.

Krusekoff, *Soil Survey of St. Louis County, Missouri*. Washington, D.C.: U.S. Bureau of the Soils, 1923.

Landesco, John. *Organized Crime in Chicago*. 3 pts. Chicago: Illinois Crime Survey, 1929.

Lane, Franklin. "What Is It to Be an American?" *National Geographic Magazine* 33 (April 1918): 348–54.

Lauer, Jeanette C. "St. Louis and the 1880 Census: The Shock of Collective Failure." *Missouri Historical Review* 76 (1982): 151–64.

Lieberson, Stanley. *A Piece of the Pie: Blacks and White Immigrants Since 1880.* Berkeley: University of California Press, 1980.

Little, James T., and Hugh Nourse. *The Neighborhood Succession Process.* Institute for Urban and Regional Studies. St. Louis: Washington University, 1975.

Litt, Edgar. *Beyond Pluralism: Ethnic Politics in America.* Glenview, Ill.: Scott Foresman, 1970.

"Little Italy in Wartime." *Literary Digest* 50 (June 12, 1915): 1409–14.

Lopreato, Joseph. *Italian Americans.* New York: Random House, 1970.

Lotchin, Roger. "Power and Policy: American City Politics Between Two World Wars." In *Ethnics, Machines, and the American Urban Future.* ed. Scott Greer. Cambridge, Mass.: Schenkman Publishing Co., 1981.

Luebke, Frederick. *Immigrants and Politics: Germans of Nebraska, 1880–90.* Lincoln: University of Nebraska Press, 1969.

MacDonald, John S. "Chain Migration, Ethnic Neighborhoods and Social Network." *Milbank Memorial Fund Quarterly* 32 (1964): 82–97.

———. "Italy's Rural Social Structure and Emigration." *Occidente: An International Review of Politics* 22 (1956): 437–56.

———. "Some Socio-Economic Emigration Differentials in Rural Italy, 1902–13." *Economic Development and Cultural Change* 7 (October 1958).

Mack Smith, Denis. *Italy.* Ann Arbor: University of Michigan Press, 1969.

MacKay, Alexander. *The Western World.* London: Richard Bentley, 1849.

Manfredini, Delores. "The Italians Come to Herrin." Illinois State Historical Society *Journal* 37 (December 1944): 317–28.

Mangold, George. *The Challenge of St. Louis.* New York: Missionary Educational Movement, 1917.

McAvoy, Thomas. *A History of the Catholic Church in the United States.* Notre Dame, Ind.: University of Notre Dame Press, 1969.

Meister, Richard. "Ethnics, Blacks, and Machine Politics in Contemporary America." In *Ethnics, Machines and the American Urban Future.* ed. Scott Greer. Cambridge, Mass.: Schenkman Publishing Co., 1981.

Meriwether, Lee. "The Reign of Boodle and the Rape of the Ballot in St. Louis." *The Arena* 33 (1905).

Merton, Robert. "The Latent Functions of the Machine." In *Urban Bosses, Machines and Progressive Reformers.* ed. Bruce Stave. Lexington, Mass.: Heath, 1972.

Michaels, Marguerite. "St. Louis: Pride on the Hill." *Time* (April 29, 1973): 27.

Missouri Crime Survey. New York: Macmillan and Co., 1926.

Mitchell, Franklin. *Embattled Democracy: Missouri Democratic Politics, 1919–32*. Columbia: University of Missouri Press, 1968.

Moberg, David. *The Church as a Social Institution: The Sociology of American Religion*. Englewood Cliffs, N.J.: Prentice-Hall, 1962.

Montagu, Ashley. *The Nature of Human Aggression*. New York: Oxford University Press, 1976.

Mormino, Gary. "St. Louis Italo-Americans and the First World War." Missouri Historical Society *Bulletin* 30 (1973): 44–53.

———. "'We Worked Hard and Took Care of Our Own': Oral History and Italians in Tampa." *Labor History* 23 (1982): 395–415.

Moyers, William. *Listening to America*. New York: Harper's Magazine Press, 1971.

Mumford, Lewis. *The City in History: Its Origins, Its Transformation, Its Prospects*. New York: Harcourt, Brace and World, 1961.

Muraskin, Jack. "St. Louis Municipal Reform in the 1890s: A Study in Failure." Missouri Historical Society *Bulletin* 25 (October 1968): 38–50.

———. "Municipal Reform in Two Missouri Cities." Missouri Historical Society *Bulletin* 25 (1969): 38–50.

Nelli, Humbert. *The Business of Crime: Italians and Syndicate Crime in the United States*. New York: Oxford University Press, 1976.

———. *The Italians in Chicago, 1880–1930: A Study in Ethnic Mobility*. Urban Life in America Series. New York: Oxford University Press, 1970.

———. "The Myth of Urban Renewal: Chicago's Near West Community in the 1960s." *I-A Identity* 2 (April 1977): 51–54.

Niebuhr, Richard H. *The Social Sources of Denominationalism*. New York: Meridian Books, 1929.

Novak, Michael. *The Rise of the Unmeltable Ethnics*. New York: Macmillan, 1971.

Nuova Chiesa Italiana di Sant' Ambrogio Dedicata il 27 Giugno, 1926. St. Louis: n.p., 1926.

Olson, Sister Audrey. "The Nature of an Immigrant Community: St. Louis Germans, 1850–1920." *Missouri Historical Review* 66 (1972): 342–59.

Otto, Steve, "St. Louis Isn't a Bad Place to Be on Independence Day." *Tampa Tribune*, July 4, 1984.

Owens, Sister Lilliana. *Loretto in Missouri*. St. Louis: B. Herder, 1965.

Parenti, Michael. "The Blessings of Private Enterprise." *Italian-Americana* 1 (Autumn 1974): 94–97.

Paths of Progress for St. Louis. St. Louis: Ford Foundation Study, 1957.

Park, Robert, Ernest Burgess, and Roderick McKenzie. *The City*. 4th ed. Chicago: University of Chicago Press, 1967.

Paxson, Frederick. "The Rise of Sport." *Mississippi Valley Historical Review* 4 (1917): 142–68.

Perogalli, Carlo and Paolo Favole. *Ville dei Navigli Lombardi.* Milan: Edizioni Sisar, 1967.

Pileggi, Nicholas. "The Risorgimento of Italian Power: The Red, White and Greening of New York." *New York* 4 (June 7, 1971): 26–31.

Polenberg, Richard, ed. *America at War: The Home Front, 1941–45.* Englewood Cliffs, N.J.: Prentice-Hall, 1968.

———. *One Nation Divisible: Class, Race and Ethnicity in the United States Since 1938.* New York: Viking Press, 1980.

———, ed. *War and Society: The United States, 1941–45.* Philadelphia: Lippincott, 1972.

Pooley, John C. "Ethnic Soccer Clubs in Milwaukee." In *Sport in the Sociocultural Process.* ed. Marie Hart. Dubuque, Iowa: Wm. C. Brown Co., 1976.

Pozzetta, George, ed. *Pane e Lavoro: The Italian-American Working Class.* Toronto: Multicultural Institute, 1980.

Primm, James Neal. *The Lion of the Valley: St. Louis, Missouri.* Boulder, Colo.: Pruett Publishing Co., 1981.

———. "Locational Factors in the Development of St. Louis: The First Century." *Gateway Heritage* 4 (Fall 1983): 10–18.

———. "Yankee Merchants in a Border City: St. Louis Businessmen in the 1850s." *Missouri Historical Review* 78 (1984): 375–87.

Proetz, Arthur. *I Remember You St. Louis.* St. Louis: Zimmerman-Petty, 1963.

Puzo, Mario. "Choosing a Dream: Italians in Hell's Kitchen." In *The Immigrant Experience.* ed. Thomas Wheeler. New York: Dial Press, 1971.

Rader, Benjamin G. "The Quest for Subcommunities and the Rise of American Sport." *American Quarterly* 29 (Fall 1977): 355–69.

Rallo, Joseph, and Mary Hulbert. *The Rallo Family.* New York: Frederick Fell, 1966.

Rammelkamp, Julius. "St. Louis in the Early 'Eighties.'" Missouri Historical Society *Bulletin* 19 (July 1963): 328–40.

———. *Pulitzer's Post-Dispatch, 1878–83.* Princeton, N.J.: Princeton University Press, 1967.

Re, Vittorio. *Michigan's Italian Community: A Historical Perspective.* Monographs in International and Ethnic Studies. Detroit: Wayne State University, 1981.

Reid, Ed. *The Grim Reapers.* Chicago: Bantam Books, 1969.

Renner, G. K. "Prohibition Comes to Missouri." *Missouri Historical Review* 64 (1964): 363–97.

Revolutionary Radicalism. 8 vols. New York State Legislature. Lusk Committee. New York: De Capo Press, 1971.

Ries, Heinrich, and Henry Leighton. *History of the Clay-Working Industry in the U.S.* New York: John Wiley and Son, 1909.

Riess, Steven R. "Race and Ethnicity in American Baseball: 1900–1919." *The Journal of Ethnic Studies* 4 (1977): 39–56.

———. *Touching Base: Professional Baseball and American Culture in the Progressive Era.* Westport, Conn.: Greenwood Press, 1980.

Roberts, Kenneth. "The Worst of Citizenship." *Saturday Evening Post* 194 (February 18, 1922): 3, 74–77.

Rolle, Andrew. *The Immigrant Upraised.* Norman: University of Oklahoma Press, 1968.

Ross, Edward. *The Old World in the New.* New York: Century Co., 1914.

Rothensteiner, John. *History of the Archdiocese of St. Louis.* St. Louis: Blackwell-Weillandy, 1928.

Royko, Mike. *Boss: Richard J. Daley of Chicago.* New York: Dutton, 1971.

Rumbold, Charlotte. *Housing Conditions in St. Louis.* Report of the Housing Commission, St. Louis, 1908.

Russo, Nicholas John. "Three Generations of Italians in New York City: Their Religious Acculturation." *International Migration Review* 1 (Spring 1969): 5–17.

Ryan, Jack, and H. W. Lannigan. *Happy Days Are Here Again.* St. Louis: P. Curran Printing Co., 1933.

Salamone-Marino, Salvatore. *Customs and Habits of the Sicilian Peasants.* trans. Rosalie Norris. Rutherford, N.J.: Fairleigh Dickinson Press, 1981.

Salutos, Theodore. "The Greeks of Milwaukee." *Wisconsin Magazine of History* 61 (Spring 1971): 175–93.

Schiavo, Giovanni. *The Italians in Missouri.* Chicago: Italian Publishing Co., 1929.

Serpieri, Arrigo. *Il Contratto Agratio e le Condizione dei Contadini nell' Alto Milanese.* Milan: n.p., 1910.

Shaw, Clifford, and Harry McKay. *Juvenile Delinquency and Urban Areas.* Chicago: University of Chicago Press, 1943.

Shover, John. "Ethnicity and Religion in Philadelphia Politics, 1924–40." *American Quarterly* 25 (December 1973): 499–515.

Simon, Roger T. "Housing and Services in an Immigrant Neighborhood." *Journal of Urban History* 2 (August 1976): 435–59.

Sinclair, Andrew. *Prohibition: The Era of Excess.* New York: Harper and Row, 1962.

Sjoberg, Gideon. "Community." In *Dictionary of American Sociology.* ed. J. Gould. London: Routledge, 1965.

Slawson, John. "The Adolescent in a World at War." *Mental Hygiene* 27 (October 1943): 534.

Smith, Timothy. "Immigrant Social Aspirations and American Education, 1880–1930." *American Quarterly* 21 (Fall 1969): 527–31.

Snyder, Eldon, and Elmer Spreitzer. "Sociology of Sport: An Overview." *Sociological Quarterly* 15 (Autumn 1974): 467–87.

Società Unione e Fratellanza Italiana. Seventy-fifth Anniversary. St. Louis: n.p., 1941.

Somers, Dale. *The Rise of Sports in New Orleans, 1850–1900.* Baton Rouge: Louisiana State University Press, 1972.

Sorrell, Richard. "Sports and Franco-Americans in Woonsocket, 1870–1930." *Rhode Island History* 31 (November 1972): 117–26.

Sowell, Thomas. *Ethnic America: A History.* New York: Basic Books, 1981.

Statuto della Società di Mutuo Soccorso degli Operai e Contadini di Cuggiono. rev. ed. Cuggiono: Tipografia Enrico Gasloli, 1914.

Steffens, Joseph Lincoln. *The Shame of the Cities.* New York: McClure, Phillips and Co., 1904.

Steiner, Edward. "How Returning Emigrants Are Americanizing Europe." *Review of Reviews* 39 (1909): 701.

Sterns, Peter N. *European Society in Upheaval: Social History Since 1800.* New York: Macmillan, 1967.

Stolarik, Mark. "Immigration, Education, and the Social Mobility of Slovaks, 1870–1930." In *Immigrants and Religion in Urban America.* ed. Randall Miller. Philadelphia: Temple University Press, 1977.

La Storia San Giorgio, Chiesa di Cuggiono. Cuggiono: n.p. 1973.

Sullivan, Margaret. "Constitutionalism, Revolution and Culture: Irish-American Nationalism in St. Louis, 1902–14." Missouri Historical Society *Bulletin* 28 (1972): 234–45.

Suttles, Gerald D. *The Social Order of the Slum: Ethnicity and Territory in the Inner City.* Chicago: University of Chicago Press, 1968.

Swieranga, Robert. "Ethno-cultural Political Analysis: A New Approach to Ethnic Studies." *Journal of American Studies* 10 (1971): 111–30.

Thernstrom, Stephan. *The Other Bostonians: Poverty and Progress in an American Metropolis, 1880–1970.* Harvard Studies in Urban History. Cambridge, Mass.: Harvard University Press, 1973.

Thistlethwaite, Frank. "Migration from Europe Overseas in the Nineteenth and Twentieth Centuries." In *Population Movements in Modern European History.* ed. Herbert Moller. New York: Macmillan, 1964.

Thomas, Lewis F. "Climate of St. Louis, Mo." *Washington University Studies* 12 (1924): 1–14.

———. "Decline of St. Louis as a Midwest Metropolis." *Economic Geography* 25 (April 1949): 118–27.

———. "Sequence of Areal Occupance in a Section of St. Louis, Missouri." Association of American Geographers *Annals* 21 (1931): 75–90.

Thrasher, Frederic. *The Gang: A Study of 1,313 Gangs in Chicago.* Chicago: University of Chicago Press, 1927.

Tilly, Charles. "Migration in Modern European History." In *Human Migration.* ed. William McNeil. Bloomington: Indiana University Press, 1978.

Tilly, Louise A. "Urban Growth, Industrialization and Women's Employment in Milan, Italy, 1881–1911." *Journal of Urban History* 3 (August 1977): 467–84.

Tomasi, Silvano. *Piety and Power: The Role of the Italian Parishes in the New York Metropolitan Area, 1880–1930.* New York: Center for Migration Studies, 1975.

Tricarico, Donald. *The Italians of Greenwich Village.* New York: Center for Migration Studies, 1984.

Trout, Charles. *Boston, the Great Depression, and the New Deal.* New York: Oxford University Press, 1977.

Tuchman, Barbara. "Distinguishing Between the Significant and the Insignificant." *Radcliffe Quarterly* 56 (October 1972): 9–10.

Twain, Mark. *Life on the Mississippi.* 3d ed. New York: P. F. Collier and Son, 1917.

Urban Decay in St. Louis. St. Louis: Institute for Urban and Regional Studies, Washington University, 1972.

Vecoli, Rudolph. "*Contadini* in Chicago: Critique of *The Uprooted.*" *Journal of American History* 51 (December 1964): 404–17.

———. "Cult and Occult in Italian-American Culture: The Persistence of a Religious Heritage." In *Immigrants and Religion in Urban America.* ed. Randall Miller and Thomas Merzik. Philadelphia: Temple University Press, 1977.

———. "Italian American Workers, 1880–1920: Padrone Slaves or Primitive Rebels?" In *Perspectives in Italian Immigration and Ethnicity.* ed. Lydio Tomasi. New York: Center for Migration Studies, 1977.

———. "Prelates and Peasants: Italian Immigrants and the Catholic Church." *Journal of Social History* 2 (Spring 1969): 217–68.

Venturelli, Peter. "Institutions in an Ethnic District." *Human Organization* 41 (1982): 26–35.

Villari, Luigi. *Italian Life in Town and Country.* New York: G. P. Putnam's Sons, 1902.

Vismara, John C. "Coming of the Italians to Detroit." *Michigan Historical Magazine* (1918): 110–24.

Wade, Richard. *The Urban Frontier: Western Urban Growth, 1790–1830.* Cambridge, Mass.: Harvard University Press, 1959.

Walsh, Denny. "Detroit Hoods Call Many Shots for Mob Leaders Here." *St. Louis Globe-Democrat*, January 12, 1968.

Ward, David. *Cities and Immigrants: A Geography of Change in Nineteenth-Century America.* New York: Oxford University Press, 1971.

Warner, Sam, and Colin B. Burke. "Cultural Change and the Ghetto." *Journal of Contemporary History* 4 (1969): 173–87.

Weber, Eugen. "Gymnastics and Sports in Fin-de-Siecle France: Opium of the Classes." *American Historical Review* 76 (February 1971): 70–98.

———. *Peasants into Frenchmen: The Modernization of Rural France, 1870–1914.* Stanford, Calif.: Stanford University Press, 1976.

Whyte, William Foote. *Street Corner Society.* Chicago: University of Chicago Press, 1943.

Wiebe, Robert. *The Search for Order, 1877–1920.* American Century Series. New York: Hill and Wang, 1967.

Williams, Barbara. *St. Louis: A City and Its Suburbs.* Santa Monica, Calif.: Rand Corp., 1973.

Williams, Phyllis. *South Italian Folkways in Europe and America.* New Haven, Conn.: Yale University Press, 1938.

Wilson, Samuel Paynter. "Ice Cream Joints." In *Chicago by Gaslight.* Chicago: n.p., 1950.

Wirth, Louis. "Urbanism as a Way of Life." *American Journal of Sociology* 44 (1938): 1–24.

Wittke, Carl. "The German Language Press in America." *Missouri Historical Review* 52 (1958): 352–86.

———. *We Who Built America.* Cleveland, Ohio: Press of Western Reserve University, 1964.

Yancey, William, and Richard N. Juliani. "Emergent Ethnicity: A Review and Reformulation." *American Sociological Review* 41 (1976): 91–403.

Yans-McLaughlin, Virginia. *Family and Community: Italian Immigrants in Buffalo, 1880–1930.* Ithaca, N.Y.: Cornell University Press, 1977.

Zorbaugh, Harvey Warren. *The Gold Coast and the Slum: A Sociological Study of Chicago's Near North Side.* Chicago: University of Chicago Press, 1929.

V. UNPUBLISHED MATERIALS

Aschemeyer, Esther Louise. "The Urban Geography of the Clay Products Industry of Metropolitan St. Louis." Master's thesis, Washington University, 1943.

Bernhard, Jessie. "An Instrument for the Measurement of Neighborhood with Experimental Application." Ph.D. dissertation, Washington University, 1935.

Binz, Ronald. "German Gymnastic Societies in St. Louis, 1850–1913: Emergent Socio-Cultural Institutions." Master's thesis, Washington University, 1983.

Christensen, Lawrence O. "Black St. Louis: A Study in Race Relations." Ph.D. dissertation, University of Missouri, 1972.

Correnti, Joe. "The History of Correnti's Soccer Team, 1946–47." Ms. Author's files, n.d.

Cowgill, Donald. "Residential Mobility of an Urban Population." Master's thesis, Washington University, 1935.

Cunetto, Dominic. "Italian Language Clubs in St. Louis, 1910–50." Master's thesis, University of Florida, 1960.

Fainsod, Merle. "The Influence of Racial and National Groups in St. Louis Politics, 1908–28." Master's thesis, Washington University, 1929.

Fendelman, Maxine F. "St. Louis Shoe Manufacturing." Master's thesis, Washington University, 1947.

Fenton, Edwin. "Immigrants and Unions, A Case Study: Italians and Organized Labor, 1870–1920." Ph.D. dissertation, Harvard University, 1957.

Galus, Walter John. "The History of the Catholic Italians in St. Louis." Master's thesis, St. Louis University, 1936.

Gilkey, George. "The Effects of Emigration on Italy, 1900–1923." Ph.D. dissertation, Northwestern University, 1950.

Hodes, Frederick Anthony. "The Urbanization of St. Louis: A Study in Urban Residential Patterns in the Nineteenth Century." Ph.D. dissertation, St. Louis University, 1973.

Holt, Glen E. "The Shaping of St. Louis, 1763–1860." Ph.D. dissertation, University of Chicago, 1975.

Keating, Grace Marie. "A Study of Americanization of the Italian Immigrant in That District of Southwest St. Louis Known as 'The Hill.'" Master's thesis, St. Louis University, 1935.

McAuliffe, Harold James. "Monsignor Timothy Dempsey: An Historical Study of Charitable Enterprises in St. Louis." Master's thesis, St. Louis University, 1940.

McBride, Robert Bruce. "Prohibition in Oswego, New York, 1920–33." Master's thesis, State University of New York, College at Oswego, 1973.

McCurdy, Phillip, and Daniel Smith. "An Urban Design Study for the Hill." Master's thesis, Washington University, 1969.

Mihanovich, Clement. "Americanization of the Croats of St. Louis During the Last Thirty Years." Master's thesis, St. Louis University, 1936.

Mysliwiec, John Stanislaus. "History of the Catholic Poles of St. Louis." Master's thesis, St. Louis University, 1936.

O'Leary, Timothy. "Ethnicity in Defense of Class." Ph.D. dissertation, Washington University, 1977.

Olson, Sister Audrey. "St. Louis Germans, 1850–1920. The Nature of an Immigrant Community and Its Relation to the Assimilation Process." Ph.D. dissertation, University of Kansas, 1970.

Perrotta, Christopher. "Catholic Care of the Italian Immigrant in the United States." Master's thesis, Catholic University, 1925.

Polizzi, Salvatore. "The Edwards Street Overpass Controversy: A Lesson in Political Expediency." Master's thesis, St. Louis University, 1972.

Pucci, Silvio. "My Memories of the Hill." Ms. Author's files, n.d..

Robinson, James Francis. "The History of Soccer in the City of St. Louis." Ph.D. dissertation, St. Louis University, 1966.

Stellos, Marie Helen. "The Greek Community in St. Louis, 1900–1967." Ph.D. dissertation, St. Louis University, 1968.

Sullivan, Margaret Justine. "Hyphenism in St. Louis, 1900–1921: The View from the Outside." Ph.D. dissertation, St. Louis University, 1968.

Tilly, Louise A. "The Working Class of Milan, 1881–1911." Ph.D. dissertation, University of Toronto, 1973.

Wood, Elmer Shorb. "Fairmount Heights: An Italian Colony in St. Louis." Master's thesis, Washington University, 1936.

Index

About the Author

Gary Ross Mormino is Duckwall Professor of History at the University of South Florida. He is the author or coauthor of numerous books, including *The Immigrant World of Ybor City: Italians and Their Latin Neighbors.*